QUEER MOVIE MEDIEVALISMS

Queer Interventions

Series editors:
Noreen Giffney and Michael O'Rourke
University College Dublin, Ireland

Queer Interventions is an exciting, fresh and unique new series designed to publish innovative, experimental and theoretically engaged work in the burgeoning field of queer studies.

The aim of the series is to interrogate, develop and challenge queer theory, publishing queer work which intersects with other theoretical schools and is accessible whilst valuing difficulty; empirical work which is metatheoretical in focus; ethical and political projects and most importantly work which is self-reflexive about methodological and geographical location.

The series is interdisciplinary in focus and publishes monographs and collections of essays by new and established scholars. The editors intend the series to promote and maintain high scholarly standards of research and to be attentive to queer theory's shortcomings, silences, hegemonies and exclusions. They aim to encourage independence, creativity and experimentation: to make a queer theory that matters and to recreate it as something important; a space where new and exciting things can happen.

Titles in this series:

Jewish/Christian/Queer
Frederick Roden
ISBN: 978-0-7546-7375-0

Queering the Non/Human
Noreen Giffney and Myra J. Hird
ISBN: 978-0-7546-7128-2

Cinesexuality
Patricia MacCormack
ISBN: 978-0-7546-7175-6

Queer Attachments
Sally R. Munt
ISBN: 978-0-7546-4923-6

Queer Movie Medievalisms

Edited by

KATHLEEN COYNE KELLY
Northeastern University, USA

TISON PUGH
University of Central Florida, USA

ASHGATE

Published by
Ashgate Publishing Limited
Wey Court East
Union Road
Farnham
Surrey, GU9 7PT
England

Ashgate Publishing Company
Suite 420
101 Cherry Street
Burlington
VT 05401-4405
USA

www.ashgate.com

British Library Cataloguing in Publication Data
Queer movie medievalisms. -- (Queer interventions)
    1. Middle Ages in motion pictures. 2. Gender identity in
    motion pictures. 3. Historical films--History and
    criticism.
    I. Series II. Kelly, Kathleen Coyne. III. Pugh, Tison.
    791.4'36358207-dc22

Library of Congress Cataloging-in-Publication Data
Queer movie medievalisms / [edited] by Kathleen Coyne Kelly and Tison Pugh.
        p. cm.
    Includes bibliographical references and index.
    ISBN 978-0-7546-7592-1 (alk. paper)
    1. Homosexuality in motion pictures. 2. Middle Ages in motion pictures. 3. Homosexuality and motion pictures. I. Kelly, Kathleen Coyne. II. Pugh, Tison.

    PN1995.9.H55Q45 2009
    791.43'652664--dc22

                                                                        2009003421
    ISBN 978-0-7546-7592-1

Mixed Sources
Product group from well-managed
forests and other controlled sources
www.fsc.org Cert no. SGS-COC-2482
© 1996 Forest Stewardship Council

Printed and bound in Great Britain by
TJ International Ltd, Padstow, Cornwall.

Contents

Notes on Contributors

Susan Aronstein is Professor of English at the University of Wyoming. She has published articles on medieval Welsh and French Arthurian romances, medievalism and popular culture, and Arthurian film. She is also the author of *Hollywood Knights: Arthurian Cinema and the Politics of Nostalgia* and is co-authoring a book on Steven Spielberg entitled *Mourning in America: Loss and Redemption in the Cinema of Steven Spielberg*.

Martha Bayless is Associate Professor of English at the University of Oregon. She focuses on the intersection between literature and culture in the Middle Ages, and her works include *Parody in the Middle Ages: The Latin Tradition*, as well as scholarship and journalism on medieval entertainment and on modern film.

Michelle Bolduc is Associate Professor in French, Italian, and Comparative Literature at the University of Wisconsin, Milwaukee, where she frequently teaches medieval cinema. Her publications include *The Medieval Poetics of Contraries* and numerous articles on thirteenth-century French and Occitan literature and manuscript contexts. Her current research probes marginal and interlinear glosses and the uses of translation in the reception of vernacular authority in late medieval manuscripts.

Glenn Burger is Professor of English and Medieval Studies at Queens College and The Graduate Center, CUNY. He has edited Hetoum's *A Lytell Cronycle* and (with Steven Kruger) *Queering the Middle Ages*. He is author of *Chaucer's Queer Nation* and numerous articles on queer, gender, and postcolonial issues in Chaucerian texts. He is currently completing a book titled *Conduct Becoming: Representing the Good Wife in the Late Middle Ages*.

Jane Chance is Andrew W. Mellon Distinguished Chair in English at Rice University. She edits three book series and has published twenty-two books and over 100 articles, interviews, and reviews. Her most recent book on J. R. R. Tolkien is a co-edited collection, *Tolkien's Modern Middle Ages*; her latest monograph, *The Literary Subversions of Medieval Women*, received the 2008 SCMLA Prize. Her other essays on the Tolkien films include "Is There a Text in this Hobbit? Peter Jackson's *Fellowship of the Ring*," in *Literature/Film Quarterly*, and "Tolkien's Women (and Men): The Film and the Book," in *Tolkien on Film*.

Susan Hayward is the Established Chair of Cinema Studies at Exeter University where she is the Director of the Centre for Research into Film Studies. Professor Hayward is the author of several books on French cinema, including *French National Cinema*; *Simone Signoret: The Star as Cultural Sign*; *Luc Besson*; *French Film: Texts and Contexts* (with Ginette Vincendeau); *Les Diaboliques*; and *Nikita*. She is also the author of *Cinema Studies: The Key Concepts*.

Cary Howie is Assistant Professor of Romance Studies at Cornell University, where he teaches medieval French and Italian literature, critical theory, and gender studies. He is the author of *Claustrophilia: The Erotics of Enclosure in Medieval Literature* and, with William Burgwinkle, *Sanctity and Pornography in Medieval Culture: On the Verge*.

Kathleen Coyne Kelly has published in *Allegorica*, *Arthuriana*, *Assays*, *Exemplaria*, *Parergon*, *PRE/TEXT*, and *Studies in Philology*. She is author of *Performing Virginity and Testing Chastity in the Middle Ages* and co-editor, with Marina Leslie, of *Menacing Virgins: Representing Virginity in the Middle Ages and Renaissance*. Her current projects include a book on Sir Thomas Malory's *Morte D'Arthur*, titled *Malory's Desire for History and the History of Desire*, and essays on movie medievalism. She also has a cyberpunk trilogy in progress, the first volume of which is titled "Upon a Peak in Darien."

Anna Kłosowska is Associate Professor of French at Miami University. She is the author of *Queer Love in the Middle Ages* and the editor of *Violence against Women in Medieval Texts*. Her edition of newly discovered texts by a Renaissance poet, Madeleine de l'Aubespine, was published by the University of Chicago Press in 2007, and she is currently at work on *Medieval Subjects: Camp, Space, Fault*, as well as preparing a critical edition of the complete works of Madeleine de l'Aubespine for Honoré Champion Editeur.

Steven F. Kruger is Professor of English and Medieval Studies at Queens College and The Graduate Center, CUNY. He is currently Executive Officer of the Ph.D. Program in English at the Graduate Center. His books include *Dreaming in the Middle Ages*, *AIDS Narratives: Gender and Sexuality*, *Fiction and Science*, *Approaching the Millennium: Essays on* Angels in America (co-edited with Deborah R. Geis), *Queering the Middle Ages* (co-edited with Glenn Burger), and *The Spectral Jew: Conversion and Embodiment in Medieval Europe*. His current work concerns medieval Jewish converts to Christianity who became spokesmen for Christian orthodoxy.

Lisa Manter is Professor at Saint Mary's College of California, where she teaches courses in medieval studies and film. She has published articles on medieval mystics, including the article "The Savior of Her Desire: Margery Kempe's Passionate Gaze," *Exemplaria* 13.1 (Spring 2001), which examines Kempe's autobiography through the lens of feminist film theory. She is currently working in the area of camp studies and has recently completed an article that reads Chaucer's Wife of Bath as a camp icon. She was also the co-organizer of a conference on camp studies entitled "Many Camps: Subcultures and the Art of Survival," held at San Francisco State University, October 2006.

R. Barton Palmer is Calhoun Lemon Professor of Literature at Clemson University. As a medievalist, Palmer has published volumes devoted to Geoffrey Chaucer, Guillaume de Machaut, Jean Froissart, and Charles d'Orleans. His books on film include *Joel and Ethan Coen, After Hitchcock* (with David Boyd), and, most recently, *19ᵗʰ and 20ᵗʰ Century American Fiction on Screen*. He is the general editor of *Routledge Medieval Texts* and *Traditions in World Cinema*. His *Hollywood's Tennessee: The Williams Films and Postwar America* (with Robert Bray) and *To Kill a Mockingbird: The Relationship Between Text and Film* appeared this year.

Tison Pugh is an Associate Professor and Director of the Ph.D. Program in Texts and Technology in the Department of English at the University of Central Florida. He is the author of *Queering Medieval Genres* and *Sexuality and Its Queer Discontents in Middle English Literature*, as well as numerous articles on medieval literature in such journals as *Chaucer Review, College English, Arthuriana, Philological Quarterly,* and *Studies in Medieval and Renaissance Teaching*. With Angela Jane Weisl of Seton Hall University, he co-edited *Approaches to Teaching Chaucer's* Troilus and Criseyde *and the Shorter Poems;* with Lynn Ramey of Vanderbilt University, he co-edited *Race, Class, and Gender in "Medieval" Cinema*.

Lorraine Kochanske Stock is Associate Professor of English at the University of Houston, where she teaches a course on the Reel/Real Middle Ages. She has published numerous articles on authors including Dante, Langland, the *Pearl-*Poet, Froissart, Chaucer, and Malory, and on topics including medieval drama, Robin Hood, Arthurian romance, primitivism, the Wild Man, the Green Man, and the Sheela na Gig. She appeared in the A&E television documentary series *History vs. Hollywood,* and she is currently completing her study *The Medieval Wild Man: Primitivism and Civilization in Medieval Culture*. She was awarded the University of Houston's 2008 prize for Innovative Use of Technology in Teaching for her creation of a Hybrid Chaucer course.

Series Editors' Preface

Always, Already, Still Medieval

What cultural functions might 'bad cinematic history' have if not to re-enact the past? What insights might cinematic representations of the Middle Ages provide into contemporary understandings of gender, sexuality and other identitarian forms? What might queer theory contribute to this discussion? These are the central questions guiding the essays in *Queer Movie Medievalisms*. This book is concerned not with scrutinising the historical accuracy of movie medievalisms for, as Cary Howie reminds us, 'there is no unadulterated time to be restored or rescued', but rather seeks, what Kathleen Coyne Kelly and Tison Pugh term, 'another "Middle Ages"'—a space for reflection and reinvention unfettered from the demands of historical accuracy and charges of anachronism.

Queer Movie Medievalisms is an exercise in textual analysis. Each contributor displays a close attention to detail in their careful readings of individual films, generic conventions, audience reception patterns and star personae. This collection, as its title makes clear, centres on relationships and the staging of encounters between and inbetween entities: the past and the present, the viewer and film, the stage and the screen, fantasy and reality, not forgetting the three fields alluded to in this book's title: queer studies, film studies and medieval studies. This collection makes it impossible to ignore the 'middle' in Middle Ages because, as Gilles Deleuze and Félix Guattari put it, the middle 'is where things pick up speed'. Traversing Hollywood blockbusters, historical epics, westerns, comedies and musicals, *Queer Movie Medievalisms* sets up a creative space for thinking about what Jeffrey Jerome Cohen calls, 'temporal interlacement'. The theoretical proclivities of this book echo those of Alexander Doty: 'any text is always already potentially queer' or available for scrutiny by 'a queer eye'. It is not so much *what* but *how* one watches.

'We are, it may be argued, always, already, still, medieval'. The 'medieval' is presented as the Other in the field of history; it is the Other against which the 'modern' defines itself as more civilised, more relevant and thus more important. Medieval studies itself is sometimes predicated upon the abjection of so-called less professional, popularised and anachronistic approaches that have been designated 'medievalism' in a dismissive gesture. *Queer Movie Medievalisms* elides these unproductive schisms by bringing the insights of medieval studies and cultural criticism to bear on films which employ the Middle Ages as a way of exploring contemporary issues governing identities and relationships. The past is not a foreign country for the contributors to this volume. 'Modernity', the editors insist, 'does not figure a break with the past; rather, it expresses itself through quotation, imitation, invocation, and allusion to the past'.

Queer Movie Medievalisms forwards Michel Foucault's notion of a 'history of the present', a politicised engagement with the past for the purposes of understanding how the present has come into being and to strategise around how to move beyond the current situation without replicating past scripts. It is a tactile history, a 'getting medieval' which, for Carolyn Dinshaw, signifies 'The process of touching, of making partial connections between incommensurate entities...using ideas of the past, creating relations with the past'. Historical accuracy might be of little concern to film producers who seek to exploit the medieval for its entertainment value but the latent and blatant (mis)appropriation of the Middle Ages for cinematic pleasure also impacts on the desire of the cinema-going populace to know more about the Middle Ages while also affecting what and how they learn about the period.

Queer, 'a protean and contested term', is put to work by the contributors as 'a disruptive mode of inquiry, one that destabilizes expectations of normativity', primarily through interdisciplinary, intertextual, interdiscursive and intertemporal reading strategies and an attendance to camp and othering as a critical lens for interrogating how particular films promote, make visible, challenge and subvert—sometimes simultaneously—compulsory heterosexuality. *Queer Movie Medievalisms* makes an intervention into queer work on film. Queer theoretical engagements with film studies include a number of different approaches: the discursive examination of the representation of sexual and gender identity categories and those who sport them across a range of films, as well as how gender and sexuality intersect with other forms of identification such as race, ethnicity, nationality, class, age, religion and dis/ability. There is a concerted effort to attend to heteronormativity by discussing how particular films promote, make visible, challenge and subvert—sometimes simultaneously— compulsory heterosexuality. These analyses treat films—either singly or in more broad-based studies—as texts and undertake close readings of, for example, characters, dialogue, particular scenes, intertextual elements as cues to latent themes, and diagetic elements such as light and sound. They are based on the understanding that the viewer creates meaning in the text as much as those behind the camera.

B. Ruby Rich coined 'New Queer Cinema' in the early 1990s as a loose descriptor for independently produced films exhibiting a flagrant disregard for and defiance of norms, conventions and rules, and those sporting an unapologetic attitude towards representing the complexity of queer lives. New Queer Cinema is not useful as a moniker for the films discussed in this book. 'Queer Movie Medievalisms', the nonce taxonomy put forward by the book's editors, serves to illustrate better the multiple ways in which the past is (re)enacted through the prism of popular culture and the ways in which we as viewers collude in this. *Queer Movie Medievalisms* is, above all, a book about pleasure: the pleasure involved in producing and viewing, reading, writing and talking about films. Such pleasure is palpable throughout the chapters for these writers are not just scholars but fans of the movies, the historical figures, the actors they focus on. *Queer Movie Medievalisms* invites us to partake of such pleasure, not just to entertain us, but also in the hope of transforming us, perhaps unwittingly, into 'medievalism*ists*'.

Noreen Giffney and Michael O'Rourke

Acknowledgements

We would like to thank the Series Editors of *Queer Interventions*, Noreen Giffney and Michael O'Rourke, for their encouragement and support through the creation of this volume, as well as Ashgate's Neil Jordan, Gemma Lowle, and Carolyn Court for their expert advice. The volume is much improved due to the suggestions of its anonymous reviewers, and we appreciate their candid assessments of its earlier drafts. We also appreciate the support of our home institutions: the Department of English of Northeastern University, and in particular Laura Green, Chair, for providing Kathleen Kelly with funding for the cover image and the stills reproduced in her chapter; and the College of Arts and Humanities of the University of Central Florida, for providing Tison Pugh with sabbatical leave to complete this project.

Introduction

Queer History, Cinematic Medievalism, and the Impossibility of Sexuality

Kathleen Coyne Kelly and Tison Pugh

"The queer present negotiates with the past, knowing full well that the future is at stake," observes B. Ruby Rich, as she points to history's complicity in the continual creation and re-creation of contemporary queerness.[1] Surely history matters in the fraught dialectic between the past and the present as we discover new paths into the future, but we must also ponder how history is even possible, since it involves the recuperation of that which is, by definition, already lost. In the urge to understand history—and, often, out of a desire to experience history—period films attempt to re-create the past, but can only do so through a revisioning that inevitably replicates modernity and its concerns. To say so is to invoke a familiar trope on which scholars depend when writing about films set in any period earlier than our own, and in the following Introduction and chapters, we hope to test the boundaries of this trope through foregrounding the queerness of movie medievalisms. Queer past, queer present, and queer future merge in films of the Middle Ages as they address issues of gender and sexuality relevant to contemporary audiences yet nonetheless mediated through a fictionalized and historicized past.

In combining these terms—*queer* and *movie medievalism*—we take as a premise that modernity is a "condition" (to borrow from Lyotard), a condition characterized by an elaborate and conflicted preoccupation with the past, and therefore deserving of interrogation.[2] Building on this premise, we hope to make two points: that queer theory is a useful mode by which to begin such an interrogation, in part because queer theory has the power to disrupt our notions of linearity and of a differentiating temporality (that is, how difference might

---

1 B. Ruby Rich, "The New Queer Cinema," *Queer Cinema*, eds. Harry Benshoff and Sean Griffin (New York: Routledge, 2004), 53-59, at p. 58.

2 Jean-François Lyotard, *The Postmodern Condition*, trans. Geoff Bennington and Brian Massumi (1979; Minneapolis: U of Minnesota P, 1984).

be experienced as past/present/future); and second, that we see the cinematic Middle Ages as an especially rich and even singular site for queer/ing study, in part because moderns so often construct the medieval period as emphatically opposed to modernity.

Modernity—and its hyperbolic epiphenomenon that we sometimes call postmodernity—might be said to manifest itself as a relation to the past. Modernity, in spite of those moderns who phantasize otherwise, does not necessitate a break with the past; rather, it expresses itself through quotation, imitation, invocation, and allusion to the past. Modernity represents a kind of temporal hybridity, as it were. Queerness has often been constructed as a modernist project in part because of the Foucauldian narrative of a *before* and an *after* of homosexuality, a binary upon which modernity depends for the construction of today's sexualities.[3] However, many scholars, and many medieval scholars among them, demonstrate the falsity of this binary with respect to subject formation. There is no *before* the subject; there are historically specific subjectivities as well as historically specific queer subjectivities. Queerness and its theorizations ask us to question the assumptions that progression and direction are evolutionary processes that result in stable identities; queerness might be said to run not along a linear, straight path, but along a helical, looping arc.

Scott Bravmann offers an alternative to a rigid historicist project when he articulates the need for scholars of queer history "to stretch rather than reinforce the boundaries that define queer history and its academic study, to think outside the historically specific formations that distinguish absolutely between the literal and the figurative, the real and the imaginary—between, in other words, 'fact' and 'fiction.'"[4] Several medieval scholars, including Judith Bennett, Carolyn Dinshaw, Karma Lochrie, and James Schultz articulate the value of exploring the figurative and the imaginary with respect to queer subjectivities in the Middle Ages.[5] As is well known, post-Foucauldian scholars have maintained that the "birth" of homosexuality, and hence heterosexuality, can be located in the nineteenth century, and Lochrie and Schultz provocatively argue for the paradoxical scene of the Middle Ages as innocent of heterosexuality, urging us

---

3 Foucault famously dates the birth of the homosexual to the 1870s, in which a transformation of perception occurred: "The sodomite had been a temporary aberration; the homosexual was now a species" (*The History of Sexuality: Volume 1, An Introduction*, trans. Robert Hurley [New York: Vintage, 1990], p. 43).

4 Scott Bravmann, *Queer Fictions of the Past* (Cambridge: Cambridge UP, 1997), p. 129.

5 See Judith Bennett, "'Lesbian-Like' and the Social History of Lesbianisms," *Journal of the History of Sexuality* 9.1-2 (2000): 1-24; Carolyn Dinshaw, *Getting Medieval* (Durham, NC: Duke UP, 1999); Karma Lochrie, *Heterosyncrasies: Female Sexuality When Normal Wasn't* (Minneapolis: U of Minnesota P, 2005); and James Schultz, *Courtly Love, the Love of Courtliness, and the History of Sexuality* (Chicago: U of Chicago P, 2006).

2

to reconsider using heterosexuality as the default hermeneutic for understanding medieval sexuality.[6] Such scholarship has already influenced how we read the Western European Middle Ages; that is, the texts, the visual and plastic arts, and the monuments and artifacts produced between 500 and 1500 C.E. We define the Middle Ages rather ploddingly as a time or period (albeit with fuzzy borders) to make the point that there is another "Middle Ages"; that is, all the accretions since, thereof and thereon. It is *this* Middle Ages in which we are interested in this collection—a Middle Ages that has been historically recast as a place and a time of an intransigent and romanticized vision of heterosexuality.

Contributors to this collection work on several levels, for they must be familiar with the insights of medieval scholars who address queer territory and current queer theory, attend to the medieval "source" texts themselves as well as to cinematic retellings of medieval texts, and utilize current film theory. Contributors do so to demonstrate, even showcase, how rich readings of movie medievalisms can be by undercutting notions of linear temporality. Contributors ask over and over again, "what is 'queer' anyway?" It is a question that informs each essay in this collection, and one that we are not invested in answering fixedly, for we acknowledge that it is a protean and contested term. A partial answer, useful for introducing this collection, is that we believe that *queer* is used most energetically as a disruptive mode of inquiry, one that destabilizes expectations of normativity. Queer theory has the power to disrupt not only the normativity of heterosexuality, but also the normativity of history, for it is how history is written, received, and understood that establishes master narratives in the first place. To queer "medieval" cinema is challenging work, in that we must contend with two separate time periods— the medieval past and the filmmaker's present—and two different phantasies—again, that of the medieval past and the filmmaker's present—and tease out how historical coherence (another phantasy) and the possibility of a unified sexual subject (yet another) play out in narratives created to tell a tale relevant to the present through negotiations of the past.

We posit that negotiating past and present in "medieval" films is often a queering process because it strips away foundational arguments of gender and sexuality as embodied in time. Past and present cannot be neatly distinguished from each other because the present uses the past to confront itself, and these confrontations are often intimately connected to issues of gender and sexuality. Think, for instance, of Disney's cinematic princesses and the marketing juggernaut that they have sparked, as well as the ways in which they introduce, if not inculcate, young girls into paradigms both archaic and contemporary, yet seamlessly and insistently heterosexual: what are the personal, cultural, and ideological ramifications of young girls locating role models of identity in a

---

6 See Lochrie, *Heterosyncrasies*, pp. xi-xxviii, and Schultz, *Courtly Love*, pp. 51-62.

medievalized past, when these models are both connected to and severed from modern conceptions of female identity? Here is where we see the queerness of gender formation in the negotiations of past and present: that the seamlessness of such unions between present and past proclaims a normativity phantastically and historically implausible yet nonetheless stunningly persuasive.

Many scholars decry the ubiquitous solecisms of films set in the Middle Ages, but anachronisms are not always to be lamented; rather, might they not be embraced as a means of understanding the cultural work of medievalism? Ostensible flubs (a twelfth-century Norman woman wouldn't wear that!) can indicate the ways in which contemporary filmmakers infuse their work with modern concerns—often political, especially with respect to gender and sexuality. For in the mediation between past and present, history becomes misty, and so, too, do constructions of gender and sexuality as incarnated by the historical and/or fictional characters who populate these films. Time fluctuates according to perspective, as Johannes Fabian notes, and in his work he takes anthropologists to task for a locational presentism, as it were: too often, according to Fabian, anthropologists situate themselves in the "here and now" and the peoples under study in the "there and then." The place and space of the Other are constructed as earlier in time—as "primitive"—when, of course, the researchers and their subjects of study are contemporaneous. Fabian calls this confusion of categories in which space is figured as time the "denial of coevalness."[7] While medievals are indeed separated from us by time, and only traces of medieval places remain, it strikes us that there is another kind of "denial of coevalness" operating here, resulting in what has, to date, served as a fortuitous divide between "modern us" and "pre-modern them" when we are, to take the long view, still coeval. We are, it may be argued, always, already, still, medieval.[8] From high culture to low culture—from Denis de Rougemont to Disney—the break with the past that constructs the Middle Ages as indeed another country also creates the medieval period as an important, if not primary, site for culturally productive and serious, phantastical play.

When it comes to cinematic representation, what sets apart the Middle Ages from ancient Rome, say, or Shakespeare's time, or the Victorian era, is the master narrative of courtly love, a trope that itself defies boundaries, for it is a result of the cooperation and the connivance of the medieval and the modern. Courtly love was heterosexualized by medievals, but also relentlessly so by moderns, who have also metonomized the clichéd materialities of a certain kind of medievalism—the knight in shining armor, the damsel in distress—as heterosexual. Thus, courtly love (a unifying modern term for a diverse medieval

---

7 Johannes Fabian, *Time and the Other* (New York: Columbia UP, 1983).

8 This conceit is reverse-mirrored in Bruno Latour's *We Have Never Been Modern*, trans. Catherine Porter (Cambridge, MA: Harvard UP, 1993).

phenomenon: it is not a fact of history; it is a phenomenon of literary history) invokes the Middle Ages through an iconic shorthand of heterosexuality that resonates powerfully in today's culture.[9] Because of the power of the master narrative of courtly love, the Middle Ages as a site for modern films differs intrinsically from films set in other eras; in fact, many of the films discussed in this collection include some representation of what is thought to be courtly love—or what is phantasized thereof. As all those who teach medieval humanities know, courtly love remains an extremely tenacious idea in popular culture; its premises, descriptions, and definitions are rarely questioned. Even though courtly love is often parodied, such parodies point to a "belief" in courtly love in the first place. As with most robust master narratives, tenor and vehicle have collapsed together in the popular imaginary, admitting of no interrogation of the concept. Queering movie medievalisms helps to prise apart the tenor and vehicle of courtly love to allow for alternative readings along the axes of time and space. Movies set either in the Middle Ages or in contemporary times with medievalized themes, in part through their sheer popularity, ask their audiences to think metadiscursively about the representation of the past.

While archetypal figures of jousting knights and fair maidens may well be put to use to create a recognizable though othered medieval past, such knights and maidens simultaneously serve as models of behavior for modern-day audiences engaged in complex identifications with who, or what, is projected on the screen. If, as we are arguing, history moves in two directions, so too does the experience of viewing and consuming a film. Janet Staiger identifies spectatorship as a perverse dynamic between viewer and viewed, in which "each act of deviant (*and normative*) viewing requires historical and political analysis to locate its effects and 'judge' its politics."[10] "Medieval" sexualities on screen represent a modern revisioning of the past, yet the past nonetheless provides a historical model for its own depiction, and viewers likewise participate in the construction of meaning as an oscillating effect between past and present. Hence the impossibility of heterosexuality, or of any sexuality, predicated upon cinematic medievalism: identity as constructed through the past cannot escape the charge of presentism, and thus queerness serves as a defining metaphor for studying both sexuality and historical films. The medievalism of modern movies presents a vision of reality, all the while not being what it ostensibly *is*.

---

9 For the literary history and invention of courtly love, see David Hult, "Gaston Paris and the Invention of Courtly Love," *Medievalism and the Modernist Temper*, eds. Howard Bloch and Stephen Nichols (Baltimore, MD: Johns Hopkins UP, 1996), pp. 192-224.

10 Janet Staiger, *Perverse Spectators* (New York: New York UP, 2000), p. 32; her italics.

Consider, for example, the website www.kiltmen.com, where one may read a manifesto against "trouser tyranny"—that is, against the Western cultural imperative that men wear trousers. Historically, men from around the world have worn more anatomically appropriate clothing than trousers, such as robes, caftans, tunics—and, of course, kilts. Some men who prefer kilts call themselves "Bravehearts," and these Bravehearts deny that wearing kilts represents any interest in crossdressing. Instead, they argue that, since so many women (in the West) now wear trousers, "if a man wishes to distinguish his masculinity through clothing, he would do much better by strapping on a real Scottish kilt."[11] Mel Gibson's *Braveheart* (1995) provides the eponymous and cinematically "authentic" inspiration for modern kilt-wearing identity, despite the fact that no Scot wore a belted plaid or anything kilt-like in the late thirteenth century.[12] Costume is only one of many historical inaccuracies in this cinematic phantasy about William Wallace, as reviewers and critics have noted since the film's release. Still, bad cinematic history has its uses, not only for Bravehearts, but also for the many medievalists, fans, and armchair critics who investigate movie medievalisms to explore representations of the past and their cultural function in the present. By embracing an anachronistic and cinematic reconstruction of the past, Bravehearts mediate their masculinities through a queering historical process in which the performance of masculinity is made possible by the movies, yet is undone by history. In this move, they unite themselves more closely with the fans of Disney's princesses (with their phantasies of heterosexuality) than with medieval men (and a version of masculinity that these men never lived).

Thus it would be useful to return to *Braveheart* to read the costumes, not in terms of their historical egregiousness, but in terms of how masculinity is made manifest. Indeed, masculinity splits along English/Scottish lines in the film: the English (and the French Queen) wear bright silks, elaborate chain mail, and careful coifs; the Scots, hair braided or wild, wear rough homespun, leather, and kilts. The English are well-groomed and orderly soldiers; the Scots are mud-stained and ragged guerillas. And therein lies another queer tale, only to be suggested here: is the English claim to Scotland illegitimate because the English aristocracy minces in such effeminate trappings? After all, the film ends as King Edward II, who was reputedly homosexual and possibly executed with an iron rod inserted into his anus, ascends to the throne.[13] Is Scotland's

---

11 See www.kiltmen.com, last accessed on 10/08/2008.

12 See Colin McArthur, "*Braveheart* and the Scottish Aesthetic Dementia," *Screening the Past*, ed. Tony Barta (Westport, CT: Praeger, 1998), 167-87, who points out that both the English and Scots were "of Anglo-Norman origin, had attained broadly the level of material development, [and] inhabited the same European code of chivalry" (p. 168).

13 For Edward II's possible homosexuality and his relationship with Piers Gaveston, see Roy Martin Haines, *King Edward II* (Montreal: McGill-Queen's UP, 2003), pp. 42-

claim to freedom also a claim to a nationalized masculinity, as signified by the overdetermined and anachronistic kilt?

In *Queer Movie Medievalisms*, we turn to films set in the Middle Ages not only to explore the uses of the medieval past to investigate, represent, or even challenge modern concerns, but also to foreground the queer tales that so often underwrite the projections of modern desires regarding gender and sexuality onto the medieval past. In 1992, film critic B. Ruby Rich published a meditation on the "New Queer Cinema"—that is, what she saw as an innovative trend to interrogate heteronormative representations on the screen and to address the tensions between cinematic representation and cultural ideology.[14] Since Rich, film critics speak simply of "Queer Cinema": it has (already) arrived. Thus we think it is time to turn a critical eye to movie medievalisms and the ways in which they complicate notions of cinematic queerness. "Medieval" films receive a good deal of scholarly attention these days,[15] yet the relationships between the medieval material and the director, as well as between the material and the audience, need continually deeper exploration. What has gotten in the way of doing so, of taking movie medievalism on its own terms, is the desire, even obsession, to expose the many anachronisms and inaccuracies that often characterize films about the Middle Ages. But let the artistic voices speak for themselves on this issue. For example, Mark Twain's *A Connecticut Yankee in King Arthur's Court* may be seen as the novelistic precursor of much movie medievalism in its deployment of the oft-repeated trope of time travel to the Middle Ages, but Twain cared little about historical accuracy, as he announced in his Preface:

> The ungentle laws and customs touched upon in this tale are historical, and the episodes which are used to illustrate them are also historical. It is not pretended that these laws and customs existed in England in the sixth century; no, it is only pretended that inasmuch as they existed in the English and other civilizations of

---

43; see also John Boswell, *Christianity, Social Tolerance, and Homosexuality* (Chicago: U of Chicago P, 1980), pp. 298–300, for a discussion of Edward's purported anal execution.

14 B. Ruby Rich, "The New Queer Cinema," pp. 53–59.

15 Recent studies of "medieval" films include Lynn Ramey and Tison Pugh, eds., *Race, Class, and Gender in "Medieval" Cinema* (New York: Palgrave, 2007); Susan Aronstein, *Hollywood Knights: Arthurian Cinema and the Politics of Nostalgia* (New York: Palgrave, 2005); Martha Driver and Sid Ray, eds., *The Medieval Hero on Screen* (Jefferson, NC: McFarland, 2004); John Aberth, *A Knight at the Movies: Medieval History on Film* (New York: Routledge, 2003); Kevin Harty, ed., *Cinema Arthuriana: Twenty Essays*, rev. ed. (Jefferson, NC: McFarland, 2002) and *King Arthur on Film* (Jefferson, NC: McFarland, 1999). See also the special issue of *Exemplaria*, "Movie Medievalism," 19.2 (2007).

far later times, it is safe to consider that it is no libel upon the sixth century to suppose them to have been in practice in that day also.[16]

It appears that Twain excused himself from much library research during his creation of *Connecticut Yankee*; he cites the historicity of his fictions only to dismiss the necessity of historical accuracy to engage in his social critique of nineteenth-century America through the lens of the medieval past. In the cinematic milieu, a similar sentiment is expressed in "Life Could Not Better Be," the jaunty opening song of Danny Kaye's comedy *The Court Jester* (1955):

> We did research,
> Authenticity was a must.
> Zooks! Did we search!
> And what did we find? (Achoo!)
> A lot of dust![17]

With its humorous and dismissive sneeze, this tune highlights the spirit in which many films revisit the Middle Ages: the cinematic experience, above virtually all other considerations, should be fun, and if history becomes too taxing in the re-creation of the medieval past, the artists can return to the pleasure of the narrative at hand, leaving those musty tomes in the archive far behind.

The contributors to this volume take as a starting point that most of the artistic forces behind the medieval film genre, including directors, writers, stars, cinematographers, and set and costume designers, are not as concerned with constructing a historically accurate past as much as they are attempting to make an artistic piece of entertainment (within the financial restraints of the profit-driven economy of most cinemas). For scholars to focus attention solely on anachronism is thus to miss the ways in which medieval films create a fictional world largely independent of a verifiable historical past. We are thus free to consider seriously the popularity of medieval film, and to study how the legendary and mythic aura of the Middle Ages serves the interests of modern artists and viewers, and in ways often detached from anything

---

16 Mark Twain, *A Connecticut Yankee in King Arthur's Court*, The Oxford Mark Twain, series editor Shelley Fisher Fishkin (New York: Oxford UP, 1996), p. xv.

17 *The Court Jester*, dir. Melvin Frank and Norman Panama, perf. Danny Kaye and Glynis Johns, 1955. For another Hollywood version of "research," see Kathleen Coyne Kelly, who, in her study of the marketing for *The Knights of the Round Table* (Richard Thorpe, 1953), quotes the souvenir booklet: "A staff of research experts . . . started the most intensive search yet made of the habits and customs of sixth century Britain." History, as she says, is fungible, whether real or invented ("Hollywood Simulacrum: *The Knights of the Round Table* [1953]," *Exemplaria* 19 [2007]: 270-89).

medievalists would recognize as their area of study. Although films reflect the artistic decisions of their creators, they also participate in dominant ideological structures that further imbue such structures with meaning. Ideology does not depend upon historical accuracy to inculcate its values successfully, and, in this manner, modern ideologies can be encoded through medievalism, as they can also be resisted through medievalism.[18] It should be further noted that "medieval" does not mean the same thing to a French or an American director, say, or to an actor/actress working in the 1930s, the 1960s, or now. The Western European Middle Ages was not a monologic entity (as much as the phrase suggests otherwise), and its histories, modern appropriations of, and influences are indeed various yet culturally specific.

It also bears mentioning that our sense of queer cinema differs markedly from traditional uses of the term in film studies. Quite simply, most analysis of queer cinema focuses on films depicting homosexuals and homosexual relationships, and numerous excellent studies elucidate Hollywood's history in this regard. In *The Celluloid Closet* Vitto Russo pioneered the study of cinematic representations of homosexuals, and now numerous scholars examine film's portrayal of homosexuality, often in terms of varying tactics among national cinemas.[19] Our approach, however, takes queer cinema as a tactic of interpretation rather than primarily as a subject matter for portrayal. What is queer about movie medievalisms is markedly different from the queerness of, say, *Making Love* (1982), *The Incredibly True Adventure of Two Girls in Love* (1995), *The Birdcage* (1996), *Beautiful Thing* (1996), or *Brokeback Mountain* (2005), in that these representative films focus on gay love and relationships, whereas the queer movies under examination in this collection appear to focus on heterosexuality in the Middle Ages only to show the historical and representational implausibility of transhistorical sexuality.

Thus, we focus, as our pluralized title suggests, on representations of genders and sexualities in films with medieval settings. We are interested in exploring why the Middle Ages proves to be such a fruitful period for filmmakers interested in critiquing gender roles and/or in offering alternative sexualities. The chapters in

---

18 For a theoretical basis of ideology, we rely on Louis Althusser, who suggests that "ideology has no history, which emphatically does not mean that there is no history in it (on the contrary, for it is merely the pale, empty and inverted reflection of real history) but that it has no history *of its own*" (*On Ideology* [1971; London: Verso, 2008], p. 34).

19 Vito Russo, *The Celluloid Closet: Homosexuality in the Movies*, rev. ed. (Harper & Row, 1987). For examples of queer studies of national cinemas, see Alica Kuzniar, *The Queer German Cinema* (Stanford, CA: Stanford UP, 2000); Robin Griffiths, ed., *British Queer Cinema* (London: Routledge, 2006); Raz Yosef, *Beyond Flesh: Queer Masculinities and Nationalism in Israelia Cinema* (New Brunswick, NJ: Rutgers UP, 2004); and David Foster, *Queer Issues in Contemporary Latin American Cinema* (Austin: U of Texas P, 2003).

this collection begin with the premise that modern preoccupations with gender and sexuality are often inserted, intentionally or not, into a setting that would normally be considered incompatible with modern ideologies concerning these concepts. The Middle Ages provides an imaginary space far enough removed from the present day to allow for critical analysis of contemporary gender and sexuality. The result, as we hope to show, is a queered vision of medieval and modern sexualities, for both dialectically underscore the impossibility of maintaining the illusion of a normative (hetero)sexuality. Indeed, as we have noted, recent critical work on the Middle Ages argues it is misleading to assume that heterosexuality is the default position when studying medieval sexuality. From this perspective, the possibility of medieval normative heterosexuality—whether as reflective of reality in the Middle Ages or as an interpretive tool today—appears ever more chimerical.

Two terms should be introduced at this point, not necessarily to define them, but to note the difficulties attached to each, and to keep in mind that such difficulties have their uses. These are not terms that are usually discussed together, but both are essential to our project in this collection: namely, *camp* and *medievalism*—or, better, *camps* and, as we have been saying, *medievalisms*. The queer may be campy, and the campy may be queer, but they are not always and everywhere synonymous terms. At the most general level, *camp* might be described as a subversively humorous intervention in the union of form and content. However, where to locate that intervention proves problematic: is camp lodged in a given performance or artifact, or is it found in the sensibility of readers, viewers, and consumers? To what degree are disjunctions between form and content historically specific? What sort of aesthetic sensibility produces and perceives camp, and to what degree does this sensibility exist along a trajectory that includes the stuff of high culture and the schlock of low culture? Moreover, to what degree is camp the result of, or the province of, an exclusively gay aesthetic? Consider the "knowing wink" in cinematic medievalisms that might inform the audience that the performers intend to deflate their performances of any hint of gravitas, and which might just signal the queer. Locating that wink—whether it is found in the artist, the art, the viewer, or their complex interaction—proves to be the elusive yet distinctive feature of camp(s). Defining camp, then, faces similar critical cruxes notable in defining humor and pornography: when dissecting humor, one faces the likely possibility of bleeding the comic from it, and when parsing pornography, one is faced with a critical category so nebulous that U.S. Supreme Court Justice Potter Stewart's famous nondefinition—"I know it when I see it"—best sums it up by refusing to taxonomize it at all. Despite Susan Sontag's landmark analysis of camp in which she pinpoints no less than fifty-eight articles lining its parameters, the protean humor of camp resists and undermines efforts to pin it down and name it.[20]

Andrew Ross succinctly describes camp as the "mimicry of existing cultural forms."[21] In this view, camp is a symbiotic effect that needs a foundation upon which to build its subversive meaning. Fabio Cleto, also understanding camp as derivative, declares: "Representational excess, heterogeneity, and *gratuitousness* of reference . . . both signal and contribute to an overall resistance to [a] definition" of camp.[22] In its dependence upon reference points in history and culture, camp sometimes faces the possibility of its own belatedness, and, in some cases, of becoming entirely static, as Quentin Crisp humorously observed of some drag queens:

> The strange thing about "camp" is that it has become fossilized. The mannerisms have never changed. If I were to see a woman sitting with her knees clamped together, one hand on her hip and the other lightly touching her back hair, I should think, "Either she scored her last social triumph in 1926 or it is a man in drag."[23]

Camp in this respect always needs the past; it is an aesthetic and artistic response, however sly and knowing, to what comes before. And thus campiness—which often defines visions of the Middle Ages through excess citationality overdetermined with meanings—pervades much movie medievalism.

But Moe Meyer argues that such descriptions of camp wrongly conflate camp and pop, thus evacuating camp of its political power to signify the queer. In fact Meyer argues against a plurality of camp altogether:

> [T]here are not different kinds of camp. There is only one. And it is queer. It can be engaged directly by the queer to produce social visibility in the praxis of everyday life, or it can be manifested as the camp trace by the un-queer in order . . . to provide queer access to the apparatus of representation.[24]

Meyer's understanding of camp makes "camp" and "queer" synonymous, if we understand queerness as a destabilizing feature of dominant discourses of power. Here camp participates in the representation of queerness as its defining

20 Susan Sontag, "Notes on 'Camp,'" *Camp,* ed. Fabio Cleto (Ann Arbor: U of Michigan P, 1999), 53-65.

21 Andrew Ross, "Uses of Camp," *Camp,* 308-29, at p. 325.

22 Fabio Cleto, "Introduction: Queering the Camp," *Camp,* 1-42, at p. 3.

23 Quentin Crisp, *The Naked Civil Servant* (1968; New York: Penguin, 1997), p. 21.

24 Moe Meyer, "Introduction: Reclaiming the Discourse of Camp," *The Politics and Poetics of Camp,* ed. Moe Meyer (London: Routledge, 1994), 1-22, at p. 5.

feature. Queerness and camp, in this formulation, are always already *here*. Since ideology can never fully shield itself from its own contradictions, queerness works from the inside to achieve its contradictory effects of reproduction and resistance. In this volume, we make room for both camps and recognize that they may well manifest themselves simultaneously, and that movie medievalisms, in their hyperbolic historical play, provide fruitful settings for camp to flourish.

Understanding camp as effects, or even celebrations, of tensions between high and low culture (differences that are contingent, not fixed), and understanding camp as contested critical ground, also helps us to understand some of the critical difficulties attendant upon defining medievalism. Umberto Eco juxtaposes icons from high and low culture (Jacques Le Goff and Darth Vader, Rabelais and Monty Python, manuscripts and comic books), and thus dramatizes the differences between a medievalism that is taken as a serious, scholarly subject and a medievalism that manifests itself in pop culture and is a consumable product.[25] The medievalism located on each end of this spectrum elicits laments from the ostensibly opposed factions: stereotypically humorless professors who bemoan students with an encyclopedic knowledge of Tolkien's *Lord of the Rings* but with little interest in the medieval sources that underlie these narratives, or the medieval fair enthusiasts who resent interruptions into their pastime by eggheads with a good deal of knowledge yet little sense of fun. Finding common ground between these factions often proves difficult, despite that their shared appreciation of the Middle Ages should smooth over many of the disagreements arising from differences in perspective.

As we consider the problem of defining *medievalism*, we begin with a simple, although deliberately tautological, definition: it is the postmedieval representation of the medieval. Part of the tautology, of course, lies in defining "medieval" itself. As Eco famously puts it, "every time one speaks of a dream of the Middle Ages, one should first ask which Middle Ages one is dreaming of."[26] Medievalism as a subject has created medievalism*ists*, as it were. Every historical period subsequent to the Middle Ages reinvents the era in its own artistic media, and scholars of these periods are perpetually interested in contending with the longstanding influence of medievalisms upon more recent histories. From Shakespeare's readings of Chaucer to southern slaveholders' post-bellum turn to Anglo-Saxonism, from eighteenth-century novelists reimagining the meaning of Gothicism to twentieth-century science fiction and fantasy, the allure of the Middle Ages invites the present to consider itself through the past.[27]

---

25 Umberto Eco, "Living in the New Middle Ages," trans. William Weaver, *Travels in Hyperreality* (1973; New York: Harcourt, 1986), pp. 73-85.

26 Umberto Eco, "Living in the New Middle Ages," p. 68.

27 The range of medievalist studies is too wide to capture in a footnote, but representative studies touching these various re-creations of the medieval past include

Medievalism is often construed as the unwanted stepchild, as it were, of medieval studies, and we do not believe that we should suture over these difficulties. Rather, by highlighting them, we ask our readers to consider the purposes behind such roadblocks between scholarly and pop-culture constructions of the Middle Ages. For us, medievalism includes the possibility of a virtually inherent queerness, in that medievalism obliterates historical foundations of subject and object. The scholarly subject, who ostensibly leads the inquiry, is lured into a relationship with the past as object, but these foundational positions are subverted due to the dissolution of past and present through their interconnections. Likewise, the essayists in this collection explore how and why movie makers exploit the Middle Ages to tell their stories; they do not tally anachronisms but play with the queer potential of "intertemporality." Furthermore, they are interested in how actors, screenwriters, and other creative forces behind a film play with medieval material while remaining mindful of the debates about cinematic historical accuracy. That is to say, these artists depend on historical reality in strikingly different ways, and the multiplicity of medievalisms at play in cinema offers a vantage point into how and why present artists turn to the past. For example, Susan Hayward, Lisa Manter, and Lorraine Stock discuss films set in the Middle Ages in the context of a director's oeuvre. Tison Pugh, Kathleen Kelly, and Martha Bayless address the Hollywood star system and how star personalities are mediated through medievalism. Most essayists take note of the initial reception of a given film, and explore the trajectory of a film's cultural status, which indeed returns us to history—not of the Middle Ages, but of the times and places that produced the film(s) under examination. Both histories—the past and the present—mingle in a given movie, and thus queerly dissolve the gendered fiction of past and present as separate.

Intertemporality, the fusion or combination of *then* and *now*, nicely complicates current theories of the gaze: the medieval scene into which a viewer inserts her/himself, either as seeing or been seen, being or having, is doubly phantasmatic, in that the medieval scene never existed *then* and does not exist *now*—whether filmed on site (always already not there) or on a set (a simulacrum). There is no "medieval" body, but only an actor whose body is an overdetermined signifier. Gendered identifications—plural, for the gaze is not the absolute Mulveyian male (white) heterosexual gaze, but is various and diverse, and even multiple within any given spectator—thus must traverse time as well as the terrain of

Talbot Donaldson, *The Swan at the Well: Shakespeare Reading Chaucer* (New Haven: Yale UP, 1985); Bernard Rosenthal and Paul Szarmach, eds., *Medievalism in American Culture* (Binghamton, NY: MRTS, 1989); Allen Frantzen and John Niles, eds., *Anglo-Saxonism and the Construction of Social Identity* (Gainesville: UP of Florida, 1997); Chris Brooks, *The Gothic Revival* (London: Phaidon, 1999); and Angela Jane Weisl, *The Persistence of Medievalism* (New York: Palgrave, 2003).

cinematic convention and codes that allow for, even propel, queer viewing.[28] We know an effeminate courtier or prince in hose and hyperbolic hat when we see one; we recognize the virginal heroine by her jeweled cross and modest dress—which shall we be, and which shall we have? Is our gazing desire to be or to have William Wallace or Mel Gibson? Morgan le Fay or Myrna Loy? This *frisson* of pleasure is thus many-layered, and located, perhaps, in a perverse experience of the anachronistic body—incongruous, impossible, *then* and *now* and *never* but mediated through a gaze that likewise shifts through time and body. Our cover image captures this shift: modernity confronts the queered medieval in the 1931 *A Connecticut Yankee* as Hank Martin/Will Rogers, dressed in a contemporary white shirt and black overcoat, looks awry at Amyas le Poulet/Frank Albertson in his pageboy, tunic and hose. Under interrogation is gender, for Martin is uncertain how to read Amyas' body—but also under interrogation is the gaze itself, for who is looking at whom—actor or character? Can we intervene and triangulate this gaze? Must we, do we, choose—or be chosen—to identify with the modern gaze that questions, or the medieval/ized recipient of that gaze *who looks back* without a qualm?

Our volume begins with a series of chapters that interrogates the meaning and function of male relationships, in that the propagation of the family ostensibly depends upon heterosexuality in reproduction, yet families are often inflected with queerness despite any struggle to define the nuclear unit as normative. In "The Law of the Daughter: Queer Family Politics in Bertrand Tavernier's *La Passion Béatrice*," Lisa Manter looks at the ways in which the family is queerly reimagined in terms of paternal and maternal alignments. Tavernier's retelling of the Cenci family tragedy upends expectations of familial normativity by queerly reconfiguring the meaning of patriarchy. In "Queering the Lionheart: Richard I in *The Lion in Winter* on Stage and Screen," Barton Palmer explores the ways in which familial and patriarchal masculinity defines the film's narrative tension: which of Henry II's sons is man enough to be his heir? Questions of masculinity are inflected through suspicions concerning (homo)sexuality, and thus the film reveals the ways in which masculinity and sexuality are staged as competitive factors in a successionary struggle. Lorraine Stock, in her "'He's not an ardent suitor, is he, brother?': Richard the Lionheart's Ambiguous Sexuality in Cecil B. DeMille's *The Crusades*," likewise turns a critical

---

28 Laura Mulvey's essay, "Visual Pleasure and Narrative Cinema" (*Screen* 16.3 [1975]: 6-18) changed film theory profoundly, even when (if not *especially* when) other critics disagree with her. For examples of work that has opened up the theory of the gaze in productive ways, see Steven Cohan and Ina Rae Clark, eds., *Screening the Male* (Routledge: London and New York, 1993), Richard Dyer, ed., *Gays and Film* (1977; New York: Zoetrope, 1984), and Patricia White, *Uninvited: Classic Hollywood Cinema and Lesbian Representability* (Bloomington: Indiana UP, 1999).

eye to the legend of Richard the Lionhearted, examining the ways in which DeMille's depiction of the famed king in *The Crusades* tackles historiographical questions concerning Richard's sexuality in regard to his hesitancy surrounding heterosexual union in marriage. In her reading of Peter Jackson's *Lord of the Rings* trilogy, "'In the Company of Orcs': Peter Jackson's Queer Tolkien," Jane Chance moves our collection from the domestic sphere of the family to the homosocial milieu of hobbits, demonstrating that masculinities are performed with various inflections of male homosociality, and that these performances reflect a queer tension in which masculinity must be assessed through attempts to control the feminine. Chance's reading of *Lord of the Rings* depends upon issues of cinematic intertextuality, most notably the film's engagement with contemporary cinema in its construction of homosocial/erotic masculinity.

Campy queerness underscores the tension between the historical past and its current re-creations, and the following chapters explore the potential of camp to subvert the gendered fictions of medieval films. Few fans would link archetypal western hero John Wayne with queerness, yet Anna Kłosowska, in "The Eastern Western: Camp as a Response to Cultural Failure in *The Conqueror*," explores how this campy epic queerly erases cultural boundaries between East and West by casting Wayne as Genghis Khan. By so doing, the film obscures the cultural differences that must be in place to make the narrative intelligible. Extending the analysis of camp in this volume, Susan Aronstein, in "'In my own idiom': Social Critique, Campy Gender, and Queer Performance in *Monty Python and the Holy Grail*," explores the performance of homosocial and fraternal bonds. The Monty Python troupe is famous for its cross-dressing antics (campy, according to some definitions), but Aronstein argues that this parodic impulse cannot contain the queer potential unleashed in the deliberate, winking, performance of gender. Susan Hayward analyzes the queerness inherent in the Joan of Arc legend with her "Performance, Camp, and Queering History in Luc Besson's *Jeanne d'Arc*." Joan's crossdressing ostensibly casts her as a queer figure, yet Hayward articulates the ways in which queerness is thrust upon Joan—both historically and cinematically—in ways antithetical to her own desires; furthermore, in her attention to Milla Jovavich's performance as Joan, Hawyard explores how film stars engage with the medieval past to address modern concerns over gender through the performativity of celebrity.

Celebrity culture is inextricably tied to movie performances and star personae, and Tison Pugh, Kathleen Kelly, and Martha Bayless examine this phenomenon in their respective chapters. In "Sean Connery's Star Persona and the Queer Middle Ages," Pugh interrogates the ways in which Connery's masculinity, defined iconically as super-spy James Bond, is reimagined and queered through "medieval" films that posit other paradigms of masculinity for an aging action hero. In "Will Rogers' Pink Spot: *A Connecticut Yankee*," Kelly investigates postures of celebrity and heterosexuality, reading Rogers' iconic cowboy figure as one who fears heterosexual consummation and thus queers his own image for comic effect. Bayless questions the myth of Danny Kaye's homosexuality in relation to his comic performances in the "medieval" past. Her essay, "Danny Kaye and the 'Fairy Tale' of Queerness in *The Court Jester*," traces the tension between cultural expectations of modern male normativity against the medieval antics of un-masculinity in the film. Kaye's film roles queered him in real life, as the contaminative force of his characters left him a sexually suspect subject despite great evidence of his heterosexuality. Surely this is perhaps the queerest of movie medievalisms, as it creates a "real world" homosexual out of movie fantasies.

The final chapters of *Queer Movie Medievalisms* consider queerness as a constitutive method of interrogating cinema itself. In "Mourning and Sexual Difference in Hans-Jürgen Syberberg's *Parsifal*," Michelle Bolduc examines the multiplicity of gender depicted in the film to consider the melancholic register of movie medievalism and its role in cultural mourning. In his "Superficial Medievalism and the Queer Futures of Film," Cary Howie interrogates the meaning of the past and how the future is mediated through a melancholic view of medievalism. History cannot help but be lost, but melancholia imbues it with a hazy and queerly informative perspective on the present. In their Afterword, Glenn Burger and Steven F. Kruger offer their views on how the queerness of movie medievalisms kaleidoscopically refracts startling visions of historical and anti-historical sexualities.

In sum, the contributors to this volume articulate a belief in the "double queerness" of medieval film in both its deployment of time and its constructions of sexuality and gender. Understanding the past is ultimately a queering process that undermines coherent conceptions of the self in the present, and the process of defining the self in relation to history is richly tied to the construction of gender and sexuality, as so clearly illustrated by the Bravehearts and any number of people who re-create the past (such as the members of the Society for Creative Anachronism and gamers) while re-imagining their genders and sexual identities in the present day. This queer tension between past and present, between genders and sexualities of yesterday and of today—between, even, medieval studies and medievalism as a process, mode, or subject of study—is fundamentally illustrated in virtually every film that addresses the medieval past, and this volume articulates this diachronic queer tension between past and present as mediated by the movies.

For certainly (queer) tensions still exist even as western society makes great strides in dismantling the ideological structures of homophobia. Frequently such tensions surface in silences—the job letter unanswered, the promotion ungranted, the invitation unextended—and indeed, we encountered such queer silences when requesting permission to use film stills for many of the chapters in this contribution to queer studies. We recognize that film stills add a necessary component to the scholarly interpretation of cinema, and we apologize to our readers for their relative dearth in this volume. But many of these requests went unanswered, and thus these silences trouble us as to the meaning accorded queer studies within the culture at large. We cannot know who—whether singularly or collectively—made the decisions to ignore our requests, but we offer these chapters despite the silence that was the film studios' response to our invitation to partake in this project. The work of queer scholarship continues apace, with no apologies, but with some appeal to the imagination and the memory.

Chapter 1
The Law of the Daughter: Queer Family Politics in Bertrand Tavernier's *La Passion Béatrice*

Lisa Manter

Having just murdered her father François de Cortemare (Bernard-Pierre Donnadieu), Béatrice de Cortemare (Julie Delpy) sits in profile with her bloody hand resting on the face of a wooden statue of the Virgin, their mirrored postures creating a closed form.[1] On the film's soundtrack, Lili Boulanger's uncanny voice adds a musical commentary to the image: "Pie Jesu domine/Dona eis requiem" (Merciful Lord Jesus/Give them rest). This mesmerizing closing shot of Bertrand Tavernier's *La Passion Béatrice* (1987) presents a haunting portrayal of gynocentric insularity that stands in stark contrast with the public validation of medieval *patria potestas* that opens the film. Between these two scenes unfolds the film's queer project, a critical examination of the insalubrious roots of the modern conception of the heteronormative family.

The initial sequence of *La Passion Béatrice* underscores the tie between the patriarchal power of the father and aristocratic privilege by opening with a priest blessing the Lord de Cortemare (Béatrice's grandfather) and his family in preparation for the lord's departure for war in the presence of his extended household. The ensuing voice-over introduces this opening flashback as the *sine qua non* of the upcoming conflict between Béatrice and her father:

> Il est des histoires comme de certaines arbres dont il est necessaire de connaître
> la racine pour mieux saisir la maladive contorsion des branches, l'afflux de sang
> dans le feuillage, le poison dans la sève.
> (There are some stories that are like certain trees, of which it is necessary to
> know the roots in order to better grasp the sickly twisting of the branches, the
> rush of blood in the foliage, the poison in the sap.)

---

1 *La Passion Béatrice* (English title: *The Passion of Beatrice*), dir. Bertrand Tavernier, perf. Bernard-Pierre Donnadieu, Julie Delpy, and Nils Tavernier, VHS (AMLF, et al., 1987; Samuel Goldwyn, 1988).

This statement, in Tavernier's own voice,[2] accompanies an image of François as a ten-year old boy running from his mother to his departing father, shouting "Père! Père!", establishing cinematically the importance of the triangular paradigm of the heteronormative family, with the son abandoning the mother to pursue his allegiance to the father. The flashback's closing scene of the young François stabbing his mother's lover to preserve his father's honor drives home Tavernier's presentation of the aristocratic family as the locus of the exercise of power, both sexual and social.

When François becomes the Lord de Cortemare in his turn, his brutal exercise of patriarchal power—which reaches its climax with the rape of his daughter—becomes the focus of Tavernier's study of the perversity of the gendered familial roles handed down to young François. The ideology of *paterfamilias* in the film, rather than prohibiting François's abusive excesses, makes possible the very terrors it promises to prevent: murder, pillage, rape, and incest. Even more scandalous is that his cruelties are visited on those the system vows to protect, namely his family and his subjects.

In juxtaposition to François's excesses, which reveal a system that is "both culpable and morally insupportable, a system of terrifying perversion,"[3] is the passion, in all senses of the term, of young Béatrice. As the "good" daughter, Béatrice at first attempts to uphold her father's privilege; then, in the face of François's unrelenting viciousness, she seeks recourse through other patriarchal channels. Finally, as she discovers the queer kernel of the Law of the Father, she institutes her own law, enforcing her personal claims to power by taking up the phallic dagger and using it against her father. Out of her process of suffering, purgation, and sacrifice emerges the possibility of manifesting an alternative, although equally queer, space from which to heal the "sickness that twists the branches" of the heteronormative family.

As in a Mirror, Queerly: Projecting (on) the Past

"The one duty we owe to history is to re-write it."
— Oscar Wilde, *The Critic as Artist*

---

2 As Stephen Hay notes, this voice-over, as spoken by Tavernier, suggests the director's "special attachment to the work" (*Bertrand Tavernier* [New York: Tauris, 2001], p. 122).

3 Stephen Behrendt, "Beatrice Cenci and the Tragic Myth of History," *History & Myth*, ed. Stephen Behrendt (Detroit, MI: Wayne State UP, 1990), p. 215. This quote from Behrendt refers to Shelley's *The Cenci*, but the "grinding system of institutionalized patriarchal domination" (215) that he finds in Shelley's version is shared by Tavernier's film.

The broad outlines of Tavernier's film are taken from the "true crime story" of the Cenci family. In brief, the story, recorded in legal documents, chronicles, and popular legend, concerns the patricide of Francesco Cenci, a Roman nobleman, who had a record of violence and sexual license. After years of abuse, his wife Lucrezia, eldest son Giacomo, and daughter Beatrice (both from a previous marriage) arranged to have him killed. Their conspiracy came to light, and Pope Clement VIII sentenced them to public execution in 1599. The youngest son, Bernard, was spared but forced to watch his family executed.[4] The sensationalist elements of the case, including the possibility of incest between Francesco and his daughter Beatrice, captured the public's imagination and became a popular theme for writers and artists.[5]

La Passion Béatrice clearly shows the influence of these earlier works, in particular Percy Bysshe Shelley's influential dramatization of the legend, *The Cenci: A Tragedy in Five Acts*, written in 1819, and the work of Tavernier's two compatriots, Stendhal and Antonin Artaud, whose versions of the story draw upon Shelley's.[6] A number of elements, however, set Tavernier's version apart: 1) the shift in setting from Renaissance Rome to late medieval France, 2) a greater development of the character of the father, 3) an emphasis on misogynistic discourse and Béatrice's uneasy relationship to it, 4) an explicit portrayal of the father-daughter incest, and 5) the ending of the story with the death of François at the hands of Béatrice. Tavernier's temporal and spatial shift of the story from early modern Italy to rural medieval France is placed at the forefront of my analysis of these directorial alterations because it is this decision regarding the setting of the story that underwrites the remaining dramatic changes.[7]

During the development of the screenplay, Tavernier asked his wife Colo Tavernier-O'Hagan to transfer the setting of the story from Renaissance Rome

---

4 See Belinda Jack, *Beatrice's Spell: The Enduring Legend of Beatrice Cenci* (New York: Other Press, 2005), Part I, for a detailed description of the historical details of the Cenci case. Jack draws her materials from Corrado Ricci's study, originally published in Italian in 1923, *Beatrice Cenci*, trans. Morris Bishop and Henry Stuart (New York: Liveright, 1925).

5 See Charles Nicholl, "Screaming in the Castle," *London Review of Books*, July 2, 1998, http://www.lrb.co.uk/v20/n13/nich02_.html, for a list of texts, operas, and films based on the Cenci story.

6 Percy Bysshe Shelley, *The Cenci: A Tragedy in Five Acts, Shelley's Poetry and Prose*, eds. Donald Reiman and Sharon Powers (New York: Norton, 1977); Stendhal, "The Cenci," *Three Italian Chronicles*, trans. C. Scott-Moncrieff (New York: New Direction, 1946); and Antonin Artaud, *The Cenci*, trans. Simon Taylor (New York: Grove, 1970).

7 For a detailed description of the historical setting of the film, see Laurence de Looze, "Modern Approaches and the 'Real' Middle Ages: Bertrand Tavernier's *La Passion Béatrice*," *Studies in Medievalism*, ed. Leslie J. Workman (Cambridge: Brewer, 1994), pp. 183-85.

to southern France during the Hundred Years' War.[8] Although the script of *La Passion Béatrice* follows its predecessors in its focus on Beatrice as a beautiful and spirited young woman faced with an impossible dilemma, the story is sharply dissociated from its early modern urban backdrop. Tavernier is thus able to take advantage of the popular belief in a "vast epistemic shift [between the Middle Ages and the Renaissance] that ushers in modernity"[9] while at the same time making use of the Middle Ages as a time that, as Umberto Eco cannily observed, has "never been reconstructed from scratch" but has always been "mended or patched up, as something in which we still live."[10] *Béatrice* makes use of this "queerness" of portraying the Middle Ages on film by playing upon the distancing effect of an amorphous and alien "Dark Ages" *and* the popularity of medieval settings in cinema as a space of continuous re-examination of issues of Western culture. In this sense, the film appears to participate in what Glenn Burger and Steven Kruger label "the logic of the queer" because it "effects a disturbance of temporality that is precisely 'preposterous'" and because there needs to be a "certain stabilization of temporal sequence into narratives of causation" if "sexual norms [are to] be given their necessary and inescapable history."[11]

But it may be argued that by projecting this Renaissance story backward onto the Middle Ages, to a time of shifting norms and instability, the narrative of *Béatrice* can be read as supporting a history that is "continuist and teleological" since the events of the tragedy should never have occurred in the modern period.[12] In other words, if the brutality and sexual deviance of the Cencis are transferred to the de Cortemare family, with their roots firmly planted in a period considered, if not lawless by modern standards, at least less subject to centralized power than Renaissance Europe, then the dramatic action is fittingly barbaric rather than perverse. In that case, the behavior of François de Cortemare, especially his pursuit of father-daughter incest, can be read as merely part of the medieval "color," and therefore not subject to modern heteronormative constraints. The film would thus seem to support "mainstream historicism['s insistence] on understanding the 'flow of time' as uninterruptedly 'progressive.'"[13]

---

8 Hay, *Bertrand Tavernier*, p. 122.

9 Jonathan Goldberg, "The History That Will Be," *Premodern Sexualities*, eds. Louise Fradenburg and Carla Freccero (New York: Routledge, 1996), 3-21, at p. 9.

10 Umberto Eco, "Dreaming of the Middle Ages," *Travels in Hyperreality*, trans. William Weaver (San Diego: Harcourt, 1986), pp. 67-68.

11 Glenn Burger and Steven Kruger, eds., *Queering the Middle Ages* (Minneapolis: U of Minnesota P, 2001), p. xii.

12 Carolyn Dinshaw, *Getting Medieval* (Durham, NC: Duke UP, 1999), p. 17.

13 Burger and Kruger, *Queering the Middle Ages*, p. xii.

On the other hand, the film could be seen as exploiting the ahistoricity of "medieval" film so that the Middle Ages symbolically functions as the unconscious of our present period. Such a reading is supported by Tavernier's epigraph that appears before the opening images of the film, which provides a justification for his characters' freedom from the constraints of modernity:

Leur univers est à la fois vaste et féroce, hanté par les puissances de l'Au-delà, un univers où le Sacré côtoie la Barbarie. . . . Ce sont des enfants sauvages. Ils sont ce que nous sommes encore la nuit, dans nos songes. Ils sont notre inconscient.

(Their universe is at the same time vast and fierce, haunted by the powers from up above, a universe where the Sacred brushes daily with the Barbaric. . . . These are savage children. They are what we still are at night, in our dreams. They are our unconscious.)[14]

Seen as a reflection of our culture in its "infancy,"[15] the Middle Ages can be posited as a mythic period where we can examine what we have repressed as a culture, that which we would consider "savage" because it has been successfully repressed by modern law and its enforcement.[16] The medieval setting of *Béatrice* thus allows Tavernier to create a bleak archetypal dreamscape that reshapes the singularity of one family's criminal history into a type of historical "screen memory." Viewing the medieval elements of the film in this way makes Freud's comments on the ahistoricity of screen memories particularly suggestive:

It may indeed be questioned whether we have any memories at all *from* our childhood: memories *relating* to our childhood may be all that we possess. Our childhood memories show us our earliest years not as they were but as they appeared at the later periods when the memories were aroused. In these periods of arousal, the childhood memories did not, as people are accustomed to say, *emerge*; they were *formed* at that time.[17]

---

14 Translation from Hay, *Bertrand Tavernier*, p. 124. All other quotations and translations from the film are my own. A special thanks to Catherine Marachi for her help with piecing together Tavernier's version of "medieval" French.

15 Eco, "Dreaming of the Middle Ages," p. 65. As Eco goes on to comment, the Middle Ages are often seen as a "*barbaric* age, a land of elementary and outlaw feelings" (p. 69).

16 See Michel Foucault, *The History of Sexuality*, Volume I: An Introduction, trans. Robert Hurley (New York: Vintage, 1990), pp. 129-130.

17 Sigmund Freud, "Screen Memories," *The Standard Edition of the Complete Psychological Works of Sigmund Freud*, trans. James Strachey (London: Hogarth, 1962), vol. 3, p. 322.

Such a dehistoricized approach fits traditional psychoanalytic views of incest as an unspeakable fantasy rather than a lived reality under heteronormative family politics.

Both of these "straight" readings are troubled, however: the first by the "historical fact" that the film is based on events that occurred during the Renaissance, with its accompanying intricate social and judicial systems, and the second by the centrality and explicitness of the incest in the film, which underscores its existence as a realistic incident rather than as an unconscious fantasy. Neither reading, therefore, fully allows for Tavernier's adaptation of the Cenci myth to be tamed into becoming part of a "straight chronology" of the family.[18]

In sum, *La Passion Béatrice* points out 1) the "preposterousness" of reading the Cenci family drama as early modern, even though historically it was, for to do so would point out that modern "law" produces Francesco Cenci's behavior, and 2) the "preposterousness" of seeing the father-daughter incest as non-normative, even though it is perverse, for it appears to be the logical outcome of the film's medieval misogyny and patriarchal privilege. Through medieval film's queer historical potential, Tavernier is able to have it both ways, and his reconstruction of a Renaissance myth in a realistic medieval setting heightens the story's function as a critical commentary on western heteronormativity. As Emily Zants notes, it is typical of Tavernier to use realism to "engage the viewers in a familiar world, [and] then [pull] the rug of habit from beneath them, leaving them questioning their own habits and prejudices as well as those of their society."[19] As a filmmaker, he takes advantage of our willingness to see ourselves as both separated from the Middle Ages and at the same time inheritors of its traditions as a means of helping us see beyond our modern (and even postmodern) ideologies surrounding heteronormativity.

The complex set of historical "vibrations" set off by this juxtaposition of the medieval setting, the early modern material, its nineteenth- and twentieth-century retellings, the contemporary technology of cinema and its post-Freudian viewers all encourage a queer reading of the film, a reading that "finds those queer touches that its culture has tried to disavow, opens up their denaturalizing perspective on heterosexual identity and can thus contribute to the mapping of heterosexuality's long and varied history."[20] As Carolyn Dinshaw notes in

18 Burger and Kruger, *Queering the Middle Ages*, p. xii.

19 Emily Zants, *Bertrand Tavernier* (Lanham, MD: Scarecrow, 1999), p. 33. Although the medieval world is not necessarily "familiar," the realism of the piece does not allow his viewers to indulge in the romanticized world of Arthurian legend so often portrayed in "medieval" films (see Hay, *Bertrand Tavernier*, p. 122).

20 Carolyn Dinshaw, "Chaucer's Queer Touches/A Queer Touches Chaucer," *Exemplaria* 7 (1995): 75-92, at p. 91.

her work on the queer "vibrations" to be found in a juxtaposition of historical material and postmodern theory, the result of such queer work is that it "empties out the natural, the essential, empties out the conventional foundations of representation and identity, [and] shakes . . . the heterocultural edifice."[21] Tavernier's medievalization of the Cenci story, therefore, not only queers the import of the original story to the history of sexuality but encourages us to queer our own understanding of "the norms of [our] time and place and . . . to contest that normativity by tracing other kinds of relations"[22]—in this case, the links among the heteronormative family, gender roles, sexuality, power, and the incest taboo. For this reason, I retain the use of *queer* for both my discussion of the perverse elements of the Law of the Father and for Béatrice's rejection of traditional familial roles. Tavernier's exploration of the patriarchal family highlights the ways in which the term *queer* has been reclaimed by queer theorists to unsettle our sense of the normative, the perverse, and their relationship to each other. As David Halperin argues, "Queer . . . does not designate a class of already objectified pathologies or perversions, rather, it describes a horizon of possibility whose precise extent and heterogeneous scope cannot in principle be delimited in advance."[23] By retaining the term *queer*, with its manifold reverberations, I hope to preserve the ever-shifting ground of the idea of the family, especially in relation to issues of gender and sexuality.

The Law of the Son

The depiction of the de Cortemare family's "medieval barbarism" theorizes what lies behind normative modern familial relations: frustration, fear, disillusionment, and aggression. Ironically, the medieval setting, which rationalizes François's behavior to modern audiences who would otherwise find it insupportable, allows for a less demonized portrayal of his character. He is human, and painfully so both for himself and his family. It is not a question of a father who engages in inhuman acts or even the failure of the papal or aristocratic structures to punish such a man; François's behavior as a lord and father reveals that the assumed justification for patriarchy—that it ensures stability and safety for the family, and by extension, society—is disingenuous. In Tavernier's version, François serves as the very marker of the queer kernel of paternal privilege: a father who insists upon his prerogatives even at the cost of his own destruction.

To flesh out the motivations behind the Lord de Cortemare's adult behavior, Tavernier's diegesis develops François's character more than earlier. Cenci

---

21 Dinshaw, "Chaucer's Queer Touches," p. 89.

22 Dinshaw, *Getting Medieval*, p. 142.

23 David Halperin, *Saint Foucault* (New York: Oxford UP, 1995), p. 62.

variants. Scenes from François's childhood make up the opening of the film, giving him a psychological history and explaining his youthful romantic fantasies about the medieval patriarchy. The film opens with an extreme long shot of the mountainous Haute Vallée de l'Aude. The feminized backdrop, with its rolling hills and valleys, creates an anticipatory set-up for the entrance of father and son. François's father shows him the valley, as if to say, "This will all belong to you, my son," and then scoops up his son into his arms. This father-and-son pairing is then joined by the rest of society, as children, a bishop, retainers, and François's mother enter the frame. The idyllic portrait of the medieval aristocratic hierarchy, with the lord at its apex, comes together for the blessing of the Lord de Cortemare as he goes off to serve the King of France.

As this idealized *tableau vivant* visually disbands, so does the dream of family harmony. François runs after his father, begging him to take him along. Instead of doing so, he gives him a dagger and tells him to guard his mother from other men: "Apprenez d'abord à défendre votre mère. Elle est si belle, et les hommes si brutaux" (Learn first to protect your mother. She is so beautiful, and men so brutal). This symbolic transfer of phallic power over the family, particularly its female members, is François's first lesson in the preservation of the heterosexual family. As the inheritor of patriarchal law, young François enacts its violent logic in the following scene. As he returns to the castle calling "Mère! Mère!", instead of finding the dutiful wife waiting patiently for her husband's return, François discovers his mother already in her lover's embrace. Here is his first chance to use the power his father has passed down to him, and, François eagerly employs the metaphorical phallus in a very literal way: he stabs his mother's lover in his parents' bed and states: "Mon père n'a pas été vengé, car vous ne l'avez pas trompé" (My father has not been avenged because you never deceived him).

In this brief scene, Tavernier provides the film's discursive logic of heteronormativity. "*Père*," the first vernacular word of the film, is immediately tied to the land, war, abandonment, and the transferal of the phallic power of life and death (the dagger); "*mère*" is tied to the castle, sexual excess, and violence. The patriarchal family in *La Passion Béatrice*, resting on the twin pillars of heterosexuality and gender inequality, begins to reveal itself in this first sequence to be the "very institution of perversion."[24]

---

24 I borrow this phrase from Raymond Bellour's article "Psychosis, Neurosis, Perversion," *A Hitchcock Reader*, eds. Marshall Deutelbaum and Leland Poague (Ames: Iowa State UP, 1986), where he claims that film is the "very institution of perversion" (p. 329).

THE LAW OF THE DAUGHTER

The Phallic Daughter: Life without Father

The shot following the murder of his mother's lover is of François in the tower of the de Cortemare castle, awaiting a father who will never return. It is at this point that we hear Béatrice in voice-over describing her father as a boy: "C'est ainsi que je l'imagine, mon père; si petit, si blessé, si terriblement seul" (That's how I imagine him, my father; so small, so wounded, so terribly alone). Tavernier's seamless dovetailing of the portrait of François's childhood and Béatrice's daydreams suggest that her romanticizing of her father is predicated on her identification with him. She sees herself in her father's place, like him waiting faithfully for a father to return from war. In this, Tavernier deviates from the Cenci tale, in which the father was rarely, if ever, absent. Stepmother, daughter, and sons all endured constant cruelty at the hands of Francesco Cenci, and the parricide resulted from the regular abuse that appears to have increased as Lord Cenci aged. In the film's reworking of the story, the four-year absence of both father and son creates the narrative space for Béatrice's fantasies of an idyllic heteronormative family structure, in spite of the early evidence of her father's violent nature. Béatrice's whole-hearted belief in the goodness of the de Cortemare patriarchy helps her endure her own abandonment,[25] but her lack of direct experience of paternal authority results in an impossible portrait of her father and her brother Arnaud (Nils Tavernier)[26] as superlative men: "C'est lui [Arnaud] qui m'a tout appris. C'était le plus bel enfant que le royaume ait jamais porté. Mon père aussi il était beau et le plus vaillant de tous" (He taught me all I know. . . . He was the most beautiful child the kingdom ever bore, and my father was the most handsome and most valiant of men). Her fantasies of herself as adoring daughter, sister, and future wife fill her imagination but do not much impact her daily existence, which is mainly spent riding, playing with Jehan, a mentally-handicapped boy, and catching birds as pets. Béatrice's idealistic views of the family under a patriarch in part stem from the fact that, in spite of the gender-normative discourse that peppers the dialogue of her household, it is the women who exercise phallic power that would typically be the prerogative of men. As Béatrice's mother says as she takes the knife from the old curé, whose age has deprived him of his masculinity, "Laissez-moi faire . . . à votre âge on n'est plus un homme" (Let me do it . . . at your age, you're no longer a man).

---

25 Unlike the historical account, Tavernier's Béatrice has not lost her mother, but the mother figure is all but invisible in the film. In the legend, Lucrezia acts as Beatrice's second mother, and they band together against Francesco's abusive treatment.

26 This is Nils Tavernier's first role in one of his father's films. It is tempting to see Tavernier using the Cenci story to teach his son about the brutality of patriarchy by casting him in this degrading role, similar to François's lesson for his daughter.

Tavernier devotes the entire second sequence, almost a third of the film, to portraying Béatrice's life prior to her father's return: a time of youthful innocence and relative happiness. His choice to first present her to the viewer not under François's influence allows him to establish her as a light-hearted and independent girl. Our first images of her show her out riding, watching over the land, preparing for her father and brother's ransom, and giving orders in the castle. With François and his son away from home, Béatrice acts as the "man" of the house, assuming the power of the father. Although she dresses up as a lady for Lemartin (Jean-Claude Adelin), her would-be lover, when he comes to finalize the sale of her father's lands, she seems more comfortable in the simple riding gear that allows her to engage in her tomboyish pursuits. (Her cross-dressing is amplified when, toward the end of the film, her father forces her to wear her brother's hunting clothes.) Béatrice is truly "la fille du père."[27] But the incompatibility of gender fluidity and patriarchy are underscored by François's mother, who chides Béatrice for not behaving like a girl; if she weren't playing in the woods "comme un garçon" (like a boy) instead of sewing "comme il sied à une demoiselle" (as befits a young lady), she would have learned that her father was on his way home. Although her tone is teasing in this scene, Béatrice's grandmother, having previously been a victim of the violence of the patriarchy, understands the import of François's imminent arrival. The enforcement of the Law of the Father that he represents will ruthlessly return the queer world of a castle run by women to its proper state of gender hierarchy, and she sees her son's homecoming as a curse rather than a blessing.

But this is a lesson that Béatrice has yet to learn, as is shown in her loving preparation of her father's and brother's beds: "Revenez-nous ce soir, père; mon jeune coeur s'épuise à vous attendre" (Come home tonight, father! My young heart tires of waiting). Her melodramatic longing for the promised idyll of the restored de Cortemare household echoes her belief that once she has secured her father and brother's freedom, she will be able to live out her paradigmatic roles of daughter, sister, and wife-to-be. Paradoxically, the only way for Béatrice to maintain both her life as she knows it and her fantasy of the "good" father is via the continued absence of François, for his return will require her to acknowledge the reality of her queer familial relationships.

Father Knows Best: The Return of the Law of the Father

Béatrice's joy at the announcement of François's and Arnaud's return is marked by a series of jump cuts as she twirls away from her grandmother,

---

27 Her grandmother describes her thus, and it is a sentiment echoed by her father later in the film.

which simultaneously expresses her delirium and prophesizes the disorientation that her father's return will wreck upon her life. In contrast to this jubilant camera work and the warm colors of the interior of the castle, the first appearance of the adult François de Cortemare and his son occurs against a bleak, snowy background as they ride slowly into the static wintry frame. After a few establishing shots of de Cortemare's entourage, during which a newborn cries in the background, the camera quickly pans left to reveal a woman and her bloody baby in the snow. François's first words reveal his obsession with gender. "Est-ce une garce ou un garçon?" (Is it a wench or a boy?), he asks the woman, basing his decision of whether to take her along on the answer. The woman "a de la chance" (is lucky) because it is a girl and, therefore, as Arnaud voices, doesn't have a soul and can be left behind. As he says this, he looks to François for approval, suggesting that this discursive misogyny is a key element in the medieval logic of male domination passed down from father to son in the context of the film.

Although this scene is repugnant to modern sensibilities, by setting it in the Middle Ages, Tavernier attempts to frame François's behavior as the logical outcome of an unmistakably patriarchal system in which women have no souls and aristocratic sons inherit the power of the Father's phallus and thus become the arbiters and enforcers of the "law." François's brooding violence stems from his own disillusionment with this system, which promises him absolute dominion but, in the end, offers only isolation and disappointment. As a boy, not only is he abandoned by his father, who leaves him to serve as a *chevalier* in the king's army, his first act as a "man" is an act of violence that forever loses him the love of his mother. As an adult, he follows his father's martial path only to have his dreams of glorious service to his earthly and heavenly lords crushed by the reality of war—a war that he describes as a stupendous blunder motivated by greed and stupidity. Salting this wound is the failure of Arnaud to measure up to medieval ideals of masculine courage, forcing François to go back to rescue a son who is "couvert de merde" (covered in shit) resulting in the capture of them both. When he and Arnaud are finally freed from captivity through Béatrice's efforts, François returns to his family castle only to find that the land his father has promised him has been sold off to pay for his ransom.

In sum, François's experiences have taught him that the dream of the patriarchy writ large produces nightmares. When the priest asks him to recount his exploits in the war, he responds: "Demande à mes écorcheurs ils n'étaient pas des nôtres. Ils inventeront l'histoire, elle n'en sera que plus belle" (Ask the spoilers who weren't with us. They will invent a better story), and "Qu'en serait-il de la Chrétienté sans l'imagination des apôtres?" (What would Christianity be without the Apostle's imaginations?). But when Béatrice asks him to have Arnaud tell of their adventures in his place, rather than acquiesce he tells his shocking version, apparently motivated by disgust for his effeminate son and his desire not to hear more fictions. After he finishes his story of the war, he stops eating, as if the horror of realizing his own failure has caused him to lose his appetite. His son Arnaud, however, continues to eat his meal meekly, only to have his father shove his face into his food, stating, "Quand ton père a terminé, c'est terminé" (When your father is done, it is done). This is the Law of the Father stripped bare.

The resetting of the Cenci story in the overtly misogynistic Middle Ages and the description of François's patrimony renders the Lord de Cortemare's behavior as cruel but not unusual. In spite of his obvious brutality and misogyny, which is exaggerated at every turn,[28] François is not the self-congratulatory sadist of the Cenci legends; he is a man deeply tortured by his own position in society and the expectations heaped upon him by his family and household retainers. He is a man who would rather be a "Juif errant" (wandering Jew) and who chooses suicide to escape from his participation in a perverse system, only to be saved by a companion who depends upon François's status to support raids upon the villagers. Tavernier's François, like Stendhal's Francesco, is a malcontent who desires to challenge his culture's hypocrisy but, unlike Stendhal's Italian Don Juan, sees no freedom from his role as the enforcer of the Law of the Father. Bound by his position, he chooses to enact the power of the phallus as a provocateur without believing in its benefit to himself or others, and rather than perpetuate the fictions of paternalism, he chooses classless "spoilers" as comrades and beneficiaries. His female companions are likewise from the lower classes, and although his deeply engrained misogyny makes his interactions with these women brutal and sexualized, he nonetheless rips the jewels off his female relatives and gives them to these women in an act that simultaneously insults his family and challenges aristocratic privilege.

Part of what makes François's behavior as lord and father truly horrific is its juxtaposition to Béatrice's daughterly devotion. To concentrate the viewer's attention on this father-daughter conflict, Tavernier alters the Cenci story so that the roles played by the stepmother, the older and younger brothers, and the members of the church hierarchy are downplayed to emphasize the relationship between François and Béatrice. Visually, father and daughter are presented as mirror-images of one another: the opening shot of the young François with his father is matched by the closing shot of Béatrice with the Virgin Mary as mother figure, and both use the same dagger to shape the family they desire. They are repeatedly presented as opponents and equals in this battle of wills,

---

28 One of the "benefits" of moving the setting from the Renaissance to the Middle Ages is that it allows Tavernier to foreground the "fundamental misogyny that coloured the period" (Hay, *Bertrand Tavernier*, p. 123). Tavernier blamed the poor box office reception of the film on the audience's inability to "accept the misogyny of the period that the film portrayed" (Hay, *Bertrand Tavernier*, p. 130, n. 3).

as symbolized by the image of them playing chess that occurs halfway through the film.

The film's depiction of the interplay between the western heteronormative family and "medieval" misogyny as a battle between father and daughter sets up François to become the Queer Father, that is, the father who returns to his family for the sole purpose of instructing them in the perversity of the patriarchy. It is a brutal lesson.

Incest: The "Indispensable Pivot"

As the conflict between father and daughter intensifies, Béatrice's body becomes the locus of their power struggle. Tavernier's insistence on incest as the "poison in the sap," as a stain that reveals the underlying queerness of the traditional family, depends upon the film's deviations from the original Cenci story discussed above: 1) the queerness of recasting the Cenci tragedy as a "medieval" narrative, 2) the portrayal of Béatrice's father as traumatized by the expectations of patriarchy, and 3) his absence from the castle during Béatrice's maturation. The intersection of these elements provides a narrative logic for the Lord de Cortemare's incestuous advances, and in spite of his cruelty, the agenda behind his actions—to test the claims to legitimacy of the *patria potestas*—prevents him from being cast as merely a self-serving libertine.[29] In contrast to the one-dimensional portrayals of the Cenci patriarch by Shelley, Artaud, and even Stendhal, François is a man divided: although part of him wants to exercise his power as the Father without restraint, his longing for justice demands that he be punished for his social transgressions by an outside father figure. In this context, François's brutality, particularly toward Béatrice, is a strange mix of his expressing his ultimate potential as *pater familias* and his challenging the claims that patriarchy serves to uphold *pax et justica*. Therefore, only if he is punished for violating his sacred trust as patriarchal protector will the Law of the Father hold any moral validity for him.

As he soon finds there is no earthly check upon him, François turns to God as the ultimate enforcer of this promised justice. Although he has little faith in the God who took his own father from him, he is tortured by a greater fear, namely that the Law of the Father as the guarantor of morality does not exist, and through his escalating outrages, he attempts to bring down God's

---

29 Hay talks about audience's difficulties with accepting Tavernier's more complex presentation: "François's abuse of Béatrice especially was perhaps too uncomfortable for audiences to face, his character being even more disturbing because Tavernier portrayed him not simply as a monster but as a complex personality struggling against his own nature" (*Bertrand Tavernier*, p. 122).

punishment upon himself. The morning after howling "Dieu et mon amour n'éxistent pas!" (My God and my love don't exist!) in the courtyard of his castle, he rapes his daughter as a final test of the goodness of God the Father while repeating this incriminating phrase. When no punishment follows, he is left with the conclusion that the authority of the Law, as expressed ultimately through divine retribution, does not exist, or if it does, its logic is frighteningly perverse. As he descends deeper into madness, his logic turns more insidious: if God does exist, he "blesses" the absolute exercise of a father's rights, which extend even to incestuous relations with his daughter.

Tavernier's placement of this particular case of incest in the Middle Ages complicates the viewer's understanding of the historical shift from the Middle Ages to modernity by challenging twentieth-century anthropological and theoretical discussions of the incest taboo that see the patriarchy as emerging from and upholding the taboo. As Jonathan Goldberg argues, these discussions cast back a "history [of incest] that will be" to justify "the failing family, and hide the workings of power beneath the register of the sovereign, the father in all his guises." By playing upon the anachronism inherent in "medieval" film, Tavernier manifestly projects a "history that will be," but one that questions the "normalcy" of the modern family rather than redeploying "the modern discourse of repression, . . . the law of desire, and widespread anthropologies" that Goldberg finds to be typical.[30] Tavernier's queer "back projection" calls into question the very wholesomeness and integrity of the modern family by challenging the presentation of incest as beyond the pale.

The centrality of the father-daughter incest in Tavernier's film highlights the underlying relationship among law, desire, and power that inheres in the heteronormative family. In particular, the Lord de Cortemare's insistence that he will continue to "recoudre [Béatrice] ici" (resow her here), while grabbing her cunt, even in the face of losing his daughter's exchange value through marriage, marks the film's familial-sexual systems as "modern" rather than strongly tied to earlier "mechanisms of alliance." As Foucault comments,

> It may be that in societies where the mechanisms of alliance predominate, prohibition of incest is a functionally indispensable rule. But in a society such as ours, where the family is the most active site of sexuality, and where it is doubtless the exigencies of the latter which maintain and prolong its existence, incest—for different reasons altogether and in a completely different way— occupies a central place; it is constantly being solicited and refused; it is an object of obsession and attraction, a dreadful secret and an indispensable pivot. It is manifest as a thing that is strictly forbidden in the family insofar as the latter functions as a deployment of alliance; but it is also a thing that

---

30 Goldberg, "The History That Will Be," p. 9.

is continuously demanded in order for the family to be a hotbed of constant sexual incitement.[31]

But in order for the family to *remain* "a hotbed of constant sexual incitement," incest must retain its status as a "dreadful secret." As Judith Butler notes, in spite of the importance of incest as the pivot for patriarchal culture, both the act and its accompanying taboo must remain at the level of fantasy. "This dream, its power to mould men's thoughts unbeknown to them . . . the acts it evokes have never been committed, because culture opposes them at all times and all places."[32] The film, however, overtly refuses to allow incest to occupy the speculative center of the story—"did he or didn't he?"—by making the act painfully explicit. The incestuous rape of Béatrice by her father is shown on-screen followed by Béatrice, in the nude, manically attempting to barricade herself in her room and to cleanse the bloodstains from the stone floor. This bald portrayal undercuts the titillating role that incest, hiding in the narrative shadows, plays in the modern retellings of the Cenci legend.

Shelley's stance is representative in this regard. In his preface to *The Cenci*, he justifies his occlusion of the act:

> This story of the Cenci is indeed eminently fearful and monstrous: anything like a dry exhibition of it on the stage would be insupportable. The person who would treat such a subject must increase the ideal, and diminish the actual horror of the events, so that the pleasure which arises from the poetry which exists in these tempestuous sufferings and crimes may mitigate the pain of the contemplation of the moral deformity from which they spring.[33]

Of course, Shelley admits, "Every one knew what *it* must be, but *it* was never imaged in words—the nearest allusion to *it* being that portion of Cenci's curse beginning—'That, if she have a child,' etc.)."[34] Stendhal and Artaud follow in Shelley's footsteps by alluding to the rape but making a point of never representing it directly. Although perhaps a part of this indirectness stems from what Stendhal calls a sensitivity to the "sensibility" of the ladies,[35] the refusal

---

31 Foucault, *The History of Sexuality*, p. 109.

32 Claude Lévi-Strauss, "The Principles of Kinship," qtd. in Butler, *Gender Trouble* (New York: Routledge, 1989), p. 54.

33 Preface to *The Cenci: A Tragedy in Five Acts*, in *Shelley's Poetry and Prose*, pp. 239-40.

34 This quote is taken from Mary Shelley's "Note on *The Cenci*," in *The Poetical Works of Percy Bysshe Shelley*, ed. Mary Wollstonecraft Shelley (London: Moxon, 1839), p. 159. The emphasis is mine.

35 Stendhal, "The Cenci," p. 12.

to acknowledge the incest outright allows for the preservation of a plausible deniability that is central to the discussion of the Cenci narrative, both culturally and legally.[36] As long as the incest is not openly shown, one can continue in the illusion that it was never committed.

In contrast, Tavernier's film points out the impossibility that "the threshold of all culture [is] prohibited incest," even "where the mechanisms of alliance predominate."[37] Instead, Tavernier calls attention to the fact that power, law, family, and sexuality always stand in queer relation to one another. This Cenci story, dressed in its medieval drag, reveals that sexuality is not only *not* "under the sway of law and right,"[38] but that "the law which prohibits that union [incest] is the selfsame law that invites it."[39] The overt portrayal of incest in the film thus undercuts the modernist myth that strengthening patriarchal law prevents "unnatural" sexual transgressions.

La Passion de Béatrice

When the incest taboo fails, François realizes the depravity at the heart of the system that he, as a father, embodies. His own disenchantment leads him to behavior that is increasingly calculated to challenge Béatrice to abandon her idealized fantasies of the patriarchy and embrace her power to stand against it. In spite of his abusive behavior, as he comes to know his grown daughter, François clearly admires her strength of will and tells her that she should have been the son. But patriarchy, with its inveterate misogyny, twists the process of bequeathing paternal power from father to daughter, forcing a disturbingly literal and destructive method of transferring the phallus through repeated and violent rapes. Ironically, François's perverse behavior reveals the self-destructive kernel at the heart of heteronormativity, and through his actions he becomes the Queer Father who exposes his daughter's potential for reconfiguring family power dynamics. In Béatrice, François finds a phallic daughter who can mete out the punishment he desires.

To balance the film's complicating of François's relationship to his position as lord and father, Tavernier re-envisions Béatrice's role in the family drama.

---

36 More recent "legal" analyses of the story likewise hinge on whether or not incest occurred. Their presentations of the "case" are less equivocal about the question of incest than the fictional portrayals, but still preserve its "central place" as "an object of obsession and attraction" that "is constantly being solicited and refused" (Foucault, *History of Sexuality*, p. 109).

37 Foucault, *History of Sexuality*, p. 109.

38 Foucault, *History of Sexuality*, p. 110.

39 Butler, *Gender Trouble*, p. 97.

The typical casting of Francesco Cenci as an unrepentant sinner demands the portrayal of the young Beatrice as the tragic and innocent heroine. Her only taint is, in Shelley's words, that "the fit return to make to the most enormous injuries is kindness and forbearance, and a resolution to convert the injurer from his dark passions by peace and love. Revenge, retaliation, atonement, are pernicious mistakes. If Beatrice had thought in this manner she would have been wiser and better."[40] The last act of Artaud's play also presents her as an innocent, though one tainted by her parricide: "I am going to die, and I tell you that this world has always lived under the sign of injustice. With my death, life itself perishes. . . . Neither God nor man, nor any of the forces which dominate what is called our destiny, have chosen between good and evil. I die, and I have not chosen."[41] In both cases the plausible deniability of the incest places Beatrice in an impossible position in relation to the Law of the Father: on one hand she is the victim of incest and yet never shown to be sullied. Her parricide is therefore simultaneously sympathetic and unwarranted. Such a moral universe supports rather than dismantles the perversity of the heteronormative family.

Tavernier inverts this traditional view of Beatrice's process of moral corruption. Instead of becoming increasingly tainted by her disillusionment and desire for revenge, Béatrice's initial simplistic belief in the "good father" is marked as culpable. In spite of her father's antisocial behavior, Béatrice clings to her fantasy of him. As he walks out to the tower, symbol of both father and daughter's shared devotion, the return of the family patriarch, Béatrice calls after him: "On m'a souvent dit que vous étiez mauvais, mais je ne les ai pas crus. . . . Je vous ai trop aimé en votre absence pour vous haïr en l'espace d'une nuit" (They told me often that you were bad, but I did not believe them. I loved you too much in your absence to hate you in one night). This naïve devotion to society's image of the family and her refusal to acknowledge the ways in which patriarchy enables the violence inherent in her father merely propels François's destructive project. In spite of this critique, *La Passion Béatrice* does not undercut the purity of Béatrice's love—if anything, she becomes more noble as she is tested by her father—but it does suggest that the power of her love must be redirected in order to benefit herself, her family, and her community.

After François's return home, life at the de Cortemare castle becomes a continuous battering of the viewer with images of the antagonistic and disturbing relationships between lord and vassals, men and women under patriarchal law. We are subject to distasteful rapes and brutal pillaging of the countryside by François and his spoilers, the belittling of Arnaud for his gentle effeminacy, and the repeated degradation of Béatrice by their father; all the while, the male characters left behind during the war celebrate the return of

---

40 Shelley, Preface to *The Cenci*, p. 240.
41 Artaud, *The Cenci*, 4.3.

the Lord de Cortemare and his men by commenting "Oh! que je suis heureux de voir un homme!" (What a joy to see a man!) and "Cela fait tant d'anneés que je ne suis entouré que de femmes" (It's been so many years that I have been surrounded by only women). Béatrice stands against a long tradition of patriarchy rooted in misogyny.

As Béatrice's fantasy of family unravels and her lingering belief in the patriarchal dream is tested to greater and greater degrees by her father's depravity, she begins her passion. Her fantasy of the "good father" and her dream of herself as the "good daughter" are martyred, but not without an ensuing redemption. Her slow process of purgation leads her to explore all possible avenues of challenging her father's power before taking responsibility herself for ending his reign of terror.

Her *via crucis* begins with her embracing traditional realms of maternal power—prayers to the Virgin Mary and appeals to her own relatives. At first, her prayers to the wooden statue of the Virgin are in gratitude for her father's return, but these quickly turn to entreaties for aid to help her to love him in spite of his cruelties. And when she cries out, "Mère! Mère!" when François comes to rape her, neither the Mother of God, nor her grandmother, nor her mother come to her aid. In contrast to the close and supportive relationship that Beatrice shares with her stepmother in earlier renditions of the Cenci myth, in Tavernier's film, Béatrice's female relatives offer little support since both have acquiesced to the gender hierarchy, whether through a bitter, but ineffectual, hatred (François's mother) or through mute invisibility (Béatrice's mother). The subordinate role of these female figures in the patriarchal power structure is underscored by François's use of the Virgin as part of his incestuous violation of his daughter. As he enters the scene, he goes to the statue of the Virgin and her infant son, crosses himself "backwards," as Béatrice notes, and then demands that Béatrice ask pardon for the sin she will commit. Although her father is less of a believer in God than Béatrice, his actions emphasize Catholicism's tacit support of his prerogatives as a father, even in the act of incest.

Her next step is to turn to underground realms of female power she had previously ignored or rejected as the devoted daughter. Her grandmother's hatred of the system and her compassion for Béatrice's plight leads her to suggest a less holy female power—witchcraft. Prior to her father's return, Béatrice's views of her grandmother are highly misogynistic; she sees her as a bitter crone, whose hatred for her son is based on a matter as trivial as his red hair. After she is raped by her father, Béatrice turns to her grandmother, who challenges Béatrice's previous paternal identification by noting that "Tant tu me ressembles quand j'étais jeune. Tant à te regarder vivre il me revient l'envie de rire et de chanter" (You resemble me so much when I was young; so much so that when I see you the impulse to laugh and sing comes back to me). But the gynocentric witchcraft she proffers, although an expression of female resistance and anger to a world centered around God the Father, has little real-world strength to resist physical violation, as suggested by the witch's loss of her nipples to her ravishers. The magic is sympathetic but in going to the witch, Béatrice is still playing with dolls (given to her by the witch) rather than taking on the responsibility of challenging her father's authority herself.

Béatrice's last hope for outside aid lies with the men in her world—can or will they stand against her father? Her appeal to the local priest underscores François's earlier hint that the Virgin's Son is on his side.

Béatrice: Je crois bien que je le hais.
Priest: Ne dis pas cela, pas ici. Mais toi Béatrice, es-tu certaine de ne pas l'avoir tenté? Parfois les femmes sans le vouloir se font l'instument du diable. Il y a votre nature de femmes, votre nature de tentatrices.
Béatrice: Vous m'avez donné ma première communion, mon père. Me croyez-vous capable de vous mentir? . . . C'est lui l'intrument du diable.
. . . .
Priest: Je ne peux que te répéter les commandements de Dieu, que la femme doit être soumise à son père et à son mari comme à son seigneur.

(*Béatrice*: I think I hate him.
Priest: Don't say that, not here. And you, Béatrice, are you certain that you did not tempt him? Woman is the devil's instrument. It is woman's nature, your nature to beguile.
Béatrice: You gave me my first communion, Father. Do you believe that I could lie to you? . . . *He* is the devil's instrument.
. . . .
Priest: I can only repeat God's commandments. Woman must submit to father and husband as she did to God and as one of a lower stature, one cannot judge a nobleman.)

Her appeal to the priest and her father's own attempt to have him bless their incestuous union has the effect of the Bishop pressuring her father to marry her off to Lemartin. He is tempted to do it to save his soul and regain his land, but his male companion brands him a coward for agreeing to forgo his male prerogative in the face of excommunication. He chooses to remain a "man" and seizes the moment to teach Béatrice the limits of male-female love, even for someone as chivalrous as Lemartin. Like her earlier belief in her father's goodness, Béatrice trusts whole-heartedly Lemartin's romantic words:

Il n'y a qu'un pays où je desire m'enraciner, celui qui délimite votre âme. Je n'ai que faire des terres de votre pére. Je suis Chrétien, madame, et depuis que je vous ai vue pour la première fois, je ne desire m'agenouiller que devant vous, n'adorer et ne vénérer que vous.

(I have traveled, but the only land I seek to inhabit is that of your soul. I care nothing for your father's land. I am a Christian, lady, but when I saw you I only desired to kneel before you and worship you.)

Béatrice runs to the statue of the Virgin, repeating his words to herself—"I only desired to kneel before you, Béatrice." She then begs the Virgin's forgiveness for her vanity: "J'implorerai tout bas, les yeux baissés comme une douce et aimante épouse; mon coeur se meurt d'amour" (I'll beg him softly, eyes downcast, as befits a good and loving wife; my heart is dying of love). Her father cuts short this reverie of the "good wife": "Il est parti" (He's gone). Instead of saving her, Lemartin abandons her after he hears of the incest, and Béatrice's dream of romantic love is shattered. Although he promised earlier in dream-like voice-over, "Je vous aimerai toujours, toujours" (I will love you always, always), he fails to fulfill his role as male protector in her moment of greatest need. Her father's assessment that Lemartin wants only unspoiled land that he can "sow" himself lays bare the woman's role under patriarchy as property.

François completes Béatrice's final disillusionment by attacking her last male supporter—Arnaud. The assault is particularly painful because Béatrice and Arnaud's relationship as brother and sister is presented as a rare image of a positive male-female relationship in the film. Against the medieval backdrop of unreflective celebration of masculine violence and habitual degradation of women, together they offer a model of familial relations that, although marked as non-normative with respect to gender roles, is mutually supportive and affectionate. One short scene shows Béatrice in her brother's room, comforting him after his war-induced nightmare by licking his face and offering soothing words, while their father stands metaphorically and literally outside. In a following scene, Arnaud teaches his sister how to shoot and, under her adoring gaze, shoots a hawk, a gift he presents to his father who rejects it.

When Béatrice turns to Arnaud to help her abort her father's child, her father catches Arnaud kicking Béatrice in the belly. To punish him, François sets up a human hunt in which Arnaud, dressed as a girl, is pursued by François, his men, and Béatrice, dressed as a man. When Arnaud is finally caught, François orders his "wenches" to strip him and rape him. The hunt simultaneously reveals the fluidity of gender and the violence of the western gender system toward "women." This final exercise of his fatherly prerogative in this perverse hunt pushes Béatrice beyond her limits. She leaves the hunt and her brother's degradation and rides home. This ultimate ride becomes a review of the inconsistencies, arbitrary brutality, and perversity of the patriarchy. First, she comes upon Jehan, whose companionship she lost after her father's rape, eating dirt by a watering hole; the next image is of the holy anchoress of the village, who rejected her father's pleas to be forgiven, being burned by the priest; last, two servant boys who tried to run away because the de Cortemare estate could no longer provide sustenance for them are seen hanging from a tree. Upon her return to the castle, she comes upon Arnaud who begs her to take him away, to which she replies "Je suis fatiguée, si fatiguée" (I am tired, so tired). But she cannot yet rest.

If she is to end the nightmare of François's cruelty, Béatrice must leave her place in the heteronormative family behind and embrace her queer potential as the phallic daughter. That it is her father who teaches her this lesson by playing out the perversity of misogyny and patriarchal power is a fitting paternal gift; although his methods are questionable, the result is an enduring distaste for paternal domination. When she comes across the mangled body of her pet magpie, stabbed gratuitously by her father, her dreams of familial happiness under patriarchy are likewise dead. She repeats the words her father spoke upon hearing of his own father's death: "My Lord God, I hate you." She, too, has lost faith in the Father, "whose image upon earth a father is,"[42] but as she picks up the dagger, the same dagger passed down to François by his father, she takes on the responsibility of enacting a new law—the Law of the Daughter. Her father, who has brought her to this state, has been waiting for her. He lies prone upon the bed of their incestuous union, waiting for his death at her hands. From her hands he will receive punishment for his excesses that he previously sought from God the Father, and he appears at peace with his fate. Faith in her has replaced his faith in God. He asks her "M'as-tu parfois aimé?" (Did you sometimes love me?), and when she answers "Non" without wavering, he knows that the veil of paternal devotion has been rent.

His final blow is to destroy Béatrice's adherence to the divine patriarchy by showing patriarchy's disregard for even the Mother of God. As he guides her to stab him, she demands he say the act of contrition, to which he responds "Je ne crois en rien à la trinité ni à un fils de Dieu daignant s'abaisser jusqúa prendre naissance dans un corps de femme" (I don't believe in a trinity or in a son of God who would deign to abase himself by choosing to be born in a woman's body). Béatrice's thrust of the dagger cuts him short as he exposes the misogyny that would deny any place for women, even as mothers. But his final verbal jab comes across as calculated rather than heart-felt. He realizes that the time of masculine power has come to an end.

---

42 Shelley, *The Cenci*, 2.1.17.

The Law of the Daughter: Béatrice as Queer Savior

Although the film's soundtrack leaves the viewer with the lyrics "Pie Jesu domine/Dona eis requiem" (Merciful Lord Jesus/Give them rest), it is Béatrice, not Jesus, who takes away the sins of the world by sacrificing her father. As the Daughter who replaces the Son, Béatrice functions as a queer savior, but her passion is not one unto death. Instead, she must suffer under the patriarchal law into an understanding of the limits of the traditional family, and then, from that place of enlightenment, sacrifice the Father, both the idyllic father of her girlish phantasies and the perverse reality of François as father-ravager. With François's death, the phallic dagger has been turned against the very system that spawned its power. But Béatrice is still "la fille de ton pere"; she is indebted to her queer father, whose actions forced her hand, brutally insisting that she abandon a system that oppressed her by revealing its twisted roots.

It is tempting to read Tavernier's film as a tragedy, seeing Béatrice as tainted by her father's violent ways and the power of patriarchy still firmly in place. Previous versions establish this as the traditional reading of the Cenci story. Shelley's play ends with the impending death of Beatrice and her family at the hands of a corrupt papal system and the resurrection of her father's spirit. Artaud's play ends with an even more insidious triumph of father over daughter: "Oh my eyes, what a dreadful vision you will see, in dying. How can I be sure that, down there, I shall not be confronted by my father? The very notion makes my death more bitter. For I fear that death may teach me that I have ended by resembling him."[43] In spite of the cathartic death of Lord Cenci, the patriarchal power that winked at his crimes goes unchallenged in both versions.[44]

Tavernier chooses not to follow his sources in this regard and ends the film with François's ritualized murder at the hands of Béatrice, emphasizing the triumph of the daughter over her father. In this, Tavernier departs from both history and legend. The Cenci narratives distance Beatrice from this violent act as a way to preserve her innocence, even though she is the prime mover in arranging her father's death. Although the phallus has been forced upon Béatrice in multiple ways, it is the father's phallus, symbolized by the dagger that François's father passes down to him as a sign of a transfer of masculine prerogative, that is the patriarch's undoing. In their ritualized final encounter, Béatrice uses the dagger her father bequeaths to her to kill him, supporting Zants's observation about Tavernier's *oeuvre* in general: "The self-destructive nature of the hierarchical power structure lies exposed." The final moments of the film envision a "historical moment of transition when those in power . . .

---

43 Artaud, *The Cenci*, 4.3.

44 Most versions of the Cenci story are careful to preserve the narrative element of the public execution of Beatrice and her family after the death of the father.

are about to be overthrown and society has a momentary chance of developing a new system and of freeing itself from the old laws."[45]

Tavernier's reworked ending to the Cenci drama hints at alternative visions of how law, desire, and power might operate within the family. The absence of retribution for the Father's murder at the close of the film's diegesis works against the re-inscription of patriarchal power found in the historical account and its fictionalized retellings. The ending of *La Passion Béatrice* implies the possibility of building something new out of the ruins. Seizing the power of the phallus, Béatrice takes the first step toward instituting her own law, the Law of the Daughter. Her destruction of the Father allows for the reconfiguration of the family, as suggested by the image of mother and daughter in the last frame. For this last shot, the camera cuts to an anticipatory set-up of the statue of Mary to the left of the screen, and as Béatrice's hand rises to caress the Mother's face, her face enters from the right. The virgin-mother and daughter-wife share the frame in a single plane of focus, creating a visual symbol of a potential new family dynamic. This balanced, mirror image of mother and daughter echoes and replaces the opening shot of François and his father, bonding over the female landscape in which they are unequal shareholders. The locus of power has shifted, and to reach this point, every element of the heteronormative family has been queered: fathers have become husbands to their daughters, daughters have become mothers to their siblings, and sisters have usurped their brothers' prerogatives as the inheritors of phallic power. In the final scene, the suppression of a woman's control over her own sexuality, represented by the young François's killing of his mother's lover and the adult François's raping of his daughter, has been restored through another blood sacrifice: the sacrifice of the father. The "poison in the sap" from the twisted roots of the Law of the Father produced a strange fruit: the *patria potens* has been supplanted by a *gyna potens*. The film's final feminine homosocial pair promises a new, yet unimaginable, future—a New Jerusalem, if you will.[46] Although there is no guarantee that this new family structure will be utopian, after tracing the perversity of the western heteronormative family through the de Cortemare family, it is hard to image a worse system of human interaction.

---

45 Zants, *Bertrand Tavernier*, pp. 68 and 55.

46 Asked by her father in their final dialogue where she will go now, Béatrice responds "Jerusalem." Whether she is going there as a penance or a place of refuge—a new Holy Land—is left unsaid.

The Queerness of (This) Medieval Film

The utopian implications of *La Passion Béatrice* are not arrived at without effort; what is required is a queer eye. For, like queer theory, the film is "[u]topic in its negativity, . . curv[ing] endlessly toward a realization that its realization remains impossible."[47] The potential for a new vision of gender and sexuality within the constraints of the family is largely left off-screen, implied only by its negative image, represented by the medieval de Cortemare family. This reading of Tavernier's film is made available in part because as a "medieval" film it is not bound by the same historical or academic constraints as scholarly analyses of medieval texts. As Martha Driver notes, "ironically, the version of history employed in much of medieval film resembles in many ways the version of history employed in the Middle Ages, before histori*cism* had been invented, when, as Glenn Burgess says, 'The study of history was not so much the need to seek the truth about the past as the need to seek truths that would be valid in the present.'"[48] Looking at our constructions of the Middle Ages on film, especially in their more "realist" forms, may help us to recognize how our unconscious assumptions about the medieval world shape even our more careful philological reconstructions of the period. Although there is much to be gained by careful study of texts from the Middle Ages itself, the "Middle Ages" of Tavernier's medieval film, released from the straightjacket of nineteenth-century historicism, allows us to see—though through a lens, queerly—that gender, sexuality, and family relations, whether in early modern Rome or late medieval France, are no more normal today than they were then, and that the early formulations of the heteronormative family under the misogynist hand of patriarchy is perverse at its very core.[49] In other words, whether looking at medieval or modern families, we would do better to leave behind the idea of heteronormativity in favor of multiple normativities, and recognizing, as Karma Lochrie cautions, that "the problem is not confined to the efforts of scholars to imagine a sexual past. It begins with the presumption that everyone knows what heterosexuality and heteronormativity are in the present."[50]

---

47 Lee Edelman, "Queer Theory: Unstating Desire" *GLQ* 2.4 (1995): 343-348, at p. 346.

48 Martha Driver, Preface to *The Medieval Hero on Screen*, eds. Martha Driver and Sid Ray (Jefferson, NC: McFarland, 2004), p. 10.

49 For this insight, I am indebted to the work of Carolyn Dinshaw and Umberto Eco, who are two of the strongest voices calling upon medievalists to examine the inescapability of our own historical, cultural, and personal subjectivities even in our most careful philological examinations of texts from the Middle Ages.

50 Lochrie, *Heterosyncrasies* (Minneapolis: U of Minnesota P, 2005), p. xviii.

In *La Passion Béatrice*, the taint of deviance, historically associated with homosexuality, so fully infects the heterosexual interactions of the de Cortemare family that it is only by rejecting the ideal of the normative completely that Béatrice is able to see clearly her family's unique "heterosyncracies" (to borrow Lochrie's term) and to recognize how sexuality functions within the family as an exercise of law, desire, and power. Reconceptualizing familial sexual and gender dynamics in this way leads to "finding the queer in much more diffuse and diverse sexual places and imagining a future without heteronormativity, or just perhaps with normativities claimed by other sexualities and identities as well as heterosexuality."[51] Viewed from this slant, Béatrice's use of the phallus to kill her father is the film's most surprisingly queer move of all. In her hands it is transformed in that moment into a subversive tool that, like the term *queer* itself, "will have to remain that which is, in the present, never fully owned, but always and only redeployed, twisted, queered from a prior usage and in the direction of urgent and expanding political purposes, and perhaps also yielded in favor of terms [and tools] that do that political work more effectively."[52] Whether that tool of subversion is the phallus or the film, in the final cut what is revealed is that heteronormativity is the greatest perversion of all.

---

51 Lochrie, *Heterosyncrasies*, p. xvi.
52 Judith Butler, *Bodies That Matter* (New York: Routledge, 1993), p. 228.

Chapter 2
Queering the Lionheart: Richard I in *The Lion in Winter* on Stage and Screen

R. Barton Palmer

This Past is Always a Present

All performance art depends on the spectator's recognition of the doubleness of the body, whose physical presence must be understood as belonging to both the actor and the character incarnated. The actor's body comes to represent, continuously if not seamlessly, two identities. Historical dramatizations further problematize the representational capacity of the performing body, installing a doubleness of the second degree. Characters based on personages from a bygone era are also, in terms of reference, reanimations of the dead. They are simultaneously fictional and historical, and the actor's body comes to bear an additional representational weight, standing in as it does for a person who once lived. As is well known, the co-presence of the actor's self and his assumed character creates an unresolved tension that can damage the drama's fictional effect if the disparity between self and character becomes unintriguingly obtrusive, but it can also become a source of intense pleasure, a quality exploited, for example, to immense profitability in the classic Hollywood star system, whose luminaries were always understood (and consumed) as both their perdurable selves and as the characters of the moment.

Similarly, in historical dramatizations, the tension between fictionality and historicity (whatever those modes of understanding might be taken separately to mean) poses a danger to the effectiveness of textual re-creation if the evoked character violates the spectator's sense of historical truth. Yet this violation can provide pleasure if the character provocatively contests received opinions of the past, underlining how a confected/evoked self exists between times as well as between the contiguous realms of the fictional and the historical. Such a conflicted representation, to put this another way, commands a belief that is always already undermined, but never discredited, making a reference to the real that is also immediately understood, *stricto sensu*, as fabulation.

History imposes no unbearable limits on this (re)creative process. Although characters in historical dramatizations must be drawn, as James Goldman declares in his preface to the theatrical version of *The Lion in Winter*, "consistent with the facts we have," the writer is left largely free to exercise his imagination because "their characters and passions . . . are fictions." Goldman describes his encounter with this contradiction in giving dramatic life to England's Henry II, his quarrelsome sons, and rebellious wife: "I made them up. I read about the things they did, I studied them and then imagined what they felt and thought and said and wanted from their lives." Such a project, he recognizes, never yields the truth, which is always elusive: "What they were really like, of course, no one will ever know."[1] The successful failure of this kind of imagining, naturally, is the essence of historical writing of every kind. The figures from the past we study and then make live again, whether in fiction or non-fictional accounts, exist for us. They cannot, naturally enough, speak to the desires or interests of their own bygone era.

And yet the impossible standard we deploy for judging their authenticity is furnished by "the facts we have." To make the obvious point, these facts are hardly exempt from never-ending hermeneutic inquiry, from the interrogation that precedes the writer's imaginative engagement. Artists interested in historical fiction, to use Goldman's phrase, not only make up their characters. They also determine what the "facts" at their disposal can be taken to mean. Goldman withholds comment about this form of re-imagining, evidently preferring to let the finished work speak for him.

In *The Lion in Winter*, Goldman thus not only (re)creates four of the most fascinating and enigmatic personages of the Middle Ages for our time, but he also furthers historical inquiry into the truths of their identities. In the case of Richard, he provides us with a fictional figure who reflects the post-Kinsey transformation of Victorian repression of the forces and vagaries of sexual urges (whose objects and practices, as we now think, are determined by circumstance and, as best we can tell, predisposition). For Goldman's Richard proclaims and acknowledges same-sex desire, which he describes not simply as lust but as an enduring love. And this Richard, with inevitable anachronism, speaks in the fashion so brilliantly anatomized by Michel Foucault, who observes that our present age offers not the reversal of a culture that had condemned sex to "prohibition, nonexistence, and silence," but an incomplete rejection of such discursive injunctions. For Richard, much as we do, finds "it difficult to speak

---

1 James Goldman, *The Lion in Winter* (1966; New York: Random House, 2004), pp. xi, ix. The film (1968) is directed by Anthony Harvey, screenplay by James Goldman, starring Peter O'Toole as Henry II, Katharine Hepburn as Eleanor of Aquitaine, and Anthony Hopkins as Richard.

on the subject without striking a different pose . . . [as] our tone of voice shows that we know we are being subversive," as Foucault observes.[2]

At the same time, the character called Richard figures as yet another version of his historical referent, in which regard his acknowledgement of homosexual desire offers a challenge to the "affirmation of nonexistence . . . [the] admission that there was nothing to say about such things, nothing to see, and nothing to know," as Foucault puts it.[3] Goldman's Richard, in short, is not only an updating, a version of the past fabulized for us, but also something of an "outing" of his historical self, a contribution to what Carolyn Dinshaw imagines as the "queer historical impulse," which is nothing less than

> an impulse toward making connections across time between, on the one hand, lives, texts, and other cultural phenomena left out of sexual categories back then and, on the other, those left out of current sexual categories now. Such an impulse extends the resources for self- and community building into even the distant past.[4]

Closeting a Legend

It is certainly true, as Goldman suggests, that historical records of Henry II's reign, and those of his sons Richard and John, give us detailed information about the "outcome of relationships—such things as who kills whom and when," but these same sources "say little if anything about the quality and content of those relationships," in Goldman's view.[5] Goldman is correct for the most part, but not in the case of Henry's son, Richard, by common consent of chroniclers then and historians ever since, a study in violent contrasts whose personal life was in his own time (and sporadically in our own) the subject of much speculation and controversy.

One of his sympathetic recent biographers, James Brundage, acknowledges how strange was the career of one of the most fascinating and enduring personalities of the Middle Ages: "He was certainly one of the worst rulers that England has ever had. He visited the island only twice during the ten years of his reign and the total duration of those two visits amounted to about six months." As to Richard's performance as king, the most praiseworthy comment Brundage feels authorized to make is that "during the other nine-and-a-half

---

2 Michel Foucault, *The History of Sexuality: Volume I*, trans. by Robert Hurley (New York: Random House, 1980), p. 6.

3 Foucault, *History of Sexuality*, p. 4.

4 Carolyn Dinshaw, *Getting Medieval* (Durham, NC: Duke UP, 1999), p. 1.

5 Goldman, *The Lion in Winter*, p. xxi.

years of his reign . . . he left it in the care of agents who were in many respects better fitted to rule than he was." His absence thus "was more beneficial for the English than his presence," a doubtful virtue that speaks perhaps to the way Richard came to function as the long-expected good king in the Robin Hood legend as reshaped by the sixteenth-century Scots antiquarian John Mair in his *Historia majoris Britannae, tam Angliae quam Scotiae* (1521). Although a monarch of dubious worthiness (and little national importance), Richard quickly became, as Brundage points out, "a genuine folk-hero whose exploits were further dramatized and elaborated by numerous legends which . . . testify to his popularity."[6] These legends never take into account, the biographer continues, how Richard's relationships "were almost uniformly unsatisfactory," and this was due to his "instability and immaturity . . . his ungovernable temper, his quick changes of moods, and the generally uneven tenor of his personal life." Richard was from such evidence "an unhappy, unsatisfied, and unsatisfiable person," but it was likely because of his good looks and incontestable military prowess that he was so "widely revered during his lifetime and has enjoyed a posthumous fame such as no other English king has ever achieved."[7]

Acting the modern psychologist, Brundage finds a significant symptom of Richard's obvious defects in character and behavior in his inability to refrain from "all too human vices," especially a homosexuality that, for Brundage, is the most obvious manifestation of his failure to become a fully functioning male. Here the historian (writing in the early 1970s) accepts the position of postwar neo-Freudianism that homosexuality represents a developmental problem, to be cured by therapy urging the acceptance of mature male responsibilities.[8] Brundage declares that "his contemporaries were very unwilling to discuss the matter openly," contenting themselves with "dark hints," but this is something of a mischaracterization of the evidence, which is as direct as comments on such behavior were likely to be in the twelfth century, as we shall soon see.[9]

Married late in life, and somewhat unwillingly, Richard spent little time with his wife, Berengaria, and left no heirs. In fact, an indifference to his wife is seen to be but one manifestation of a "wider aversion to women" and a correlative

---

6 James Brundage, *Richard Lion Heart* (New York: Scribner's, 1974), pp. 258, 261.

7 Brundage, *Richard Lion Heart*, p. 261.

8 For accessible commentary on this point, see Barbara Ehrenreich, *The Hearts of Men: American Dreams and the Flight from Commitment* (Garden City, NJ: Doubleday, 1983), pp. 14-41.

9 See the impressive survey of the extensive twelfth-century material about same-sex desire in John Boswell, *Christianity, Social Tolerance, and Homosexuality* (Chicago: U of Chicago P, 1980), pp. 207-66. Boswell concludes: "Even allowing for poetic hyperbole, contemporary claims for the extreme frequency of homosexual behavior were impressive" (p. 232).

to Richard's obvious preference for "exclusively male company." His personal qualities, for Brundage, thus led him to fail "in one of the primary obligations of a medieval king," for he "produced no male heir, indeed no heir at all."[10] We can safely discount as "evidence" of Richard's supposed sexual orientation Brundage's oversimplifying comments that he was overly attached to his mother and had a difficult relationship with Henry II, his father, and this is a tack Goldman follows as well.

Readers of Brundage would be surprised, perhaps, to discover that the biographer's acknowledgement of Richard's sexual orientation is not shared by others who have portrayed the king's life, including, and especially, the most respected and *au courant* authorities. In fact, as John Boswell reports, "of the many biographies of Richard, only Brundage is frank about his homosexuality, although he discusses it in highly derogatory terms."[11] More prevalent among twentieth-century historians and biographers is some Foucauldian "affirmation of nonexistence" with regard to Richard's sexual proclivities, of which there is substantial enough written evidence to require some comment, however dismissive. In any case, such affirmations paradoxically always say what they are not going to say, continuing a trope of unspeakable mentionability about same-sex desire that, interestingly enough, has its origins in the later Middle Ages.[12]

In a book that amounts to something like hagiography, tellingly entitled *Coeur de Lion*, Clennell Wilkinson mentions a personal life that reflected Richard's "dark, passionate Angevin background," but concludes that he is "no subject for the psychological dissecting table" because "his simple heart lies open for all to see." It is hard to know what exactly to make of this mystifying assertion, except that it stipulates as irrelevant any consideration of the private life of historical figures, even when that private life is demonstrably public as well. For Richard's great love, it seems from the evidence, was the young man who would become Phillip II of France and the bitter enemy of his Angevin neighbors, a historical theme that Goldman pursues in depth in *The Lion in Winter*. Wilkinson, not surprisingly, contents himself instead with trying "to illustrate his character by telling of his deeds," in support of the view that "the average Englishman is right," while professional historians (because they fault his performance as

---

10 Brundage, *Richard Lion Heart*, pp. 263, 259, 257. Brundage's view of Richard's same-sex desire was anticipated some twenty-five years earlier by J. H. Harvey, who congratulated himself on "breaking the conspiracy of silence surrounding the popular hero Richard" (*The Plantagenets* [London: Batsford, 1948], pp. 33-34). Harvey and Brundage, however, have not persuaded the majority of their colleagues, despite the abundant evidence.

11 Boswell, *Christianity, Social Tolerance, and Homosexuality*, p. 232 n.82.

12 On this point, see Mark Jordan, *The Invention of Sodomy in Christian Theology* (Chicago: U of Chicago P, 1997), pp. 1-9.

ruler of the kingdom) are wrong about Richard being "the supreme type of the Crusading soldier-king."[13]

But even less jingoistic, more sober-minded biographers have sought to ignore or discount the evidence, which is considerable, that Richard was homosexual (as we would now say) and that his personal relationships suffered as a result. Philip Henderson follows the course of least resistance in simply refusing to broach the subject.[14] Most prominently, and revealingly, in what has rightly become the contemporary standard biography of Richard, John Gillingham states categorically that: "Although there is strong evidence that Richard committed adultery, there is no evidence that he was homosexual—or bisexual—either before or after marriage. We simply do not know. Naturally, we can speculate or, if we prefer, 'unnaturally.'"[15]

An Eminently Obvious Monolith?

The above-quoted passage from Gillingham manifests a palpable uneasiness, and for this reason it holds no little interest for us in evaluating the cultural significance of Goldman's portrait of Richard, reflecting as it does an unwillingness on his part to admit that a figure he admires could have behaved in a manner he obviously abhors. But if there is no evidence of the Lionheart's homosexuality, then, one might ask, why would we be interested in or moved to speculate about it? What would call the presumption of heteronormality into question? Perhaps of even more interest, the historian's uncharacteristic attempt at humor, which, we might say, de-naturalizes the weakly commentative "naturally," and connects thereby to a medieval intellectual preoccupation about the role of Nature in regard to sexual conduct, suggests a nervousness in broaching the question, presumably because others like Brundage have interpreted the evidence differently. Perhaps, Gillingham also senses, and if so perceptively, a certain calculated indeterminacy in the very material whose meaning he declares is, on the one hand, so overwhelmingly determined ("there is no evidence") and yet, on the other, is acknowledged as giving rise to the very speculation Gillingham, ever the highly competent scholar, duly footnotes, calling attention to the very controversy he says is no controversy.

In her discussion of the difficulty in reconstructing a medieval queer sensibility ("How can we trace something that has been deemed unspeakable?"), Carolyn Dinshaw observes that:

---

13 Clennell Wilkinson, *Coeur de Lion* (New York: Appleton-Century, 1933), p. vi.

14 Philip Henderson, *Richard Coeur de Lion* (Westport, CT: Greenwood Press, 1958).

15 John Gillingham, *Richard I* (New Haven: Yale UP, 1999), p. 264.

If postmodern history has established that its objects are heterogeneous and multiple, it continues to be important to assert, however, *especially* to postmodern thinkers, the indeterminate nature of medieval cultural phenomena. In some very influential theoretical and critical work developing out of postmodernism, the Middle Ages is still made the dense, unvarying, and eminently obvious monolith against which modernity and postmodernity groovily emerge.[16]

The force of the monolith, buttressed by an unconvincing appeal to cultural relativism that seems instead another strategy for ducking, yet paradoxically facing, the issue, asserts itself in Gillingham's claim that: "Roger of Hoveden's report that, in 1187, Philip Augustus and Richard shared a bed was meant to be understood in political, not sexual, terms."[17] Gillingham, however, offers no evidence why we should understand Roger's report (to be examined in detail below) in political terms, whatever those might be. Is it really credible that such sleeping arrangements were made to further not the personal affection that is the main subject of this passage, but a political agenda of some kind, producing a cooperative pair who might, in the modern metaphor, be understood as "bedfellows"? Close friends as young men, Richard and Philip later became bitter political rivals, but there is no reason to read this later development into a comment from a much earlier era.

Transparently an attempt to keep an admired figure in a closet not of his own making, the historian's energetic defense of Richard against "misinterpretation" soon degenerates into something approaching farce when he attempts to explain away an even stronger and more unusual bit of evidence. According to the chronicler Richard of Hoveden (or Howden), a hermit appeared before Richard in 1195 (the king was then 38) and asked him to recall the destruction visited upon Sodom and so refrain from what was unlawful. The story is worth quoting at some length:

> There came a hermit to King Richard, and, preaching the words of eternal salvation to him, said: "Be thou mindful of the destruction of Sodom, and abstain from what is unlawful; for if thou dost not, a vengeance worthy of God shall overtake thee." The king, however, intent upon the things of this world, and not those that are of God, was not able so readily to withdraw his mind from what was unlawful. . . . Hence it was, that on the Lord's day in Easter . . . the Lord scourged him with a severe attack of illness, so that he was ashamed to confess the guiltiness of his life, and after receiving absolution, took back his wife, whom for a long time he had not known, and putting away all illicit

---

16 Dinshaw, *Getting Medieval*, pp. 15-16.
17 Gillingham, *Richard I*, p. 264.

intercourse, he remained constant to his wife and the two became one flesh and the Lord gave him health of both body and soul.[18]

Gillingham suggests that references to the "destruction of Sodom" are generally just that—"allusions not so much to the nature of the offences as to the terrible and awe-inspiring nature of the punishment."[19] While this particular episode from Genesis often figured in earlier periods as an exemplum illustrating the power of Jehovah's dissatisfaction, it was certainly not the case when this hermit daringly presumed to chastise his king. By the end of the twelfth century, references to the story of Sodom had acquired two connected interpretations that emphasized the nature of the sinful behavior involved more than its apocalyptic consequences. Historian Mark Jordan reports that, on the one hand, "that complicated and disturbing story was simplified until it became the story of the punishment of a single sin, a sin that could be called eponymously the sin of the Sodomites." On the other hand, there was "another process, more diffuse, but no less important, [that] had to do with grouping together a number of sins under the old Roman category of *luxuria*," which "came to be seen as the source of sinfulness in diverse acts, many of them having to do with the genitals."[20]

This second process of development, Jordan reports, would under the influence of Peter Damian's *Book of Gomorrah*, written in the 1050s, soon coalesce into the first, gaining considerable currency by the time Roger came to write his chronicle. The point is that by 1195 references to Sodom and the destruction visited upon its inhabitants had primarily one meaning. These were punishments for the "illicit intercourse" that Roger of Hoveden emphasizes from which Richard thereafter refrained. Interestingly, Gillingham fails to report what Hoveden says about "illicit intercourse" in his brief summary of the passage. Given Richard's famous lack of interest in women (apparent enough to be something of a joke among his contemporaries), it seems wishful thinking for Gillingham to conclude that this passage indicts the king for adultery in the customary sense, but does not refer to Richard's sexual interest in men.

One further comment: it is important to note that Peter Damian's highly influential anatomizing of same-sex desire did not postulate that such urges and resultant behavior constituted an "identity" or an "orientation," as we now mostly think. Instead, "the hortatory structure of the *Book of Gomorrah* supposes that the Sodomite can be reformed by exhortation," although such a

---

18 Roger of Hoveden, *The Annals*, trans. Henry Riley, 2 vols. (London: Bohn, 1853; repr. New York: AMS Press, 1968). The quotation is from vol. 2, pp. 356-57.

19 Gillingham, *Richard I*, p. 265.

20 Jordan, *Invention of Sodomy*, p. 29.

turning aside from the practice would be exceptional, of which more below.[21]
Roger of Hoveden's story of Richard's sickbed resolve to mend his ways, which
led him to turn from illicit intercourse to spousal constancy, should perhaps be
understood within the context of the theological and reformatory developments
traced by Jordan, among others.

Perhaps the main point of Hoveden's story, then, is not so much to indict
Richard, as does the hermit, for a practice then increasingly seen as odious
to God, but more to praise him for the strength of character to effect so
complete and lasting a transformation. The two historians, though separated
by almost eight centuries, share much in common. Like Gillingham, Roger is
eager to defend the character of a man he obviously admires. For his modern
counterpart, however, who sees sodomy as the outward sign of an inalterable
aspect of individual identity, Richard cannot be allowed such a hermit-prompted
conversion, unless it be unconvincingly interpreted as a turn away from that
most common (and generally unmentioned) of the faults of powerful medieval
monarchs: their interest in and dalliance with women other than their wives.
But, we might ask, do hermits risk royal displeasure to inveigh against such
customary infractions against conventional standards of sexual purity? And,
even if they do, what would lead admiring clerkly chroniclers to give such
weight to this kind of episode?

Roger's account of Richard's late in life turning from "illicit intercourse"
clarifies the more famous story Roger tells of him as a young man:

> Richard, the duke of Aquitaine, son of the king of England, remained behind
> with Philip, then king of France, who paid him such honor for a long time
> that every day they ate at the same table and drank from the same cup, and at
> night the bed did not separate them. And the king of France loved him as his
> own soul; and they cared so deeply for one another that because of the fervent
> affection they shared, his majesty the king of England, completely stupefied,
> wondered that it might be so [or, alternatively, *what it might be*].[22]

The main point of this story, *contra* Gillingham, is not that the two men are said
to spend their nights together in the same bed, but the unusual nature of their
relationship. It could be argued with some plausibility that, for adolescent young
men then as now, such a practice need not mean they were lovers. But what
makes this interpretation unlikely is the detail that follows. For we are told that
Richard's father, a man of no little experience in matters personal and sexual,
is so amazed by this "fervent affection" as to be stupefied, perhaps reduced to

---

21 Jordan, *Invention of Sodomy*, p. 57.

22 William Stubbs, *Gesta Regis Henrici Secundi Benedicti abbatis,* 2 vols. (London: Bohn,
1853). The passage referenced is in vol. 2, pp. 63-64; translation mine.

incomprehension. No wonder that this episode fired the imagination of James Goldman and is a central element as well in Anthony Harvey's film version of *The Lion in Winter*, which treats a fictitious Christmas court held in Chinon, at which Henry, still vital but knowing that at fifty he cannot hope to live much longer, intends to put an end to the bitter feuds with wife and sons that marred his otherwise prosperous and successful reign. Two of the invited guests are Richard and Phillip, brought together for the first time in some years.

Two Years on Every Street in Hell

The moment of dramatic reversal in Harvey's film comes, as in Goldman's play, after Henry (Peter O'Toole) has apparently succeeded in insuring the bequest of his considerable empire to John (Nigel Terry) by fending off the attempts of his two older surviving sons, Geoffrey (John Castle) and Richard (Anthony Hopkins), aided by the *agent provocateur* Philip of France (Timothy Dalton), to form an alliance against him and John. Henry's estranged wife Eleanor of Aquitaine (Katharine Hepburn) has done her best to further their intrigues, with a particular view to insuring that Richard, her favorite, succeeds his father. In an at-first farcical scene right out of Restoration comedy, the three sons come separately to Philip's room, there to be hidden in the closet *seriatim*. Richard is the last of the sons to arrive, and although his avowed purpose is political (to get Philip to agree to become his ally and make war upon Henry), the scene between them suddenly turns personal:

> *Richard*: I never wrote because I thought you'd never answer. You got married.
> *Philip*: Does that make a difference?
> *Richard*: Doesn't it?
> *Philip*: I've spent two years on every street in hell.
> *Richard*: That's odd: I didn't see you there.

The tone of this exchange is complex, and it is played by Hopkins and Dalton with a passionate, if uncertain, intensity. If poignantly romantic, this encounter quickly turns lustful, as the two make for the bed, even though (or perhaps because?) Philip knows Richard's brothers are watching and listening. But this lovers' reunion also emphasizes Richard's doubt and incomprehension, as he seems to require instruction in the nature of the very desire that has taken hold of him. The arrogant, audacious warrior who fears no man on the battlefield suddenly confesses to an apprehension of rejection. The pair are lovers in hell not only because of their separation, but because they had hitherto, it seems, no idea how to proceed. How are they to accommodate their mutual desire within the hidden spaces of the lives they are otherwise called upon to live, including and especially the heteronormative imperative to which Philip (but not Richard, at least not yet) submits?

The shared reference to the place of eternal damnation, moreover, hardly seems accidental, invoking as it does the loss of salvation that the restless, disturbing urgings of the sodomitical must entail, or so late twelfth-century theology proclaimed. This desire is metaphorized as traveling a path from which the possibility of salvation is precluded. Although the influential Peter Damian insists on the one hand that the sodomite must abandon his unnatural practices and by repentance find salvation, as Mark Jordan reports, he seems also "to conceive Sodomy as a sin that cannot be repented. This conception violates the fundamental Christian teaching about sins of the flesh, namely that they are always repentable." Sodomy, in this way, is "a sin from which there is no return in this life. The Sodomite is dead in the way the dead are, and he dwells already in the house of the dead."[23]

The streets of hell that Philip and Richard walk are thus also the streets of this world. Goldman, whose screenplay follows the playscript closely here, succeeds perhaps better than he knew in re-imagining the painful alienation of gay men in an era when their status was rapidly changing, separated from those they loved by social convention and their own fears, but also fearful that salvation lay always beyond their grasp. Although in hell together, Richard and Philip endure their pain separately, prevented from acting on their love for one another. This sense of living death was undoubtedly increased by a suddenly restrictive social environment, as John Boswell describes: "During the 200 years from 1150-1350, homosexual behavior appears to have changed, in the eyes of the public, from the personal preference of a prosperous minority . . . to a dangerous, antisocial, and severely sinful aberration."[24]

A Whiskered Thing?

At the time that *Lion in Winter* was written and then produced on Broadway in the middle 1960s, American attitudes toward homosexuality were only slightly more liberal than those of the High Middle Ages. A 1966 *Time* magazine essay on the subject (which had at least emerged from unmentionability) concluded with a strident condemnation:

> It is a pathetic little second-rate substitute for reality, a pitiable flight from life. As such it deserves fairness, compassion, understanding, and, when possible, treatment. But it deserves no encouragement, no glamorization, no

---

23 Jordan, *Invention of Sodomy*, pp. 66, 57.
24 Boswell, *Christianity, Social Tolerance, and Homosexuality*, p. 295.

rationalization, no fake status as minority martyrdom . . . and above all, no pretense that it is anything but a pernicious sickness.[25]

Goldman's Richard, if only in part, reflects this view, as the play stages an "outing" that is crucial to its dramatic structure. Easily besting the less-experienced Philip in a quick series of exchanges about relations between the two kingdoms, Henry quickly withdraws, boasting that "I've found out the way your mind works and the kind of man you are. I know your plans and expectations . . . and I've told you exactly nothing." Angered and humiliated, Philip recalls that Henry did much the same to Philip's father: "You—you made my father nothing." But Philip proves to have more power than Henry suspected, for he confesses to have learned "how much fathers live in sons."

"What's the official line on sodomy?" he asks Henry, who seems prepared to dismiss this charge, which he immediately understands is directed at Richard, although unnamed. Richard, Philip says, "found me first when I was fifteen." He was repelled by those advances, submitting only so that "one day I could tell you all about it." His sense of shock and betrayal stronger than his desire to remain hidden (how could it be otherwise?) within his appointed closet, Richard shows himself to proclaim "you loved me" to Henry's evident dismay. Rejected once again by the father against whom he has been in revolt of one kind or another for years, Richard responds with a bitter question. Henry should look within for the source of his disappointment: "So the royal corkscrew finds me twisted, does he?" But the father refuses any responsibility for the son: "How completely hers you are." Richard is not the only son who comes out of the closet in this scene: Geoffrey and John do so as well in turn, but their secret is more conventional. They admit to plotting to prevent Henry from choosing which of them will succeed to the throne upon his death. For the father, these revelations are all forms of betrayal. He proclaims in a fit of anguish and rage: "King Henry had no sons. He had three whiskered things but he disowned them. You're not mine."

It is not only his father who condemns Richard for being a freak of nature, a "whiskered thing" who can hardly register as human because of his lack of natural feelings, his indulgence in what, according to Alan of Lille, a Parisian academic and rough contemporary of Richard's, has brought flooding tears to the eyes of Nature. In Alan's text, this allegorical figure is prompted to utter a long complaint condemning mankind's transgressions against her principles.[26] Although he is her favorite, Eleanor later in the play chides Richard for being

25 *Time*, January 21, 1966, p. 41, quoted in John D'Emilio, *Sexual Politics, Sexual Communities*, 2nd edition (Chicago: U of Chicago P, 1983), p. 138.

26 Alain of Lille, *The Plaint of Nature*, trans. James J. Sheridan (Toronto: Pontifical Institute of Medieval Studies, 1980).

"unnatural." This time he has more of a response than the adolescent "you made me who I am," although Richard does blame her for shaping him in the very image of her own hatred for Henry. The real question, however, or so it seems to him, is not which parent to blame for the wreckage we make of our lives, but what precisely is the nature of the created order in which monstrousness of every kind can come into being. What is in nature, he reasons, must come from nature. And since there is nothing that does not come from nature, who is the very principle of generation, then how can we maintain that anything violates natural law? The question that Richard asks his mother in both the play and the film has proven difficult, as much in the twelfth century as the twenty-first, to answer: "If poisoned mushrooms grow and babies come with crooked backs, if goiters thrive and dogs go mad and wives kill husbands, what's unnatural?"

What's Natural?

Michel Foucault suggests how we might understand Richard's dramatically sudden interest in defending himself against parental condemnation. Because speaking about sex, Foucault maintains, puts the speaker "outside the reach of power" and thereby upsets "established law," this entry into a hitherto forbidden form of discourse "somehow anticipates the coming freedom." That is, it imagines however dimly a time when repression and the need to confront repression have passed from the scene and the utopian moment of freedom has arrived. Outed by his own refusal to deny the truth of his individual experience—he exits the closet to proclaim the genuineness of his love for Philip, not the more abstract concept of a "sexual orientation"—Richard later shows in this defiant response to Eleanor that he has come to feel less shame for who he is, his "difference" a part of the natural order, not a deviance from it. And so he takes advantage of what Foucault terms the opportunity "to speak out against the powers that be," perhaps looking forward to "the coming age of a different law."[27]

In *The Lion in Winter*, James Goldman rewrites what had become the accepted view of Richard Lionheart, restoring to the historical character what historians like John Gillingham repressed, often in a startling rejection of the plain truths contained in the surviving evidence, which as we have seen is considerable. In a climactic scene that registers Henry's dissatisfaction with the truth, long suspected but never faced, about his oldest surviving son, who he admits is the best of the three, Goldman thus offers us a *mise-en-abîme* for his project as a whole, which is, as he suggests, to say something about "the quality and content

---

27 Foucault, *History of Sexuality*, p. 607.

of the relationships" between a quintet of super-sized historical figures.[28] Revealing Richard's same-sex desire, of which the vast majority of filmgoers at the time were likely ignorant, undermines the sense in which the Middle Ages, in the words of Carolyn Dinshaw, can continue to be understood as the "dense, unvarying, and eminently obvious monolith" against which the supposed eruption of modern polymorphousness has taken shape, in the minds of some, at least, under the evil-priest leadership of Alfred Kinsey. Such a restoration, to quote Dinshaw once again, provides us with the "Middle Ages Foucault most deeply desires"—"a time whose lack of unified sexuality is *preferable* to the present with its 'fictitious unity' of normative heterosexuality."[29]

But what about the "fictional" Richard whom Goldman offers us, that character who, the playwright admits, is "imaginary"? Let us consider for a moment Richard's place within cinematic history. Hollywood began treating homosexual themes more directly and substantially by the early 1960s (even if the word "homosexual" could not be uttered), ending a prohibition solemnized in the Production Code, which had been promulgated in 1934. By the late 1950s, audiences had demonstrated that they would accept homosexual characters, and so the Code was modified to remove "sex perversion" from the forbidden category. Dominating these early film treatments is the dramatic movement of the outing, often complexly developed (in, for example, *The Children's Hour* or *Advise and Consent*, both 1962) as a movement that acknowledges the existence and power of same-sex desire, which is brought into the light only to provoke a terrible, self-inflicted punishment that is meant to be understood as a kind of redemption.

By the middle of the decade, Goldman's *The Lion in Winter*, play and film, exemplified how homosexuality could be represented differently. Indignant that Philip, eager to hurt Henry by giving his son pain, would characterize their relationship as a loveless coupling, which the younger "boy" permitted only to gain a future advantage, Richard refuses to let stand what he sees as a lie. It is a gesture that speaks to the essence of the play's action, like much modern drama organized around the revelation of inner truths, however difficult to bear. Henry is disabused of his own confidence to control what will happen upon his death, discovering not only that he has three sons whom he would disinherit yet cannot bring himself to execute, but also that there is no possibility of siring another brood with Alais, the young woman he loves. And Richard, in turn, must bear the pain of his betrayal by Philip, but he is permitted a dignity that allows him to remain the man he was, despite the making public of a private truth he had hitherto kept hidden. It is beyond doubt, as Vito Russo declares, commenting on the cinema from which *The Lion in Winter* had emerged, that

---

28 Goldman, *The Lion in Winter*, p. xi.
29 Dinshaw, *Getting Medieval*, pp. 16, 205.

"the 1970s would continue to reflect the freak show aspects of homosexual villains, fools and queens."[30] Goldman's Richard, on both stage and screen, successfully resists the demeaning power of those stereotypes, refusing in the name of historical truth the category of the unnatural (and its close kin, the abnormal and immoral) their traditional purchase on the representation of sexual experience and identity.

---

30 Vito Russo, *The Celluloid Closet*, rev. edn. (New York: Harper & Row, 1985), p. 178.

Chapter 3

"He's not an ardent suitor, is he, brother?": Richard the Lionheart's Ambiguous Sexuality in Cecil B. DeMille's *The Crusades* (1935)

Lorraine Kochanske Stock

Introduction: Historians' Constructions of Richard I's Sexuality

King Richard I, nicknamed "the Lionheart," is arguably the most famous medieval English monarch, renowned for his military valor at the Third Crusade, but also, as I discovered, for something else. At a recent dinner party, I announced to Warren and Lila, a well-educated pair of antique collectors and avid anglophiles, that I was writing about Richard Lionheart. Unprompted, Warren immediately quipped (anachronistically or not), "You know he was gay, don't you?" The "vexed subject of Richard's sexual tastes" not only has engaged the popular imagination,[1] as Warren's immediate response suggests, but also has provoked controversy among historians of twelfth-century England. Although John Gillingham, the most prolific historian of Richard's career, insists that the construction of a "gay" Richard came into prominence only in the mid-twentieth century when J. H. Harvey broke "the conspiracy of silence" surrounding Richard's homosexuality,[2] he acknowledges its earlier currency in a 1732 *History of England* alluding to Richard's "sins against nature" and the effect Philip's "caresses" had on him.[3] Moreover, the veiled as well as more blatant hints of chroniclers of Richard's own era suggest that Richard's contemporaries suspected him of more expansive sexual proclivities than medieval mores allowed. There is still no consensus regarding this unanswered question about Richard's personal life.

---

1 Antony Bridge, *Richard the Lionheart* (New York: Evans, 1989), p. 141.

2 J. H. Harvey, *The Plantagenets*, (London: Batsford, 1948), pp. 33, 34. See also John Gillingham, *Richard Coeur de Lion: Kingship, Chivalry and War in the Twelfth Century* (London: Hambledon, 1994), p. 189.

3 Paul de Rapin-Thoyras, *History of England* (London, 1732), pp. 241, 257.

Two recent biographers epitomize polarized views. Supplying the "conditioning factors," such as Richard's close relationship with his domineering mother Eleanor of Aquitaine, his upbringing in the "predominantly feminine environment of the queen's court at Poitiers," and the emotional distance between himself and his father Henry II, James Brundage insists that Richard "chose men, rather than women, as his usual sexual partners."[4] He presumes Richard's "aversion to women" because of the absence of mistresses, his rather late marriage at age thirty-four, his failure to spend more than minimal time with his wife Berengaria once he did marry, his failure to sire a legitimate male heir, and his banning of women (and Jews) from his coronation. Besides Richard's lifelong preference for male company, these other factors lead Brundage to conclude "that Richard was by preference a homosexual."[5]

Perhaps overreacting to Brundage's certainty concerning Richard's enjoyment of sex with males, Antony Bridge defends his biographical subject from the accusation of homosexuality. He emphasizes reports of Richard's heterosexual exploits: illicit affairs, "lusting after all sorts of women," including a king's daughter while imprisoned in Germany and a nun at Fontrevauld Abbey, whom he "wanted so badly that he threatened to burn the place down."[6] Labeling Richard "something of a sexual athlete subject to bouts of self-recrimination," Bridge insists that when in 1195 a hermit heaped recriminations against Richard's "illicit acts" in the context of asking him to recall the destruction of Sodom, the holy man was warning "not against the sin of sodomy in particular, but against sin in general . . . idolatry, faithlessness, pride, greed, fornication, or *what-have-you*."[7] That the "what-have-you" might include "amorous adventures with sailors or other long-tailed Englishmen" in Messina, Bridge denies.[8] Writing for a "popular" audience, these clashing biographers might be excused for using broad strokes and inflammatory rhetoric in assembling their arguments and for omitting scholarly documentation to substantiate their contradictory claims about Richard I's sexuality.

---

4 James Brundage, *Richard the Lionheart* (New York: Scribner's, 1974), p. 38.

5 Brundage, *Richard the Lionheart*, pp. 257-58.

6 Bridge, *Richard the Lionheart*, p. 141. Bridge neglects to mention that these reports of Richard's heterosexual proclivities were attributed to him after the fact by thirteenth-century chroniclers.

7 Bridge, *Richard the Lionheart*, p. 247; my emphasis.

8 Bridge, *Richard the Lionheart*, p. 131. Ann Trindade explains that while Richard and his army remained in Messina while awaiting sailing to Palestine, for their offensive behavior, the English were reviled by Greeks, Franks, and Muslims as the "long-tailed Englishmen (*caudati*),though whether this referred to their devilish hooliganism or their physical endowments is not clear" (*Berengaria: In Search of Richard the Lionheart's Queen* [Dublin: Four Courts, 1999], p. 78).

However, even the most respected professional historians of Richard's reign are equally polarized about Richard's sexual orientation, though supporting their positions with scrupulous documentation and finely parsed analysis of the language of twelfth-century chroniclers' Latin reports. They also pay attention to the legend that contributed to a revised version of Richard's reputation after his death found in the reports of later medieval chroniclers, romance writers, historiographers, and post-medieval creators of popular culture representations of his life and personality, such as James Goldman, whose play/screenplay *The Lion in Winter*, discussed in Chapter 2, constructs Richard as a homosexual. Some of the most vexing and still inconclusive aspects of the Lionheart's character involve his aborted engagement to Alice, sister of King Philip Augustus of France; his subsequent marriage to Berengaria of Navarre and the failure of their union to produce even a single heir to the throne, evidence for some that Richard was "*perversely* indifferent"[9] to fulfilling his royal responsibility; and contemporary reports of Richard's culpability of and penance for *peccatum illud* or "*that* sin."

Richard's apparent aversion to marrying Alice, with whom he had been affianced since age four, problematized political relations between England and France.[10] His personal relationship with Philip Augustus has been construed variously. Chronicler Roger of Howden reports that when Richard and Philip met for a truce in 1187, they ate their food from the same plate, shared a common bed, and that the latter claimed he loved Richard like "his own very soul." Confronted by this "partnership" between the young men, Richard's father Henry II expressed shock and dismay, which some historians construe as repugnance at Richard's homosexuality and others claim reflected his unease at his son's political alliance with the French monarch, seemingly against his own father.[11]

---

9 Gillingham, *Richard Coeur de Lion*, p. 189; my emphasis.

10 John Gillingham, *Richard the Lionheart* (London: Weidenfeld and Nicholson, 1978), p. 160.

11 Those who defend Richard and Philip from practicing nothing more than kingly homosociality include Gillingham, *Richard Coeur de Lion*, pp. 134-35; M. Bennett, "Military Masculinity in England and Northern France c. 1050-c. 1225," *Masculinity in Medieval Europe*, ed. D. M. Hadley (London: Longman, 1999), 71-88, at p. 83; Bridge, *Richard the Lionheart*, p. 90; and C. Stephen Jaeger, *Ennobling Love* (Philadelphia: U of Pennsylvania P, 1999), pp. 26, 129, 133. Those who see the meeting with Philip as evidence of Richard's homosexuality include: Brundage, *Richard the Lionheart*, p. 258; John Boswell, *Christianity, Social Tolerance, and Homosexuality* (Chicago: U of Chicago P, 1980), pp. 271-72; James Reston, *Warriors of God: Richard the Lionheart and Saladin in the Third Crusade* (New York: Doubleday, 2001), p. 67; Trindade, *Berengaria*, p. 72; and Jean Flori, *Richard the Lionheart: King and Knight*, trans. Jean Birrell (Westport CT: Praeger, 2006), p. 382.

The match with Berengaria, daughter of Sancho of Navarre, whose land bordered Richard's holdings in southern France, arranged either by Richard himself or by his mother Eleanor of Aquitaine, likely was a union of mere political expedience to secure the support of Berengaria's father and brother in defense of Richard's estates during his lengthy absences abroad.[12] All biographers and historians concur that Richard and Berengaria were seldom together, officially or "privately," typically traveling in separate ships. After their wedding in Cyprus, before embarking to Palestine, they seldom saw each other. Berengaria saw Richard's sister Joan, her traveling companion to and in the East, more than her husband.[13] Berengaria and all other women were excluded from Richard's coronation, which Brundage dubs "a bachelor party."[14] No concrete evidence exists that Berengaria ever set foot in England. As to the lack of an heir, Gillingham, Bridge, and others automatically presume Berengaria's barrenness, rather than that the couple did not couple often enough (if ever) to achieve a pregnancy.

The aspects of Richard's complex attitude to sexuality most analyzed by scholars are contained in several chroniclers' reports about his confession of his various sins to a group of bishops and archbishops in his entourage. Proffering three sticks from which the bark had been peeled, he prostrated himself naked at their feet and confessed his sins while they subjected him to penance with the impromptu flails. On another occasion after his marriage, a hermit warned Richard about changing his behavior: "Remember the destruction of Sodom and give up forbidden pleasures; otherwise you will receive from God the punishment you deserve!"[15] According to Roger of Howden, Richard initially ignored the warning; later, suffering a serious illness, he recognized the hermit as a divine messenger, confessed his "shameful conduct," and did penance. Afterwards, he received Berengaria, with whom he had not had marital relations for some time, forswore the "forbidden forms of love" for which he had been chastised, and reunited with his wife, thereupon regaining his health. Despite the claims of Gillingham and Bridge, the staunchest defenders of Richard's heterosexuality, that a reference to "Sodom" would not necessarily connote "sodomy," William Burgwinkle aptly represents the position taken by the opposing historians about what the "Sodom" warning meant: "Claiming Richard as a heterosexual is like claiming that there are no gays in the US military because they do not 'tell.' Lack of evidence can be a cover for not knowing how, rather than where, to look behind the blinders of ideological fantasies, with monolithic

---

12 This is the conclusion of Trindade and most other historians.

13 Gillingham, *Richard the Lionheart*, p. 160.

14 Brundage, *Richard the Lionheart*, p. 257.

15 William Burgwinkle, *Sodomy, Masculinity, and Law in Medieval Literature* (Cambridge: Cambridge UP, 2004), p. 79.

heterosexuality as the inevitable default setting."[16] If the "apologists" conclude that Richard's relationship with Philip expressed innocent homosocial bonding or expected regal deportment, others read his relationship with Philip and the hermit's reference to Sodom as signs of homosexuality. A recent biographer of Berengaria agrees with Brundage, Boswell, and Burgwinkle that the bond between Richard and Philip was at least homoerotic.[17] Richard's most recent biographer, Jean Flori, subjects all the evidence on both sides to careful analysis and, unable to accept Gillingham's explanation, concludes: "Rather than an out-and-out exclusive homosexual, Richard seems to have been, like his father and his ancestors before him, above all a hedonist; almost certainly less of a paedophile than his father, but probably a bisexual; in a word, a versatile lecher."[18]

Such controversy and insecurity about Richard's sexual proclivities leave the field wide open for cinematic interpreters of the Lionheart legend. Training his camera lens on Richard's character in his 1935 epic black-and-white film, *The Crusades*, director Cecil B. DeMille anticipates and reflects the ambivalence of the scholars noted above.[19] In portraying Richard's character and his imputed sexual orientation, DeMille has it both ways. In the first third to half of the film, Richard's behavior creates the impression that he finds women abhorrent, greatly prefers the company of men, and will do anything to extricate himself from his arranged engagement to Princess Alice of France. Despite his admitted lack of Christian devotion, he pledges to wage the Third Crusade as an excuse not to marry Alice. With the historical fact of Richard's marriage to Berengaria of Navarre an inescapable aspect of his biography, in the second half of the film, DeMille hetero-normalizes Richard by romanticizing his union with Berengaria well beyond the historical reality of their practically sham marriage. The film's transformative construction of a gay-to-straight Richard uncannily anticipates later historians' vexed polarity about the king's sexuality. To accomplish this, DeMille employs two provocative triangulations of desire to portray the complicated sexual politics of Richard's biography: the first triangle between Richard, Philip, and Alice; and later in the film, another between Richard, Saladin, and Berengaria. Moreover, this director famed for his historical and epic spectacles incorporates much documentary and legendary material about Richard Lionheart, but literally reframes "history" through a revisionist cinematic lens. He also effectively invents the character of Berengaria,

16 Burgwinkle, *Sodomy, Masculinity and Law,* p. 85.
17 Trindade, *Berengaria,* pp. 71-72.
18 Jean Flori, *Richard the Lionheart,* p. 393.
19 Informing my discussion of other aspects of DeMille's film is the analysis of John Aberth, *A Knight at the Movies* (New York: Routledge, 2003), pp. 86-91. Aberth omits examination of Richard's sexual orientation.

about whom almost nothing is recorded. Finally, this early film about a much earlier historical period provides intriguingly fluid gender constructions of the principal characters inhabiting the two above-mentioned triangulations. As I discuss below, DeMille's interpretation of the homosocial/homoerotic Richard did not spring *ex nihilo* from this creative director's imagination.

A Cinematic Model for DeMille's Construction of Richard's Sexual Orientation

DeMille's depiction of Richard's ambiguous sexual orientation had a significant cinematic precedent in another blockbuster example of movie medievalism, Alan Dwan's 1922 *Robin Hood*. Starring Douglas Fairbanks as the gentrified outlaw, *Robin Hood*, in its New York premiere drew over 100,000 people, and the movie grossed over five million dollars for Fairbanks' studio.[20] Late medieval ballads about Robin Hood neither situate the yeoman outlaw in any specific medieval century nor identify in which king's reign the outlaw lived. However, Sir Walter Scott's 1819 novel *Ivanhoe* permanently connected the popular culture image of Robin Hood with the Third Crusade. Set in the twelfth-century reign of Richard I, whose extended Plantagenet family, Prince John and Queen Mother Eleanor of Aquitaine, became fixtures in the cinematic Robin Hood canon, *Ivanhoe* places neither Richard I nor Robin Hood physically at the Third Crusade. Nevertheless, as the English king of *Ivanhoe* became firmly identified as the definitive western hero of the Third Crusade and the ideal European crusader, Robin Hood also became connected inextricably with the Third Crusade. Movies about him typically relate his post-Crusade adventures in England where, disinherited from his patrimony, the Earl of Huntingdon (or Locksley) remains a loyal subject of King Richard (absent at the Crusade), thwarting the plots against the crown by Richard's enemies. In the cinematic Robin Hood canon, Richard is an influential, if offstage presence, making a brief obligatory appearance upon returning from crusading or imprisonment by Duke Leopold V of Austria, usually pardoning Robin and endorsing his loyal comrade's marriage to the royal ward Marian at film's end.[21] Breaking this rule, Richard (Wallace Beery) plays a major part in Douglas Fairbanks' *Robin Hood*,

20 Aberth, *A Knight at the Movies*, p. 164.
21 See *The Adventures of Robin Hood* (Michael Curtiz and William Keighley, 1938), starring Errol Flynn as the "fluently treasonous" Earl of Locksley, and *Robin Hood: Prince of Thieves* (Kevin Reynolds, 1991), starring Kevin Costner as Locksley. Ridley Scott's 2005 *Kingdom of Heaven* continues this tradition by having Richard make a brief appearance on his way to the Third Crusade, meeting Balian of Ibelin at the film's end.

which is almost as much about Richard's campaign in the Holy Land as about Robin's famously benevolent activities on behalf of downtrodden Saxons. Dwan's film thus offers a baseline against which later cinematic characterizations of Richard may be compared.

Wallace Beery, billed in the credits as "the Lion-Hearted," portrays Richard as a physically robust "man's man," given more to fleshly pleasures than to religious devotion, anticipating DeMille's conception of Richard in *The Crusades*. In most of his scenes, Beery eats heartily or presides over a groaning board, both at home and at war. One caption identifying his character describes him as "immortal, impulsive, generous and brave." Despite Richard's famed military skill, this movie visually showcases his impetuous, irascible personality rather than his valor. Historians have often criticized Richard for spending a mere six months of his entire reign in England. Indeed, Beery's Richard does not wear the crown comfortably; in one scene, he doffs it with weary irritation. Further, *Robin Hood* inaugurates for cinematic versions of the monarch the traditional and ongoing uncertainty about Richard's sexuality in scenes between Richard I and Huntingdon suggestive of the historical/mythical construction of Richard I as a homosexual summarized above. As I have argued elsewhere, homosocial relations between Richard and his "favorite" the Earl of Huntingdon verge perilously on the homoerotic in Dwan's film.[22] Beery's vigorous, excessively enthusiastic physical gestures to Fairbanks' Huntingdon (such as slapping and patting his body), Richard's peevish jealousy at Huntingdon's romantic attraction for Maid Marian whom he dubs "the wench," and his frantic pounding on the door of Robin and Marian's wedding-night chamber, indefinitely delaying their marriage's physical consummation in the last frames of the film, all suggest Richard's inordinate attraction to one of his male comrades. Moreover, Beery's Richard displays no interest in the many pretty female extras who inhabit his court, nor does the film allude whatsoever to Richard's longtime problematic engagement to Princess Alice of France or his eventual politically engineered marriage to Berengaria of Navarre, who accompanied Richard to Palestine. The wedding historically occurred before they arrived in the Holy Land, where most of Beery's scenes in the film take place. Berengaria's otherwise puzzling absence in *Robin Hood* allows for a more expansive development of the relationship "between men" of Richard and Huntingdon. Thus, Fairbanks' silent

---

22 See Lorraine Stock and Candace Gregory-Abbott, "The 'Other' Women of Sherwood: The Construction of Difference and Gender in Cinematic Treatments of the Robin Hood Legend," *Race, Class, and Gender in Medieval Cinema*, eds. Lynn Ramey and Tison Pugh (New York: Palgrave Macmillan, 2007), pp. 119-214 and Lorraine Stock, "Now Starring in the Third Crusade: Depictions of Richard I and Saladin in Films and Television Series," *Hollywood in the Holy Land*, eds. Nikolas Haydock and E. L. Risden (Jefferson, NC: McFarland, 2009, pp. 93-122).

foundational blockbuster *Robin Hood* inaugurated the cinematic ambiguity about Richard I's sexuality in a mainstream Hollywood vehicle. Thirteen years later, in an even more lavish and spectacular treatment of Richard at the Third Crusade, DeMille continued to engage in cinematic speculation about the Lionheart's sexual orientation, mirroring the historical uncertainty about this issue.

Richard's Amatory Reluctance in De Mille's *The Crusades*

DeMille's blockbuster "talkie" *The Crusades* pits Richard against his charismatic Third Crusade foil, Saladin, who does not figure in Dwan's *Robin Hood*. Further, he introduces in major roles the two women who historically vied for Richard's unenthusiastic marital commitment, Alice of France and Berengaria of Navarre. If Dwan's *Robin Hood* was inspired by Sir Walter Scott's *Ivanhoe*, *The Crusades'* screenplay by Harold Lamb and Waldemar Young is heavily influenced by the romantic medievalism of Scott's 1825 Crusades novel, *The Talisman*.[23] DeMille's epic mirrors that novel's entertainingly improbable erotic triangle[24] among the crusading Richard I (Henry Wilcoxen), his infatuated bride of convenience, Berengaria of Navarre (Loretta Young), and his military antagonist/romantic rival, Saladin (Ian Keith). Before exploring that triangulation, DeMille first proposes another one, among Richard, his purported onetime "soul-mate" King Philip, and Philip's sister Alice, to whom Richard is affianced. However, DeMille's film is not titled *Richard and Saladin*, or *Richard and Philip*, but rather *The Crusades*, and yet another triangle introduced comprises the city of Jerusalem itself, troped as a "bride" or damsel in distress, with the contending other points of the triangle being the European crusaders and her Muslim captors. The violation of a feminized Jerusalem opens the film and the restoration of that city's freedom and the rescue of its women conclude it, returning the arc of the film's plot back to its opening sequence.

DeMille's establishing shots provide not only necessary historical exposition for the audience, but also an important context for framing his interpretation of Richard's sexuality and gender construction. The film's title and credits are projected over a series of still shots, first of heralds announcing the start of both the film and the Holy War, then an image of a mighty, well built warrior

---

23 Harold Lamb, a historian who published a 1930 two-volume history of the Crusades titled *The Flame of Islam* and *Iron Men and Saints*, republished in one volume in 1931 as *The Crusades*, was hired as scriptwriter and technical consultant on the film's historical authenticity.

24 Scott's triangle involves Saladin, Richard's kinswoman, Lady Edith, and a Scots knight, Sir Kenneth. Saladin and Kenneth vie for the favors of Edith, as depicted in the movie adaptation of Scott's *The Talisman*, *King Richard and the Crusaders*.

in armor, astride a charger—the quintessential crusading knight. Although the visor of his huge steel helmet obscures his face, the hauberk displays couchant lions (the Plantagenet heraldic device) announcing the identity of Richard with a visual reference to his nickname, "Lionheart." After cutting to an image of the heraldic shields of the other European crusaders, DeMille adds a montage of shots of Richard's winged helmet and his iconic sword, a prop that plays a significant role in the film's construction of his masculinity and sexuality. This powerful phallic image is replaced by a view of a city, identified in the caption as, "Jerusalem: through the ages, the city sacred to men." Jerusalem is apparently not sacred to women, for the next shot reveals a looming phallic minaret behind a caption identifying the year, 1187, when Saracens swept over Asia and took the Holy Land, subjecting its Christian inhabitants to death or slavery. The troping of the feminized Jerusalem as a bride despoiled by Muslim rapists is literalized in the next sequence, wherein Muslims desecrate crucifixes, burn bibles and holy books, and auction to the highest bidders pale-skinned European women with "gold Christian hair," including a nun—her ripped habit telegraphs that her captors do not even spare the religious—who provides spiritual solace and a crucifix to kiss to her terrified companions in bondage. These female captives sold into white slavery will suffer unspoken but implicit sexual depredations by their leering Arab buyers, who are portrayed as sexual predators.

Here DeMille sexualizes (and complicates) the ideology of the Crusades ethic by subtly alluding to two prominent legends about Richard that level the moral playing field between Christians and Muslims. According to twelfth-century chronicler Roger of Howden, before the Crusade, Richard had treated his subjects in Aquitaine to similar sexual devastations, forcibly abducting his subjects' wives, daughters and kinswomen, making them his concubines, and after sating his own lust on them, handing them over to his troops to enjoy similarly.[25] Historians who defend his sexual reputation cite this incident as proof of Richard's heteronormativity. If it is true, it implicates him as no less a violent sexual offender than the "evil" Muslims in DeMille's account of the Crusade. In another thirteenth-century revisionist legend, Richard desired a nun in Fontevraud Abbey so passionately that he threatened to burn down the abbey unless she acquiesced. Inquiring what attracted him to her, she was told it was her beautiful eyes; she excised them and sent Richard what he so much desired.[26] If the slave auction scene recalls some important Ricardian lore, it also anticipates a similar selling of a European woman to the highest bidder, this time by her Spanish father, when Sancho of Navarre includes Berengaria as part of a lucrative package deal of cattle and supplies to Richard, a negotiation between men over a commodified female. Betrothing her to the king of England,

---

25 John Gillingham, *Richard I* (New Haven: Yale UP, 1999), pp. 66-67, 263.

26 Gillingham, *Richard the Lionheart*, p. 162.

Sancho both gains status and unloads a "strong-willed" daughter. Richard does not give the bartered bride a second thought, so focused is he on the logistics of feeding his hungry army and transporting them to Palestine. By the film's end, both Jerusalem and Berengaria are brides fought over by the respective sides of the triangles in which each is the apex: Jerusalem disputed over by her Christian liberators and her Muslim captors, and Berengaria by her Christian husband Richard and her Muslim admirer Saladin.

Gendering Philip Augustus, Richard I, and Saladin

Before considering the way DeMille suggests Richard's erotic relations with male and female characters, it is useful to reveal how this most visual of filmmakers constructs gender through costume, body language, and *mise-en-scène*. The first European king presented visually is Philip Augustus of France (Henry Gordon) as he pledges to join the Crusade at the invitation of the preaching hermit. Viewed from behind, Philip's body is kneeling in supplication before the altar of a cathedral, his elaborate ermine-trimmed velvet mantle fanning out widely around his kneeling body like the unfurled trumpet of the heraldic lily of France. Signifying his royal position, the cape also feminizes him for a 1935 American audience. A medium shot of Philip's upper torso shows off his jeweled crown, the heavily embellished *fleur de lis* medallion suspended across his chest above the wide ermine collar. Transfixed by a religious epiphany, his face looks appropriately radiant, a pageboy hairstyle softly framing his face. As he exits the church, pages must carry his heavy mantle, further weakening his physical image. Under the robe is more costume glamour: another wide, jeweled girdle encircling a gold lamé robe. Overall, the costume assigned to give the first impression of Philip is that of royal dandy rather than warrior king, despite his vow to wage war in Jerusalem. Philip's religiosity feminizes him, with the ecclesiastical setting further softening his masculine image. His kneeling posture is submissive, not masculine-aggressive. As soon as he leaves the cathedral, he and Conrad of Montferrat mention Richard for the first time, Conrad noting Richard's "Lionheart" persona. Although Philip claims the "lion will be caged" when Richard marries his sister Alice, he underestimates his former royal companion and (perhaps) lover.

A quick dissolve from the Conrad-Phillip conversation provides Richard's dramatic entrance, so different from Philip's soft, passive introduction, setting them up as visual and political foils. Richard races a warhorse onscreen full tilt toward a wooden target—and the audience—making several passes at the target "knight" with his long lance. When Richard pauses to doff his face-concealing helmet, DeMille provides the first close-up shot of the rugged features, hard lantern jaw, and short-cropped hair of the king's visage, which mirror the ideal features of a twelfth-century warrior: pale skin, well proportioned eyes, nose, and mouth.[27] Henry Wilcoxen's muscular body is shown to maximum masculine advantage in the form-fitting military costumes that his Richard wears throughout the film. This actor's physiognomy reflects the ideal medieval warrior's physique, "which should be that of a horseman: broad shouldered, slender at the waist and with a good *forcheure* (fork: long legs, well-joined at the pelvis)."[28] Wilcoxen's "Lionheart" believably fulfills the thirteenth-century legend about how his character earned his nickname. A romance about Richard's captivity in Germany claimed that, attracted to Richard, a German king's daughter enjoyed sexual trysts with him. Her enraged father plotted Richard's murder by releasing a hungry lion into his cell. His hand protected by forty silk scarves (furnished by the daughter), Richard rammed his fist down the lion's maw, extracted the beast's heart from its carcass, sprinkled it with salt, and consumed it raw before the dumfounded German monarch.[29] The posthumous legend was intended to demonstrate both Richard's heterosexuality and his masculinity (real men eat lion-heart, not quiche), but it also provided the silk scarf motif that DeMille would use to great effect later in the movie to construct Richard's masculinity.

Further in the scene that establishes Richard's character, when the blond, long-haired foppish-looking royal minstrel Blondel (Alan Hale) sings an unflattering song about his master, Richard playfully gallops after him aiming his long, phallic lance at Blondel's backside, a bit of homosocial horseplay that borders on the homoerotic. The encounter references another posthumous Ricardian legend about his relationship with Blondel, which was sometimes construed as a sexual one.[30] Chasing him into the forge of Hercules the blacksmith, Richard shouts, "Blondel, come out and fight like a man," to which Blondel, holding his lute upright, replies, "I can't fight you with this." Richard demands his new sword from the smithy. Raising it aloft, Hercules offers, "Here it is sire, a fair sweet blade!" Richard impetuously grabs the untempered steel and begins hammering it himself; whereupon Hercules warns "Nay, sire, you can't shape steel with love taps!" Insulted, Richard invites his smith to an exchange of blows, reminding him, "and no love taps, remember!" When powerful Hercules reluctantly takes a hard swing at the king, he dazes Richard, who insists that the stunning blow had been "nothing but a love tap." When Richard returns the punch, he knocks Hercules to the floor and Blondel into a trough of water, inviting the raucous laughter of the rest of Richard's men at arms. The scene concludes with the entrance of Leicester, announcing the arrival of Philip, whom Richard terms

---

27 Bennett, "Military Masculinity," p. 79.
28 Bennett, "Military Masculinity," p. 79.
29 Gillingham, *Richard I*, p. 263.
30 Bradford Broughton, *The Legends of King Richard I, Coeur de Lion:* (The Hague: Mouton, 1966), pp. 126-28; cf. Gillingham, *Richard I*, pp. 233, 254, 265.

his "saintly cousin," and his sister Alice, Richard's intended, whom he labels a "surly-tempered wench" and about whom Richard mutters in consternation, "she's no dove with an olive branch!" The next scene presents the meeting between the members of this triangle, discussed below. However, the rough-and-tumble mayhem of this extended scene on the jousting field and in the forge establishes the strong homosocial bonds between Richard, Blondel, Hercules, and his vassals, who enjoy sustained physical contact and masculine camaraderie. This is the masculine company in which Richard is clearly most comfortable, and his appearance indicates that, unlike the "saintly" Philip, this king eschews regalia in preference for the costume of a warrior and tolerates no royal pomp. However, all the backside-chasing, physical horseplay among men, and numerous references to "love" taps exceed what Bennett defines as the "companionship central to the 'homosocial' link between . . . two men" characterizing the ideal "military masculinity in England and northern France c. 1050-1225."[31] By seeking companionship with his social inferiors and avoiding his royal peers, Richard does not perform the proper royal masculinity expected of a monarch.

The other major male lead is, of course, Saladin. Throughout *The Crusades*, DeMille orientalizes Saladin. In his gaudy entrance after the slave auction scene, Ian Keith's "Sultan of Asia" mounts a white Arabian stallion, heralded by a parade of drum-beating turbaned "Turks" and protected by black-skinned, bare-chested, scimitar-wielding Nubian guards, garbed in skimpy leopard-skin loincloths. Saladin's costume signifies visually to the audience the famed splendor of the Orient: flowing robes of luxurious fabrics embroidered in precious metals; silken sashes criss-crossing his chest; and jeweled crescents ornamenting sash and turban, topped by a gold minaret-like spike. Compared to Richard— uniformed in utilitarian chain mail hauberk under heraldic tabard—Saladin, whose body disappears under his flowing robes, appears exotically feminized, though not so feminized as Philip, who, retaining his kingly regalia throughout the film, is rarely presented in warrior garb despite his pledged military service in Jerusalem. Evaluated on a continuum of masculinity labeling these three political leaders in contemporary (though anachronistic) terminology of same-sex relations, Richard appears "butch," Philip looks "femme," and Saladin ranks somewhere between them. Wilcoxen's matinee idol Richard would appeal to women in DeMille's audience, while his muscular masculinity would also be attractive to men. This bivalent presentation of Richard's gender construction adroitly parallels the mixed signals of his sexual behavior in *The Crusades*, discussed below.

---

31 Bennett, "Military Masculinity", pp. 82, 71.

Gendering Alice of France and Berengaria of Navarre

As with the male leads, DeMille's visual presentation of the female characters provides extreme contrasts. During the conversation between Philip and Conrad outside the cathedral, the camera cuts to a shot framing Richard's pearl-crowned fiancée Alice, seated as if for a royal portrait. Played by Katherine DeMille (the director's daughter) with bosom rising in cool self-possession and an unflinching stare, Alice palpably exudes "sultry," as if a hard-boiled *film noir* heroine had been transported to the Middle Ages. Rising from her throne with ramrod straight carriage, Alice stands even taller than Philip and Conrad. Although a regal costume, Alice's dark gown is far less fussy than her brother's fur-festooned garments, signaling her no-nonsense demeanor. Her luxuriant brunette hair—nearly all the film's women have floor-length locks—is plaited and bound in a business-like (for the period) coiffeur, unlike the equally long but loose, blonde tresses of Loretta Young's Berengaria, introduced a few scenes later.

Berengaria of Navarre is first shown on the balcony of her father's house in Marseilles, reviewing the arriving crusaders, particularly excited to see the legendary Richard Lionheart. A study of ultra-femininity, she is costumed in a virginal white gown carrying a basket of flowers as her luxuriant blonde hair flows to the floor. If Alice is cynical and hard-boiled, Berengaria is innocent and idealistic, expressing her devout support of the Holy War and her desire to carry a sword, nurse the sick, or do whatever will help the war effort. She offers her basket of flowers to Richard, about whom she has heard minstrels' songs of his legendary "chivalry, bravery, and gentleness." She is soon disabused of this fantasy when an angry Richard, trying to jockey a mangonel through narrow streets, punches and threatens to hang someone who injured his horse's leg. Knowing that Richard requires the cattle and provisions her father can supply, a disillusioned Berengaria curses him, wishing that he "starve." Described as a "fair sweet girl, a flower," by her father, Berengaria is temperamentally the opposite of Princess Alice, whose gender construction is as much a visual foil for Berengaria's far softer femininity as Richard's hard warrior persona is for Philip's fussy regality and Saladin's Oriental exoticism. Overall, Alice and Berengaria comprise a study of dark and fair looks, black and white costumes, and "butch" and "femme" visual stereotypes.

Richard as a Reluctant Suitor of Women

Adding another layer of sex/gender complication, *The Crusades* continues the tradition of Richard's ambiguous sexuality suggested in 1922's *Robin Hood*. An establishing shot in Richard's castle reveals *mise-en-scène* incorporating various props blatantly advertising aspects of Richard's legendary personae: several large statues of rampant lions; lion pelts serving as floor rugs; and a book stand registering his status as a sometime troubadour poet. Composing the shot are an impatient-looking but self-possessed Alice seated on screen left, Philip pacing nervously center screen, and on the right, oily Prince John, smug at Richard's discourteous failure to appear promptly. At the meeting of Richard, Philip, and Philip's sister, the many-years-waiting Alice emphasizes Richard's palpable reluctance to marry her when she archly observes to the indignant Philip, "He's not an ardent suitor, is he, brother?" This remark so encapsulates one construction of Richard's sexual orientation in the film (preferring men to women) that it merits my chapter's title.

When Richard finally makes his rudely tardy entrance, he is announced with all his impressive seigneurial titles, "King of England, Duke of Normandy and Aquitaine, Count of Anjou." Instead of greeting his fiancée, as would be proper courtly etiquette, his first salutation is to Philip (for some historians and chroniclers, Richard's purported ex-lover and soul-mate), whose shoulder he grasps. Philip reciprocates the gesture with an additional shoulder squeeze, and they exchange and hold a significant look for a moment. Both then look askance across the room toward the seated princess, whom Richard acknowledges, "Ah, the Lady Alice." When he crosses the set to greet her, she curtsies and coolly reprimands, "I'm not accustomed to waiting, Richard, even for a betrothal kiss." Richard replies, "Well then let's postpone it," continuing to defer the long-projected union. Proposing a drink of wine, Richard calls for Blondel to entertain them with a song, who suggests, "Shall it be of love?" to which Richard demurs, "No, no, no, hunting." At every attempt to bring the conversation to the engagement, Richard changes the subject or runs out of wine to toast, at Philip's suggestion, the impending union with Alice. Katherine DeMille's Alice trains a steely glare at Richard throughout the scene and when Philip insists that Richard fulfill the contracted marriage to his sister, Alice observes wryly, "The lion squirms in the net." The arrival of the hermit preaching the Crusade provides Richard's pretext to supplant his marriage pledge with a pledge to fight the Holy War. Rather than join the military campaign for spiritual or ideological reasons—he "fears no devil and prays to no God," a lack of faith that Prince John describes "an open scandal"—the blatantly irreligious Richard uses the Crusade as an excuse to avoid marriage to Alice. DeMille's presentation of Richard's amatory proclivities thus mirrors his sexual ambivalence noted by chroniclers and historians.

A Second Triangulation: Richard, Berengaria, and Saladin

Driving a hard bargain for the provisions Richard needs to send his troops to Palestine, Sancho of Navarre extracts from the unenthusiastic Richard the promise to marry his daughter Berengaria as part of the price of their business, with her dower being the cattle, grain, horsefodder, and foodstuffs Richard requires. Although Richard huffs, "You can marry your wench to the devil," ultimately he accepts "the wench." However, preoccupied with organizing his departure to Palestine, he quickly forgets his promise of that night's wedding. A friar must interrupt his carousing with his men, a reprise of the scene of homosocial bonhomie at the film's beginning, to tell him he must now attend his nuptials. Summing up Richard's attitude about marital union with a woman by singing, "O, Richard is no ladies' man, though something of a sinner," Blondel encapsulates the two major charges lodged against Richard by his twelfth-century chroniclers—his reputed sexual affinity for males and his culpability of "that sin," for which he supposedly was assigned thirty-three years of Purgatory.[32]

Because marriage to Berengaria is as unwelcome as union with Alice, Richard sends his sword as a personal token, delivered by his jester-like minstrel Blondel, his proxy representing him at their wedding ceremony, the ultimate insult. The bride awaits her groom resplendent in an elaborate wedding gown, while an extreme close-up reveals the deep humiliation and disappointment on Young's luminous face as he fails to appear. Only for the sake of the Crusade, to which she remains committed, does she accept this sham marriage to the king's weapon, not the man. As the priest officiating the marriage intones the trope— that they are gathered together so that "we may couple together these two bodies"—and the rest of the vows are recited, the dramatic irony of his words is stunning. At the film's last frame, Richard and Berengaria remain uncoupled, for they never consummate their marriage, as may have been true historically. Berengaria pledges herself in wedlock to Richard's token, a sword, which she is required to kiss, in some mortification, at the ceremony. She also sends her own token, her long silk wedding veil, which Blondel presents to Richard. Richard's careless employment of her length of silk cloth to bandage his horse's wounded leg indicates both his priorities (horse trumps bride) and utter contempt for "the wench" he has just married. It also recalls the legend of how he earned his sobriquet "Lionheart," by wrapping forty scarves of silk around his hand to rip the lion's heart from its body. Richard consistently uses silk cloths bestowed by women for his own self-aggrandizement. In a later scene with Berengaria and Saladin, a similar length of silk reveals the shortcomings of both his diplomacy and his valor, as we shall see.

---

32 Gillingham, *Richard Coeur de Lion*, p. 186.

As Richard rides through Marseilles before embarking for Palestine, he sees Berengaria standing on her balcony and admires her beauty, unaware of her actual identity as his wife. In most other movies, this would be a *Romeo and Juliet* moment, which Richard's insensitivity botches. He notes her beautiful eyes (he mistakes them for "stars"), a possible reference to the Fontevraud nun, whose eyes attracted him and who excised them rather than submit to Richard's improper desires. His admission, "I confess my sin and ask your forgiveness," is another reminder of "that sin." His supplication, "I'm in the dust at your feet," merits Berengaria's bitter rejoinder, "So is my veil," to which Richard's clumsy explanation, "My horse was wounded," is countered by, "Yes, so am I."

Although DeMille later purports that Richard desires her, his ardor may be fueled more by her stubborn rejections of him from her bed than by love. Medieval chroniclers accused Richard of rape in the Holy Land and in Aquitaine, though the reliability of these sources is not airtight.[33] In the scenes between Richard and Berengaria in her tent, her fearful reluctance to allow her serving woman Tina to leave her company (at Richard's insistence) and her invoking the protection of the thick bedposts of her four-poster—named for the Evangelists, Matthew, Mark, Luke, and John—signal both her religious devotion and her fear that Richard intends to claim, against her will, his conjugal right to her body as her husband, effectively raping her. Before Richard has a chance to make good on this threat, he is called to deal with an attack on the crusaders' camp, preventing the consummation, whether voluntary or forced. Despite his late conversion and reluctant prayer to God to possess Berengaria at the close of the film, their marriage still remains unconsummated, mirroring the historical marriage engineered for Richard by his mother Eleanor, which appeared to be one of political convenience, the spouses spending almost no time together, and producing no heir.

A Second Triangulation: Richard, Berengaria, and Saladin

After Saladin's archers kill the Europeans' herald, Saladin appears at the council of European kings to negotiate a truce. Arriving on his white charger, wearing sumptuous fur-trimmed garments, a crescent-adorned breastplate, and a helmet evoking "Egyptian Pharaoh," Saladin is announced as "the conqueror, Sultan of Islam," boasting, "There is room in Asia to bury all of you." When Richard commits the blunder of offering wine to "the infidel," Saladin politely reminds him, "We of the true faith drink no wine." Richard demands, "A goblet of water for the King of the infidels." When Saladin's emir fears that the water may be poisoned, Richard's new bride Berengaria volunteers to taste Saladin's water,

---

33 Gillingham, *Richard I*, p. 66, n. 44.

thus smoothing over her husband's diplomatic gaffe. Earlier she had observed, "They told me [Saladin] had horns like the devil. I think he's magnificent." As she departs the tent, Saladin's attraction to her is obvious. Thus DeMille sets up a second triangle among Richard, his still virginal bride, and his "infidel" foe. Richard threatens, "With this sword, I'll cut my way through Jerusalem." To this Saladin counters, "No, You'll find the blade too dull." Rising to this challenge, Richard wields his sword upon an outstretched iron mace, breaking it in half. Saladin cleverly observes, "The Lion King has shown us the strength of his arm, not the sharpness of his sword." Extending a gossamer length of silk, Saladin defies Richard to cut through the scarf in midair with his blade. When Richard argues that this is impossible, Saladin tosses the scarf aloft and allows it to fall gently upon the edge of his saber, slicing it neatly in two. He warns, "Just as easily will I cut your Crusade to pieces," and vows, "By Allah, [Richard] shall never pass the gates of Jerusalem." Saladin's prediction proves correct, for by the end of *The Crusades*, Richard neither enters the holy city nor consummates his marriage to Berengaria, with whom he shares a mere kiss in the entire film. All the allusions to Richard's iconic sword, his masculine (and phallic) substitute at his nuptials, as being dull are too ironic to be coincidental. DeMille devalues Richard's masculinity as well as his ability to negotiate successfully with another man, a leader with whom he reaches homosocial affinity near the film's end.

In a series of romanticized complications, Berengaria decides that only by committing suicide will she save Richard's political reputation and further the cause of the Crusade. A Saracen arrow inadvertently wounds her as she walks on the ramparts. Acting on his infatuation with Berengaria, as he finds her wounded by one of his own men, Saladin abducts her to his Jerusalem palace, whose orientalized *mise-en-scène* suggests the luxury of Persian manuscript miniatures. There, illustrating Crusades movies' association of the East with medical advancements, Saladin cures her wound, professes courtly love to her, and strikes a bargain: she must ransom her affection to him to spare Richard's life, another commodification of Berengaria. If Saladin has transmogrified from Oriental other to courtly lover, Richard has undergone a similar (if less plausible) transformation, from religious apostate to convert, praying to God to regain his wife.

Conclusion

According to the truce Richard and Saladin negotiate, access to Jerusalem, the ravished bride, is restored to the Christian pilgrims, Berengaria is returned to Richard, but Richard must never enter the holy city himself, just as, within the world of the film, his consummation with his wife remains indefinitely suspended, however much the couple seem to want to couple. By creating deliberately slippery gender identities of the male and female leads through costuming, by using significant sexual symbolism in his choice of props and setting (phallic minarets, iconic swords, long lances, silk scarves), and by alluding to various contemporary and posthumous histories and legends about Richard Lionheart's sexual proclivities and homosocial alliances, DeMille anticipates and replicates the quandary about Richard I's sexual orientation that has engaged medieval chroniclers and modern historians. Was he or wasn't he? DeMille ultimately equivocates. In the first half of *The Crusades*, Richard is definitely not an "ardent suitor, is he?" Later in the film, the director creates a fantasy about a romantic attraction between Richard and his historical wife. However, the film's fictive Berengaria (as well, perhaps, as the actual woman) remains a bride, never achieving the status of sexually experienced wife, leaving any determination about Richard's possible homosexuality up to the interpretation of moviegoers like Warren, who read the cinematic signs and "know he was gay."[34]

34 I thank Margarethe and Guy, who introduced me to Warren and Lila, watched *The Crusades*, and offered advice as I developed my argument.

Chapter 4
"In the Company of Orcs":
Peter Jackson's Queer Tolkien

Jane Chance

Peter Jackson's many omissions and additions to J. R. R. Tolkien's text of *The Lord of the Rings* in his film trilogy have been for the most part disparaged by Tolkien fans and critics. Only a grudging acknowledgment of the difference in the nature of the film medium from that of text has rationalized Jackson's redaction and the Hollywood establishment's prioritizing of dramatic suspense and entertainment over fidelity to written word.[1] Despite the validity of such reactions to the film trilogy, one of Jackson's most interesting embellishments of Tolkien's medievalized epic is scene 62 (special extended DVD version), "In the Company of Orcs," in the third film, *The Return of the King.*[2] This scene title bears no similarity to any chapter title in Tolkien, although the event it presents does appear in book 6, in *The Return of the King*, chapter 2, "The Land of Shadow" (the latter, the title for the film's next scene, 63). During Jackson's "In the Company of Orcs," Hobbits Frodo and Sam, while en route to their final destination, Mount Doom—where they must return the One Ring to its fiery origins—don Orc armor, heavy, metal, and medieval in appearance, which allows them to be concealed as deserters within an Orc phalanx moving across Mordor.[3] Tolkien, however, in the equivalent scene takes care to specify

---

1 See, for an example of the disparagement of Jackson's changes in the film on the one hand and of the acknowledgement of the film medium's differences in the other, David Bratman, "Summa Jacksonica: A Reply to Defenses of Peter Jackson's *The Lord of the Rings* Films, After St. Thomas Aquinas," *Tolkien on Film: Essays on Peter Jackson's* The Lord of the Rings, ed. Janet Croft (Altadena, CA: Mythopoeic Press, 2004), pp. 27-62; and Janet Croft, "Mithril Coats and Tin Ears: 'Anticipation' and 'Flattening' in Peter Jackson's *The Lord of the Rings* Trilogy," *Tolkien on Film*, pp. 63-80.

2 *The Lord of the Rings: The Fellowship of the Ring, The Two Towers, Return of the King*, Special Extended DVD Editions, dir. Peter Jackson, screenplay by Peter Jackson, Fran Walsh, and Philippa Boyens, perf. Elijah Wood, et al. (United States: New Line, 2002-04). This scene does not appear in the shorter theatrical version (two hundred minutes instead of two hundred fifty).

3 All references to *The Lord of the Rings* (cited within the text by the abbreviation *LOTR* and book, chapter, and page[s] within parentheses) derive from J. R. R. Tolkien,

only items of Orc clothing that conceal their Hobbitness. In part, Jackson's production of this scene is colored by Rankin and Bass's humorous treatment in the 1979 animated film *The Return of the King*, in which Tolkien's Orc jeer "Where there's a whip, there's a will" transforms into a joyous and upbeat all-male marching song.[4] But the sadism of Jackson's Orcs is neither homosocial nor humorous.

To dramatize a range of queer ontologies in Tolkien's Middle-earth, Jackson instead borrows the title for his scene from a more contemporary film directed by Neil LaBute, *In the Company of Men* (1997). The parodic title—in its substitution of Tolkien's "Orcs" for LaBute's "Men"—suggests that there is an equivalence—or a contrast—between Orcs and Men, and that the "company" each race provides for Hobbits Sam and Frodo both defines and subverts their masculinities. To this end, Jackson's key visual irony in scene 62 is that Frodo and Sam appear in Orc armor. As Hobbits they are not in fact Orcs, but they are also certainly not Men, even though Hobbits "liked and disliked much the same things as Men did" (*FR*, Prologue 2). As Halflings, Hobbits are half Men, at least in stature; what does it mean for a Half Man to perform as an Orc, even for purposes of survival? How does Jackson's invocation of LaBute's film help to answer this question that remains so much less sharply defined in Tolkien's text?

In *The Lord of the Rings*, Tolkien defines both Orcs and Hobbits in relation to Men. Holly Crocker has suggested that if masculinity represents a universal in the epic—an invisible standard of heteronormativity—then Hobbits and Orcs, like the Black Númenóreans (the Ringwraiths), reflect disfigurations, or inversions, of Men:

> The Orcs and their lands are twisted into degenerate forms by wastrel habits; bred from Elves, they are similar to the Black Númenóreans, whose captain is so distorted by his evil practice that he retains affiliation with his former kind only through the overt declaration that he is not a Ringwraith but a "living man" (*RK*, V, x, 191); like those decayed worthies who were corrupted by their desire

---

The Lord of the Rings, 2nd edn., with Note on the Text by Douglas Anderson (Boston: Houghton Mifflin, 1994).

4 *The Return of the King*, prod. and dir. Arthur Rankin, Jr. and Jules Bass, adapted by Romeo Muller Production, perf. Orson Bean, John Huston, Roddy McDowell et al., VHS Home Video (United States: Warner, 1993). In 1978 Ralph Bakshi had also directed an unfinished animated film of *The Lord of the Rings*, but it did not reach this point in the text. See *The Lord of the Rings*, dir. Ralph Bakshi and prod. Saul Zaentz, screenplay by Chris Conkling and Peter Beagle, VHS edition (United States: Republic Pictures, 1978).

for power, such ruined figures highlight the trilogy's recurring concern with the failures responsible for the distinctions that divide groups.[5]

Thus, Crocker continues, "in crossing the very divides of difference that it maintains for others, masculinity may assert its boundless universality. By positing kind as a racializing geography that exceeds the human, Tolkien's trilogy calls attention to the status of masculinity as 'the apparatus of cultural difference,' as Homi K. Bhabha puts it."[6] The future king Aragorn may epitomize that ideal of masculinity in the support that he receives from the Free Peoples, yet the "invisible masculinity" he promotes lies in his quiet dominion: Crocker notes that "the masculinity that Aragorn promises is defined by disavowal, a refusal to assume authority over others through visible gestures."[7]

Within this heteronormative context, Tolkien invests both Orcs and Hobbits with cultural difference. The epithet most descriptive of their mutual alterity is *queer*. The Orcs—mutants bred by Sauron from captured Elves—represent the monstrous Other, not unlike the queer gnome-like Hobbits with their furry feet who isolate themselves geographically from Men and all other races. In this respect, as Alexander Doty argues, "queerness has been set up to challenge and break apart conventional categories."[8] Doty uses *queer*

to mark a flexible space for the expression of all aspects of non- (anti-, contra-) straight cultural production and reception. . . . When a colleague heard I had begun using the word *queer* in my cultural studies work, she asked if I did so in order to "nostalgically" recapture and reassert the "romance" of the culturally

---

5 Holly Crocker, "Masculinity," *Reading* The Lord of the Rings: *New Writings on Tolkien's Classic,* ed. Robert Eaglestone (London: Continuum, 2005), 111-123, at p. 111.

6 Crocker, "Masculinity," pp. 122-123. Crocker also observes that "The central place in field of sight that Aragorn finally assumes, I suggest, asserts masculinity's invisibility by defining it as the standard of identity that will consolidate all kinds in this new reign" (p. 122). The citation from Homi Bhabha comes from "Are You a Man or a Mouse?," *Constructing Masculinity,* eds. Maurice Berger, Brian Wallis and Simon Watson (New York: Routledge, 1995), 57-65, at p. 58.

7 Crocker, "Masculinity," p. 121. Crocker notes: "Instead, Aragorn must refashion the masculinity of his kind to avoid their missteps, ultimately by taking a role in the Fellowship that reveals his leadership through gestures of service that avoid visibility. His support of Frodo's errand, therefore, is simply the culmination of a long formation of masculinity that is fostered by contact with groups who protect Middle-earth using quiet modes of dominion" (p. 117). She also adds, "Before he becomes king, then, the new masculinity that Aragorn realizes is enabled by its ability to pass unseen amongst those it protects" (p. 117).

8 Alexander Doty, *Making Things Perfectly Queer* (Minneapolis: U of Minnesota P, 1993), p. xv.

marginal in the face of trends within straight capitalistic societies to co-opt or contain aspects of queer cultures. . . . By using *queer*, I want to recapture and reassert a militant sense of difference that views the erotically "marginal" as both (in bell hooks' words) a consciously chosen "site of resistance" and a "location of radical openness and possibility."[9]

The adjective *queer*, then, as Doty defines it, does not necessarily denote "homosexual," nor, as an existential situation, does the noun depend upon or proscribe a limiting essentialism. Tison Pugh cautions that

The term *queer* need not be limited to the sexual, as it also describes relations of power predicated upon relations of sexuality. . . . *[T]o queer* means to disrupt a character's and/or the reader's sense of self by undermining his or her sense of heteronormatively inscribed sexuality, whereas *homosexual* and *homosexuality* are used to describe sexual relationships between members of the same sex (of whatever degree, from kissing to intercourse). Thus, heteronormative identity stands at stake in the queer as much as any specific sexual act.[10]

How this identity stake works depends upon a kind of queer gender parallaxis. Doty observes that "gender" within the queer either mirrors conventional forms of "feminine" and "masculine," parodies external behaviors without complete identification with straight ideology, or resists (or combines) gender codes to transcend straight formulations of female and male; only in the latter two instances does a queer gender identification exist.[11] In this chapter, *queer*, then, substitutes for the female as the Derridean trace of difference set in continual opposition to an essentialized male norm, although it might be more accurate to recognize it as a gender trope used to describe a continuum of differences, racial, national, cultural, sexual.

That director and screenplay-writer Jackson understands this mutual difference of Orcs and Hobbits as queer is clear from the way both are cast in the filmic trilogy. In his figuration of the Orcs and Orcish behavior, Jackson deploys a hypermasculinity theorized as *queer* by Pugh and other film critics because of its exaggeration of male physical characteristics.[12] The all-male group of Orcs, with their Neanderthal, bulked-up forms, long hairy arms, low brows,

9 Doty, *Making Things Perfectly Queer*, p. 3. Doty cites bell hooks's essay "Choosing the Margins as a Space of Radical Openness," reprinted in hooks, *Yearning: Race, Gender, and Cultural Politics* (Boston: South End, 1990), p. 153.

10 Tison Pugh, *Queering Medieval Genres* (New York: Palgrave Macmillan, 2004), p. 5.

11 Doty, *Making Things Perfectly Queer*, p. 5.

12 See Tison Pugh, "Queering the Medieval Dead: History, Horror, and Masculinity in Sam Raimi's *Evil Dead* Trilogy," *Race, Class, and Gender in 'Medieval' Cinema*, eds. Lynn

incisor-like teeth, phallic-snouted helmets, and bestial rage, project a campy, monstrous masculinity at odds with that of the idealized and nonauthoritarian Aragorn or the more gentle, even childlike (feminized) Halflings. Barely post-adolescent, Frodo Baggins (Elijah Wood), Sam Gamgee (Sean Astin), Merry Brandybuck (Dominic Monaghan), and Pippin Took (Billy Boyd) hardly resemble the middle-aged Hobbits (and Men) of Tolkien's epic. (Frodo is over fifty when he begins his adventure in *The Fellowship of the Ring,* as is Aragorn [Viggo Mortensen].) Yet Jackson keeps Frodo permanently queer throughout the film—perpetually youthful, if scarred, and childlike, if not infantilized.[13]

The symbolic act of Orc re-dressing by the two heroes in "In the Company of Orcs" not only enables the next step in the two Hobbits' journey to return the Ring but also situates the couple within a context of extreme and monstrous masculinization necessary for their survival in the savage and warlike world of Mordor. Jackson's Orc armor resembles medieval armor with its metal helmets bearing protective guards for noses and cheeks, even if noses and cheeks grotesque and deformed. So also this scene parodies a medieval chivalric engagement and feudal relationship: the Orcs savage one another with emotional abuse and demeaning epithets and their captain brutalizes them with whips and other weapons. For Frodo and Sam to join the group out of survival, even to ensure and protect their progress across Mordor, suggests that they both become—and also fail to become—one with this group. That is, the Hobbits fail to embrace the Orcish rupture/displacement of the feudal bond between lord and serf, which in the film depends upon a sadistic imbalance between master and slave, or prisoner. Thus Frodo and Sam remove the armor after this important scene because both it and the Orcish hypermasculinity it symbolizes are too heavy. In a sense, as Halflings they remain children; they do not "grow up" to become "men" in Jackson's bizarre Orc parody of masculinity. Like the Orcs, the hypomasculine Hobbits remain queer.

One key aspect of Orc queerness in both the text of Tolkien and the films of Rankin and Bass and Jackson is sadistic. The Orcs in Jackson's scene 62 whip their captured deserters into moving faster, both captain and soldier serving the ultimate purpose of Sauron to dominate Middle-earth by means of war and

---

Ramey and Tison Pugh (New York: Palgrave Macmillan, 2007), pp. 123-36; also, Lee Edelman, *No Future: Queer Theory and the Death Drive* (Durham: Duke UP, 2004).

13 See Jane Chance, "Is There a Text in this Hobbit? Peter Jackson's *Fellowship of the Ring,*" *Literature/Film Quarterly* 30.2 (2002): 79-85; and Jane Chance, "Tolkien's Women (and Men): The Film and the Book," *Tolkien on Film,* pp. 175-93. In addition, Daniel Timmons, "Frodo on Film: Peter Jackson's Problematic Portrayal," *Tolkien on Film,* pp. 123-48, contrasts the unheroic and "witless" filmic Hobbit very specifically with Tolkien's protagonist to demonstrate Jackson's attempt to build suspense leading to the climax at Sammath Naur.

conquest. While Jackson tones down the camp of the Rankin and Bass original, in which Tolkien's poem "Where There's a Whip, There's a Will" is set to catchy music, he retains the sadistic tone in his creepy Jason-like main guard ("Shut this rabble down!") and its echo in the diversionary scrap between "Orc" Frodo and Sam so they can escape scrutiny and, therefore, discovery by the guards.

Jackson intends this filmic embodiment of Orcish hypermasculinity in scene 62, "In the Company of Orcs," to invoke the ruthless, cruel competition between the two central male characters of the Neil LaBute film *In the Company of Men* (1997).[14] In LaBute's tough, dog-eat-dog, corporate world, deceitful Chad Piercewell (Aaron Eckhart) competes successfully in a game with newly promoted manager Howard (Matt Malloy) for the love of deaf Christine (Stacy Edwards) in order to distract him sufficiently and thereby take over his job. Chad reenacts a spectrum of misogynistic behaviors to win and therefore to empower himself as a man. Jackson's scene appropriates that behavior to gloss Tolkien's text and redefine the necessary masculinity of Middle-earth in the coming Fourth Age, of Men, as necessarily queer. By "outing" Tolkien's heroes as queer, this crucial scene will figuratively and by contrast permit the more romantic and feminized bonding and inverse "marriage" of the two Hobbits at the end of the film. As we shall see, the scene of Frodo and Sam as Orcs invariably foreshadows the important quadruple (and seemingly endless) endings in which Frodo bears some increasingly tenuous queer relationship with Sam that eventually ends altogether with his complete separation and departure to the Grey Havens. This scene also casts a similarly queer shadow on the rough, hypermasculine heroism of Hobbits Merry and Pippin at the end of the epic— both of whom endured an involuntary Orc captivity at the beginning of *The Two Towers* during which Pippin found an Orc blade.

The film of *The Return of the King*, in visualizing the relationship of Frodo and Sam and other relationships between male characters in terms of their appearance in "In the Company of Orcs," pushes the envelope of these medievalized feudal or chivalric relationships between Hobbit and Hobbit. Esther Saxey perceives Jackson's *The Lord of the Rings* as a bridge that makes explicit the homosocial in the book when she interprets "practically every pairing" of males as homoerotic.[15] In LaBute's film, in addition, the pairing of the two main characters depends upon a sexual relationship with a mediating woman who is symbolically damaged—she cannot hear. In reference to the bonding of the two corporate men through their dual but separate seductions of this vulnerable female victim, helpful is Doty's acknowledgement that one

---

14 *In the Company of Men*, dir. Neil LaBute (United States: Sony Picture Classics, 1998).

15 Esther Saxey, "Homoeroticism," *Reading* The Lord of the Rings, 124-137, at p. 131.

conventional device in film "to mediate and diffuse male-male erotics" is in fact a woman.[16] The rapacious and patriarchal corporate culture in which the appropriately named Chad Piercewell (suggestive of phallic penetration) and his superior, boyish, bespectacled Howard—called Howie by Chad—participate expects middle managers to fend off inroads by junior employees and interns and simultaneously appeal to demanding bosses. But Chad and Howie go beyond mere corporate competition. Envious Chad dupes manager Howie into making a woman fall in love and then dumping her by means of the pretense that his own girlfriend has suddenly moved out, leaving him just a futon and a poster of *American Gigolo* (again, both quickie-bed and stud-film an appropriate emblem of Chad's promiscuity and exploitation of others). When Piercewell intones that "we are doomed as a race," he proceeds to convince the viewers of that truth by the excellence of his acting during scenes with the appropriately named and Christlike victim, Christine, who, only gradually coming to believe that he loves her, inadvertently leads Howie into a love that she does not reciprocate. Chad further tricks Howie into missing an important job deadline—which Chad meets instead—so that Chad make Howie look weak and inept. After Christine learns that Chad was only playing a game with Howie, the fall-out so unnerves Howie that Chad—a fellow alumnus—can step into Howie's managerial shoes by film's end and back into bed with his own girlfriend.

Women in this film are registers of corporate power; the bonding, if it can be called bonding, that does occur exists between men. Piercewell, in particular, is by turns sadistic toward Howie and toward the woman pawn that they both bed and, in his sexual sharing of the woman with Howie, latently homosexual. To justify the "game" of exploiting a woman's vulnerability so egregiously, Chad, in a mood of black misanthropy at the beginning after his girlfriend appears to have left him, inadvertently warns Howie of his true nature: "I do not give a shit about anybody" (scene 2, "Chad and Howard"). At the end, after Chad explains the game he has played to Howie, as a joke he adds in a note of perfectly dehumanized predation, "I don't trust anything that bleeds for a week and doesn't die" (scene 3, "The Game"). It is no accident that an African-American colleague of Howie declares he would not be caught dead in a relationship with a woman like Christine—meaning deaf—in a corporation "like this with these men around" (scene 12, "Copy Line").

But Chad is not only a monster of maleness. There is a homoerotic desire underlying much of what he does within the firm, beginning with his relationship with Howie, the feminine partner of the two. "You're not pussing out on this, Howie?" Chad asks in the men's room when they talk about the "perfect candidate," knowing boyish Howie will, indeed, "puss out" by falling in love with Christine (scene 6, "A Perfect Candidate"). Meeting in mens'

---

16 Doty, *Making Things Perfectly Queer*, p. 11.

rooms throughout the film (indeed, proposing the game while Howie spends an interminable time on the toilet), Chad and Howie parody a long-married couple when sadistic Chad (knowing already how humiliated Howie must feel) again and again queries Howie how he feels. At the airport Chad asks how Howie's ear feels after a woman offended by Howie's asking the time rakes it with her nails. Chad also inquires about Howie's feelings after Howie admits to Christine that Chad's "love" for her was only a game. Further, Chad has made love initially and at the end, when Christine discovers his lies, in Howie's hotel room (by telling the maid he forgot the key), making Howie's bed the site of Chad's own seduction of Christine. If Howie is a masochistic victim of Chad's sadism, Howie similarly inflicts suffering on Christine by calling her "handicapped" after she confesses she loves Chad. And after Chad has admitted he has also screwed Howie out of a job, Howie throws up and later demands crazily, again and again, that deaf Christine listen to him. Chad sees the "game" as "fun," something he did "because I could" (as he says to Howie at the end, scene 27, "Weeks Later").

The viciousness of employee-employer relations in the capitalist culture of LaBute's film is not far removed from the sadism of the Orcs in the Jackson film. In the most outrageous scene in *In the Company of Men*, Chad demands of an African-American intern (Jason Dixie) who has mispronounced both "asked" ("axed") and his own name ("Keif")—for which Chad viciously chastises him—that he "show me your balls" (scene 22, "The Intern"). Chad means, "Do you have the balls to associate with money and power," but he insists that the intern literally lower his pants. The scene of humiliation in which Chad gazes at Keith's genitals is both nakedly voyeuristic and sadistic/homoerotic. All of these businessmen must serve their employer, Chad implies, even if such service demands self-sacrifice; as the employer ignores the needs of his employees, so both together unite in their goal of overcoming competition in winning the consumer's dollar. The (male) corporate analogy illuminates the sexualized game between Chad and Howie for the love of the innocent (female) consumer, Christine.

Does Jackson's use of the LaBute film appropriately sexualize Tolkien's feudalized epic-romance? The presence of sexuality in *The Lord of the Rings* was, in the earliest criticism, generally ignored or denied, or perceived only in the female central characters whose behavior can be validated by means of medieval antecedents such as the Valkyries or the women of *Beowulf*. The denial of sexuality began when Edwin Muir first typified all Tolkien's male characters as "boys masquerading as adult heroes. The hobbits . . . are ordinary boys, the fully human heroes have reached the fifth form; but hardly one of them knows anything about women, except by hearsay. Even the elves and dwarves and the ents are boys irretrievably, and will never come to puberty."[17] In one of the earliest essays on this subject, Brenda Partridge, in "No Sex Please— We're Hobbits: The Construction of Female Sexuality in *The Lord of the Rings*," argues that "the claim that *The Lord of the Rings* contains no sex must be strongly refuted: it is there, though it is closely interwoven with and often masked by the various other themes and symbolism."[18] Partridge's discussion of the lack of female characters in *The Lord of the Rings*, the idealization of those who do appear as goddess or romantic heroine figures (Eowyn, Goldberry, and Galadriel), the "stilted and distant" relations between male and female characters (Gimli and Galadriel), and the paternalistic, even feudalistic, relations between Hobbits and other male characters during wartime (Merry and Théoden, Pippin and Denethor, Frodo and Sam) provides insight into the concealed sexuality of Tolkien's medievalized world. Partridge's take on Tolkienian sexuality culminates in the view of the battle between Sam and Shelob as a violent, even sadistic, sexual altercation between male and female. Her view derives from a prior comment by Catharine Stimpson that "The scene . . . oozes a distasteful, vengeful quality as the small, but brave, male figure really gets the enormous, stenching bitch-castrator."[19]

If some later critical treatments regarding his women characters similarly argue Tolkien's misogyny, others see his handling of male characters as justified by his own day or that of the Middle Ages from which he borrows.[20] In

---

17 Edwin Muir, "A Boy's World," *Sunday Observer* (London), 27 November 1955, 11.

18 Brenda Partridge, "No Sex Please—We're Hobbits: The Construction of Female Sexuality in *The Lord of the Rings*," *J. R. R. Tolkien: This Far Land,* ed. Robert Giddings (London: Vision, 1983), 179-97, at p. 179.

19 Catharine Stimpson, *J. R. R. Tolkien* (New York: Columbia UP, 1969), p. 19. See also Partridge, "No Sex Please—We're Hobbits," pp. 187-91.

20 For the former view—Tolkien's misogyny—see Tanya Wood, "'Is Tolkien a Renaissance Man?' Sir Philip Sidney's *Defense of Poesy* and J. R. R. Tolkien's 'On Fairy-Stories,'" *J. R. R. Tolkien and His Literary Resonances: Views of Middle-earth,* eds. George Clark and Daniel Timmons (Westport, CT: Greenwood, 2000), 95-108; Faye Ringel, "Women Fantasists: In the Shadow of the Ring," *J. R. R. Tolkien and His Literary Resonances,* pp. 159-71; C. Frederick and S. McBride, eds., *Women among the Inklings: Gender in C. S. Lewis, J. R. R. Tolkien, and Charles Williams* (Westport, CT: Greenwood, 2001). For the latter view—the justification of Tolkien's misogyny by his medieval sources—see, for Old Norse antecedents, Leslie Donovan, "The Valkyrie Reflex in J. R. R. Tolkien's *The Lord of the Rings*: Galadriel, Shelob, Eowyn, and Arwen," *Tolkien the Medievalist,* ed. Jane Chance (London: Routledge, 2003), pp. 106-32. For a third, related, view, that Tolkien borrows from Old English literature, particularly, *Beowulf,* for his women, but still underestimates them, see Jennifer Neville, "Women," *Reading* The Lord of the Rings, pp. 101-110.

relation to the male characters in Tolkien's book, D. M. Craig acknowledges that the absence of women during wartime in World War I facilitated closer male friendships.[21] And as late as 2001, in a return to the desexualized version of the epic—this time understood as demanded by medieval models—Dan Timmons promotes the relationship between Frodo and Sam as a spiritual bond between two males as depicted in the romance *Sir Gawain and the Green Knight.* Timmons concludes that "One of Frodo's wounds from his experiences, a sort of metaphorical castration, is that he will never experience such joys (marriage, family life) available to mortals in Middle-earth."[22]

Certainly there is some evidence in Tolkien's own life for a homosociality that bordered on the erotic. Partridge's examination of homosociality in male groups in Tolkien's life, particularly the Inklings, and male friendships, especially with C. S. Lewis, takes note of Tolkien's exclusion of his wife Edith from both, his Roman Catholic disapproval of Lewis's late-life marriage to divorcee Joy Davidman, and his jealousy of Lewis's friendship with Charles Williams.[23] And, whatever Tolkien may have felt for Lewis, Lewis more explicitly expresses what Partridge describes as "ambiguous sexuality and latent sadism" in Lewis's diary comment that Tolkien "thinks all literature is written for the amusement of *men* between thirty and forty . . . No harm in him: only needs a smack or so" (Lewis's italics).[24]

Recent analyses of male characters in *The Lord of the Rings* enable a queering of sexuality in Tolkien. I have argued for the implications of the word *queer* to label Bilbo and Frodo (and others viewed by the locals as alien or different from the norm) in the opening chapter of *The Lord of the Rings* as reflective of the larger problem of alterity in the epic.[25] Queerness is also found in specifically medieval paradigms invoked throughout the epic. Tolkien fully rehearses homosocial relationships in scenes involving the Hobbits as they each fulfill a slightly different role as medieval vassal or thane who serves some lord or master, willingly or no, to suggest the possibility of the misuse of domination

---

21 D. N. Craig, "Queer Lodgings," *Mallorn: The Journal of the Tolkien Society* 38 (2001): 11-18.

22 Dan Timmons, "Hobbit Sex and Sensuality in *The Lord of the Rings*," *Mythlore* 23.3 (2001): 70-79, at p. 78.

23 Partridge, "No Sex Please—We're Hobbits," pp. 180-82.

24 C. S. Lewis's diary remark, from *The Lewis Papers*, vol. 9, pp. 89-90, is quoted by Humphrey Carpenter, *The Inklings: C. S. Lewis, J. R. R. Tolkien, Charles Williams and Their Friends* (London: Allen & Unwin, 1978), pp. 22-23, and picked up by Partridge, "No Sex Please—We're Hobbits," p. 182.

25 See Jane Chance, "The Problem of Difference in 'The Birthday Party,'" chapter 5 of *The Lord of the Rings: The Mythology of Power* (New York: Twayne, 1992), pp. 27-35; recast as chapter 2, "'Queer' Hobbits: The Problem of Difference in the Shire," in the rev. ed. (Lexington: U of Kentucky P, 2001), pp. 26-37.

and, therefore, to hint at exaggerated masculinity. From the very beginning, Sam's service to his master, Frodo, represents a backdrop against which more minor relationships involving service are replayed. Sam initially serves as gardener before the quest begins, but he becomes a squire to his lord in *The Two Towers* after they are separated from the Fellowship and, eventually, in *The Return of the King*, serves as a deeply compassionate friend whose love transcends the ordinary. Gollum, also a Hobbit, if degenerate in form, represents a parody of Sam as servant, as Frodo parodies the Dark Lord, Sauron, in Tolkien's version of how self-aggrandizement, greed, and pride pervert masculine relationships. Tolkien portrays their mutual emotional enslavement by the Ring (called the "Precious" by Gollum in an ironic reference both to valuable items and to the beloved) in the most medieval, feudal, scene of oath-swearing in the epic, in "The Taming of Sméagol," when Gollum swears to the Master—Frodo—by the Precious, or tries to: "Sméagol will swear never, never, to let Him have it. Never! Sméagol will save it. But he must swear on the Precious." At the moment Frodo insists Gollum swear instead *by* the Ring, Sam imagines that "his master had grown and Gollum had shrunk: *a tall stern shadow, a mighty lord who hid his brightness in grey cloud,* and at his feet a little whining dog. Yet the two were in some way akin and not *alien*: they could reach one another's minds" (*LOTR*, 4:1, 618; my emphasis). In *The Return of the King*, in "Minas Tirith," this scene of feudal domination is varied by Hobbit Pippin, who, like Gollum attempting to swear on the Ring, similarly swears to the House of Denethor his allegiance as vassal, but as compensation for the loss of Denethor's son Boromir while defending the Hobbits: "Here do I swear fealty and service to Gondor, and to the Lord and Steward of the realm, to speak and to be silent, to do and to let be, to come and to go, in need or plenty, in peace or war, in living or dying, from this hour henceforth, until my lord release me, or death take me, or the world end" (*LOTR*, 5:1, 756). After constructing these contrasting scenes of medieval fealty, Tolkien provides a *tertium quid* when Hobbit Merry willingly and joyfully offers his service to King Théoden of Rohan in "The Passing of the Grey Company": "Filled suddenly with love for this old man, he knelt on one knee, and took his hand and kissed it: 'May I lay the sword of Meriadoc of the Shire on your lap, Théoden King?' he cried. 'Receive my service, if you will!'" (*LOTR*, 5:2, 777).

When Jackson queers Tolkien—adds this homosocially inflected scene with its own title that does not exist per se as a separate chapter in *The Return of the King*—he simultaneously uses it to parody the three other medieval *comitatus* or indenture scenes just described in Tolkien's *The Two Towers* and *The Return of the King* between Hobbit and Hobbit or Hobbit and Man. The queering of Tolkien, then, depends on how Orclike either Man or Hobbit appears in the film, given the author's definitions of Orcishness (Elven decline into mutation), set against masculinity. Either to Orcs or to Men the Fourth Age ushered in at the end of *The Return of the King* will belong, Helms reminds us. As far as the latter are concerned, "In arguing that masculinity is a mode that subsumes all kinds," Holly Crocker also claims, "the narrative's preservation of differences among groups is ultimately a way to install hierarchy in an empire where one *kind* of Men—the High Men of the West—gives order to those others who inhabit their realm."[26] The High Men of the West preserve the hierarchy of rational (hetero)normativity against which all differences are measured, including the ugly Orcness of masculinity as Other and individual difference as aberrance. The Orc chieftain is described in *The Two Towers* as "almost manhigh," a phrase Tolkien uses to differentiate the Orc from the human norm (*LOTR*, 2:5, 325); interestingly, when Men are corrupted they look more like Orcs (*LOTR*, 2:5, 566).

Tolkien's Orcs differ from Men in their broad flat faces, coal-black eyes, and a red tongue; they speak their own language, which further isolates them (*LOTR*, 2:5, 325). Bearing yellow fangs, Orcs have "no time to play," meaning that they must work, that is, kill and torture, and they are quarrelsome, dominating, disloyal, and vengeful, differentiated only by a military chain-of-command, not by individual personal or temperamental characteristics (*LOTR*, 3.3, 445-46). Cruel—they jeer at Merry when he puts "medicine" on his wound and promise that "We shall have some fun later" (*LOTR*, 3.3, 448)—they are regularly abusive and sadistic verbally, physically, and even sexually. For example, Uglúk, leader of the Uruk-hai of Saruman's Isengard (who have been further mutated so they can march by day), insults Grishnákh of Sauron's Lugbúrz by calling his Orcs swine and maggots: "Don't stand slavering there! Get your rabble together! The other swine are legging it to the forest" (*LOTR*, 3.3, 452). When Grishnákh steals Merry and Pippin away from the other Orcs because he thinks they have the Ring, Tolkien portrays his search for it as disturbingly sexualized. Grishnákh's "long hairy arm" and "foul breath' are apparent when "He began to paw them and feel them. Pippin shuddered as hard cold fingers groped down his back. . . . His fingers continued to grope" (*LOTR*, 3.3, 455). Angry that he has not found the Ring, Grishnákh threatens the Hobbits with torture if he does not find it: "I'll cut you both to quivering shreds" (*LOTR*, 3.3, 457).[27] Ironically, after Grishnákh is killed by an arrow, which permits Pippin to locate the Orc leader's knife, Pippin can cut their bonds and escape. The acquisition of this phallic weapon—the carved handle of an Orc blade is shaped like a hideous head with "squinting eyes" and "leering mouth" (*LOTR*, 3.3, 489)—

---

26 Crocker, "Masculinity," p. 113.

27 In Jackson's film *Two Towers*, scene 12, "The Fate of Merry and Pippin," compresses three different text scenes without any identification of Grishnákh as the Orc who steals and gropes the two Hobbits, perhaps because his actions in the film would have hinted at pedophilia and male rape.

represents both a re-arming and Orcish masculinization of this Hobbit hero. It is after this escape that Pippin "grows" while traveling with the Ents and then in Gondor offers his indenture as servant to tyrannical and mad King Denethor as compensation for the loss of the Gondor king's son Boromir while defending Pippin and Merry against the Orcs.

In addition, Orcs, as repressed sexuality, brute animality, and the hypermasculine Other, represent the queer polar opposite of the Hobbit as a desexualized and even idealized feminine Other. According to a letter to his son Michael, Tolkien believed that men, unlike women, "when uncorrupt," are not monogamous because of their "very animal nature."[28] In this binary system, men would be, figuratively, Orcs. According to Randel Helms writing on Tolkien, Orcs are projections of the id, derived from William Blake's more positive, revolutionary figure, Orc, although, we might add, suggestive of the militant resistance of difference, even if they merely parody the masculine without identification:

> Both Orcs are symbols or representatives of a disruptive power inimical to established order, whose function is to rebel against and overthrow the status quo. . . . In Blake, Orc appears as a symbolic picture of the return of the repressed to the level of consciousness by the vehicle of political revolution; he is the inevitable result of sexual repercussion, which Blake, unlike Freud, regarded as inimical rather than necessary to civilized life. Though disagreeing with Freud about the necessity of repression, Blake anticipated by more than a hundred years the psychoanalytic insight that the energies of the id, when denied outlet in one form, will find an exit in another form, often with terrible psychic or physical violence. . . . *The Lord of the Rings* can likewise be seen as a political fantasy expressed in covert sexual symbols.[29]

Helms sees the very nature of the Orcs as threatening to Middle-earth: "Indeed Tolkien's revulsion from the Orcs is a chief motivating force behind *The Lord of the Rings;* they *must* be pushed back into Mordor and held there. Tolkien wants Orc-hood sealed in precisely the same underworld of the mind from which Blake wants it to erupt; the one, that is, accepts the necessity of repression, the other argues that repression in any form is damaging to the soul."[30] The carryover to *The Return of the King* is one of misogynous and sadistic machismo with an overlay of homoeroticism based on power relations.

---

28 J. R. R. Tolkien, *Letters*, ed. Humphrey Carpenter (Boston: Houghton Mifflin, 1981), p. 51.

29 Randel Helms, *Tolkien's World* (Boston: Houghton Mifflin, 1974), pp. 69-70.

30 Helms, *Tolkien's World*, p. 72.

Just as Tolkien in *The Two Towers* uses the Orc re-arming of Pippin once his bonds have been cut to signal the Hobbit's metamorphosis into a being more hypermasculinized and military than a Hobbit, more queer, he changes the costume of Sam and Frodo throughout the epic in their encounters with other beings to signal the breaking of boundaries and borders in their epic quest. Indeed, *who* they are, as they evolve, confuses the enemy, who rely on external signs for racial identity: one small black-skinned tracker Orc quarrels over the object of their search, the two Hobbits, with a larger warrior Orc who bears the sign of the Eye: "First they say it's a great Elf in bright armour, then it's a sort of small dwarf-man, then it must be a pack of rebel Uruk-hai; or maybe it's all the lot together" (*LOTR* 6:2, 925). But the Hobbits are all three: Frodo's Dwarf mithril-coat, given to him by Bilbo, not only protects this newly heroic Hobbit[31] from death during the attack by the Orcs at the abandoned Dwarf mine at Khazad-dûm but also reveals him, in a sense, *as* a Dwarf defending his ancient home: he valiantly stabs the foot of an Orc who is attempting to break down the door (*LOTR*, 2:5, 324). Later, in Lothlórien, the grey-green and silver Elven hood and cloak Galadriel gives to the Hobbits offer camouflage in any forest setting, near-invisibility from enemies, and lightness and warmth in wearing, but also mark them more symbolically as Elven in their song-making and wisdom (*LOTR*, 2:8, 370).[32] So also when Sam and Frodo put on Orc armor to disguise themselves from Saruman's Orcs searching for them, the Orcs themselves perceive Sam as a big Orc. For Frodo, this assumption of Orc armor is necessary because the Orcs who captured him have stripped him of all clothing, including the garments and "armor" given to him by others—the coat of mithril mail from Bilbo and the Elven cloak with the Elven-brooch; for Sam, the Elven blade he uses against Shelob has failed (*LOTR*, 4:10, 728) and the short sword he carries has been taken by the Orcs (*LOTR*, 5:10, 889).

This stripping and queered epic re-arming of the hero(es) in *The Return of the King* alerts us to an important stage in their journey together—what might be called a defensive identification of the Other with the Other for self-protection as they cross Mordor, which is indicated by the donning of Orc apparel. The Orc clothing they put on includes long hairy breeches, a dirty leather tunic, a coat of ring mail, a belt with a sword, and, for Frodo, a black cap on which a red Evil Eye has been painted with iron rim and "beaklike nose-guard" (*LOTR*,

---

31 The developing hero Frodo at the end of book 1 has so mastered the Ring he carries that he resists the summons of the Black Riders in "Flight to the Ford" and lifts his sword at them (*LOTR* 1:12, 214).

32 In relation to Tolkien's essentialism in assigning a specific garb to each race, note that the leader of the wise Elves tells the Hobbits that "we put the thought of all that we love into all that we make. Yet they are garments, not armour, and they will not turn shaft or blade" (*LOTR* 2:8, 370).

5:1, 913). So effective is this garb that both Hobbits appear to be Orcs: captured Frodo, dazed and dreaming in "The Tower of Cirith Ungol," in anticipation of Sam's appropriation of Orc costume, sees "an orc with a whip, and then it turns into Sam" (*LOTR*, 6:1, 910). After they don the clothing, Sam calls Frodo "a perfect little orc" or would be, if he would cover his face with a mask and if he were longer in arm and bow-legged (*LOTR*, 6:2, 913). Tolkien implies that they have in some way been symbolically transformed into Orcs, but what that means is not explicitly indicated. Further, in "The Land of Shadow," *before* they meet the Orc company, they divest themselves of some of the armor because Sam is too big and cannot wear Orc-mail over his clothing (he just wears an Orc-helm and a black cloak) and because the Orc-mail is too heavy for Frodo (he borrows Sam's Elven cloak, which he wears over the "orc-rag") (*LOTR*, 6:2, 918).

Unlike Tolkien, Jackson portrays both Hobbits as wearing their Orc armor throughout scene 62, "In the Company of Orcs," which, in underscoring the contrast between text and film and the simultaneous intervisuality of the films *The Lord of the Rings* and *In the Company of Men*, reveals how Jackson queers Tolkien. What actually occurs in Tolkien's chance meeting of the Orc company and the Hobbits? Their encounter happens at night, when the Orcs are moving very quickly to reposition themselves for battle. Smaller "breeds" of Orcs who want to get the trip over, even if it means joining Sauron's wars, comprise the group, which is guided by very large "uruks" (slave-drivers) with whips (*LOTR*, 6:2, 930). Sam and Frodo do not try to escape—they merely hope they will not be noticed, but of course they are, not as imposters, but as deserters. One of the slave-drivers whips and harasses these "slugs" into joining the front of the phalanx:

> Now and again the orc-driver fell back and jeered at them. "There now!" he laughed, flicking at their legs. "Where there's a whip there's a will, my slugs. Hold up! I'd give you a nice freshener now, only you'll get as much lash as your skins will carry when you come in late to your camp. Do you good." (*LOTR* 6:2, 931)

When the company later meets several Orc companies that converge at the road intersection, during further whippings, scuffles, and confusion Sam falls to the ground with Frodo so that Orcs fall on top and they are able to crawl off in the dark (*LOTR*, 6:2, 932). This is all there is in Tolkien.

Jackson portrays both Sam and Frodo as wearing Orc armor throughout scene 62 to indicate that the queer Hobbits have become queer Orcs. In his parodic treatment of the scene "In the Company of Men," "Company" suggests that the Hobbits Frodo and Sam join (and intend to fight) the band of Orcs—the queer Other—in a medieval military sense, but "company" (a business) also suggests entertainment and companionship, that which might be provided by a "fellowship." In Jackson's version of the scene, Frodo and Sam in their snouted black armor (it is not explained in the film where they have found it) are similarly beaten and called slugs, but instead of a chance meeting with other Orc troops and the confusion that results, which allows the Hobbits to escape, Jackson emphasizes the two Hobbits' pretense of sadomasochism—specifically, mock-abuse and submission that enable them to survive in Orc-company. When they halt for inspection, Frodo, wearing what looks like an S & M dog collar tearing into his neck (in fact the chain that holds the One Ring), almost falls and Sam insists that he "stand up!" while a guard snarls "no speech." Yet Frodo, not Sam, begs, "Hit me, Sam! Start fighting!" as a ruse to distract the Orcs so they can escape. Only in the following scene (63), "The Land of Shadow," do the Hobbits strip off the burdensome Orc armor to expose their shirts underneath, momentarily returning to truer selves when Frodo, with his head on Sam's shoulder, admits there is beauty in the light.

That Sam and Frodo have acquired an Orcish hypermasculinity in Jackson's film (but not in Tolkien) is mirrored both in their abusive treatment of Hobbit alter-ego Gollum, the "Precious," and their homoerotic relationship after his disappearance. Earlier, in scene 3 of *The Two Towers*, "The Taming of Sméagol," Frodo has exhibited pity toward the fallen Hobbit, although both Frodo and Sam grapple with him while he scratches, hits, and bites. It is Frodo who threatens aggressive Sam with Sting: "Release him [Sam] or I'll cut your throat." Then, after Gollum complains of the pain when he is dragged by the rope on his neck, Frodo removes the rope after Gollum "swears to do what you wants" and "swears to serve the Master of the Precious." Further, Jackson (but not Tolkien) also highlights the similarly sadomasochistic codependency of Orc-like Gollum and his higher Hobbit self, Sméagol, in scene 29, "Gollum and Sméagol," which involves the famous debate over killing his Master. Dominant Gollum abuses Sméagol to manipulate him into dropping his opposition to the proposal. Smeagol whines, "Master is my friend!" while Gollum replies, "No one likes you! You're a liar and a thief! Murderer!" When Sméagol resists him by telling him to go away, Gollum eats away at his self-esteem—what little he has left—by demanding, "Where would you be without me?" Although Sméagol knows he does not need Gollum now that "Master looks after us," later, in the corresponding betrayal scene of Frodo by Gollum, in scene 66, "Gollum's Plan," he loyally promises that "Sméagol will look after Master." To convince Sméagol, Gollum notes that Master broke his promise. Gollum's violence erupts in a non-Tolkienian way: "We ought to break his filthy neck! Kill him! Kill them both! Then we'll be the Master" (even "Put out his eyes"). When Sméagol answers that it is too risky to kill him, Gollum understands he has won and comes up with the possibility that "she" (Shelob) could do it, absolving them of responsibility. The violence of Jackson's last scene involving the three Hobbits, scene 68, "Mount Doom," when Gollum attempts to seize the Ring and jumps on Sam and Frodo, Sam hits Gollum with a rock, and Gollum bites Sam, has been previously foreshadowed by this violent Jacksonian psychomachia.

In echo of the name used by Gollum to address both the Ring and himself, Tolkien allows Shagrat the Orc guard, who realizes Frodo, as a commodity, a treasure, is still alive, to call him "precious" in "The Tower of Cirith Ungol" (*LOTR*, 5: 10, 741). As a name, it reflects the endearments for the beloved in a heterosexual relationship and thus invokes the intratextual queerness of the Orc. In Jackson's film, this scene—a touchstone for the blossoming of the relationship between Frodo and Sam—leads to the pairing, repairing, and reuniting of the two in at least three to four scenes in what appears to be "endless endings" for Jackson's trilogy but which are summed up by Frodo and Sam's love for one another. This love climaxes in the appropriation of the conjugal "ring" by their jealous Hobbit alter-ego Gollum at the moment of dis-consummation, or, in another sense, Gollum's "union" with the sexualized female fires of Orodruin. (Here it is important to note the vaginal fiery eye of Sauron with which those fires are matched.) After the destruction of the Ring, in scene 70, "The Crack of Doom," when Frodo hangs from a precipice with two hands, Sam appeals to Frodo, "Don't let go," and offers his hand to him. Visually, Jackson here uses Michelangelo's "Creation of Adam" as a context, zooming in on the entwined hands to invoke God's loving clasp of Adam's hand. In the next scene, "Sauron Defeated," as the Hobbits touch hands and Mount Doom spews fire, Sam is reminded of sex and love—he would have married Rosie Cotton if he had been able to return home—while Frodo comforts and embraces him: "I'm glad to be with you, Samwise . . . here at the end of all things." "The End of All Things" is also the title of scene 72, in which the giant Eagles rescue them from fiery doom by clutching them in their talons like Jove's eagle lifting Ganymede, the classical myth of the rape of the Cup Bearer for the gods and medieval code for gay love.[33] But it is not the end of all things, for when Frodo awakens at last, safe in bed at Rivendell, the last of the homely figures he sees, after Merry and Pippin jump into his bed like boys, embracing, and Gandalf, Gimli, Legolas, and Aragorn appear in quick succession, is beloved Sam. Their eyes meet as if they were long-parted lovers (scene 73, "The Fellowship Reunited").

Neither culture—that of chivalry in which the knight owes fealty to his lord in battle nor that of matters of love in court involving his liege lady— mirrors the idealized feudalism of medieval epic and romance, but their fusion occurs in the bonding of Frodo and Sam. Jackson's crucial scene in his film,

---

33 John Boswell, "The Triumph of Ganymede: Gay Literature of the High Middle Ages," *Christianity, Social Tolerance, and Homosexuality: Gay People in Western Europe from the Beginning of the Christian Era to the Fourteenth Century* (Chicago: U of Chicago P, 1980), 243-66.

"In the Company of Orcs," in echoing LaBute's film *In the Company of Men*, queers Tolkien by accentuating the hypermasculinity and sadism of the Orcs and the hypomasculinity and gentleness of the disguised lovers Frodo and Sam. Underlying the feudal relationships of all the Hobbits, Tolkien's queerness tropes gender binaries throughout the epic. Whatever encoding Tolkien uses in his masterpiece is decoded by Jackson through this appropriately named filmic scene, in which brutish Orcs and feminized Hobbits keep queer company.[34]

---

34 Some of the ideas in this essay first emerged in the guest lecture "The Endless Endings of Peter Jackson's *Lord of the Rings*" for the Rice University Young Alumni Association, at the Houston Museum of Natural Science, in conjunction with the Jackson film exhibit, on 21 June 2005. As a short paper it was delivered in a session on "Reconsidering Sexuality" at the Annual Rice University Graduate Student Symposium, on "Pathologies: Scientific and Cultural Representations of the Normal and Abnormal," in Houston, Texas, 17 March 2007. Portions of the current essay were included in the plenary lecture, "Tough Love: Teaching the New Medievalisms," at the Eighteenth Annual Texas Medieval Association Conference, Texas Tech University, Lubbock, Texas, on 3 October 2008. The entire essay was also presented as the keynote speech at the Sixth Annual Tolkien Symposium, on "Sex and Gender in Tolkien's Middle-earth," sponsored by the English Department, University of Vermont, Burlington, VT, 11 April 2009. I am grateful to Rice University research assistant (and English graduate student) Ryan Kehoe for his help in rechecking citations and bibliography.

Chapter 5

The Eastern Western: Camp as a Response to Cultural Failure in *The Conqueror*

Anna Kłosowska

Surely, Gilles Deleuze and Félix Guattari were not the first to note that:

> America has inversed directions: she put her Orient in the West, as if the Earth became round precisely in America; her West is the very margin of the East (it is not India . . . that mediates between the West and the Orient, it is America that constitutes the tipping point and the inversion mechanism).[1]

What happens when the quintessentially American genre of the Western (which occupies an analogous phantasmatic space to the one taken up in Europe by the Oriental novel) is translated into the geographical and imaginary space of the Orient? The answer is, of course, that worlds collapse; the time-space continuum experiences a rift. Something similar happened when John Wayne starred as Genghis Khan in a famous 1956 RKO flop produced by Howard Hughes and directed by actor Dick Powell, *The Conqueror*. Lore about the film has it that "if half the cast died of cancer, the other half died of humiliation." I submit that the translation of the conventions of the Western into the Orient precipitated an unbearable understanding of the facticity, and, at the same time, of the "disgusting" operations of the Western. This unbearable understanding of the failure of the Western as a cultural project is being experienced, in the case of *The Conqueror* (often described as one of the worst movies ever made), as camp: a relationship to the Real that is, at the same time, respectful and disrespectful, intimate and distant.

Camp is an "and/or" type of relation that allows two mutually exclusive positions to operate at the same time. By allowing that illogical excess, camp opens a possibility of reinterpretation in which disgust can be transmuted into another form of pleasure, and a class of objects of desire can be produced that

---

1 Gilles Deleuze and Félix Guattari, *Mille plateaux* (Paris: Minuit, 1980), pp. 29-30. All translations are mine.

differs from the original ones while maintaining their characteristics. One way to define the specificity of camp is to say that it differs from parody and irony in that it does not destroy the objects of its attention. It is a recuperative strategy that takes disgusting objects (e.g., femme women or macho men) and reinvests them with value, but at the same time transforms them into another class of objects (lovely drag queens and transwomen or macho camp men or transmen) that can only mistakenly or at some cost operate in the primary structure where they originated.

Camp is also an optimistic space where the categories of gender and forms of desire are expanded. A classic marker of that cost, as well as a declaration of optimism concerning the expansion of the class of desirable objects, is the discovery scene and the ending of *The Crying Game* (1992), the first mainstream U.S. hit about a transgender/transsexual hero: the protagonist discovers that Dil, the object of his binding affection, has a penis, and leaves, but then returns and sacrifices his freedom to save her. Camp opens a zone of indistinction in the sense that it is at the same time a testimony to the existence of sexual categories and a means to undermine them. It is a paradox in that it both expands the spectrum of, and maintains the existence of, sexually charged differences. This paradoxical operation of camp is apparent in many definitions that typically describe it as a "loving assassination."

Finally, camp is an aesthetic movement and a drag practice that is also political. Camp can be explained in terms of the Lacanian theory of disgust. Camp is one of the means to overcome the disgust that overwhelms us when what was known but kept secret becomes public. In Lacan's theory of repulsion, disgust is a mechanism that prevents us from excessive enjoyment: at the moment when the inside is outside, the more intimate is the inside, the more disgusting it seems. Slavoj Žižek proposes a "mental experiment" to demonstrate this working of repulsion: we constantly swallow our saliva, but if we spit into our own glass of water, we are unable to drink it.[2] Our reaction has nothing to do with the substances involved, and everything to do with the intimate becoming public. Žižek extends that operation to the revelation of a "public secret" (in one of Žižek's examples, the public revelation of what was always known, that a democratic state like the U.S. uses torture at Abu Ghraib): "nobody learned anything new, and yet everybody changed." Similarly, when an intimate structure of enjoyment is made public, according to Žižek, its economy is interrupted, the economy of "self-staging for the impossible gaze structure." Under that gaze, we keep the obscene logic secret; a state, a group, contends Žižek, functions jointly at these two levels of official and obscene logic. When the gaze is confronted and its secret presence revealed (by interrupting the

---

2 Slavoj Žižek, "Is There A Proper Way to Remake a Hitchcock Film," www.lacan.com/hitch.html.

self-staging and rendering the intimate and the obscene public), the structure collapses. The unbearable pain of that collapse is experienced as disgust and thus avoided.

When it happens, though—when a cultural artifact like *The Conqueror* comes to inhabit the cultural scene—an operation is necessary to integrate it. That operation is already available: it can take the form of denial, or of disgust. Another of its forms is camp (drag). The fact that camp joins denial and disgust as a productive alternative, a form of integration of the revelation of the obscene, is not surprising. Camp has a very peculiar relationship to the real that precisely answers the needs of the integration of the disgusting element: it allows the emergence of a position where two incompatible relations, disgust and longing, can be occupied simultaneously. If we are to continue consuming an artifact like *The Conqueror*, camp is the means through which we can accomplish that. To continue Žižek's example of the glass of water, if instead of drinking it we perform for others the act of drinking it, or mediate our experience in other ways (for instance, by talking about it), we can continue to enjoy it, and the trauma of disgust is recuperated as fun. But how was the object of our campy recuperation produced in the first place?

"GENGHIS KHAN! The world trembled at his name!": The Making of an Unintentional Camp Classic[3]

The Conqueror was a mega-budget battle movie starring John Wayne as Genghis Khan (1162?-1227). Casting alone—John Wayne as founding father of Mongolia—explains the powerful appeal of the movie as one of the most notorious and unintentional comedies in Hollywood history. One contemporary reviewer called *The Conqueror* an "Oriental 'Western.'"[4] He continued: "the facts appeared to have been lost in a Technicolor cloud of charging horsemen, childish dialogue and rudimentary romance." The script, he wagered, "should get a few unintentional laughs," many of them directed at the macho posturing of the main character:

---

3 As the trailer has it. *The Conqueror*, dir. Dick Powell, script by Oscar Millard, perf. John Wayne, Susan Hayward, and Agnes Moorehead, DVD (1953 or 1954, released in 1956; VHS releases: Universal City, CA: MCA Universal Home Video, 1983, 1993; DVD releases, GoodTimes Home Video and *John Wayne, an American Icon Collection: Seven Sinners/The Shepherd of the Hills/Pittsburgh/The Conqueror/Jet Pilot*).

4 Title of the *New York Times* review, A. H. Wheeler, March 31, 1956: "'The Conqueror': John Wayne Stars in Oriental 'Western.'"

Temujin/Wayne (to resisting Bortai/Susan Hayward): Your life will be full of difficulties.

. . . .

Temujin (to Bortai): Know this, woman, I take you for wife.

Bortai: For me, there is no peace while you live, Mongol.

Temujin: You're beautiful in your wrath.

[*Bortai tries to escape*]

Temujin: I stole you. I will keep you. Before the sun sets you will come willingly to my arms.

. . . .

Temujin: She is a woman—much woman. Should her perfidy be less than that of other women?

. . . .

Temujin (to Bortai's father): While I live, while my blood burns hot, your daughter is not safe in her tent.

These lines characterize Temujin/Wayne as a barbarian—a stereotype announced in the trailer for the movie: "Spectacular as its barbaric passions and savage conquests!"—but irreconcilable both with Wayne's screen persona and with the film's intention to create a romantic fantasy. A measure of *The Conqueror*'s failure is how improbable the film appears in spite of the fact that that the script is unusually well-grounded in research; disproportionate care was bestowed on historical details, including some of the sets and costumes. The principal source for the biography of Genghis Khan, or Temujin, is *The Secret History of the Mongols*, the first Mongol written literary work preserved in a Chinese transliteration and translation from the fourteenth century.[5] Current popular biographies of Genghis could also have been the source of the screenplay.[6] In view of the fact that the movie follows its historical source relatively closely, I would like to suggest that it is not the lack of historical research but a deeply

---

5 The popular paperback edition is Paul Kahn and Francis Cleaves, *The Secret History of the Mongols: The Origins of Chingis Khan,* expanded edn. (Boston: Cheng and Tsui, 1998). Francis Cleaves's edition was completed in 1956 but only came out in 1982: *The Secret History of the Mongols* (Cambridge, MA: Harvard UP, 1982). An earlier partial translation by Arthur Waley and a different translation and notes were published between 1971 and 1985 by Igor de Rachewiltz, *The Secret History of the Mongols: A Mongolian Epic Chronicle of the Thirteenth Century* (Leiden: Brill, 2004). For Genghis Khan's biography, see Paul Ratchnevsky, *Genghis Khan: His Life and Legacy*, trans. Thomas Haining (Oxford: Blackwell, 1991), and John Man, *Genghis Khan: Life, Death and Resurrection* (New York: St. Martin's, 2005).

6 For instance, Harold Lamb, who also wrote fiction and screenplays, authored a popular biography, his first popular success: *Genghis Khan, the Emperor of All Men* (New York: McBride, 1927).

flawed conceptual integration of well-researched facts that contributes to *The Conqueror*'s failure. In other words, it is not an absence of history, but a failure of theory, amplified by the resources of cinema. Here is how the crawl at the beginning of the movie characterizes Genghis Khan:

> In the 12th century the Gobi Desert seethed with unrest. . . Petty chieftains pursued their small ambitions with cunning and wanton cruelty. Plunder and rapine were a way of life and no man trusted his brother. Out of this welter of treachery and violence there arose one of the greatest warriors the world has ever known, a conqueror whose coming changed the face of the world.

Note how "treachery and violence" and "conqueror" are contrasted here. Since conquering typically involves a massive performance of treachery and violence, the distinction is absurd, and must be legitimated by a superposition of a sentimental scheme: Temujin fights for his love, the woman he kidnaps secretly wants him, and his enemies are fundamentally bad—they are, as in the Western convention, "the men that killed his pa." Belying first appearances, Wayne plays his standard screen persona, a man bent on righteous revenge. The camp value of *The Conqueror* is linked to the fact that the work of translation from Western to Oriental setting exposes the romanticization of bloodshed as a complete fiction. Our disbelief is no longer suspended, our fetishist disavowal ("I know, but . . .") cannot withstand the pressure of knowledge. In fact, considering the proverbial nature of Genghis Khan as a cultural signifier, one must ask oneself under what conditions did the film's producers think that moviegoers might say, "I know who Genghis Khan is, but he's a lonely orphan, a passionate lover, and a devoted family man, too," as they convinced themselves the film would appeal to a mass audience.

The romanticization of the Genghis Khan figure in the film is not only at odds with the cultural stereotype, it is also at odds with the traditional historical assessment of Genghis Khan's legacy. In turn, this assessment is disputed in a typically incisive passage in *A Thousand Plateaus*, where Deleuze and Guattari devote a chapter to "nomadology" and conceptualize Genghis's conquest as a "war machine," a multifarious "device" that combines nomadism and warfare. Deleuze and Guattari focus on the fact that Genghis Khan's conquest of Asia did not survive as a centralized state. That, according to traditional historians, points to a fundamental failure in Genghis Khan's functioning as a conqueror:

> Sometimes historians . . . follow that negative tradition, and explain that Genghis Khan does not understand anything: he "does not understand" the phenomenon of the state, he "does not understand" the phenomenon of urbanism. That's easy for them to say. It's because the exteriority of the war machine with respect to the State apparatus is visible everywhere, but it is difficult to think about.

It's not enough to say that the war machine is external with respect to the State apparatus. One has to conceptualize the war machine as a pure form of exteriority, while the State apparatus is a form of interiority that we normally use as a model.[7]

While traditional historians see Genghis Khan as a flawed ruler, a failure as the head of a "State apparatus," Deleuze and Guattari claim to see him more appropriately as having realized his potential as a head of a "war machine." A war machine, they postulate, does not lead to state formation, but perpetuates itself. While the opening lines of *The Conqueror* say that Genghis Khan "arose" and "changed the face of the world," the ending depicts Genghis surrounded by innumerable troops. I would suggest that *The Conqueror*'s failure—"lost in a Technicolor cloud of charging horsemen"—derives in part from the nervous appreciation of the fact (rendered quite inescapable by the resources and professionalism of 1950s historical filmmaking) that a war machine glorified by the Western romantic veneer is still a war machine, not a civilizing state- and city-building machine. This point apparently escaped traditional historians both in the East and the West (i.e., on both sides of the Iron Curtain) until Deleuze and Guattari's *mise à point*—making the fact that it escaped *The Conqueror*'s producers less peculiar.

This is not an abstract philosophical or historiographical quibble. The figure of Genghis Khan is a commonplace cultural referent, usually negative. In 1941, Churchill compared German mass executions in Russia to Mongol horde invasions: "There has never [since] been methodical, merciless butchery on such a scale."[8] This "butchery" makes a positive appearance in Hitler's speeches, and the fact that Himmler gave Genghis's biography to all high SS officers as a Christmas present, the more significant.[9] As Richard Breitman shows, Genghis Khan "the state builder" was one of Hitler's frequent references, including in the speech of August 22, 1939, a week before the invasion of Poland: "Our strength is in our quickness and our brutality. Genghis Khan had millions of women and children killed by his own will and with a gay heart. History sees only in him a great state builder." And, as Breitman shows, Hitler's belief in the

---

7 Deleuze and Guattari, *Mille plateaux*, pp. 434-35.

8 Richard Breitman, "Hitler and Genghis Khan," *Journal of Contemporary History* 25 (1990): 337-351, at p. 337. Breitman notes that a popular biography of Genghis Khan appeared in Germany in 1934, "selling 20,000 copies by 1938," followed by translations (Spanish 1953, Dutch 1943), including an English translation that appeared in London in 1940: "writing in 1969 on Genghis Khan's military strategy, a retired United States army colonel praised the English translation of Prawdin's books as the most consistent account available in English" (pp. 339, 349 n.11 and 12).

9 Breitman, "Hitler and Genghis Khan," pp. 340 and 345-46.

mellowing optic of history and his obsession with "Genghis Khan's methods" was concomitant with the loathing of what he perceived as the modern Mongol horde (Russia and the East), manifested in his inclusion in the Final Solution of the "inferior races of Asia," to whom he referred as the "Mongol problem."[10]

The Conqueror discredits its representation of Genghis Khan as the exemplar of "civilized warfare" in that nothing short of divine intervention—a booming voice from the heavens—is necessary to reassure us that all is well in the end, making it painfully clear that we cannot draw this conclusion from the narrative itself. The movie's illogic also explodes when the movie portrays Genghis as an Oriental and a lover. While the main lines of the *Secret History* are maintained, the story of Genghis's romance is a 1950s rape fantasy. The movie begins with Temujin, falcon in hand, and his "blood brother" Jamuga, sweeping upon the caravan including Bortai's husband on horseback and herself reclining on a canopied cart pulled by oxen (here, longhorn cattle). Her decorative yurt (on an even larger cart) brings up the rear. The yurts are quite believable; in a later scene, Temujin cuts out a back door to escape from his yurt, and the camera captures the thickness of the felt. On their first meeting, Temujin and Bortai exchange smoldering looks, and she derides her fiancé, laying the groundwork for her double role as a proud and unwilling captive who secretly loves her abductor, Temujin. She takes turns violently resisting him and yielding to him. This double dealing, which the actors pull off quite admirably, is a translation of marriage practices of Central Asia and twelfth-century Mongol legend of the birth of the nation (*The Secret History*), into the 1950s vernacular of date rape. The most frequently cited lines of dialogue emerge from this fantasy like a symptom: "Dance for me, Tatar woman."

In another oft-cited line, towards the end of *The Conqueror*, Bortai the "wife" shares a moment of identification with "blood brother" and chief councilor Jamuga, by asking: "Why do you love [Genghis] so?" In blatant contrast with the accurate portrayal of the yurt, Bortai is played by the vertiginously curvy Susan Hayward, an Irish American (red hair, pale complexion) shrink-wrapped in Oscar-gala dresses (including one in silver lamé that makes her look like a female Oscar statuette). Jamuga is played by the Mexican heartthrob of the 1940s and 1950s, Pedro Armendáriz. Unlike in a Western, where we suspend our disbelief (viz. John Wayne becomes his character), in *The Conqueror*, a movie whose pleasure consists in the fact that we are not able to suspend our disbelief, Bortai's question to Jamuga proliferates into a number of incompatible, simultaneous strains of thought: why do Irish-American women and Mexican men equally love the tough but fair Wayne, whose real-life reactionary politics must always be bracketed in order to allow the romance of his onscreen Western persona and the queerness of his physique (young Wayne's beautiful girly face)

10 Breitman, "Hitler and Genghis Khan," pp. 337, 341-48.

to emerge? Why do abducted women and adopted brothers love a conqueror? Why does a famous Mexican actor play a Mongol character in a Hollywood movie? Apparently, the syllogism goes like this: Mongol = Oriental = non-white = Mexican celebrity. Why, on the other hand, must both principal actors be white? The casting of Wayne as Genghis displaces another hidden scandal of the movie: the refusal to cast an Asian-American actor as a heroic conqueror in a mega-budget film in 1956. And why is Wayne a conqueror and not, as usual, an underdog or a maverick to the end? The premise of *The Conqueror* is that this conqueror is, in fact, an underdog and a maverick: Genghis is a nomad and an outcast looking for the guy who killed his pa. However, the classic Western scheme is not as obvious to us in the new, unfamiliar setting of Mongolia. We recognize the familiar Western fiction structure, but it is not opaque; rather, it is a see-through device that allows us to glimpse the essential characteristics (Irish-American star, Mexican heartthrob, Wayne as Genghis). This see-through quality defines camp.

While the failure of *The Conqueror* is realized in a wide-ranging field of parodies and dissonances—sexual, racial, ethical, historical—the early, excoriating critiques reserved particular contempt for the script, as the following examples show:

> *Temujin:* There are moments for wisdom, Jamuga, then I listen to you. And there are moments for action, then I listen to my blood. I feel this Tartar woman is for me, and my blood says, "Take her!"

> *Bortai:* The Conqueror? Mighty armies cannot stop him. But one touch of my lips . . . Yes, he captured me—but he cannot tame me.

> *Kumlek (to Temujin):* Joint by joint from the toe and fingertip upward shall you be cut to pieces, and each carrion piece, hour by hour and day by day, shall be cast to the dogs before your very eyes until they too shall be plucked out as morsels for the vultures.

The robust machismo can be ascribed to an attempt at cultural authenticity (portraying barbarians), and yet it is perceived as over-the-top, partly because it blatantly contrasts with the movie's conventions, in their sexy strictness not unlike the Aristotelian rules of Greek tragedy or the *bienséances* of the classical, seventeenth-century French theater. If the sentimental redeeming of rape anchors this mainstream movie squarely in the 1950s, another aspect that dates it with as much accuracy are the images that are not shown: Hayward's naked bosom after she is stripped by her attackers (at the moment when the naked breasts are expected to appear, we see instead the awestruck, leering expressions on the attackers' faces), or Temujin hacking up the Shaman (off camera; the noise of blows indicates a thorough, protracted dismembering).

Another moment where *jouissance* comes at the ready expense of Mongolian *couleur locale* is the turnabout where Temujin/Wayne roughly embraces and kisses Bortai/Hayward and she, finally, unexpectedly, yields. The sequence begins with Wayne, who escapes with Bortai in his arms, wedging himself and her under a ledge over which the enemy riders jump. As the cavalcade ends, Bortai attempts to extricate herself, but then she swings her arm over Temujin's back in a gesture of submission (already anticipated because of the telling looks with which she appraises Temujin's torso; and yet, her loud resistance in a number of scenes was buildup enough that we are shocked). The night scene fades to the glowing constellation of five white dots—Hayward's French manicure on Wayne's back.

Much of the humor of the script derives from this situation: the main character abducts the heroine, alternating between rape and seduction. She fights his advances but, as her throwaway looks and his persistent commentary on her make clear, she wants him. In a crisis, she saves his life—"and for a hundred years, the children of their loins ruled half the world" (closing scene). The combination of rape and dynastic romance, while it is coherent with Freud's classic essay on the subject, "Family Romances of the Neurotics," appears campy when presented as a historical fact rather than as a neurotic fantasy, mythology, or tragedy; in other words, when it is taken out of the sphere of the sacred where it is reserved as forbidden.[11]

Other camp highlights of the film can similarly be understood in terms of the "category mistake" or *mélange* of genres. The failure (or campy humor) attaches to the contrast between authenticity and formula, between a desperate wish to remain straight and the irresistible pull of queer reality, between attention to historical detail and Hollywood mainstays-that-may-not-be-missed: the leading couple's love/hate magnetism, the expert battle scenes. After the fast-paced abduction, the slow-paced celebration in Temujin's camp features a folkloric vocal and instrumental ensemble opening with a doleful tune intended to assuage the spirited abductee. The contrast between the horseback chase and the close-up of the musicians' wide-eyed faces in fur hats, plucking their simple Mongol tune, is killing. It's the fur hats that put us over the edge. Otherwise, a chase followed by a lyric moment around the fire is a stock Western device. Here, the Central Asian desert costumes effect a travesty of stock Western elements, literally and metaphorically. The displacement produces a comic effect. While we are habituated to experience lyric emotions in the original genre (Western),

---

11 Sigmund Freud, "Family Romances," *The Standard Edition of the Complete Psychological Works of Sigmund Freud*, ed. and trans. James Strachey (London: Hogarth, 1953-74), vol. 9, pp. 235-242.

laughter is our response to displacement; it is a defense mechanism. At the same time, we are more likely to laugh because these are stock situations where we expect to be manipulated expertly. Here, the manipulation is impeded, the mood is highjacked by the "winter at the Kremlin/Charlie Chaplin in *The Gold Rush*" fashions, and our laughter is that of someone manipulated too clumsily to yield. It is an indulgent laugh.

I want to emphasize again that the campy effect arises not in the absence of, but in spite of, historical accuracy. Other examples of the use of historical research include Genghis's standard (nine white yak tails arranged in three rows, four, three, and two in descending order), the use of signal arrows (whistling arrows during the day, flaming by night), and others. What also interests me is that the fascination with historical accuracy does not only define the interests of the movie creators, but is an integral part of the current experience of the movie. In that history of reception, the historical accuracy of the movie is validated within frames that are themselves characterized by various degrees of historical accuracy. At the "expert" end, *Strategypage*, a military blog, provides the following review:

> the bows seem to be standard-issue Robin Hood longbows from the studio armory, not the short composite recurved bows Mongol horsemen actually used. We see the use of lances with hooks, to unhorse an opponent, but there is little mounted archery . . . The swords are all wrong: exotic scimitars and Japanese samurai swords that look "Oriental," rather than the practical, slightly curved sabers. . . . The costumes range from utterly whimsical to just about right—metal-studded leather jackets and steel caps with soft fabric flaps to protect the nape of the neck from sun and wind. . . . The film's only concept of Mongol warfare seems to be sudden charges down impossibly steep gravel slopes. To be fair, the sophisticated Mongol tactics of feigned retreat and encirclement would be difficult to capture, even on the wide screen, without costly helicopter shots, and lots of mounted extras. The horses, of course, are too big to be steppe nomad ponies, and they wear Western bridles and saddles.[12]

Given the context, the reference to helicopter shots prompts the remark that aerial photography at the time did not involve helicopters but planes, whose use in film was specifically associated with Howard Hughes.[13] This seems to confirm

---

12 Review by Mike Markowitz, http://www.strategypage.com/moviereviews/default.asp?target=The%20Conqueror, accessed Jan 15, 2006.

13 The first civilian helicopter was licensed in the U.S. in 1946, and helicopters were apparently not used for aerial photography at the time (the first program on helicopter on TV dates to 1957). Helicopters fully displaced plane shots as the main technique of aerial photography in the late 1960s. Howard Hughes, the producer of *The Conqueror,*

one of the theses of this collection—that playing "catch the anachronism" is a symptom of the refusal to acknowledge the present. At the same time, the failure to catch the anachronism (or other form of displacement) can also be a refusal of the present. For instance, signifiers for "Oriental" between 1956 and now remain fluid, even as the difference between Sunni and Shiya is being integrated as the touchstone of expertise (a point famously escaping Britain's Prime Minister, Gordon Brown). The "pan-Oriental," undifferentiated "other" seems impossible to anchor fully in an authentic historical and geographic specificity, and attempts at authenticity only emphasize the general inability to achieve it. One of the places where that fluidity is apparent is the fact that knowledge about Mongolia remains the vanishing point of the reception of *The Conqueror*: one current online blog review of *The Conqueror*, while bemoaning unauthentic casting, describes Genghis's armies as "Arabs." It is as if the critique of the historical accuracy of *The Conqueror* was the touchstone endeavor through which those incapable of accuracy can be identified.

Because *The Conqueror*'s frame of reference is fractured and heterogeneous, we assume that the unfamiliar elements, even if they are in fact culturally accurate, are instead a clumsy attempt at signaling cultural difference through the use of empty signs (Samurai swords instead of curved cavalry sabers)—just as the campy allure of a drag queen resides in the fact that her secondary, ostensible sexual characteristics are at the opposite end of the gender spectrum to her primary, hidden ones. In other words, camp consists of two frames superimposed in a performance that does not merge, but rather exacerbates the differences between them ("see-through"). *The Conqueror* is camp because we always assume that referents are inaccurate, displaced. Since Wayne is miscast as Genghis, we anticipate that the entire movie misrepresents its cultural frame.

A case in point is the scene of divination in Ong Khan's palace, conducted by the Shaman. His method of divination is traditional for the geographical area and period: reading the network of cracks on a roasted shoulder of lamb. When the Shaman announces that is what he is about to do, those of us (myself) without background in Central Asian divination assume that this outrageous detail is a hoax, as inauthentic as Wayne's blue eyes. But, in fact:

> In Late Shang divination as practiced during the reign of Wu-ting (*c.* 1200–1180 BC), cattle scapulae or turtle plastrons, in a refinement of Neolithic practice, were first planed and bored with hollow depressions to which an intense heat

---

was no foe to innovation in the area; he was responsible for the development of aerial photography early on, with *Hell's Angels* (1930). *Society of Camera Operators Magazine*, http://www.soc.org/opcam/08_sps96/mg08_aerial.html.

source was then applied. The resulting T-shaped stress cracks were interpreted as lucky or unlucky.[14]

Our disbelief is nourished by the scene that immediately precedes the culturally accurate Central Asian divination reference: a protracted dance sequence plunging us into 1950s burlesque. The scene features belly dancers in pink, with a solo by the dancer-choreographer Sylvia Lewis clad in strategically placed strips of red fringe, and Bortai/Hayward in a seductive veil dance (she appears to be caressing . . . the veil) followed by her amateurish sword dance (she threatens to kill herself, but concludes by hurling the sword at her audience in a gesture of defiance).

Moreover, the Shaman is none other than John Hoyt, in a marvelous performance as a sinister pervert. Hoyt was a member of Orson Welles's Mercury Theatre, and he was typically typecast as a villain. Famously, in the 1974 sci-fi soft porn movie *Flesh Gordon*, Hoyt played the evil Emperor Wang the Perverted, who shoots his nefarious Sex Ray at the Earth from his planet Porno, causing the entire Earth population to be obsessed with sex. In *The Conqueror*, our intuition that the Shaman is morally perverted, murderous, and double-dealing is first awakened by the nature of his desire: his conspicuous oral fixation. The first inkling of the Shaman's deviation is during the veil dance performed by Bortai/Hayward, when he ignores her bouncing curves and fixates on the cracker he is consuming, a sequence cross-cut with Hayward greedily licking the long veil she uses as a dance prop. This is not so much sexual innuendo as sexual stereotype, and it is reinforced by Hoyt's comical overperformance. Throughout the movie, the direction is exaggerated, camped up, with standout, simple but sure, traditional touches, for instance, the timing of Hoyt's entrance in one of the scenes. The Shaman/Hoyt is spying, and enters the secret meeting much too fast after being called in—an overachievement that his gullible master attributes to his prophetic ability rather than to his eavesdropping at the door. It appears that the Shaman is not only camping it up on his own initiative, but was directed to do so. Apparently the director and others believed that the movie's serious content could withstand a little comic relief. If so, they were greatly mistaken.

While Hoyt's over-the-top performance appears to be directed, his fellow Mercury Theater collaborator (who played the mother of the hero in *Citizen Kane*), Agnes Moorehead skulks around like Igor from *Young Frankenstein* and seems part of the panicked response to the movie's unintentional campiness sensed by the seasoned cast. When Temujin decides to capture Bortai, his mother (Moorehead) upbraids him for consorting with the enemy, a task in which she is asked to persevere through the remainder of the script. Moorehead

---

14 *Encyclopedia Britannica*, "Late Shang divination and religion."

is a fantastic addition to the comic high of *The Conqueror*. Her petite frame (next to Wayne, who was 6 feet 4), her pasted-on scowl, and her folkloric outfit, complete with a head scarf, are a foil to Bortai's glamorous gowns, seemingly spray-painted onto the pointy "twin peaks" foundation of her 1950s brassiere. The authentic costume and the scowl set off both Hoelun/Moorehead's drag and that of Bortai/Hayward. Caught in that dynamic, Moorehead's character becomes frozen, stock, caricatural—an effect forwarded by comic repetition. Each time Wayne rides his horse into his home camp after a blood-rousing skirmish, he mutters "Greetings, Mother," and a scowling Moorehead appears:

> *Hoelun*: She will bring woe to you and your people, my son! A woman made wife against her will, can be a dangerous foe!
> . . . .
> *Hoelun*: My son has won the world. Still he must conquer that redheaded Jezebel.

Here, Moorehead plays the kind of female role that turned her into a lesbian icon, and which runs the gamut from tragically unloved schemer who ruins everybody's chance at happiness in Welles's *The Magnificent Ambersons* (for which she received the New York Film Critics Circle Award for Best Actress and an Oscar nomination in 1942), to flamboyantly attired, strong-willed, "older witch" on the TV show *Bewitched*, her famous contribution to pop culture as Samantha's mother. It is but one small step in the unusually long career of this fine actress, but in terms of the camp potential of any single movie, what could be more satisfying than *The Conqueror* with John Hoyt as Effete Devil and Agnes Moorehead as Older Witch?

I want to suggest that *The Conqueror's* camp potential relies on a combination of several factors. The first is the script's fidelity to the stock epic elements of *The Secret History*'s narrative of the origins of Mongol nation, a narrative whose relationship to historical truth is probably as direct as in the case of Homer, Virgil, or Wace. The fictional character of the nation-building legend is compounded by the fact that historical details provide no pleasure of recognition for the Western audience. Another element is the juxtaposition of Hollywood conventions for love story and historical movie, for instance, in the mutually amplifying effect of Bortai/Hayward's glamorous 1950s gowns and Hoenlun/Moorehead's folkloric garb. The stylistic conventions of the script, including florid metaphors, archaisms, unflinching reference to bodily functions, understatement, parataxis, simplified grammar that's supposed to suggest the origins of time, seal the fate of the film as an unintentional parody.

The Irresistible Pull of Camp: Queering Genres, Category Mistakes, and Saïd's *Orientalism*

The Conqueror was destined to be a camp classic rather than a successful straight movie. What fascinates me is the fact that this shift into camp was already noted in the initial moment of cultural consumption of the movie in 1956, although it was amplified later as a result of changes that directly affected the fantasy of the movie (postcolonialism, women's rights, globalism with its attendant increase in actual knowledge of others). Camp's takeover of *The Conqueror* was first noted by the movie's reviewers and even earlier, in the performance by the actors themselves, who famously undermined the project (both in the main and in the [un]supporting roles). In spite of its $6,000,000 budget (impressive for the time and providing for unlimited crowded horseback battle scenes), queering the genre of Western by making it Oriental results in camp, as if queering a genre necessarily results in exposing the fiction of heterosexual orthodoxy. This example could be aligned with Tison Pugh's proposition that queering genres is tantamount to queering gender and sexuality.[15] As in Pugh's analysis where cross-contamination between genres allows the expression of sexual fantasies that are unorthodox and do not fit the heteronormative ideal, making an Eastern Western results in the representation of unorthodox desires and subject positions. In Pugh's examples, queering the genre provides agency, in the form of discourse and narrative, for sexually queer subjects embodied by characters in the story, such as the Wife of Bath who queers heterosexual marriage, or the Green Knight who queers chivalric masculinity. In *The Conqueror*, we witness a similar effect. When the towering, blue-eyed Wayne fails to convince as Genghis, *The Conqueror* consequently fails to convince as a fiction of justified violence. The realization of the absurdity of the movie's premise is greatly aided by the fact that the plot also features rape and kidnapping as a means to love and marriage. As a quick comparison with the *Secret History* shows, rape is supposed to translate historical authenticity in *The Conqueror*, but only reveals sexual fantasies of the 1950s.

In a Western, good and evil are grounded in national politics, but an Oriental Western makes the flimsiness of that grounding palpable. The genre of the Western allows viewers to abandon the stifling atmosphere of the bourgeois living room for the open prairie, and ends with the ride into the sunset instead of the disappointing conclusion (death or matrimony) of a bourgeois comedy of manners, deflating all attempts at heroism by miring the characters in everyday mediocrity. The Western is never everyday. It is a heroic fantasy genre that everyday bourgeois existence needs and therefore allows. The Western is situated, metaphorically and literally, at the outer borders of the bourgeois

---

15 Tison Pugh, *Queering Medieval Genres* (New York: Palgrave Macmillan, 2004).

"nation," and its heroes are allowed mobility because they patrol the borders (U.S. and white vs. Native, good vs. evil, peacefully settled and agrarian vs. nomadic, violent, armed). Moving the Western to a different context seems like a logical enough move—an "us vs. them" mentality seems easy enough to recreate anywhere—but it turns out that the move then allows for an objective stance that reveals the artificial character of the "us vs. them" relation. As a result, rather than reinforce the structures of the Western, the Eastern Western discredits them.

The functioning of a Western, a "roaming adventure," resembles the functioning of the Oriental novel, as described by Edward Saïd. The world of the Oriental novel, such as Rudyard Kipling's *Kim*, is:

> very different . . . from the dull, mediocre and lusterless world of the European bourgeoisie . . . Hence the antithesis offered by Kipling's fiction: his world, because it is set in an India dominated by Britain, appears to hold nothing back from the expatriate European. *Kim,* therefore, is expressly designed as a novel to show how a white sahib can enjoy himself in this lush complexity; and, I would argue, the apparent absence of resistance to European intervention in it . . . is due precisely to the imperialist vision of the world.[16]

Kipling himself reveals the mechanism denounced by Saïd when, in one of his private letters, he refuses to leave India for the more competitive literary scene of London:

> My home's out here. . . . Any fool can put up rhymes and the market is full of boys who could undersell me as soon as I put foot in it. . . . [O]ut here one lives and writes more in the centre of history with one's hands on everything than in a land where by reason of its hugeness every one is on the outskirts of everything; watching ministers, policies and financiers from afar.[17]

Just as for the British the possibility of exotic adventure was geographically located in the British colonies and its fiction was the Oriental novel, North Americans located that adventure in the encounter with the "West," and its fiction was the Western and *The Little House on the Prairie*.[18] But a move from the West to the East in the setting of a Western brings to the forefront the irreducible conflicts that are erased under the Western contract and replaced

---

16 Edward Saïd, "*Kim* as Imperialist Novel," introduction to Rudyard Kipling, *Kim,* ed. Edward Saïd (Harmondsworth: Penguin, 1987), p. 43.

17 Letter to E. Robinson, 30 April 1886, in Rudyard Kipling, *Kim,* ed. Zohreh Sullivan (New York: Norton, 2002), p. 270.

18 Laura Ingalls Wilder, *Little House on the Prairie* (New York: Harper, 1935).

by white/North American fantasy. As an "Eastern Western," *The Conqueror* precipitates the unasked question of legitimacy (of sex, violence, execution, war, invasion, imperialism), most visibly because the racial white *fails* to impersonate Genghis.

I also want to suggest that this nervousness concerning these irreducible conflicts is displaced onto the legend of *The Conqueror*. Generations of viewers have created a substantial legend that extends the comedy and pathos of *The Conqueror* in several directions. One of the most persistent stories is that the nuclear fallout present at the filming site caused a high rate of cancer deaths among the cast. Wayne supposedly carried a Geiger counter during the shooting, while Agnes Moorehead and other actors are said to have linked the film to their illnesses. While the link is under dispute (while staggering, the rates of cancer for that cast may not be higher than the average at the time, a high level linked to the use of tobacco and alcohol), the story itself is like a symptom, a visible mark of a hidden malaise: an autoimmune disorder related to military nuclear testing conducted near the site where the movie was made. Another element tied to the movie's camp status is the history of its release, specifically the acquisition of the film by its producer, Howard Hughes, a Citizen Kane-like tragic hero, Wells's sponsor, and denizen of bad taste. Hughes bought the rights to the movie (and, story has it, all the existing copies) when he sold his production company, RKO Radio Pictures, in 1957. Hughes never released *The Conqueror* until 1974 (but he reputedly often screened the movie in his private theater for his own gratification). As a result, the film was not in wide release for twenty years, a fact that helped it acquire a cultish cachet. What can be simply explained as a business decision (the movie, initially unsuccessful, was not expected to bring revenue), generated more complex and novel-like explanations: supposedly, Hughes felt implicated in the cancer deaths, or constantly viewed the movie privately.

My own fantasy concerning this particular story is that Hughes bought out the copies of the movie because he didn't want his fetish exposed to public ridicule, to avoid the fate of the protagonist in Welles's *Citizen Kane*, who neurotically enacts his fantasies by forcing his mistress to perform as an opera star in spite of the evidence that she's just an ordinary girl. *The Conqueror* plunged into a farce. That humiliation can only be released or recuperated as camp, a result of our shifting between two frames and anticipating that referents are cut from their matrix of origin and grafted onto a competing, unfamiliar one. Camp in *The Conqueror* extends in many directions: political (the Cold War), racial (Mexican and Native American actors and extras, and Wayne's redesigned eyebrows, representing Asia), sexual (the brutal treatment and objectification of the female lead in the film, framed as one of the defining characteristics of Asia and nomadism), and colonial (the "Eastern Western" fantasy). The camp reading, the only one possible today, is the response to cultural failure, especially because the values and structures inscribed by the movie are condemned by a new social consensus.

Thus, the camp reading of *The Conqueror* is the only reading possible. And, actually, it is almost the only reading of *The Conqueror* performed and relished by today's viewers, alongside the "historical accuracy" viewing, whose vicissitudes I hope to have demonstrated earlier. Is not the double option of viewing *The Conqueror* a figure of our own relationship to the Middle Ages? Some of us caught up in examining facts (eternally, delightfully, but also pathetically unable to get them all right), others camping in the space they digest. Affirming the meaning of camp as "political opposition," Moe Meyer argues for reaffirming the power of camp as a political movement, thereby denouncing and counteracting the appropriation of the term *camp* to describe a purely aesthetic concept, which he detected in Susan Sontag's well-known essay on camp.[19] I argue that the camp reading is the response to the initial multiple impossibility of the *The Conqueror* as an Eastern Western, too uncomfortable not only today, but already in 1956, to be explored in terms other than camp. Similar to the campy cult of *The Conqueror*, other forms of camp (drag, macho camp) respond to the cultural failure of gender normativity and the oppressive regime of sexual, erotic, affective, and gender simulacra. Camp digests social malfunction and makes it palatable. Its subversive movement reclaims what is otherwise a cultural breakdown.

To emphasize the political importance of camp, I want to point out that the "category panic" experienced by the conservative elements of American society *vis à vis* gay culture, especially drag, transvestism, and transgendering (and perhaps also the unease experienced by some gay constituencies *vis à vis* bisexuality, effeminacy, femmes, or passivity), is often expressed in terms of concern for shifting boundaries. This "category panic" typically uses a biopolitical argument: gay marriage is a threat to the family, and as such should be disallowed by the state. Casting the opposition to gay marriage as the fight for the nation's fertility is precisely the operation that Giorgio Agamben denounces in his work: it is an illegitimate intervention, predicated on the structure of unlimited biopolitics. There are no bodies that are not biopolitical—only banned ones.[20] As Agamben shows *contra* Foucault, Western democracy is always already a biopolitics. (Foucault traces the origins of modernity and biopolitics to the French revolution.) The work of *Homo Sacer* is to denounce the deadly alternative between biopolitics and banishment that, as Agamben contends, is not modern but always inherent in Western democracy inasmuch as it is always already based on the Aristotelian distinction between *zoe* (bare life) and *bios*

---

19 Moe Meyer, "Introduction: Reclaiming the Discourse of Camp," *The Politics and Poetics of Camp*, ed. Moe Meyer (London: Routledge, 1994), pp. 1-22.

20 Giorgio Agamben, *Homo Sacer: Sovereign Power and Bare Life*, trans. Daniel Heller-Roazen (Stanford: Stanford UP, 1998).

(qualified, political life). It is on that level that I can best explain the positive operation of queer camp. Queer camp does not establish a non-biopolitical zone; on the contrary, as Myers insists, camp is political. However, camp's functioning is a powerful alternative to biopolitics because it does not replicate, but rather it restages, reposesses, and reinterprets the "bio" of the biopolitical. It is not excepted from biopolitics, it does not elude, but it perverts the rules. Queer camp is a productive, optimistic recuperation and expansion of gender performances and cultural artifacts.

When I say that camp is an optimistic and productive alternative to disgust, I evoke the possibility that Žižek also notes when he contends that carnival is not always liberating but can be the most horrible ethical fiasco, in the context of Mikhail Bakhtin's work on carnivalesque reversal. Žižek mentions Boris Groys's research implying that Bakhtin himself was well aware of that double possibility, and that his work on carnival was related to the horror of Stalinist purges as a form of carnival, "the world inside out" ("today you are on the Central Committee, tomorrow . . .").[21] According to Žižek, the work of ethics must be conducted on two levels as dictated by both the written rules and the obscene rules that become operative in the episodic space of the carnival. Žižek points out that the written rules of what is acceptable are changing (the U.S. policy defying the Geneva Convention on torture) as well as the unwritten ones. If we have to argue against torture, we have lost ethical ground, if not the battle; just as the battle would have been lost if we had to argue against racism. It seems to me that Žižek's position on "discipline" is campy in the sense that Žižek emphasizes the need to maintain boundaries and that he denounces the rhetoric of *"lignes de fuite"* in Michael Hardt and Antonio Negri, and Agamben's "playing with the law."[22] According to its common definitions, queer camp is a strategy that paradoxically both unlocks and maintains boundaries, and it is in that sense a suitable answer to Žižek's call for discipline.

---

21 Žižek, interview with *Soft Targets*, March 14, 2007, http://www.softtargetsjournal. com/web/Žižek.html; on the violence of carnivalesque reversals overlooked by Bakhtinian criticism, see Žižek, *Metastases of Enjoyment* (London: Verso, 1994), p. 55.

22 Michael Hardt and Antonio Negri, *Empire* (Cambridge, MA: Harvard UP, 2000) and their *Multitude: War and Democracy in the Age of Empire* (New York: Penguin, 2004).

Chapter 6
"In my own idiom":
Social Critique, Campy Gender, and Queer Performance in *Monty Python and the Holy Grail*

Susan Aronstein

Monty Python's send-up of 900 years of British history in *Monty Python and the Holy Grail* (1975) has been widely recognized as a masterpiece of parody and pastiche—a film that merrily takes apart everything from Malory and Tennyson to Bergman and *Camelot*; however, very little of this discussion takes into account the film's treatment of gender and what does tends to focus on "The Tale of Sir Lancelot" as an isolated instance of gender confusion.[1] In many ways this is not surprising; the Pythons' desire to question conventions of narrative, history, and authority does not seem to extend to the conventions of gender and heteronormativity. Indeed, the troupe's portrayal of women and homosexuality rarely breaks free of conservative clichés and prurient winks. As Marcia Landy observes: "the Pythons' caricatures of femininity, heterosexuality and homosexuality are not congenial to supporters of identity politics; they do not present desirable and affirmative gendered images to emulate." Yet she also argues that "gender reversal in the *Flying Circus* is parallel to the series' practice of inverting all roles involving social class and national and generational identities."[2] This seeming contradiction in Landy's argument identifies a strange

---

1 *Monty Python and the Holy Grail,* dir. Terry Gilliam and Terry Jones, perf. Graham Chapman, John Cleese, Terry Gilliam, Eric Idle, Terry Jones, and Michael Palin, DVD (1975; Culver City, CA: Tri-Star Home Entertainment, 2001). Explorations of gender and sexuality in "The Tale of Sir Lancelot" include Donald Hoffman, "Not Dead Yet: *Monty Python and the Holy Grail* in the Twenty-First Century," *Cinema Arthuriana*, rev. edn., ed. Kevin Harty (Jefferson, NC: McFarland, 2002), pp. 136-48 and Kevin J. Harty, "The Damsel 'in Dis Dress:' Gender Bending in the Arthuriad," *Arthuriana* 14.1 (2004): 79-82.

2 Marcia Landy, *Monty Python's Flying Circus* (Detroit, MI: Wayne State UP, 2005), pp. 79 and 71.

blind spot in the Pythons' comic project: an investment in traditional gender roles that persists in spite of its own recognition that all other identities are constructed performances. However, both the troupe's radical social agenda and its characteristic use of cross-dressing, parody and camp—which imbues its gender depictions with the queer potential to deconstruct gender through its excessive enactment—undermine this investment.

On the surface, *The Holy Grail's* gender-politics are standard Python fare: comic cross-dressing, lascivious sex objects, and school-boy sniggers. However, since it is a feature-length film rather than a series of sketches, the narrative's sustained critique of the entire British political and social system questions these politics. As *The Holy Grail* attacks British myths of national identity, monarchy, class, and government at the moment of their supposed origin, depicting aristocratic and royal identity as performance-based constructs and arguing that "idiom" creates the knight, it asks its audience to reconsider the categories of "universal" and "innate." The Pythons cannot have it both ways: by calling into question the notion of natural and stable social identity, they—whether they intend to or not—also suggest that gender, male and female, is no less a queer performance.

This chapter examines the Pythons' investment in and unwitting destabilization of traditional gender roles in *Monty Python and the Holy Grail* by placing the film in the context of both *Monty Python's Flying Circus* and the British political and social debates that frame the "Monty Python Years" (1969-1975). It begins with a brief examination of these debates and *Flying Circus's* participation in them; it then looks at standard Python gender politics in both *Flying Circus* and *Holy Grail*: static and misogynist images of women, violent hypermasculinity, and the use of a sniggering, adolescent destabilization of gender to head off homosexual panic. The chapter concludes with a re-reading of gender and queer performance in *The Holy Grail* in light of the film's anti-medievalism, which participates in Britain's heated discussion of monarchy and its discontents—a discussion that stems directly from the larger social and political upheavals that took place during what Tom Nairn has called "the break-up of Britain."[3]

Crisis and Comedy: The Python Years

This "break-up of Britain" in the late 1960s responded to a series of economic and social crises that began in the late 1950s.[4] In 1959, the Tories, campaigning

---

3 Tom Nairn, *The Break-Up of Britain* (London: Schocken, 1982).

4 See Nairn, *The Break-Up of Britain*; John Seed, "Hegemony Postponed: The Unraveling of the Culture of Consensus in Britain in the 1960s," *Cultural Revolution?*

on a platform that depicted the nation as a land of the "haves and the have mores," won the general election. However, by 1960, the poverty rate stood at 14%—nearly double that of the early 1950s—and a balance of payment crisis in 1961 (which resulted in pay freezes and spending cuts) accompanied by the rejection of the country's common market application in 1963, cost the Tories, as John Seed observes, "a significant part" of "an electoral appeal" tied to an "association with national greatness." In addition, a sense of social decay (divorce, illegitimacy, latch-key children, and rising crime) combined with a series of scandals, epitomized by the Profumo affair, undermined the Tories' traditional role as a "guarantor of moral order."[5] Economic, global, and social crises combined in 1964 to lead to a regime change. Running on a platform of modernization and progress, Harold Wilson blasted the forces of privilege and tradition that, he argued, had led to global and domestic disarray. "We are living in a jet-age but we are governed by an Edwardian establishment mentality," he claimed as he launched his campaign, "They cling to privilege and power for the few, shutting the gates on the many. Tory society is a CLOSED society, in which birth and wealth have priority, in which the master-and-servant, landlord-and-tenant mentality prevails."[6] Wilson's call to a new, modern nation echoed a spate of books analyzing the "national crisis" that, as John Seed observes, "pointed to outdated attitudes, especially towards social class, British backwardness, traditionalism (and) parochialism" as the root of the nation's woes.[7]

The electorate responded to Wilson's vision of a brave new world. Labour won by a slight margin in 1964 and a landslide in 1966. Economics, however, doomed Wilson's national optimism. In 1967, the government was forced to devalue the pound; by the end of that year, unemployment had doubled, the government was given the right to delay wage increases, and inflation and workers' strikes were on the rise—all, as Alfred Havighurst points out, "a clarion call to a reduced standard of living."[8] Furthermore, a diminishment in Britain's global status accompanied these economic woes. The nation withdrew from colonies, reduced the military, and reoriented from the United Nations to

---

The Challenge of the Arts in the 1960s, eds. Bart Moore-Gilbert and John Seed (New York: Routledge, 1992), pp. 15-44; Alfred Havighurst, Britian in Transition: The Twentieth Century (Chicago: U of Chicago P, 1979); Ron Ramdin The Making of the Black Working Class in Britain (Aldershot: Gower, 1987); and Patrick Dunleavyt, The Politics of Mass Housing in Britain, 1945-1975: A Study of Corporate Power and Professional Influence in the Welfare State (Oxford: Clarendon, 1981).

5 Seed, "Hegemony," p. 18.

6 Qtd. in Seed, "Hegemony," p. 30.

7 Seed, "Hegemony," p. 19.

8 Havighurst, Britain in Transition, p. 529.

NATO, changes that, in the words of defense secretary Dennis Healy, "set the seal on Britain's transformation from a world power to a European power."[9]

Britain's domestic make-up was also changing, particularly in its urban centers. Beginning in the late 1950s, black commonwealth immigrants from the British West Indies arrived in search of work and economic opportunity. Instead, the newcomers were economically exploited by both their landlords—who, as Ron Ramdin writes, "corralled [them] into bad housing in neglected patches of London . . . [with] conditions [that] deteriorated and rents [that] increased"—and their employers, who paid poverty wages for the menial jobs that white workers did not want.[10] In spite of the fact that black immigrants posed no threat to the white economic base, their presence alarmed a significant fraction of the native British population. Unlike the Polish immigrants who proceeded them, the West Indians were immediately visible and, as early as 1958, became the target of racial violence; their presence also triggered calls for immigration control—a technically difficult issue because, as members of the Commonwealth, West Indians held British passports. Nevertheless, a series of legislative acts moved to limit immigration even as the Labour government passed rather ineffective "race acts" to discourage discrimination. When Enoch Powell delivered his infamous "Rivers of Blood" speech in 1968, envisioning an England in which white men were "strangers in their own country," it met with the approval of three out of four people; and when, in 1970, he called to repatriate the immigrants to their country of origin, he was met with popular, if not official, support.

This time of "rapidly accelerating backwardness, economic stagnation, social decay and cultural despair" resulted, as Bart Moore-Gilbert and John Seed argue, in "the emergence of . . . self-confident and articulate 'sub-cultures,'" whose explorations of "polarization and fragmentation" characterized British art and culture in the late 1960s and 1970s.[11] The group of novelists, playwrights, and directors collectively known as "the Angry Young Men" (John Osbourne and Kingsley Amis, among others) critiqued the nation's political and social institutions. British film directors (such as John Boorman and Lindsay Anderson) exposed a hypocritical establishment and a barren society. Tom Stoppard argued that sense was nonsense; and the group that David Frost calls the "Exasperated Young Men" brought explosive comedy to such programs as *That Was the Week That Was* and *The 1948 Show*, which provided the individual Pythons with apprenticeships in which they honed and developed their comedic talent.

---

9 Qtd. in Havighurst, *Britain in Transition*, p. 524.

10 Ramdin, *The Making of the Black Working Class*, p. 193.

11 Bart Moore-Gilbert quoting Tom Nairn, "Introduction," *The Arts in the 1970s* (New York: Routledge, 1994), 1-28, at pp. 1, 6, 10.

This is the Britain in which *Monty Python's Flying Circus* premiered on the BBC on October 5, 1969—a country that had already endured a decade of economic, political, and cultural instability, resulting in an increasingly fragmented society that questioned traditional myths about class, privilege, and authority. At the same time, those who were heirs to these traditions fought to resuscitate the myths and retain their prerogatives. These debates—and the instabilities that occasioned them—intensified during the next six "Python" years (the final program of *Flying Circus* aired on December 5 1974; *The Holy Grail* opened in London on April 3, 1975). The economy continued its downward spiral into the worst recession since World War II, unemployment—especially among the young—skyrocketed, and nationalism and racial tensions spun into violence.

Monty Python's Flying Circus participates directly in the struggle between the establishment and the voices of dissent for control of the narrative of British identity. The troupe takes on traditional myths about family, sex, religion, monarchy, the military, middle-class life, medicine, nationalism, and class, as well as the vehicles—literature, film, and television—that transmitted those myths to the people, consistently demonstrating that "the most serious ideas can be subverted by the absurd."[12] The troupe's trademark camp performances combined with its use of postmodern techniques—pastiche, self-reflexiveness, abandonment of narrative continuity and closure—tear both social and narrative conventions apart, calling its audiences' attention to the fact that all narratives, from genres to political and social discourses, are merely constructs.

Colossal Bimbos and Fairy Brigades: Gender in the Python World

However, there is, as I observed earlier, a strange blind spot in the Pythons' deconstruction of "anything and everything," a blind spot that the excruciatingly awful frame to the DVD, *John Cleese's Personal Best*, calls attention to. A woman reporter asks Cleese to respond to criticism of the troupe's portrayal of women "as sex symbols or half-crazed housewives who screech a lot."[13] An irascible

12 Eric Idle, qtd. in Robert Hewison, *Irreverence, Scurrility, Profanity, Vilification and Licentious Abuse: The Case against Monty Python* (New York: Grove, 1981), p. 14. Other discussions of the Python's techniques and history can be found in Landy, *Flying Circus*; Moore-Gilbert, *The Arts in the Seventies*, pp. 176 97; George Perry, *Life of Python* (Boston: Little, Brown, 1983); and John Cleese, Terry Gilliam, Michael Palin, Eric Idle, Terry Jones, and the Estate of Graham Chapman, *The Pythons: Autobiography by the Pythons* (New York: St. Martin's, 2003).

13 *The Personal Best of Monty Python's Flying Circus*, perf. Graham Chapman, John Cleese, Terry Gilliam, Eric Idle, Terry Jones, and Michael Palin, 6 DVD boxed-set (Arts and Entertainment Television, 2006).

Cleese replies "Fair point. But you see that has been my experience in real life. All women are either rather repulsive old bags or colossal bimbos." While Cleese (who wrote the frame) is clearly trying to be funny here—as he is in the segments which comment on the Pythons' violence ("Well, life is violent, you see; it's simply all around us. You can't escape it") and anti-Semitism ("Michael Palin is Jewish. He just hasn't come out yet")—both the frame and the re-packaged sketches work to confirm Cleese's (and *Flying Circus*'s) definition of women as either sex-pot bimbos or dim housewives.

Real (as opposed to cross-dressed) women in the Python world are consistently presented as "sex-pot bimbos," a role that was usually played by Carol Cleveland, who has been identified as the unacknowledged "seventh Python." Cleese tellingly comments, "Whenever we wanted someone who was a real woman, in the sense that she was female and attractive, we asked Carol to do it."[14] During the *Flying Circus* years, Cleveland played—often in various states of undress— ladies of the manor, nurses, wives, girlfriends, and, most commonly, seductresses ("The Spanish Inquisition," "Seduced Milkman," and "Travel Agent," among many others). Cleveland's on-screen roles, combined with the series' pervasive school-boy attitude towards women and sexuality ("nudge, nudge, wink, wink"), defines young and attractive women as disruptive and confusing objects of desire, often teasingly directing the male gaze to the "naughty bits" ("Full Frontal Nudity" and "How to Recognize Different Parts of the Body"). Since "real women" are identified by their sexual attractiveness, the "repulsive old bags" are mainly portrayed by the various male members of the Python troupe. Over the years, *Flying Circus* introduced a wide array of frumpy and clueless housewives (e.g. "Mrs. Sartre," "The Pepperpots," and "Mrs. Premise and Mrs. Conclusion"), who functioned as a satire on British middle-class mores and customs even as they reified misogynist clichés.

In some ways, men fare little better in the *Flying Circus*'s world, particularly those (usually played with over-the-top relish by John Cleese) who represent a hypermasculine establishment, such as the self-defense instructor who teaches a hapless class to defend itself against fresh fruit, "killing" most of them in the process. Yet women in this world are denied even the possibility of gender transgression. The one sketch, "The Adventures of Mystic and Janet," that allows Carol Cleveland to function as a doctorate-holding secret agent dresses and poses her as a chorus-girl throughout. However, the same gender blindness that reduces women to sex-pots and old bags also operates in the series' barely disguised homosexual panic—a panic illustrated by the odd silence that surrounds Graham Chapman's openly gay sexuality. In *Flying Circus*'s explorations of male gender-bending—"Poof Judges," in which two judges disrobe to reveal sexy lingerie; "The Military Fairy Brigade," in which a military drill morphs into a

---

14 Landy, *Flying Circus*, p. 14.

ballet recital; "Scotsman on a Horse," in which the rider disrupts a wedding and carries off the groom; and, most famously, "I'm a Lumberjack," in which a tree-cutting manly man reveals his penchant for dressing up in women's clothing—the Pythons come close to a radical critique of gender and, however unwittingly, open Pandora's (or Judith Butler's) box. Each of these sketches suggests that masculine identity is a performance, one that may well, as do the judges' robes and the lumberjack's manly flannel shirt, cover up a feminine one wearing bustier and fishnets, or suspenders and a bra, and given to beauty shop gossip and pressing wildflowers. Yet, in all of these instances, the sketches attempt to shut down the radical possibilities in this suggestion, using the excessive camp of the performances to play into the homophobic stereotypes of the "poof" and the "fairy" and, in the case of the shopping and scone-eating lumberjack, linking his gender confusion to the repressed murderous inclinations of the unhappy barber whose fantasy this is. These sketches also serve to head off homosexual panic and valorize heteronormativity by confining homosexuality to the stereotype of the effeminate male, an identity that is bound to "come out."

When the Pythons turned to the Middle Ages in *Monty Python and the Holy Grail*, they carried these conservative views on women and homosexuality into the past, and, on the surface, *The Holy Grail*'s gender politics seem to be the sole depiction in the film that functions traditionally as medievalism, using the past to naturalize and universalize contemporary ideologies. Medieval and modern stereotypes meet in the film's women. Carol Cleveland, reprising her fixed role in *Flying Circus*, plays the seductress in a scene that is indebted to Bors's adventures in Malory. Sir Galahad the Chaste (Michael Palin) stumbles onto the Castle Anthrax, where "naughty Sister Zoot" has lit the Grail beacon to lure unsuspecting knights into her trap: "eight score young blondes and brunettes all between age sixteen and nineteen and a half . . . bathing, dressing, undressing, making exciting underwear." Cleveland's portrayal of Zoot (and her twin sister Dingo) wallows in hyperfemininity—high, ditzy voice, fluttering gestures, batting eyelashes—as the narrative reinforces the view of women as sex-pots, all of whom desire "a spanking" and its more graphic aftermath. It also comically warns against the dangers of female sexuality as Sir Galahad capitulates to their request—"I suppose I could stay a little longer"—and has to be rescued, protesting, by Lancelot (John Cleese), barely escaping a fate worse than death.

Zoot/Dingo plays into the misogynist stereotypes developed and deployed in *Flying Circus*, as does Dennis's mother, one of the *Circus*'s cross-dressed "dimwitted" housewives (Terry Jones) transported to the medieval past. Like them, she is obsessed with the mundane and the ludicrous ("there's lovely filth down here") and comically clueless about the social and political structure in which she lives ("Who are the Britons?"); furthermore, her non-reaction to Dennis's beating echoes countless *Circus* housewives' catatonic and indifferent responses to violence (for example, Mrs. Premise's and Mrs. Conclusion's Laundromat chat on the killing and disposal of pets and the unfazed audience of "Exploding Penguins on a T.V. Set").

Similarly, much of *The Holy Grail*'s sniggering homophobia transfers *Flying Circus*'s contemporary anxieties into the medieval past. "The Knights of the Round Table," "The Tale of Sir Robin," and the portrayal of Herbert/Alice in "The Tale of Sir Lancelot" all derive from the *Flying Circus*'s exploration of masculine cross-gendered behavior in sketches such as "The Military Fairy Brigade" and "The Lumberjack Song." In "Knights of the Round Table," King Arthur and his knights spy Camelot in the distance; Arthur suggests that they all ride to "their new home" and, using the same technique as "Fairy Brigade," the film cuts to a Broadway chorus singing and dancing the can-can, as opposed to the manly knights practicing their jousting and sword play that we might expect. "We're Knights of the Round Table," the chorus proclaims "we dance whene'er were able. We do routines and chorus scenes with footwork impeccable." These knights, as does the Lumberjack, juxtapose manly behavior ("in war we're tough and able") with gender-bending hobbies ("we're opera-mad in Camelot" "between our quests, we sequin vests / and impersonate Clark Gable"), concluding "it's a busy life in Camelot" because "I have to push the pram a lot." This number, which associates Camelot's resident knights with gay stereotypes and feminized behavior at the same time as it deconstructs the conventions of the Broadway musical (specifically Lerner and Loewe's *Camelot*), presents a masculinity that Arthur and his new knights immediately reject: "On second thought, let's not go to Camelot. It's a silly place."

Sir Robin (Eric Idle) and Herbert/Alice (Terry Jones) seem to reinforce this rejection of "silly" cross-gendered conduct. The representation of these characters echo—on the surface anyway—the sniggering homophobia of many of *Flying Circus*'s sketches. Sir Robin's non-adventures begin as he, with long locks flowing, prances "through the dark forest of Ewing, accompanied by his favorite minstrels." Robin's association with music immediately identifies him with the singing and dancing knights left behind at Camelot, casting further doubt on his masculinity, and his comic rejection of his Arthurian identity in the face of danger confirms this doubt: "Nobody, really. I'm just passing through," he stutters as he confronts the Three-Headed Knight. His final act—"he bravely turned his tail and fled"—confines unseemly behavior and cowardice safely within the stereotype of the effeminate male. As we later see, Arthur and the other knights gamely press forward when challenged by the Knights Who Say Ni.

"The Tale of Sir Lancelot" also ridicules effeminate behavior; Herbert's misrecognition of Lancelot as his knight in shining armor is an occasion for a comic hilarity that attempts to shut down any such possibility. The tale opens with the whiny, music-loving Prince Herbert—almost cross-dressed in a flowing white tunic and golden coronet—protesting his marriage to a girl with "huge . . . tracts of land." "I want the girl that I marry to have a certain special something," he intones as the music swells and the putative groom prepares to launch into song. His father (Michael Palin), unimpressed by his son's addiction to music and romantic narrative, cuts both the song and the narrative short and lays down the law: "Look, you're marrying the Princess Lucky, so you'd better get used to the idea." The gender-reversal in this scene—the plight of the boy in the tower—transforms melodrama into comedy. When Lancelot, responding to Herbert's plea for help—"I have been imprisoned by my father who wishes me to marry against my will. Please, please, please come and rescue me. I am in the tall tower of Swamp Castle"—belatedly realizes that his "fair one" is not a damsel in distress, he breaks off mid-sentence, "Oh I'm terribly sorry." Herbert, on the other hand, is undeterred by the gender-bending and its implications: "You've come to rescue me. I knew someone would; I knew that somewhere out there, there must be someone who . . ." and prepares to sing as the orchestra strikes up. Herbert's love ballad is cut short, first by his non-musical father and, then, by Lancelot who suggests that they "not jump to conclusions" that the film suggests are as impossible as they are hilarious.

The Violence Inherent in the System: Gender and Anti-Medievalism in the Holy Grail

In the scenes that I have discussed, *The Holy Grail* seems to have translated the Pythons' apparent investment in traditional gender roles to the medieval past. However, as in *The Flying Circus*, the troupe's camp performances of gender—its hyper-enactment—has the potential to undermine its own gender politics. In the case of *The Holy Grail*, the film's narrative agenda, which (as I have argued elsewhere) uses an anti-medievalism to expose the "ideal Middle Ages" and their chivalric-feudal utopia as ludicrous constructs seeking to secure acquiescent subjects and not above resorting to violence when discourse fails, realizes this potential.[15]

The Holy Grail takes on a series of myths central to the rhetoric of British national identity, such as the appropriation of Arthur for the line of English kings, the fantasy of insular union, and the valorization of monarchy and class inherent in a neo-feudal society. The film thus enters into a debate about Britain and its monarchy that (tied as it was to larger issues of national and social identity) continually resurfaced during the Python years when the series of economic, social, and political woes discussed above precipitated a crisis

15 Susan Aronstein, *Hollywood Knights: Arthurian Cinema and the Politics of Nostalgia* (New York: Palgrave Macmillan, 2005), pp. 110-16.

of authority in England that undermined such myths, powerfully articulated in General de Gaulle's 1961 words to the Queen: "Be the person in relation to whom, by virtue of your own legitimacy, all things in your Kingdom are ordered; the person in whom your people perceive their own nationhood; the person by whose presence and dignity, national unity is sustained."[16] By the late 1960s there was a growing sense that, far from symbolizing national stability, the royal family was both irrelevant and expensive. While more vocal republicans (most notably William Hamilton) called for the dissolution of the monarchy, the royal family attempted to repackage itself and the institution it represented.[17] In 1969, under the auspices of Haseltine, "the first press secretary who recognized a need to sell the monarchy to the public," two television events were planned to do just that. The first, a BBC documentary entitled *Royal Family*, attempted to establish the royal family as a "model domestic family," prompting a rhetoric of royalty based on its function as an exemplum to its people.[18] The second, the Investiture of Prince Charles in Caernarvon, Wales, reverted to older arguments of royal transcendence. As Ziegler comments, "Here was the royal family deployed in all its most formal and hierarchical array—a reminder that for all the picnics and cosy viewings of Dad's Army, there was still a mystery about the Crown, a religious and spiritual significance."[19]

Ziegler, a royalist, clearly approves of the royal reminder; more republican commentators such as Nairn and Pimlott read the event quite differently. Both comment on the ceremony's use of "Arthurian pantomime, mock medieval pageantry and Gothic revival words" as "ceremonial theatre to focus the attention of the British subjects and the Commonwealth on the self-renewing monarchy" and to establish, especially for the restless Welsh and Irish nationalists, that "Britain isn't just England in white satin breeches, but a supernal realm to which Welsh, Scots, and Irish . . . may in good conscience belong."[20] As television drama, the myth-making of the investiture was quite successful; however, the television silenced the voices of dissent—the perplex canopy that was abandoned because of fears of a Welsh marksmen, the jailing of six members of the free Army of Wales, the "third division football sized

---

16 Tom Nairn, *The Enchanted Glass: Britain and Its Monarchy* (London: Radius, 1988). Nairn quotes de Gaulle on p. 9.

17 My discussion of the debate surrounding the royal family is based on Nairn, *The Enchanted Glass*; Robert Lacy, *Majesty: Elizabeth II and the House of Windsor* (New York: Harcourt, 1977); Ben Pimlott, *The Queen: A Biography of Elizabeth I* (New York: Wiley, 1996); and Phillip Ziegler, *Crown and People* (New York: Knopf, 1978).

18 Pimlott, *The Queen*, p. 378.

19 Ziegler, *Crown and People*, p. 136.

20 Pimlott, *The Queen*, pp. 390, 388; Nairn, *Enchanted Glass*, p. 228.

. . . crowds," the bomb at Caernarvon station, and the earlier bomb that killed two men.[21]

In spite of these silenced voices, the monarchy's attempts to reestablish its currency in 1969 was reasonably successful. However, in 1971, it again came under scrutiny as the Queen was forced to ask for a revision of the Civil List—essentially a budget increase—in a time of general unemployment and economic recession. Her request resulted in the formation of the Select Committee on the Queen and both an official and popular perusal of the monarchy. Everything was debated in the newspapers—the expense to the nation, the minor non-working royals on the payroll, the royal family's tax-exemption, their private wealth. Although the Queen got her "raise" in the end, the question of the monarchy had entered into mainstream public debate; in 1975, William Hamilton published *My Queen and I,* in which he vociferously repeated his arguments for dissolution. The book and Hamilton received an unexpected boost in visibility when, a few months later, the same inflation that was wrecking havoc with the nation's economy led the Queen to ask for another revision of the Civil List.

While this debate about the monarchy may seem like a side-show in light of the nation's larger economic and social crises, the myths of monarchy and benevolent feudalism are central to a traditional vision of British nationhood, and the attempts to resuscitate the monarchy—particularly Charles's investiture—are in the tradition of the nineteenth-century's appropriation of the medieval past to instill a nostalgia for a feudal good-old-days in which the upper classes provided for and protected those below them. As such, these attempts aim to shore up an establishment Britain and silence the voices of discontent and fragmentation. In *The Holy Grail,* the Pythons deconstruct this conservative appeal to nineteenth century/medieval myths of monarchy, tradition, class and authority—a deconstruction that calls into question their own myths about gender.

While many scenes in the film ridicule medievalism's rhetoric of divine election and royal authority—from Arthur's "coconut horse" to the villagers' method of identifying their king ("he hasn't got shit all over him")—Dennis's anti-monarchical tirade provides the most succinct version of *The Holy Grail's* critique of the dominant order. In his escalating argument with Arthur, Dennis punctures the king's high rhetoric, demoting the Lady of the Lake to a "watery tart" and deriding Arthur's divine election as a "farcical aquatic ceremony." Unable to silence Dennis's insistence that his kingly identity and authority are constructed by discourse, Arthur resorts to violence and Dennis invites us all to observe "the violence inherent in the system," an invitation central to the film's larger agenda. The next two scenes, Arthur's encounter with the Black Knight, which portrays Arthur's ideal knight as a senseless killing machine, and "The

---

21 Nairn, *Enchanted Glass,* p. 227.

Witch Village," which provides a ludicrous example of authoritative discourse and illustrates that the upper-classes and their laws are both incapable of and uninterested in protecting anyone, confirm Dennis's charges.

"The Witch Village" criticizes neo-feudalism and demonstrates how the film's thematic agenda undermines the troupe's investment in traditional gender roles. The scene begins with the exuberant villagers proclaiming, "A witch! A witch! We have found a witch. May we burn her?" Bedevere, the resident knight/authority, inquires, "How do you know she's a witch?" to which the villagers reply, "She looks like one." When the "witch" (Connie Booth), sporting a witch's hat and a tied-on turnip nose, insists "I'm not a witch," Bedevere replies, "but you are dressed as one." "They," she accuses, "dressed me up like this. And this isn't my nose; it's a false one." The villagers sheepishly admit that they "did do the nose . . . and the hat." Undeterred, they continue to insist "she's a witch," an insistence that sparks the famous debate that equates witches with wood, and wood with ducks—both float on water—and concludes that "so logically, if she weighs the same as a duck, she's made of wood and therefore, she's a witch . . . burn her!" While the primary purpose of this scene is to expose Arthur and his knights as a privileged and exclusive group who, in the words of Elizabeth Murrel, "wear the same school tie"[22] and take a swipe at the authoritative discourses of science and reason, "The Witch Village" has unintended consequences. By taking a standard medieval misogynist stereotype and suggesting that women are first "dressed up"—socially constructed—to conform to cultural expectations and then condemned on the basis of a ludicrous discursive authority ("a fair cop!" as the doomed "witch" observes), the scene calls into question the other, more modern, gender stereotypes embedded in the film.

Similarly, *The Holy Grail*'s critique of "the violence inherent in the system" works against the conservative gender politics and heteronormativity of both "The Tale of Sir Robin" and "The Tale of Sir Lancelot." The comic tale of the cowardly Sir Robin unfolds against generic expectations: the unmanly Sir Robin is anything but brave. However, this tale also functions to highlight the violence that supports and enforces Arthur's chivalric order. The scene's opening vignette, in which an armed knight gallops through the film's internal modern documentary and skewers the Historian, introduces a critique of a world in which masculine identity is based on acts of senseless violence, a critique that frames Sir Robin's adventures. The lyrics to the minstrel's song—a bloodthirsty and disturbing counterpoint to the sweetness of the lilting melody—further questions the dominant discourse's masculine ideals. "He was not at all afraid," the minstrels cheerfully carol, "to be killed in nasty ways/. . . to be mashed into a pulp/or to have his eyes gouged out and his elbows broken." The catalogue of potential mutilations continues for another five lines, punctuated by the refrain, "brave

---

22 Murrell, "Revenged," p. 57.

Sir Robin," which trumpets Robin's assured place in the chivalric pecking order. However, the minstrel's graphic descriptions of the violence that this order is based on places audience sympathy with Sir Robin when, in his encounter with the Three-Headed Knight, he rejects his Arthurian identity: "Halt," he (they?) demand, "who art thou?" The minstrels, versed in the discourse of chivalric adventure, respond, "He is brave Sir Robin, brave Sir Robin." Robin contradicts them, "Shut up. Nobody, really. I'm just passing through" "What do you want?" the knight continues; again, the minstrels chime in with the proper response "to fight and . . ." and, again, Robin silences them, "Shut up." "Nothing really. Just to pass through, Sir Knight." However, in the world of Arthurian chivalry, as we saw in the Black Knight scene, "just to pass through" is not an option. Instead, both sides must test and prove their knightly mettle through combat: "I'm afraid I'm going to have to kill you," the knight declares. At this point, the scene turns to a discussion that, like the conversations of Mrs. Premise and Mrs. Confusion, exposes a world in which violence has become routine and banal, where one head concludes, "Let's kill him first and then go and have tea and biscuits." "Not biscuits," another protests. "Oh all right," the first head concedes, "not biscuits but let's kill him anyway."

Lancelot's "daring and heroic rescue in [his] own particular . . . idiom"—carried out to the tune of "Brave Sir Robin"—furthers *The Holy Grail's* critique of the connections between the Arthurian court, hyper-masculinity and violence, a critique that questions the tale's own dismissal of Herbert's desires. As Lancelot (John Cleese, in a medieval-version of his fruit-obsessed martial arts instructor) single-mindedly carries out his task, he charges and cuts down a flower-bedecked guard, slashes through a group of dancing maidens, fells servants, stabs guests, and takes impromptu detours to kick the bride and destroy a vase of flowers. In response to the father's blustering protest, "Did you kill all those guards? . . . You killed eight wedding guests in all . . . Killed the bride's father . . . kicked the bride," Lancelot shame-facedly replies, "I'm afraid that when I'm in this idiom, I sometimes get a bit carried away." The camera then cuts to a scene of bloody mayhem and sobbing survivors, suggesting that Arthurian protection is the last thing anyone would desire. Furthermore, the fact that Lancelot and Herbert's father seem to be natural allies casts a jaundiced eye on the status quo and its willingness, as Dennis has observed, to use violence to "exploit the masses"—or, in the father's case, his own son and prospective daughter in law. The father sees the young couple as a means to an end—"huge tracts of land" or Camelot's "good pig country"—and is certainly not himself above the use of violence to attain these ends. When Lancelot seems a better bet as an ally, he himself cuts the rope and sends Herbert plunging to his supposed death. When the bride's father is found to be "not quite dead" and, indeed, "getting better," he tacitly orders one of his henchmen to dispatch him, concluding that he has now "gained a daughter . . . in a very real and legally binding sense" and happily anticipating the "merger . . . union between the princess and the brave but dangerous Sir Lancelot." He casually dismisses the slaughter that makes this union possible, initially only concerned with "the fortune" it will cost him and, when it becomes clear that it might bring him a fortune, chiding his surviving guests: "Let's not bicker about who killed who."

"The Tale of Sir Lancelot" strengthens the connection, central to *The Holy Grail's* deconstruction of the medieval myths employed by the establishment to revalorize a neo-feudal vision of a glorious national tradition and ideal social structure, between hyper-masculinity and senseless violence that runs—from Arthur's encounter with the Black Knight, through the killing of the Historian, and into the minstrels' bloody song—throughout the film. Lancelot's violent idiom, combined with Arthur's empty rhetoric, exposes the founding legend of Arthur, at its origin, as a suspect tool, designed to convince people—through violence, if necessary—that coconuts are horses, beacons are Grails, and Camelot is something more than "a silly place." However, as it does so, the film inadvertently argues against its own gender politics. If Lancelot's hyper-masculine identity is a mere "idiom," it may be no more "natural" then Herbert's feminized one. Furthermore, as the scene leaves Lancelot—who insists that his idiom demands that he escape dramatically—dangling by a rope, begging for a "push," and Herbert, singing "I'm here to tell," holding center stage, the *Holy Grail's* critique of the dominant discourse opens the space for Herbert's marginal one, allowing him a moment of triumph.

While *The Holy Grail,* as we have seen, attempts to shut down the gendered implications of its larger social and political critique—Herbert may have the last word, but the possibility of a union between him and Lancelot has been raised only to be laughed out of court—the cat, so to speak, is already out of the bag, as the 2005 musical *Monty Python's Spamalot* recognizes.[23] Its retelling of "The Tale of Sir Lancelot" embraces the gender-bending possibilities that the film denies. In *Spamalot,* Herbert does not misrecognize Lancelot. He is the only one to see him as he truly is: as a knight who—similar to the "Poof Judges"—sports "a glittering, glimmering, shimmering outrageous body costume with silver lame tights" underneath his shining armor. This recognition allows Lancelot to escape his "idiom"—"To kill / I will / it gives me such a thrill" and to embrace gay exuberance—"He must finally come out and say that he is G. A. YMCA . . . He's gay!" so that he may enter into a marriage that "will still be controversial 2000 years from now."

---

23 Disappointingly, *Spamalot* itself, in the end, uses the scene conservatively, as Laurie Finke and I discuss in "'Got Grail?': Monty Python and the Broadway Stage," *Theater Survey* 48.2 (2007): 289-312.

Chapter 7
Performance, Camp, and Queering History in Luc Besson's *Jeanne d'Arc*

Susan Hayward

In terms of generic film types, the epic more often says less about the history it purports to portray than something about the precise social moment it emanates from. History as heterotopia! The epic functions, whether consciously or not, through displacements of time and culture, allowing the present to masquerade as some queered representation of the past. I take queer in its established theoretical sense to refer to the desire in any art form to challenge and push debates on gender and sexuality. Further, I take queer as a concept that embraces all "non-straight" approaches to living practice—including, within our context, film and popular culture. As a politics, or a practice, queering seeks to confuse binary essentialisms around issues of identity, expose their limitations and to suggest that things are more "blurred" than one might initially suspect. With this in mind, let us begin from the beginning, that is to say, where the Joan of Arc story is located.

Setting History Straight—Joan of Arc (1412-1431)

History for its own part is not necessarily free from accusations of misrepresentation. Where Joan is concerned, however, two vital sets of transcripts of events allow us to discern more readily than in most cases where truth more or less lies (in both senses of that intentional pun). The first is the transcript of her trial of May 1431, including transcripts of the hearings that preceded the trial running from February to April; the second is the transcript of the various testimonies brought to bear for her rehabilitation some twenty years later—the so-named Rehabilitation Trial (a process begun in 1450 and completed in 1456). It is the second text that allows us to see the hypocrisy and lies of the first—for, although Joan was burnt as a heretic, it is clear that the whole procedure and the decision to execute her was a political one. Why were the judges (the Burgundian allies of the English) so keen to have her burn?

Because, had she been kept as a political prisoner (or prisoner of war, as the Duke Charles of Orléans had been held during the same period), she could not have been executed and, therefore, her charisma would have continued to hold significant sway for the French. Burning her as a heretic would send warnings to the French—and this is what the English and their Burgundian allies wanted in their attempts to regain supremacy over the Valois Royal dynasty as embodied by Charles VII, the former Dauphin for whom Joan had fought so hard to claim the French throne.

We need to recall that the Hundred Years War was still underway (1337-1453). This complex war—waged between the English and the French, but also between the French themselves—was precipitated by Edward III's claim to the French throne (through his mother Isabella of France). By the early fifteenth century, Henry V of England had been granted eventual title to France through marriage to Catherine de Valois (and settled by the Treaty of Troyes, of whom one of the negotiators was the infamous Pierre Cauchon, Bishop of Beauvais and Joan's eventual inquisitor). The Dauphin, Charles, was disinherited and France was more or less shared between Henry V and the Duke of Burgundy. Only the territories south of Orléans and north of Bordeaux remained in the purview of the Dauphin. France thus became divided between the Orléanists (true to the Valois dynasty) and their Burgundian rivals who, from the beginning of the war, allied themselves with the English and recognized the latter's claim to the throne. As a measure of how close-knit (even slightly incestuous) all this factionalism was, it is worth remembering that—at the time of the war period which concerns Joan's life (the mid to late 1420s)—the Duke of Bedford was married to Anne of Burgundy; that the Duke of Brittany had mostly sided with the Burgundians and the English, finally, after Orléans, coming down on the side of the Orléanists; that Georges de la Trémoille was a political schemer, formerly a Burgundian who finally switched sides and joined the Dauphin; and that—most treacherous of all—the Dauphin's own mother sided with the Burgundians (having also impugned her son's claims to the throne by suggesting to him that he was illegitimate). Charles the Dauphin was, however, the last remaining son of the Valois family and therefore to all intents and purposes the true heir to the French throne. Yet he was bound within his own land by his enemies, hemmed in from virtually all sides. All territories north of the Loire river were English-occupied or owned either by the Burgundians or by pro-English Brittany. The Dauphin was also bound from the south by the English-occupied territories south of the Gironde river (Aquitaine). Essentially his royal court and government were besieged. For security reasons he had to decamp from Bourges (which was too close to the enemy, north of the Loire) further west to Chinon. So what hope did he have of consecrating his kingship if he could not even make it to Reims—held as that royal city was within English enemy occupied territory? The hope was Joan, whose arrival in Chinon on March 4, 1429, changed the political landscape drastically.

Joan's impact was huge. Where before the Dauphin had little support from the nobles, doubtless because he had lost so many of the most important cities and territories, now Joan galvanized their support. More, while much of the population were still loyal to the Dauphin, it took Joan's inspired speeches and charismatic persona to urge them to fight—even when all seemed lost. This was how she won Orléans back from the English. She made the impossible seem possible. This was how she got the Dauphin through enemy territory to Reims and crowned king, taking the English-held cities of Montargis, Troyes, and Chalons on her way. The English and the Burgundians were not mistaken when they realized how much moral and morale-boosting power she wielded. She obviously had phenomenal energy: in her brief twelve-month life as a warrior (of which nine months were spent on the road), she rode some 2573 kilometers, leading men into battle and her king to Reims. She was the French court's secret weapon—something they understood only too briefly by failing to support her campaigns after the Dauphin was crowned. Nonetheless, she was undoubtedly the catalyst for the beginning of the change in the fortunes of the French. Twenty years after her execution, the English would be expelled.

The English wanted Joan dead. So too did the Burgundians. But the problem was how to obtain this sentence? Only through finding her guilty of heresy. Yet throughout the trial this objective proved virtually impossible. Until, that is, the prosecuting inquisitor (the pro-Burgundian) Bishop Cauchon came up with an ingenious trap. And here is where history got queered in its own time.

Let us recall the spirit of late medieval Europe. It was an "era of doubt, fear and uncertainty, war, destruction and depopulation, disease, decay and death." It was also a time that witnessed the "emergence of centralised monarchical powers in both Church and state."[1] Indeed, for its part the Catholic Church had become a totalitarian organization—ruling with a fist of iron thanks in large part to the Fourth Lateran Council (1215), which sought to impose a grand plan of re-Christianization upon an increasingly pluralistic (and therefore unruly) society.[2] The intention was to gain control over the lives and beliefs of the laity—by the most repressive means. As such, confession became established as the main ritual of truth-production—confessional conduct, bearing witness against one's self, became part of everyday life.[3] With regard to sexuality, the Church advocated purity and chastity—lust was a sin and, within marriage, sexual intercourse was regulated. In confession, scrutiny of sin as an intention

---

1 Jeffrey Richards, *Sex, Dissidence, and Damnation: Minority Groups in the Middle Ages* (London: Routledge, 1991), pp. 18, 9.

2 Richards, *Sex, Dissidence*, p. 42.

3 José Merquior, *Foucault* (London: Fontana, 1985), pp. 119-20.

and acknowledgment of lust acted as part and parcel of this system of self-denunciation.

It was not just the individual who was repressed, however, in that the Lateran Council sought the total suppression of religious groups who challenged the status quo, labelling them as heretic. As part of this repressive practice, its most draconian measure was the institutionalization of the process of the Inquisition whereby legal procedures could be initiated without private accusation—denunciation would suffice. This radically altered the former legal system of communal self-policing and trial by ordeal. Under the new system an accused could be condemned "on the testimony of two eye-witnesses or by confession. If the evidence was circumstantial or partial there was no conviction."[4] Thus, in essence obtaining a confession was fundamental to getting a conviction. And to obtain a confession—that most difficult of things—authorities sanctioned torture. (Incredibly, torture became part of the ordinary criminal procedure lasting until the end of the eighteenth century.) When we come back to considering Joan, we will see how key these issues are.

And yet at the same time, in Europe but particularly in medieval France, there was a growing sense of national identity "sharpened by war with England, by conflict with the Papacy and by the promotion of Paris as the national capital"[5]—a promotion pushed for presumably by the Burgundian intellectuals who resided at the University of Paris. This thrust for national identity brought shifts in its wake, most importantly the development of the concept of citizens with rights and duties as opposed to the concept of subjects who must obey their lord and master. This search for self-knowledge did not detract from the drive to penitential confession; rather, it accentuated it. As Jeffrey Richards explains, there was a "desire of ordinary people to attain a state of religious perfection *by their own acts* . . . while remaining in the world." As far as the Fourth Lateran Council was concerned, this rise of Christian fundamentalism was nothing short of heresy—and yet there was nothing anti-Christian about its motivation. It was "for the most part popular religious dissent . . . a fundamentalist Christian impulse of the purist kind, to return to the truth of the Gospels."[6] This dissent had its intellectual leaders and religious reformers who clearly threatened the Catholic establishment. John Wycliffe (1329-84) in England criticized the Church and was condemned as a heretic and forced into retirement. Nonetheless, he oversaw the translation of the Bible into English and can be seen as a forerunner of Protestantism. Jan Hus (1369-1415) of Bohemia criticized the established Church on moral grounds, repudiated close control of the Papacy, and advocated a vernacular liturgy. Hus was condemned

---

4 Richards, *Sex, Dissidence*, p. 12.

5 Richards, *Sex, Dissidence*, p. 5.

6 Richards, *Sex, Dissidence*, pp. 45 (italics mine) and 44.

as a heretic and burnt at the stake. His followers, the Hussites (who were Joan's contemporaries), demanded a reformed national Church, but they were swiftly repressed, surviving Hus by a bare twenty years (1415-34).

It is not difficult to see how Joan embodies both these trends: an obedient servant of the Church on the one hand and, on the other, a fundamental nationalist. In the former she emblematized the concept of confession as a daily practice. Her piety is well documented[7]—and Besson in his film *Jeanne d'Arc* (1999), makes much of it in the first sequences depicting her early life.[8] She strove for chastity and religious purity at all times. She chased the impure, in the form of prostitutes, out of the army's retinue. She called for daily confessions in the army; she forbad swearing. She acted as a true anti-heretic, frequently inveighing against the Saracens and threatening them with military action. She also sent an ultimatum to the Hussites—addressing them as the "Heretics of Bohemia"—warning them she would lead a crusade against them if they failed to return to the Catholic faith.[9]

But she was also driven by a notion of nationhood that aligns her more readily with the second trend. She sought out her Dauphin, galvanized the troops to fight in the interests of France, and saw the Dauphin sacralized as the true monarch of France. Signs of religious fervor, even fundamentalism, are not hard to discern in her pursuit of the dictates from the visions she had. She claimed repeatedly that it was the voices of saints that sent her to serve and rescue her Dauphin and liberate France. It would be easy to read into this an avocation of the return to apostolic simplicity—a Hussite practice and therefore heretical. In battle she consistently invoked "Jésus, Marie" as her battle cry— showing perhaps an over-zealous identification with Christ, a form of heresy according to the Church. Her banner can also be seen as a site of this seeming (essentially political) contradiction she embodied—adorned as it was with the Fleur de Lys (the emblem of the French monarchy) and the image of Jesus or the Almighty (accounts differ) sitting in judgment in the clouds and, written upon it, the names of "Jésus, Marie."[10] On the one hand, it could be read as emblematic of her spiritual purpose; on the other hand (albeit for precisely those same reasons but differently read as exemplifying the arrogance of the individual assuming spiritual or religious purpose on earth), it could be read as

---

7 See Allen Williamson, *Biography of Joan of Arc,* http://joan-of-arc.org/joanofarc_ biography.html (accessed Oct. 1, 2008).

8 *Jeanne d'Arc*, dir. Luc Besson, perf. Milla Jovovich and John Malkovich, DVD (1999; Gaumont: Leeloo Productions, 1999). In the United States, the film was released as *The Messenger*.

9 See Allen Williamson, *Joan of Arc, Brief Biography*, http://archive.joan-of-arc.org/ joanofarc_short_biography.html (copyright 2002-2007, accessed Oct. 1, 2008).

10 Williamson, *Joan of Arc, Brief Biography*.

incorporating all that the Church could read as fundamentalist. Certainly, at the trial, an attempt was made to read it as proof of her heresy, as indeed were the other apparent indications noted above (her invocation of saints and her battle cry).

For those intent on condemning Joan, nowhere was evidence of her ambiguity more clearly on display than in her cross-dressing. And in the end, because she persisted in not confessing to any heresy, this matter of cross-dressing was the route taken to speed her downfall. During her captivity in prison, Joan retained her male attire to protect herself against rape. Flouting standard Inquisitorial practice, authorities ordered Joan to be held in an English secular prison in Rouen instead of an ecclesiastical one where her guards would have been nuns. Thus, she was under constant threat of rape by her male English guards. Indeed, her commitment to chastity (a tenet of the Catholic Church) would in the final analysis be her undoing. At her trial, which lasted the month of May 1431, Cauchon tried by all means possible to convict her of heresy. Finally he found the way. On May 24, the tribunal threatened her with summary execution (which would entail no opportunity to be absolved by a priest) if she did not renounce her male clothing. We must remember that Joan had been in prison now for a year, without any form of religious confession—the only way to confess would be to abjure the divine nature of her mission and don a dress. This she did. Much good it did her. Four days later she was forced to resume male clothing, to protect herself against rape once more. Documents testify to the increase in attempts to violate her once she was in a dress. On the fourth day of this abuse, she was deprived of her dress and given back her male attire as the only clothes available. Since, according to Cauchon, the donning of male attire was a relapse on her abjuration, this allowed him to pronounce her a relapsed heretic and condemn her to death.[11]

The cruellest of ironies has to be that, unlike women of the Middle Ages who cross-dressed, it was never Joan's intention to pass as a man, even though as a warrior she showed herself to be man's equal and capable of military strategy worthy of any military leader. Truly, there was nothing queer about her intentions, despite Cauchon's insistence that there was. And it is here that we can now show how he queered theological history to achieve his ends.

Joan was well aware of her rights, and she pointed these out at her trial. Most importantly, she asserted that she had committed no sin in cross-dressing. Indeed, as she argued, medieval theology sanctioned necessity-based cross-dressing as appropriate protective clothing either when travelling or when given titular command of an army.[12] Moreover, she had received permission from a

---

11 For more details on these events, see http://archive.joan-of-arc.org/joanofarc_male_clothing.html (accessed Oct. 1, 2008).

12 Williamson, *Biography of Joan of Arc*.

number of influential clergy to wear male attire during her military campaigns.[13] Nor, when she was forced to resume male clothing in prison, had she committed a heretical act. The thirteenth-century *Summa Theologica* is very clear on this issue: "this [cross-dressing] may be done without sin due to some necessity, whether for the purpose of concealing oneself from enemies, or *due to any other lack of clothing.*"[14]

It was not as if the Church were unaware of the rulings on female cross-dressing. Moreover, there were many examples of cross-dressing women in the Middle Ages. Technically the Bible forbad it, but women somehow seemed to be able to bypass the rulings—primarily because of the medieval theological emphasis on chastity, but, as we shall see below, for a somewhat queerer reason also. As Vern Bullough tells us, during this period there were a "number of female transvestite saints, in fact as least forty of them, most of whom lived their adult lives as males and were discovered to be females only after they had died."[15] Furthermore, women who had cross-dressed during the medieval period had never been prosecuted or penalized, and most significantly had not been burnt.[16] A major reason why this practice was tolerated among women (but not men) was the (queer) belief that women, in striving to become more male-like, would become better persons—because women were considered inferior to men. As Bullough tells us, "the easiest way for women to approach the male level of rationality was for women to *deny their sexuality*, to remain virgins." In the eyes of the Church, then, cross-dressing women had higher status than their fellow mortal women, were more rational and holy, and "much admired for their ability to live among men as a man."[17] This queerest of reasoning asserted, first, that cross-dressing affirmed the supremacy of the male and, second, that chastity was next to holiness and therefore to maleness.

Thus cross-dressing females were not considered material for accusations of heresy—especially if they successfully passed. Joan dressed as a man, but there was no intention to deceive or deny her sexuality, merely to be accepted as an equal—and, implicit in that, to be perceived as an equal in gendered terms. However, in so doing, she failed in fact to live up in one crucial way (total

---

13 Allen Williamson, "Primary Sources and Contexts Concerning Joan of Arc's Male Clothing," *Historical Academy of Joan of Arc Studies*, 2006, p. 3.

14 Williamson, "Primary Sources and Contexts Concerning Joan of Arc's Male Clothing," p. 11 (my parenthesis added and emphasis).

15 Vern Bullough, "On Being Male in the Middle Ages," *Medieval Masculinities*, ed. Clare Lees (Minneapolis: U of Minnesota P, 1994), 31-45, at p. 34.

16 Vern Bullough, "Cross Dressing and Gender Role Change in the Middle Ages," *Handbook of Medieval Sexuality*, eds. Vern Bullough and James Brundage (New York: Garland, 1996), 223-42, at p. 228.

17 Bullough, "Cross Dressing," pp. 227 (my emphasis) and 229.

masquerade) to the traditional standards of transvestite saints sanctioned by the Church—although she did maintain her chastity and therefore purity. In her lack of desire to "pass" (as a man) yet to ensure her chastity, she asserted her female gender (and of course in being a virgin this meant that she could not be possessed by the Devil either). But, because she was so effective as a warrior (strategically and in the battle field), she challenged through her asserted femaleness the notion that women were inferior.

Joan was as good as a man when in battle—but her cross-dressing in this context was not unique, except in relation to class. Other women, usually aristocratic women to be sure, were given titular command when they oversaw their family's forces at war. In terms of class, however, Joan transcended her humble origins and attained a form of noble status by default—as indeed the gifts of finery she was given by the Dauphin after her success at Orléans make clear (a rich robe of Brussels vermillion cloth, lined with satin, as well as a tunic). Her cross-dressing had given her franchise ("franc" as in free)—a quality of being usually only enjoyed by nobility—something she would never have enjoyed as a peasant girl.

Thus, while it is clear that Cauchon's condemning Joan to death for cross-dressing was an illegal act and a gross misinterpretation of theological law (since the conditions she found herself in permitted it)—a first queering—it was also the case that he was condemning her for something she was not doing—a further, rather abject kind of queering. For he was, after all, condemning her for cross-dressing as a man when in fact she was cross-dressing as a woman—to keep her womanhood intact. By not relinquishing her identity ("I am Joan the Maid"), she exposed the masquerade ("I am *not* Joan the *Man*"). So for his part, Cauchon had in fact queered an act that at the time had nothing incoherent (or heretic) about it. There was no transcendent disregard, on Joan's part, for systems of gender, merely a desire to maintain her chastity. In so doing, she sought gender-neutrality so that her sex would not matter and she could engage in battle. However, the effects of her gender-neutral performance were such that they led to her own queering of boundaries—especially those of gender and class, some of which exposed the contradictions and hypocrisies of the Church's reasoning on heresy—a queering which made her condemnation ineluctable. A woman could never be an equal to man either in body or in reason.

Queering History—Besson's *Jeanne D'Arc* (1999)

If Cauchon queered history to his own ends, then so too did Besson, but for entirely different reasons, it must be added. Whereas Cauchon wanted to eradicate the femaleness of Joan, Besson wanted to get behind the myth and understand the woman and her emotions, to reveal her doubts and to show that no one can come out of the experience of war intact.[18] But to do this, he falsified history almost as blatantly as Cauchon distorted theological rulings. Besson offers us a double motivation for Joan's individual mission for her Dauphin. The first is the one we all know—the visions and voices that instruct her to free France and to crown her king. The second is complete fiction. According to Besson's story of Joan, a desire for vengeance equally fuels her mission. Having witnessed English looters and pillagers rape and murder her sister, the young Joan is so traumatized that even the heavenly commandment "thou shalt not kill" seems to have no meaning for her anymore. And, in essence, what then follows from this moment on, in the film's narrative, is Joan's increased confusion with regard to God's commandments and mankind's brutal behavior especially in wartime. So which is it that motivates her, as onto war she goes? For into battle she goes astride her white horse, carrying her banner—so that she might not have to kill anyone—but also at times forced to at least brandish a sword. When she spares an Englishman's life (his captor wanting to chop off his head so he can have his teeth!), is it the horror of the bloodshed around her that brings her to this act of compassion to the extent that she ransoms him? Or is it the memory of her sister who sacrificed her life and chastity to save Joan hidden away in the cupboard?

In truth, Domrémy, Joan's village, was sacked by the Burgundians (allies of the English). Joan and her family had escaped to nearby Neufchâteau, so all were spared. Her sister Catherine went on to marry and have children. Two of Joan's brothers, Pierre and Jean, joined her army and fought by her side and, when she entered Orléans, they rode in behind her. Significantly, in this domain of family engagement, both her parents came to the coronation of the king at Reims.[19] Certainly, Besson does not have to insert all historical truths, but as a filmmaker well-known for representing the family as dysfunctional—one that fails its youth generation, one which in his films is always absent—perhaps this cavalier disregard for historical accuracy surrounding Joan's family should not surprise too much. (Her father is represented as ineffectual and her mother even more so; they pack her off to stay with her aunt.)

Besson's distortion of history negates an understanding of the medieval context that is crucial to an understanding of Joan's behavior. The Fourth Lateran Council demanded purity of religious spiritual life, and this is what Joan sought, above all, to achieve. Revenge was not even a remote possibility in her consciousness—especially since there was nothing to be outraged by. We only have to read the transcripts of her trial to understand this. Her words were lucid and candid. She asked, pleaded even, that her rights be respected. She

---

18 Besson interview in *Ciné Live* 29 (Nov. 1999), p. 28.

19 Williamson, *Biography of Joan of Arc.*

exposed, through her truthfulness and legitimate claims, the hypocrisy and bias of the court. But even here she expressed no words of revenge. An indication of how poorly Besson has understood historical theological rulings—or his disregard for them—comes in the last section of the film that covers Joan's trial. Instead of maintaining her in male attire, Besson costumes Joan in a blue dress until the moment she abjures. At which point, he rejoins history by showing the attempts of the English, first, to rape her and then to discredit her by throwing her in the male attire not seen since her capture. He distorts matters further by having Cauchon appear almost compassionate towards Joan, once she has been condemned as a heretic, regretting that he cannot offer her absolution. Whereas in historical fact he had set the trap himself and, once she had donned the male attire, announced to the English that the deed was done.[20]

Besson's answer to this queering is twofold. He is on record as saying that he was not interested in narrating history but in pulling out of history a message that is relevant for us today—war and its effects.[21] And his second intention was to humanize Joan by exposing her moral ambiguity—something that is pure speculation on his part. (All we do know is that she grieved for the dead, and this mostly because they had not been given last rites and confession.) As I have explained above, she embodied the political contradictions of the times, she was not someone who was morally ambiguous or riddled with self-doubt. In "humanizing" Joan, Besson effectively brings her into the contemporary world as a model (literally in one sense) to whom young audiences can relate (and evidence indicates that he was successful in doing this).[22] Joan of Arc, according to Besson, is like his other heroines, someone who is marginal to society and out of synch with it.[23] In fact the real Joan was no such thing: she was born into a family of reasonable means (they owned fifty hectares of land); she was a quiet, well-behaved and spiritual child—elements she did not give up when she embarked upon her perilous quest to take Orléans and enthrone the Dauphin. In fact, of all ironies, she was (as we saw) very much in harmony with the demands of her society, governed as it was by the Fourth Lateran Council.

Besson's Joan is certainly not in the image of her predecessor, but she is in the image of contemporary youth. When in battle, the eye-bulging Joan (as played by Milla Jovovich), screaming at her men, is not quite the charismatic Joan who exhorted her troops with her battle cry of "Jésus, Marie!" and her firm invocation of God's will. Jovovich is closer to the aggressive youth class that has become so much a stereotype of France's *banlieue cités*. And, as such, she

---

20 Williamson, *Joan of Arc, Brief Biography*.

21 Besson interview in *Ciné Live*, p. 28.

22 See the interview conducted by Zoe Eisenstein of young French people who went to see the film (*The Guardian*, Feb. 29, 2000, p. 61).

23 Besson interview with *Ciné Live*, p. 31.

rings as totally false. She is aggressive and impertinent, as Besson admits, but he claims he needed to display her in this way so that we would understand her "aggressive and impertinent" behavior at the trial.[24] But again the historical point is lost. The 1431-Joan argued all her legal points with clarity and firmness. She contested the legitimacy of the court (quite rightly since the Inquisition rulings state that the tribunal must be impartial). She demanded the right to appeal to the Pope (again within her rights, but her request was ignored).[25] She knew the law. Besson's Joan, when in front of the tribunal, shows no such competence. She is cheeky and displays "attitude," which makes us cheer for her doubtless. But this part of her characterization brings her closer to contemporary youth than to the woman of history who pleaded for fairness of due legal process. Nor does this "attitude" sit easily with the self-doubting Joan in her cell with her conscience eating away at her motivation for her exploits. The real Joan was recorded as having grieved greatly for the enemy dead and asked for them to be given absolution in their death. She also cried at the sight of so many of her own men slain[26]—but what we certainly do not know is whether she questioned her motivations: what we have on record is that, when in prison, she refused to recant until forced to abjure.

When we take into account how Besson and Jovovich imagine Joan, we see how self-reflexive their purpose is and how undermining of Joan's radical power their take on her becomes. Besson wanted to make the film about one of France's national icons before any of the Americans got in on the act (is he the new Joan, one wonders!).[27] He immediately saw Jovovich in the role as Joan: "she resembles Joan, both are ill at ease in their century, both are wonderful, crazy, hyper-sensitive, capable of anything."[28] My question: how does he know this? He and Jovovich decided that Joan should have an unpredictable nature, with no rational logic motivating her actions.[29] Jovovich claims to understand Joan and sees her as lost, as confused and traumatized,[30] even slightly mad[31]—something completely contested by documents recording Joan's actions and words. Recall that she dictated letters to the Burgundians and English beseeching them to lift

---

24 Besson interview with *Ciné Live*, p. 30.

25 Williamson, *Joan of Arc, Brief Biography*.

26 Williamson, *Biography of Joan of Arc*. It is worth noting that, after Orléans, at Patay (June 18, 1429) her strategies were so strong she (apparently) lost only three men as compared to the English with 2200 dead.

27 Besson interviewed by Frodon in *Le Monde*, Oct. 27, 1999, p. 32.

28 Besson interviewed by Frodon in *Le Monde*, p. 32.

29 Jovovich in Luc Besson, *L'Histoire de Jeanne d'Arc* (Paris: Intervista, 1999), p. 63.

30 Jovovich interviewed by Philippe Trétiak in "Divine Milla," *Elle* 2807 (Oct. 18, 1999), p. 179.

31 Jovovich interviewed by François Forestier in "Milla Jovovich: La Fille de feu," *Le Nouveau Cinéma* (Nov. 1999), p. 78.

their siege of Orléans so that battle and therefore bloodshed could be avoided, a supremely rational request in those days when much of war was about posturing and negotiation. This disregard for Joan's prudence and intelligence, coupled with the lack of understanding of her tremendous charisma, precisely pinpoints what undermines any in-depth characterization Besson might have wanted for his Joan. Jovovich's Joan is monochrome in her exalted state of irrationality.

Queering the Body—Besson's *Joan of Arc*

Although dressed as a man, Joan of Arc was never a transvestite, in the sense of a person trying to pass as a member of the opposite sex. Nor indeed, according to documents about her, did she have a body that could pass as a man's. Although there is no extant image of her, descriptions of her in her armor and of her cropped hair, as well as notations on the lengths of cloth used for her gifts of finery from the Dauphin, allow us to know the following. Physically she was about five feet tall, an average height for the times. She was, according to her bodyguard Jean d'Aulon, "beautiful and shapely." Her hair was black and, to make her blend in better with the troops, it was cut in the rounded style of the times (shaped like a bowl and covering most of her ears and neck).[32] To preserve her feminine chastity she wore two layers of hosen securely fastened to the doublet with forty eyelets on the inner hose and twenty on the outer (double the normal amount).[33] She also wore her armor at night as an extra layer of protection. And her armor was specifically built to mold to her body shape.[34] In other words, her inner and outer shells were molded according to a precise gender—she did not wear the regular male war fashions that would have been more convenient, but more dangerous.

This rather flies in the face of Besson and Jovovich's view of Joan as androgyne. And we must recall that a woman cross-dressing in medieval times was about attaining greater proximity to maleness, it was not about androgyny. However, as I argue elsewhere, this should not detract from the fact that, despite coming at Joan ahistorically, Besson nonetheless offers us an interesting essay on identity politics.[35] As I shall now go on to argue, his Joan—an anachronistic remodelling of the corporeal original—re-appropriates the mythic status of France's icon

---

32 Williamson, *Biography of Joan of Arc*.

33 Williamson, "Primary Sources and Contexts Concerning Joan of Arc's Male Clothing," p. 1.

34 Williamson, *Joan of Arc, Brief Biography*.

35 See my "*Jeanne d'Arc* (1999): High Epic Style and Politicising Camp," *The Films of Luc Besson*, eds. Susan Hayward and Phil Powrie (Manchester: Manchester UP, 2006), pp. 161-74.

as a pre/text to explore contemporary androgyny. But I shall also argue that he delivers us a new take on the history of Joan, one that has been overlooked in previous films about her (some twenty-two, according to my records), a take that is located precisely in this question of gender politics. Indeed, as Kathleen Kelly and Tison Pugh point out in their introduction to this book, "anachronisms are not always to be lamented" but "should be embraced; . . . [they] can indicate ways in which contemporary filmmakers infuse their work with modern concerns—often political, especially in respect to gender and sexuality."[36] To which I would add, anachronism can also illuminate the past.

Jovovich saw reflected in her own androgyne looks those which, to her mind, would necessarily be Joan's, since she was living in a masculine environment.[37] Of her own looks she declared: "I could pass as a boy, from behind, actually I am pretty buff" (meaning expert in passing). Jovovich's Joan continues the androgynous line of Besson's female protagonists (Nikita in *La Femme Nikita* [1990], Leeloo in *The Fifth Element* [1997]) and in some ways, we have become accustomed to Besson working out his ideas about female identity through his star women. But the point here is that *this* Joan *is* performing at passing, attempting to confound, something her original did not seek to achieve. Her lack of breasts (which, after her chest wound, gets greater heightened visibility once she is bandaged, as if to say "look how inexistent my breasts are!") along with her trim hipless form and short haircut above the ears, readily mark her out as a boy—certainly as a blonde equivalent of her bodyguard d'Aulon whose armor hers mirrors—than as a shapely female.

The androgyne body—in this instance Jovovich's Joan body—serves a vital function, for it unsettles notions of gender. In signifying the fluidity of sexual characteristics, by holding them together in one performance, the androgyne body, as a rule, disorientates. With the female androgyne (Jovovich-Joan in this case), it is not simply a case of dressing like a man—for as such she would be a transvestite. Rather, in her (cross)-dressing, she performs androgyny, becomes an in-between, or even third or fourth way which surpasses ideological notions of sexuality and gender identity. In-between because s/he embodies neither a precise sexuality of heterosexual, homosexual, nor lesbian, nor a precise gender of male or female. In her performance, the androgyne female plays on the ideological function/fiction of gender as "either/or," suggesting it is not even a case of "bothness" (already better than either/or) but of moreness. Androgyny as parody—this is what Jovovich's performance as Joan offers us. That is an edge of the film, and a queering of what heteronormativity traditionally displays before us. But—and here is another, more paradoxical, edge to the film and its

---

36 Tison Pugh and Kathleen Coyne Kelly, "Queer History, Medievalism, and the Impossibility of Sexuality," p. 4.

37 Forestier, "Milla Jovovich: La Fille de feu," p. 80.

function—she offers it to us from the safety of 600 years ago, just as in *The Fifth Element* she offered it to us from the safety of the twenty-third century. Why this historical distance? After all, androgyny in late capitalism has been around since at least the 1970s, but we need to be precise. It has, but only in a liminal way and mostly for the male androgyne. We think of David Bowie and Mick Jagger in glam-rock and again of the 1980s in male fashion. The female androgyne is a more recent development, with, as its pioneer, the iconic Grace Jones of the 1980s and, a little later, Annie Lennox. While androgyny is a contemporary cultural issue, as exemplified in fashion and popular music and even in the gradual homogenization of clothing apparel, none of this has necessarily led to an easier set of attitudes around sexuality and gender performance—what therefore is the threat? And it is here that we can see how Besson looks to the past to consider a response to this question.

Besson's *Joan* points to the present and to the past. In relation to the present, it celebrates a new idea of difference—one based in the power of female androgyny. What has always interested Besson in his female characterizations is how women come to wield power since they are traditionally less strong than men. The strategies that they must adopt have been a central investigation of his ever since *La Femme Nikita* (1990)—his first female androgyne whose cross-dressing masquerade is ultimately sniffed out (literally by a hound) and arguably fails to preserve her from persecution. Besson claims that what interests him in the woman is her masculinity and that what he wants to draw out in her is both her masculinity and her femininity—male and female characteristics, the first definition of androgyny.[38] Milla Jovovich, his Joan, was the perfect body and icon for his portaiture of the female androgyne. She is variously described as a Top Model, a lesbian icon with her boyish looks and figure.[39] With her allure of glam-rock,[40] she recalls earlier male androgyne icons. She is indeed "buff" in many ways—something that is very clearly exemplified in both her roles for Besson (medieval Joan and sci-fi Leeloo) in which she engages in physically demanding exploits (either out-witting men or out-punching and kicking them on their terms).

But Besson also looks to the past with his Joan and hints at what was so transgressive in the original Joan's cross-dressing—and he does this through Jovovich's performance of androgyny-as-power. Let us unpick this.

While the original Joan may not have been interested in the possibilities of the androgyne body, Besson's Joan points to the implications of passing far more readily than does the original cross-dressed Joan. Remember that the

---

38 This was Besson's response to a question I put to him in an informal interview after the *Guardian Interview* at the National Film Theatre (Mar. 23, 2000).

39 Forestier, "Milla Jovovich: La Fille de feu," p. 78.

40 Trétiak, "Divine Milla," p. 177.

better a woman passed the better she was considered (as gaining proximity to maleness). She could, in cross-dressing, do something strictly forbidden to medieval men—pass as other, be unreadable. Indeed, it was a punishable crime for a man to attempt to pass as woman. The criminal forms this took were threefold—all associated with sex. The first and most tolerated was the cross-dressed man who might be attempting to gain entry into a female household to commit rape. The second was the drive to prostitution for financial gain. The third and most heinous was the "unnatural urge" to sodomy with another man. This latter was considered a heretical crime and was punishable by burning. The other two instances seem to have not entailed such draconian judgements.[41] But in each instance the male is considered to have debased himself (sometimes beyond repair)—in all cases they risked damnation if they did not recant (before burning) or change their ways. Male cross-dressing then is about loss of power—and arguably stands as a sign of the most extreme *mise-en-évidence* of the very complex relations of power in the pre-Renaissance moment of the late Middle Ages as power shifted away from nobles and courtiers and increasingly fell into the hands of the Church and centralized monarchical states.

Besson's Joan plays closer to what was expected of a female cross-dresser (passing), but in so doing she exposes, more clearly than the original Joan, the fragility of power relations of that time. This brings me to a consideration of camp to explain this idea more clearly.[42] Increasingly, during this period (and indeed throughout the eighteenth century where France was concerned), nobility was kept from being a threat to the monarchy (or aspiring monarchy in the case of the Dauphin) by having to be at court. In the first part of this essay I pointed out how treacherous courtiers could be and how quasi-incestuous most alliances were. Although courtiers intrigued (La Trémoille being one of the most notorious, and undoubtedly a major player in Joan's subsequent lack

---

41 A good example is the English transvestite/prostitute John/Eleanor Rykener. It is unclear whether his acts of sodomy were those of a homosexual or of a male prostitute needing money. He was arrested and prosecuted for his "detestable acts" (1394), but it is unclear from the records what happened to him. He did express a sexual preference for priests, but only because they paid more. (See Ruth Karras, *Sexuality in Medieval Europe* [London: Routledge, 2005], pp. 143-44, for more details on this case and medieval sexuality in general.)

42 What follows is a very condensed version of a longer argument about camp set out in my earlier piece on this film, "*Jeanne d'Arc* (1999): High Epic Style and Politicising Camp." My take on it this time is somewhat different. Here I develop the idea that, in her androgyny, Besson's Joan transcends camp. I also want to acknowledge Mark Booth's excellent essay on camp, which greatly helped this part of my argument: "*Campe-toi!* On the Origins and Definitions of Camp," *Camp*, ed. Fabio Cleto (Edinburgh: Edinburgh UP, 1999), pp. 66-79.

of success),[43] for the most part, once at court, it was a politics of play, display, and wit (as indeed we note upon our first entry into the Dauphin's court). In short, in the place of true politics, courtiers swanked, camped roles. Even in moments of battle, this idea of camp did not disappear. The whole court would move camps, setting up an artificial camp made up of hugely ornate tents (as we note from Besson's film). The battle-camp became the pageant. Battle was engaged in the most courtierly of manners; messages delivered from one camp to another; agreements drawn up between the two sides as to when battle would commence, and so on. In decamping to these temporary camps, the courtier did not give up his posturing, but continued to display himself, in short, to camp his role.

We see this camp posturing most readily in the film's four central male characters: Dunois (Tchéky Karyo), Gilles de Rais (Vincent Cassel), d'Alençon (Pascal Greggory), and La Hire (Richard Ridings). The costume designer Catherine Leterrier tells us that she sought to make their armor flaunt their persona. Thus Dunois, who was a man of many battles, has an armor that is all patched up (a display of his great experience). The Duc d'Alençon, who was rich and seductive, has an armor that displays his wealth and gallantry. For La Hire—whose name literally means "the irate one"—she designed a costume that reflected his crazed lust for battle. His armor is adorned with small pointed rhino-like horns. Finally, for Gilles de Rais she designed a costume that put on display his somewhat alarming persona. In fact his elegant black suit of armor says more about his future self—the notorious Barbe-bleue—than the person he was at the time of the battle of Orléans.[44]

Camp is about spectacle, performance, and excess. It is male, but, as we can see, is also apolitical (the courtiers are held in camp, as it were, by their Royal court). Thus this camp (be it in court or at battle) is a "self-mocking abdication of any pretension to power."[45] As such it is located in the feminine— the male courtier knowingly feminizes his self, ironizes his condition, makes it spectacular. Interestingly the Dauphin most clearly exemplifies this, until he is finally crowned king. He, most of all the courtiers, knows he has no power. Only his Valois heritage and the fact that he might one day be king preserves him from any treachery. But to return to our courtiers: in going to war, their disempowered status has been decamped from court to the battlefield. The difference now is that they are able to display masculine prowess as well— suggesting that camp is located in the feminine and the masculine, much like androgyny, except that their display is in the realm of the asexual and not the sexually ambiguous, since it is without real power. It is significant in this context

43 Williamson, *Joan of Arc, Brief Biography.*
44 Leterrier in Besson, *L'Histoire de Jeanne d'Arc*, p. 143.
45 Booth, "*Campe-toi!*" p. 74.

that Joan, the true androgyne, is the one who sends messages to her enemies, negotiates the battle encounters with them, sets the tactics and demonstrates to their amazed acknowledgment an ability to campaign better than they do. It is equally significant, surely, that it is she, who on several occasions, calls Dunois, La Hire, d'Alençon, and Gilles de Rais to order—as if to remind them of their disempowerment.

In comparing her androgyny to theirs, we can understand what Besson is telling us about the transgressive androgyne and power as opposed to the conforming, albeit self-ironizing campy courtier. What the Jovovich-Joan female androgyne refuses to do is to don the masquerade of womanliness any more than to give the pretense of being a man. She disturbs, however, because at the same time she expresses sexual ambiguity. She embodies a position of bothness—moreness even. And in so doing, she disrupts power. It isn't just a question of challenging the ontological status of the gendered body; she also fearlessly exposes the phallic economy for what it is (based in power relations). She occupies, therefore, the very opposite position to that of her noble warriors. In performing androgyny, she transdresses and transgresses the world of camp—that most male of courtierly positions—while dictating the rules of engagement and giving orders at Orléans. In so doing, she subverts the male-warrior role and wins the battle.[46] In short, her androgyny allows her to transcend power relations (as established by the Church and the Royal court). And because, unlike her noble warriors, she is at ease with her androgyny, she produces power of another order—one that emanates from a space of moreness, where conventional thought and hegemonic beliefs in the structures of sexuality do not prevail. Not even her conversations with her conscience at the end as to her true motivations (pride or fervor or revenge) can undermine this powerful message. Thus, if Besson's Joan rejoins her predecessor in that she takes power-politics beyond Eros, she nonetheless distinguishes herself from the real Joan in that she cuts a swathe through the unnaturalness of gender fixity and offers us a beyond-sexuality (in the sense of a transcendence of binaries) that dares to speak its name!

---

46 A subversion we readily witness when she re-appropriates the archery tower, turns it around, and uses it as a bridge to break into the battlements.

Chapter 8
Sean Connery's Star Persona and the Queer Middle Ages

Tison Pugh

In a career spanning approximately fifty years and nearly seventy films of various genres, Sean Connery's definitive role is James Bond, seducer and spy extraordinaire from his seven films in the internationally successful series: *Dr. No* (1962), *From Russia with Love* (1963), *Goldfinger* (1964), *Thunderball* (1965), *You Only Live Twice* (1967), *Diamonds Are Forever* (1971), and *Never Say Never Again* (1983). As this iconic incarnation of British charm and heterosexual derring-do, Connery performs the necessary masculinity to establish the character's allure within the film franchise and, by so doing, to construct his star persona for consumer consumption. Because his role as Bond iconically defines Connery, the actor cannot help but to bring to his non-Bond roles certain expectations for these performances congruent with his star persona as Bond. Connery's star persona, the hybridized constellation of his fictional on-screen identity as Bond that merges with genuine markers of his identity, such as his physique, nationality, and voice, defines his appeal as an actor.

Over his long career, Connery has performed in films of various genres, including spy films, caper films, war films, science-fiction films, and mysteries/thrillers,[1] and the vast majority of these films feature Connery in roles that embody the alpha-male masculinity featured in the Bond franchise and congruent to his star persona. In his many medieval movies, including *Robin and Marian* (1976), *Time Bandits* (1981), *Sword of the Valiant: The Legend of Sir Gawain and the Green Knight* (1984), *Highlander* (1986), *The Name of the Rose* (1986), *Indiana Jones and the Last Crusade* (1989), *Highlander II: The Quickening* (1991), *Robin Hood: Prince of Thieves* (1991), *First Knight* (1995), and *Dragonheart* (1996), it is likewise apparent

---

1 In addition to the Bond films, Connery's espionage films include *The Russia House* (1990) and *The Hunt for Red October* (1990). His caper films include *The Anderson Tapes* (1971), *The Great Train Robbery* (1979), *Family Business* (1989), and *Entrapment* (1999). His war films include *On the Fiddle* (1961), *The Longest Day* (1962), *The Hill* (1965), and *A Bridge Too Far* (1977). His sci-fi films include *Zardoz* (1974), *Meteor* (1979), and *Outland* (1981). His mysteries and thrillers include *Time Lock* (1957), *Marnie* (1964), *The Offense* (1973), *The Presidio* (1988), *Rising Sun* (1993), and *Just Cause* (1995).

that Connery's star persona is sufficiently matched with audience expectations for medievally themed movies that Hollywood studios cast him in such parts with relative frequency.[2] One might thus expect Connery's medieval films to feature him in historically modulated alpha-male roles—e.g., the conquering crusader, the heroic knight, or the victorious king. On the contrary, Connery's medieval films queer the alpha-male construction of heroism that provided the foundation of his career and thus allow the actor to escape the typecasting that trapped other actors who assumed the mantle of James Bond.[3]

The queer potential of the Middle Ages to reassess masculinity arises in its position as temporal Other to modernity. Time and historical eras frequently serve as defining factors of cultural difference in art, literature, and film, in that varying temporalities are depicted as enacting various ideologically inflected behaviors and values. Along these lines, the Middle Ages frequently serves as the chronological Other that delineates modernity. When modernity is depicted as civilized in a time-travel film, then the Middle Ages might serve as its barbaric foil, along the lines of Mark Twain's contempt for "historical" England in his *A Connecticut Yankee in King Arthur's Court,* as well as in its films versions. From Will Rogers's and Bing Crosby's film versions of the novel to Disney's adaptations for kids, including *Unidentified Flying Oddball* and *A Kid in*

---

2 Defining film genres is a notoriously tricky business, and one might question the categorization of some of these films as medieval. *Robin and Marian, Sword of the Valiant, The Name of the Rose, Robin Hood: Prince of Thieves, First Knight* and *Dragonheart* all fit comfortably within the genre, as they are set within the temporal and social field of the western Middle Ages. *Time Bandits* features settings of various temporalities, of which the Middle Ages are featured prominently; however, Connery plays Agamemnon and a modern-day fireman, which thus muddies his relationship to its medievalism. The *Highlander* films also feature time travel between a medieval past and the late twentieth-century; in this instance, Connery's character appears in the medieval background to the film's modern storyline. *Indiana Jones and the Last Crusade* is set during the World War II era, yet given its theme of an Arthurian quest for the Holy Grail, it is certainly medieval in its narrative arc. These ten "medieval" films constitute approximately fifteen percent of Connery's film corpus, a substantial subgenre of the actor's career.

3 In terms of typecasting and career longevity, Sean Connery and David Niven are the only actors to play Bond and to maintain successful star identities after this role. The careers of George Lazenby, Roger Moore, and Timothy Dalton did not commercially prosper in the afterlives of their Bond performances. Pierce Brosnan may fare better, but he does not yet appear to be a major box-office draw in his non-Bond films, and it is too soon to gauge Bond's effect on Daniel Craig's career trajectory. Also, in terms of the contrast between Connery and Niven, Niven's career was well established when he played Bond in *Casino Royale* whereas Connery's career was still developing when he took the role. Connery is thus the only actor both to build his career on Bond and to enjoy continued success as a leading man and box-office powerhouse after Bond.

King Arthur's Court, the *Connecticut Yankee* storyline models the ways in which the past is depicted as a problem that only a hero from the future can fix. But the opposite approach also appears frequently, in that the courtly manners of the medieval past highlight the inhumanity and incivility of modern times. Through its labile deployment as counter to modernity, whether that modernity be utopian or nightmarish, the Middle Ages allows an alternate vision of the present as much as it presents a view of the past. Its queerness thus arises in its ability to reimagine genders of the present through the past, and for Connery, such a revisioning focuses consistently on the ways in which medievalism modulates the forceful masculinity of his star persona. Through Connery's medieval film oeuvre, we see a paradigmatic lesson in homohistory, which Jonathan Goldberg and Madhavi Menon describe as a queer theoretical praxis "invested in suspending determinate sexual and chronological differences while expanding the possibilities of the nonhetero, with all its connotations of sameness, similarity, proximity, and anachronism."[4] One might think Connery would hardly be interested in creating his own homohistory, but his medieval films nonetheless allow him to "suspend determinate sexual and chronological differences" within the construction of his star persona.

The connection between stars and their roles should function symbiotically to increase the celebrity of the star and the box-office gross of the film.[5] As a result of such mutually constitutive relationships, audiences learn to associate a given celebrity with certain types of roles in particular film genres. Such relationships bear the threat of typecasting, but as Richard Dyer demonstrates, an actor's films build in themselves a genre that creates expectations both for the star and for the films of the star's corpus:

> In certain respects, a set of star vehicles is rather like a film genre such as the Western, the musical or the gangster film. As with genres proper, one can discern across a star's vehicles continuities of iconography (e.g, how they are dressed, made-up and coiffed, performance mannerisms, the setting with which they are associated), visual style (e.g. how they are lit, photographed, placed within the frame) and structure (e.g. their role in the plot, the function in the film's symbolic pattern). . . . Of course, not all films made by a star are vehicles, but looking at their films in terms of vehicles draws attention to those films that do

---

4 Jonathan Goldberg and Madhavi Menon, "Queering History," *PMLA* 120.5 (2005): 1608-17, at p. 1608.

5 For studies of the Hollywood star system and the construction and marketing of stars, see Richard Dyer, *Stars* (London: British Film Institute, 1998) and Paul McDonald, *The Star System* (London: Wallflower, 2000).

not "fit," that constitute inflections, exceptions to, subversions of the vehicle pattern and the star image.[6]

In terms of the construction of audience expectations, the genres of Connery's films merge with their identity as vehicles for him, thus establishing modulated and hybrid genres—e.g., not just a caper film, but one of Connery's caper films. Looking for patterns among the various films of Connery's career, it is apparent that Connery plays in most of his films the heroic protagonist, a variation on a Bond theme, despite the variety of film genres in which he has performed.

In the construction of Connery as a star, the actor and the role of James Bond merge to form a hybridized yet unified icon. As Tony Bennett and Janet Woollacott observe, the borders between Connery and Bond blur together in the creation of a mythic persona:

> the close association between the figure of Bond and the constructed screen and off-screen identit[y] of Connery . . . bear[s] witness to the . . . process, best exemplified in the star system, whereby "real lives" become fictionalised and blended with screen images to result in the construction of a mythic figure poised midway between the two: the cases of Marilyn Monroe and John Wayne, for example.[7]

Connery observes of his fans that "they're bound to mix up the man with the image [of Bond]," which indicates his self-awareness that he metamorphosed into a hybrid figure comprising both human actor and Bond in the process of becoming a star. Yet Connery also realized that Bond bore the potential to circumscribe his celebrity if he were not careful about his star image: "The problem . . . is to get across the fact, without breaking your arse, that one is *not* Bond, that one was functioning reasonably well *before* Bond, and that one is going to function reasonably well *after* Bond."[8] When Connery spoke these words in 1965, he appeared confident about his continued success after Bond, but such success was in no manner guaranteed. He foresaw a commercially viable future beyond 007, but, for such a long-term career, he would need to modify his star persona by moving beyond Bond as a character while retaining his appeal as an actor.

The mythic cast of stardom creates a fictionality to the star's life, as it simultaneously imbues the actor's roles with the aura of "real life." Andrew Spicer notes that Connery's characters embody the actor's personal traits: "[Connery's]

---

6 Dyer, *Stars*, p. 62.

7 Tony Bennett and Janet Woollacott, *Bond and Beyond* (New York: Methuen, 1987), p. 45.

8 "*Playboy* Interview: Sean Connery," *Playboy* 12.11 (Nov. 1965): 75-84, at p. 78.

characters are always men of talent, embodying the values of individualistic self-help which unite them with Bond and with the widely circulated accounts of his own upbringing and his often abrasive independence as an actor, to create a classless hero who appeals across the age range."[9] The construction of heroic masculinity imbues the majority of Connery's roles with an unquestioned virility, and this machismo marginalizes other male characters from the ostensible privileges of their own masculine positions. Certainly, one of Connery's most salient traits is this powerful masculinity. In an interview tellingly entitled "Sean Connery: The Superman," Oriana Fallaci records that Diane Cilento, Connery's first wife, compares his masculinity to that of other men, and he measures up admirably to her expectations: "There aren't many real men around, are there? Sean is one, without question." To the wife's appreciative assessment of her husband's virility, Fallaci agrees wholeheartedly, "He certainly is."[10] Connery's decision to play heroes and protagonists in so many of his film roles accords with his "take charge" sensibility. He asserts his belief in the supremacy of power: "I admire something done, accomplished, successfully finished, not something theorized and philosophized about. Between conquered and conquerors I choose the conquerors, always."[11] Leaving aside the unethical bent of this statement, with its "might makes right" sensibility, his words point to a vision of heroic masculinity that demands success. Defeat denotes weakness, and the construction of and constant reinforcement of Connery's masculinity depends upon his virtual invincibility. One can thus see that Bond accords well with Connery's construction of himself as an actor and as a man. In Connery's words, "Bond is important: this invincible superman that every man would like to copy, that every woman would like to conquer, this dream we all have of survival."[12]

Such macho posturing cloaks the necessary fragility of masculinity: a man can brag and bluster all he desires, but his masculinity suffers from constant duress because it must be constantly defended, and every man's defenses must eventually break down. Connery realized the possibility of losing his masculine allure and, hence, his star persona. When explaining why he avoids Hollywood hoopla and publicity, he reports that his sense of his masculinity demands that he protect it, lest he lose it altogether:

---

9 Andrew Spicer, "Sean Connery: Loosening His Bonds," *British Stars and Stardom*, ed. Bruce Babington (Manchester: Manchester UP, 2001), 218-30, at p. 228.

10 Oriana Fallaci, *The Egotists: Sixteen Surprising Interviews* (Chicago: Regnery, 1968), p. 23.

11 Fallaci, *Egotists*, p. 36.

12 Fallaci, *Egotists*, p. 29.

> To take care I don't lose my head. To keep my balance. To stay a man. I mean, when what's happened to me happens to you, your balance hovers on a razor's edge. You give way just once, and you fall onto the razor and cut off your . . . in short, you're no longer a man. And I don't want to stop being a man.[13]

The delicate elision shields the reader from the ostensibly vulgar image of Connery's imagined castration, yet the nonetheless bald statement of phallic panic highlights the inevitable infirmity of masculinity for an actor whose star persona is based on machismo. In this passage, Connery shifts from first person to second person, ascribing to his interlocutor the loss of phallic puissance in response to the razor's castrating cut, as if he could not bear to picture such a fate befalling him.

From Connery's perspective, an actor must forever maintain his masculinity to continue being a man. However, if an actor's roles define this masculinity, he faces the likelihood of eventually losing his alpha-male status because no man should be able to play the action hero forever. The simple and unavoidable truth of aging necessitates that, as no warrior can fight forever, so too should no actor play a warrior forever. Given Hollywood's enthusiasm for youth, aging threatens an actor's viability for commercial success, as Linda Dittmar explains:

> For those whose gender and sexuality place them at the hub of commodified desires hinging on the allure of youthfulness . . . aging seems especially cruel because it threatens their very access to well-being. Their power, pleasure, and income depend on their position as icons of immortality; their aging will prove so repellent a sight as to make the gaze slide over them, disavowing their visible presence.[14]

An aging alpha-male actor continually faces a metaphoric castration as the next generation of younger and presumably more virile men begin to take the hyper-masculine roles that he formerly played. And certainly numerous action heroes have faced ridicule for playing heroic figures for too long, when their aging bodies can no longer credibly perform the heroism expected in such manly roles.

The alienating and commercially deleterious effects of aging, however, ring false in regard to Connery's career. His appeal as an actor is often reinforced

---

13 Fallaci, *Egotists*, p. 25.

14 Linda Dittmar, "Of Hags and Crones: Reclaiming Lesbian Desire for the Trouble Zone of Aging," *Between the Sheets, in the Streets: Queer, Lesbian, Gay Documentary*, eds. Chris Holmlund and Cynthia Fuchs (Minneapolis: U of Minnesota P, 1997), 71–90, at p. 71.

by his ever smoldering sexuality, despite his advanced years. He was fifty-nine years old when *People* named him "Sexiest Man Alive" in 1989,[15] and the popular press repeatedly comments on his status as a geriatric sex symbol: "Connery, at 74, is still a hell of an actor, and, surprisingly, a sex symbol."[16] Films late in Connery's career depict him as a powerful action figure of unquestioned strength and masculinity even in his sixties and seventies. For example, in *The Rock* (1996), Connery plays the alpha-male of unquestioned virility, in large measure overshadowing the performance of Nicolas Cage as scientist Dr. Stanley Goodspeed, despite the thirty-four-year difference between their ages.[17] During one of his hair-raising escapes, Connery's character John Mason concedes, "I'm too old for this," but the nonstop action belies the line.[18] In preparing to attack the bad guys, Mason hands Goodspeed a gun, and Goodspeed grimly declares, "I'll do my best." Mason disparages such trite declarations of effort with a ramped-up homage to adolescent machismo: "Your best? Losers always whine about their best. Winners go home and fuck the prom queen." Despite being approximately fifty years older than most prom queens, Connery plays in *The Rock* a slight variation on the hypersexual Bond theme, a Bond a bit wizened by the years but no less the alpha-male of big guns, sly cunning, and sexual virility. If one fails to perceive the connection between Mason and Bond, Mason makes the link explicitly clear when identifying himself to General Francis X. Hummel (Ed Harris), revealing his name to be "Captain John Patrick Mason . . . of Her Majesty's SS. Retired, of course." *On Her Majesty's Secret Service* features George Lazenby as Bond, but the direct allusion to the 007 franchise nonetheless tellingly connects Mason to Bond. A major box-office success, *The Rock* confirmed Connery's commercial viability as an action hero whose masculinity is largely untouched by the effects of aging.[19]

Connery has announced his retirement from film acting, and it is thus likely that *The League of Extraordinary Gentleman* (2003) will remain his final film; as such, it is a particularly fitting tribute to his status as an ageless action hero. Again, Connery plays the alpha-male, this time as H. Rider Haggard's Alan

---

15 "*People's* Sexiest Men Alive," *People Weekly* 48 (1997): 71-74.

16 "The 50 Greatest Movie Stars of All Time," *Premiere* (April 2005): 45-77, at p. 57. In an early interview, Connery hypothesized that, in the future, he would "like to be an old man with a good face" (Pete Hamill, "Bottled in Bond: Sean Connery," *Saturday Evening Post* 237.22 [June 6, 1964]: 32-33, at p. 33); it appears that he achieved this goal, at least in the eyes of the entertainment media.

17 Sean Connery was born on August 25, 1930; Nicolas Cage was born on January 7, 1964.

18 *The Rock*, dir. Michael Bay, DVD (1996; Hollywood Pictures Criterion Collection, 2001).

19 *The Rock* was the fourth highest grossing film of 1996, following *Independence Day, Twister,* and *Mission: Impossible* (McDonald, *The Star System*, p. 102).

Quartermain in a story pitting various characters from nineteenth-century fiction against the Fantom, a criminal mastermind who conspires to incite world war. As in *The Rock*, Connery's character disparages his ability to serve as an action hero due to his age: "I'm not the man I once was," he declares after being asked to join the eponymous league. Immediately following this demurral, however, villains murder his friend, and Quartermain springs into action and kills his attackers; the only indication that his age negatively affects his martial abilities is that he needs his glasses to aim at and shoot a fleeing assassin. He makes another disparaging remark about his advanced years ("I hate getting older"), but his actions again belie his age. Connery's Quartermain leads the other protagonists throughout the film, but he does not survive the final confrontation with arch-villain Moriarty/Fantom (Richard Roxburgh). With his dying words, he bequeaths the nascent twentieth century to his compatriot Tom Sawyer (Shane West) in an allegorical moment reflecting America's eclipsing of its British roots and the incipient decline of English imperialism: "May this new century be yours, as the old one was mine." If the death of Quartermain (and by extension, the twilight of Britain) appears to argue against Connery's status as alpha-male hero, the final shots of the film indicate that Connery/Quartermain achieves heroic immortality. An African priest dances around his grave, which begins to shoot with flames, suggesting that Quartermain—and Connery as actor—can cheat death and apotheosize into a mythic figure. If Connery remains in retirement and never makes another film, his final cinematic image will remain this moment of potential rebirth and eternal heroism, as a protagonist whom even the grave cannot conquer.

The Rock and *The League of Extraordinary Gentlemen* showcase the tenacity of the Bond hero throughout Connery's career, but his medieval films construct a subgenre of his corpus that qualifies his overwhelming construction as a heroic figure. By analyzing these films as "inflections, exceptions to, subversions of the vehicle pattern and the star image,"[20] it is apparent that Connery's medieval films provide a space for the actor to undermine his Bond persona and to escape the dangers of typecasting. Also, these films acknowledge Connery's aging, a fact which most of his contemporary action films deny. The Middle Ages provides a temporal framework for Connery to grow old gracefully and to play roles subversive of narrow definitions of alpha-male masculinity that privilege youth. Connery's apparent heroic agelessness in films such as *The Rock* and *The League of Extraordinary Gentlemen* in some ways mitigates the necessity of these roles, but given his somewhat ambivalent relationship to the role that made him a star, such medieval films give a deeper pitch to his career as a hero. The queerness of the Middle Ages, as an alien land of temporal and potentially

---

20 Richard Dyer, *Stars*, quoted previously.

gendered Otherness, is thus deployed to reconsider Connery's modern male masculinity.

Medieval films allow Connery to widen the contours of his star persona, yet some aspects of Bond nevertheless accord well with his cinematic medievalism. Pam Cook and Claire Hines observe in Connery's performance as Bond an anachronistic yet nonetheless appealing construction of masculinity that was undermined by the sexual revolution of the 1960s: "It is precisely his (often cringe-making) regressive qualities, and his lack of political correctness, that underpin his enduring appeal. His sadism and habit of treating some women as disposable objects are counter-balanced by an occasional chivalric tendency."[21] This assessment of Connery's correspondence with Bond also teasingly hints at his appropriateness for medieval films. In terms of the general audience's assessment of the Middle Ages, the period is often seen as regressive and lacking political correctness. The precarious balance between the chivalric adoration and misogynistic abuse of women characterizes (with broad strokes) their treatment in medieval films, which also connects to Connery's misogynistic persona, as in his belief that violence against women can be justified: "I don't think there is anything particularly wrong about hitting a woman—although I don't recommend doing it in the same way you'd hit a man."[22] The violence promised in these words appears somewhat "medieval" in sentiment, and as Carolyn Dinshaw argues, "medieval" itself often serves as a synonym of all that which society rejects in itself.[23] Furthermore, Connery's self-described identity as a "working class Scotsman" imbues him with the appropriate biographical and semiotic cues for medieval film roles.[24] His rich voice, with its warm Scottish brogue, suits him for medieval films by providing an aural cue to audiences about the setting of the film in the mythical "England" of popular culture.[25] Indeed, in *Dragonheart*, the female lead, Kara (Dina Meyer),

---

21 Pam Cook and Claire Hines, "'Sean Connery *Is* James Bond': Re-fashioning British Masculinity in the 1960s," *Fashioning Film Stars*, ed. Rachel Moseley (London: British Film Institute, 2005), 147-159, at p. 157.

22 "*Playboy* Interview: Sean Connery," p. 76.

23 Dinshaw further notes that the "problem with alterity [is that] the Middle Ages are taken to be absolutely other but turn out to be only a refraction of the present" (*Getting Medieval* [Durham, NC: Duke UP, 1999], p. 19). Both the Other and a means by which the present confronts itself, the Middle Ages functions as a necessary counterpoint to contemporary views of the present.

24 "*Playboy* Interview: Sean Connery," p. 77.

25 It is somewhat problematic to suggest that a Scottish brogue connotes medieval "England" in a film, especially when not all of Connery's medieval films take place in England. In regard to constructing audience expectations, Connery's voice is sufficiently—and attractively—different for audiences to identify it with a chivalric medieval past. Here we see another example of Roland Barthes's "insistent fringe":

compliments Connery's Draco for his voice ("You have a beautiful voice"), and in *Highlander*, Connery gives the voice-over for the film's introduction. One might expect Christopher Lambert, the actor playing the protagonist, to provide this narration, but Connery's brogue better suits the construction of audience expectations for medieval Scotland than Lambert's French accent.

Connery's medieval films begin in 1976 with Richard Lester's *Robin and Marian,* and this film ponders the meaning of heroism and masculinity for an aging man identified as an action hero.[26] As such, it seems a particularly apt choice for an actor in his mid-forties whose career was based on Bond and alpha-male masculinity, but who was seeking to expand his range of roles. After returning from the Crusades, Little John (Nicol Williamson) suggests reconstituting the band of merry men, but Connery's Robin Hood replies that he no longer considers himself fit for such adventuring: "Not at my age." Indeed, Robin's heroic actions are now unnecessary, as evident in this dialogue with his former beloved Maid Marian (Audrey Hepburn):

> *Robin:* If you're in trouble, I can save you.
> *Marian:* I've nothing to be saved from. I don't want you, Robin.
> *Robin:* But you've got me. I like the way you look.

An action hero more due to habit than necessity, Robin still seeks to prove his masculinity, but Marian no longer needs his assistance. Instead, she chides him for his juvenile behavior: "Robin, are you ever going to grow up?" *Robin and Marian* bears the markings of a post-Vietnam War film, as its characters express their fatigue with the incessant violence that creates only death and destruction, never peace. Marian attempts to dissuade Robin from engaging in battle with the sheriff: "What will you do now? Fight the sheriff? More corpses? Aren't you sick of it?" In contrast to James Bond's perfect ease and swagger with women, Connery's Robin Hood no longer understands how to interact with Marian. In the end, after Robin defeats the sheriff in hand-to-hand combat, Marian

---

the iconic use of symbols and signs that create and fulfill viewer's expectations for historicity. In some instances, one need not do much to communicate the setting of a film: for example, togas and hair cut in bangs for Romans, dirt for the Middle Ages. Connery's voice iconically suggests the Middle Ages, no matter the geographical location of any particular film. See Roland Barthes, "The Romans in Films," *Mythologies,* trans. Annette Lavers (New York: Hill & Wang, 1972), pp. 26-28 and also Vivian Sobchack, "The Insistent Fringe: Moving Images and Historical Consciousness," *History and Theory* 36.4 (1997): 4-20.

26 *Robin and Marian,* dir. Richard Lester, DVD (1976; Culver City, CA: TriStar Home Entertainment, 2002).

poisons Robin. She declares her undying love for him—"I love you more than God"—and Robin realizes why she has killed him:

> *Robin*: I'd never have a day like this again, would I?
> (Marian slowly shakes her head no.)
> *Robin*: Then it's better this way.
> (Marian nods.)

With one last burst of alpha-male glory, Robin saves the day, but his final victory brings with it his final defeat as well. The setting of medieval England thus allows Connery to explore the limits of Bondian masculinity in a scene impossible to imagine transpiring in the 007 franchise—the death of the aging hero, with no hope of fiery rebirth as in *The League of Extraordinary Gentlemen*.

Connery's star persona as a warrior of unquestioned virility does not typically blend well with paternal roles, but *Time Bandits* allows him to reimagine heroic fatherhood and depict its limitations.[27] He plays Agamemnon, but given the sacrifice of his daughter Iphigenia prior to departing for the Trojan War, this character serves as a poor role model for fathers. Within the action depicted in the film, Agamemnon returns to Mycenae after killing the "enemy of the people," a ferocious warrior wearing a bull's head mask. While fighting this "minotaur," however, Agamemnon is defeated in battle; the monstrous antagonist prepares to administer the *coup de grace*, but the young protagonist Kevin (Craig Warnock) falls out of the sky, thus giving Agamemnon sufficient opportunity to slay his adversary. Agamemnon subsequently adopts Kevin as his son ("I have decreed that this boy shall remain here with us in our city; furthermore, he shall from this day forward be my own son and heir to the throne of Mycenae"), but the eponymous time bandits kidnap the child and deprive him of this new home that promises an escape from a stultifying suburban life with his detached parents. At the film's close, Connery, now playing a fireman, reappears when Kevin's parents explode after touching a piece of concentrated evil. One might thus expect this fireman to adopt Kevin, thereby reenacting Agamemnon's earlier adoption of him; however, both of Connery's characters act with insufficient masculine or paternal force to effect a happy ending. The film trails off with Kevin standing by himself, orphaned and alone. Locating a hero in *Time Bandits* is a difficult task, as Kevin represents a quick-witted child, but certainly not a hero. Connery shows off his fantastic and heroic physique in the film—wearing a short tunic that displays his muscular legs and draws attention to his somewhat immodest undergarments—but this heroic figure cannot resolve Kevin's search

---

27 *Time Bandits*, dir. Terry Gilliam, DVD (1981; Troy, MI: Anchor Bay Entertainment, 1999).

for a suitable father. As in *Robin and Marian,* masculinity fails to catalyze a happy ending or to showcase Connery's virility.

As Dyer points out, a star's vehicles include films that do not fit the expectations that typically surround a given actor, and certain films roles—such as a kidnapping Moroccan sheik in *The Wind and the Lion* (1975), the villainous Sir August de Wynter in *The Avengers* (1998), and the Green Knight in *Sword of the Valiant: The Legend of Sir Gawain and the Green Knight*—cast Connery as the antagonist, in apparent contradiction to his heroic star persona.[28] It is hard to take Connery's antagonistic Green Knight seriously, however, with his campy costuming and make-up. The Green Knight is heavily bronzed, as if just returned from a Riviera vacation, and glitter sparkles on his hair and face. Most ridiculous is the Green Knight's body armor, which features a large cut-out in order to show off his muscled, hairy chest. Not surprisingly, in the climactic battle between Gawain (Miles O'Keeffe) and the Green Knight in which they fight to the death, Gawain stabs him in the chest. "Stop. Stay your sword," the Green Knight pleads, as he then ages rapidly and proclaims before he dies, "Now, live on, Sir Gawain. Live on." A low-budget production from schlockmeisters Menahem Golan and Yoram Globus, *Sword of the Valiant* represents a nadir in Connery's career, but the role nonetheless depicts his facility with campy cinematic theatrics and heroics, thus further distancing him from the Bond persona of suave urbanity.

Of Connery's medieval films, *Highlander* most valorizes typical constructions of alpha-male masculinity, but Connery does not play the film's heroic lead.[29] In this tale of supernatural beings fighting for supremacy, of whom only one can triumph, Connery's character Juan Sanchez Villa-Lobos Ramirez plays a decidedly secondary and effete role to Christopher Lambert's Connor MacLeod. He apprises MacLeod of his latent identity as a quasi-immortal, but this role as MacLeod's mentor is somewhat paradoxical: he informs MacLeod, "In the end, there can be only one," but such a situation would thus require that MacLeod kill Ramirez. Regardless of the logic of a mentor training a student to execute him at some undetermined point in the future, Connery's character is repeatedly effeminized in his role as mentor, despite that, by definition, a mentor should stand in a more powerful position than the student. "You look like a woman," MacLeod tells Ramirez upon meeting him, due to his rather flamboyant costuming. Ramirez teaches MacLeod to deny himself amatory pleasures, telling him, "You must leave her, brother" and "let Heather go," ostensibly because these immortal warriors will live past the lives of their mortal lovers.

---

28 *Sword of the Valiant: The Legend of Sir Gawain and the Green Knight*, dir. Stephen Weeks, DVD (1984; MGM Home Entertainment, 2004).

29 *Highlander*, dir. Russell Mulcahy, DVD (1986; Troy, MI: Anchor Bay Entertainment, 2002).

As the hero of the series, however, MacLeod ignores this advice, maintaining his relationship with Heather (Beatie Edney) in the film's medieval past and sleeping with Brenda Wyatt (Roxanne Hart) in its contemporary scenes. As MacLeod's mentor, Connery's Ramirez must be surpassed both in terms of his sexual and martial prowess, a queer fate unimaginable for Bond.

In *The Name of the Rose*, Connery's masculinity is tempered by his religious role as a Franciscan monk, William of Baskerville.[30] In a role predicated upon the character's asexuality and imperviousness to both heterosexual and homosexual desire, Connery serves as the voice of modern reason and logic in the medieval past: he is the Sherlock Holmes of the Middle Ages, as his geographic home in Baskerville, reminiscent of Arthur Conan Doyle's famous hound, suggests. If this clue fails to connect William to Sherlock for the audience, the monk also co-opts Holmes's famous line when, in explaining the apparent suicide of a monk, he exclaims to his novice Adso (Christian Slater), "My dear Adso, it's elementary." *The Name of the Rose* plays with many queer themes, especially in its subplot involving homosexual desires among the monks that motivate some of the many murders. William, however, is never implicated by the homoerotic desires flourishing in this corrupt monastery, as his homosocial desires are predicated upon intellectual—never sexual—communion. After being seduced by a young woman, who is quite dirty and thus symbolizes the degrading force of heterosexual intercourse, Adso asks William about love:

Adso: Master, have you ever been in love?
William: In love? Yes, many times.
Adso: You were?
William: Yes, of course . . . Aristotle, Ovid, Vergil, Thomas Aquinas . . .
Adso: No, no, I meant with a . . .
William: Oh. Ah. You're not confusing love with lust . . .

The mental homosociality on display in *The Name of the Rose* contrasts sharply with the sharp intellect of James Bond. Surely, 007 relies on his keen wits throughout his many adventures, but his dash and bravado construct him as a man of action, not as an intellectual. By focusing on cerebral pursuits, William undermines a typical construction of Bondian masculinity and thus modulates Connery's star persona increasingly into a mentoring figure of impressive intelligence. Andrew Spicer argues that Connery's roles as a mentor create a new facet to his star persona as a "nonconformist tribal elder," and these mentoring roles imbue Connery's star persona with a gravitas lacking in

---

30 *The Name of the Rose*, dir. Jean-Jacques Annaud, DVD (1986; Burbank, CA: Warner, 2004).

Bond's untamed sexuality.[31] As a mentor, William teaches Adso the primacy of male homosociality over heterosexuality, and at the film's conclusion, the novice rejects the dirty girl with whom he earlier fornicated. Instead, Adso follows William, and in the ending voice-over, he reveals that William bequeathed him his eyeglasses, in a symbolic move to link Adso to the homosocial scholarly world represented by Aristotle and Aquinas.

As a quest film in which Connery plays the father of action hero Indiana Jones (Harrison Ford), *Indiana Jones and the Last Crusade* differs intrinsically from the generic expectations of most of Connery's action/adventure/espionage films.[32] Although the enemies are vanquished at the film's conclusion, the quest for the Holy Grail must fail as well. It drops into a chasm, and first Nazi collaborator Dr. Elsa Schneider (Alison Doody) dies reaching for it, and then Indy almost dies while grasping for it, until his father gently admonishes him that the quest is not worth dying for: "Indiana, Indiana, let it go." The grail, in the final analysis, was not the objective of the quest as much as the experience itself, as Indiana learns when he asks his father what he gained from their adventures:

Indiana: What did you find, dad?
Henry Jones, Sr.: Me? Illumination.

If the quest for the Holy Grail provides the film's overarching narrative structure, overcoming father/son rivalries and healing the rift between generations serves as its thematic core. As Susan Aronstein declares, "the search for the father and the search for the Grail are one and the same."[33] Certainly, the two men compete with each other throughout the film. After discovering an important clue to the location of the Grail, Indy derides his father's ability to meet the challenges of the quest: "He never would have made it past the rats." The two men also compete sexually: both father and son sleep with Elsa, as suggested by her telling Indy, "I can't forget how wonderful it was," and by Henry's surprising revelation that "she talks in her sleep." A leitmotif running throughout the film is Indy's repeated demand that he not be called "Junior," an infantilizing appellation that underscores his father's superior masculine position. In terms of Connery's career, the viewer sees traces of his alpha-male heroism, as when he points out that "In this sort of race, there's no silver medal for finishing second," but the film's deeper thematic focus appears in the reconstitution of the father/son bond that both men have largely neglected. As Connery's

---

31 Spicer, "Sean Connery: Loosening His Bonds," p. 229.

32 *Indiana Jones and the Last Crusade*, dir. Steven Spielberg, DVD (1989; Hollywod: Paramount, 2003).

33 Susan Aronstein, *Hollywood Knights* (New York: Palgrave Macmillan, 2005), p. 131.

Agamemnon in *Time Bandits* showcases the failures of heroic masculinity to merge with fatherhood, *The Last Crusade* focuses on two alpha-males learning to surpass narrow constructions of heroism by working together and reforging familial bonds. At the end of *Indiana Jones and the Last Crusade*, cooperative masculinity triumphs over its antagonistic incarnation.

In his uncredited role as Richard the Lion-Hearted in *Robin Hood: Prince of Thieves*, who appears in the film's conclusion, Connery performs with appropriate gravitas and affection when presiding unexpectedly at the marriage of Robin (Kevin Costner) and Marian (Mary Elizabeth Mastrantonio).[34] Long away fighting in the Crusades, Richard reasserts his authority, which his long absence has undermined:

> *Richard*: (Interrupting the wedding, to Friar Tuck): Hold, I speak.
> *Marian*: Richard . . .
> *Richard*: I will not allow this wedding to proceed . . .
> *Robin*: (sotto voce): My Lord . . .
> *Richard*: unless I am allowed to give the bride away.
> (Turning to Marian) You look radiant.
> *Robin*: We are deeply honored, your majesty.
> *Richard*: It is I who am honored, Lord Locksley. Thanks to you, I still have a throne. Friar, proceed.

Connery's Richard retains the right to distribute fair maidens to brave men, yet as he himself admits, it is only thanks to Robin's defense of his kingdom that he still holds it. In this film, Connery's cameo role shores up the alpha-male status of Robin Hood as character and of Kevin Costner as actor; ironically, he assists Costner to construct the same type of alpha-male protagonist that he escapes by taking such a secondary role.[35]

His penultimate medieval film, *First Knight*, features Connery's King Arthur as the unquestioned ruler of Camelot but nonetheless a lover and a warrior past his prime.[36] He is painfully aware that, despite her protests of love, Guinevere is motivated to marry him to protect her kingdom rather than due to any sexual attraction to him. In battle with the men who attacked her kingdom, Arthur

---

34 *Robin Hood, Prince of Thieves*, dir. Kevin Reynolds, DVD (1991; Burbank, CA: Warner, 1997).

35 In following Kevin Costner's career, it is apparent that, to date, he has not successfully negotiated the transition from action hero to an actor of continuing commercial success in non-action-hero roles, as he not scored a major box-office hit following the debacle of *The Postman* (1997).

36 *First Knight*, dir. Jerry Zucker, DVD (1995; Culver City, CA: Columbia TriStar Home Video, 1997).

shouts "Charge," but he does not join the combat; instead, he directs the men from the sides while Lancelot (Richard Gere) fights fiercely. Because Arthur can no longer effectively defend Camelot due to his age, he builds allegiances both homosocial and heterosexual to cement his authority. When Lancelot joins the Round Table, the knights swear to one another, "Brother to brother, yours in life and death," and this scene of homosocial "marriage" is immediately followed by the marriage of Arthur and Guinevere (Julia Ormond), which underscores the virtually identical nature of these vows. The knights then pledge to Guinevere: "I swear to love and serve Guinevere, my true and rightful queen, and to protect her honor as my own." The knights follow Arthur in his oaths, and the construction of Camelot thus depends on Arthur carefully choosing his wife and knights and then linking them to one another. After this social order fractures when Arthur discovers Lancelot and Guinevere embracing, the kingdom is vulnerable to Malagant (Ben Cross), who soon demands to Arthur that he "Kneel before me, or die." Arthur does so, apparently conceding the battle, before exhorting his people to fight:

> I have no pride left in me. What I do now, I do for my people and for Camelot, and may they forgive me. This is my last act as your king. Do not be afraid. All things change. I am Arthur of Camelot, and I command you all now to fight! Never surrender! Never surrender!

Arthur is immediately pierced with arrows—a queerly iconic penetration indicating the superior phallic strength of this rival—but Lancelot then defeats Malagant with Arthur's sword. The symbol of phallic strength passes from the aged to the young, and, on his deathbed, Arthur also bequeaths Camelot and Guinevere to his rival Lancelot. Leaving Lancelot and Guinevere alive at the film's conclusion, *First Knight* radically rewrites Malory's *Morte D'Arthur* in its final shots of Arthur's maritime funeral, as presided over by his wife and friend. The once and future king is here eclipsed in death by the adulterous couple who, as the surviving members of the erotic triangle, must now face their relationship without the crutch of their mutual, although asexual, love for Arthur. Cuckolded and then killed in battle, Connery's aging Arthur displays a masculinity queered from the privileges of his authority as king.

Dragonheart, Connery's last medieval film, tells the unlikely story of Bowen (a knight played by Dennis Quaid) and Draco (a dragon voiced by Connery), who join forces to defraud villages in a "protection" scam, in which Bowen "kills" Draco in battle so that the beast will no longer terrorize the people.[37] Despite

---

37 *Dragonheart and Dragonheart: A New Beginning*, dirs. Rob Cohen and Doug Lefler, DVD (1995; Universal City, CA: Universal Studies, 2004).

their chicanery, Bowen and Draco represent the values of the Old Code, which is threatened by the evil ruler, King Einon (David Thewlis):

> A knight is sworn to valor.
> His heart knows only virtue.
> His blade defends the helpless.
> His might upholds the weak.
> His word speaks only truth.
> His wrath undoes the wicked.

Connery's voice portrayal of Draco, the virtuous monster, allows him to perform a new role of the self-sacrificial Other, one who must die for the benefit of his human companions. He is intimately connected to King Einon as a result of an earlier ritual, such that, as Draco realizes, "For Einon to die, I must die." After Draco's death and in the final shot of Bowen, it appears that Draco's spirit lives on in the knight, as Bowen exhales and his breath frosts in the cold night air, reminiscent of Draco's smoky exhalations. Gilbert of Glockenspur (Pete Postlethwaite) makes explicit the salvific nature of Draco's death: "And in the days following Draco's sacrifice, Bowen and Kara led the people in a time of justice and brotherhood. As I remember it now, those were golden years warmed by an unworldly light. And when things became the most difficult, Draco's star shone more brightly, for all of us who knew where to look." In this vocal performance, Connery assumes a bestial and sacrificial role that nonetheless allows him to play a character whose age and wisdom merge well with the medieval mentor roles also found in *Highlander* and *The Name of the Rose*.

In sum, Connery's medieval films allow him to complicate the construction of James Bond as the defining feature of his star persona and thus to escape the alpha-male masculinity that might have uncomfortably circumscribed the contours of his career. One might expect that the Middle Ages would serve as an inhospitable setting for men to age gracefully, especially in light of its pop-culture construction as a land of knights forever jousting. Connery plays with the myths of the Middle Ages as he also plays with the mythic cast of his star persona. As an aging Robin Hood in *Robin and Marian,* an ultimately ineffectual father figure in *Time Bandits*, the glittery antagonist of *Sword of the Valiant*, an asexual monk in *The Name of the Rose*, a foppish mentor in *Highlander*, a powerless ruler in *Robin Hood: Prince of Thieves*, a cuckolded King Arthur in *First Knight*, and a salvific dragon in *Dragonheart*, Connery explores roles disruptive to cultural paradigms of alpha-male and heroic masculinity that ultimately helped his career to flourish in the many years after James Bond. Surprisingly, the queer Middle Ages allow an old man to age gracefully in the "past" while remaining a culturally constructed sex symbol in the present.

Between medieval and postmodern, then, where is the queerness of temporality? It is often found where it is necessary to perform specific ideological, and sometimes individual, work. As an actor playing roles situated across the centuries, Sean Connery offers a unique opportunity to witness the ways in which masculinity, as embodied in a star persona, metamorphoses queerly between past and present. That Sean Connery's rugged hyper-masculine persona needs the queerness of the past to prosper in the present showcases the cultural ambiguity and necessity of queerness in delineating masculinities across the ages.

Chapter 9
Will Rogers' Pink Spot:
A Connecticut Yankee (1931)

Kathleen Coyne Kelly

Bessie Smith, in *"Foolish Man Blues"* (1927), sings:

> There's two things got me puzzled,
> there's two things I can't stand,
> A mannish actin' woman
> and a skippin' twistin' woman actin' man.

What follows is a study of an "actin' man": Will Rogers. By the time he starred in *A Connecticut Yankee* (David Butler, 1931), he was already famous.[1] Rogers was known as a plain-speaking man of the people with a wry sense of humor who criticized the follies of government and the excesses of capitalism and denounced discrimination against women and people of color. Part Cherokee (which he never let people forget), Rogers was loved by almost everyone—even by such representatives of big business as Ford and Rockefeller. Rogers regularly and deliberately spoke from the margins: as he famously said in *So This Is London* (John Blystone, 1930), his ancestors didn't come over on the Mayflower; they met the boat. Rogers is always Rogers, no matter the character he plays, and he embodies, literally and figuratively, a transcultural, hybridized space.

The role of Hank Martin in *A Connecticut Yankee* was perfect for Rogers. Martin is a hero who stands up for social justice and good government—albeit

---

1 *A Connecticut Yankee*, dir. David Butler, perf. Will Rogers, Maureen O'Sullivan, Myrna Loy, Frank Albertson, and William Farnum, VHS (1931; CBS/FOX Video, 1991). Excerpts from '*A Connecticut Yankee*' ©1931 courtesy of Twentieth Century Fox. Written by William M. Conselman and Owen Davis. All rights reserved. Also courtesy of the Will Rogers estate. Figure 3 '*A Connecticut Yankee*' ©1931 Twentieth Century Fox. All rights reserved. Also courtesy of the Will Rogers estate. Figure 2 courtesy of the Will Rogers estate. Special thanks to Steven K. Gragert, Director of the Will Rogers Memorial Museums, who kindly read my essay and offered corrections on some factual matters with respect to Will Rogers' life and the screenplay of the film. All errors that remain are, of course, my own.

backed by a large fleet of knights-errant in Austin motor cars. *A Connecticut Yankee* is of its historical moment, capturing the confusion and fear of the Great Depression. The film also anticipates Roosevelt's New Deal, in that Martin brings progress and prosperity to Arthur's kingdom through the invention of new jobs to serve new technologies. This is not unproblematic, as we shall see. Rogers' Yankee, like Twain's, introduces a superior art of war that devastates the "natives," as it were.

A summary of the film is in order, in part to register how it differs from Mark Twain's *A Connecticut Yankee in King Arthur's Court*. While Twain uses the Middle Ages as a "sort of mythological stage on which to place contemporary characters," as Umberto Eco says of those for whom the Middle Ages is simply a pretext,[2] Hollywood returns to a silent film, *A Connecticut Yankee in King Arthur's Court* (Emmett Flynn, 1921), as its pretext and pre-text, with the result that Rogers' *A Connecticut Yankee* is once-removed from Twain's *A Connecticut Yankee* and thus twice-removed from the Middle Ages.[3]

Radio repairman and amateur radio host Hank Martin delivers a battery to a mock-gothic horror of a house of a crazed inventor (William Farnum), and encounters a menacing butler (Brandon Hurst), a pair of young lovers (Maureen O'Sullivan and Frank Albertson) and a threatening vamp (Myrna Loy). The inventor tells Martin that he has succeeded at listening to the past on the radio. A suit of armor then falls on Martin, knocking him unconscious. He wakes up as he is poked by Sir Sagramor le Desirous (Hurst) with a lance. Taken prisoner, he awes Arthur (Farnum) and angers Merlin (Mitchell Harris) with tricks with his cigarette lighter. He is imprisoned with the page Amyas le Poulet (Albertson), who is guilty of loving Arthur's daughter Alisande (O'Sullivan). Looking into his trusty notebook-*cum*-almanac, Martin discovers that an eclipse is in the offing, and threatens Arthur with total darkness. Once he "saves" the kingdom from the eclipse, Martin becomes "Sir Boss," and proceeds to modernize Camelot with telephones, automated knights-in-armor-washes, and the "magic" of advertising. Martin is captured by Morgan le Fay, escaping her embraces only to be condemned to death (along with Arthur and Alisande) by hanging. Amyas le Poulet/Clarence and various knights come to his rescue. They ride motorcycles, drive baby Austins and tanks, fly airplanes and helicopters, and are armed with machine guns and sawed-off shotguns. Finally, a bomb is dropped on Morgan's castle. Martin is knocked out, and wakes up to find the

---

2 Umberto Eco, "Dreaming of the Middle Ages," *Travels in Hyperreality* (1973; New York: Harcourt, 1986), p. 68.

3 Contemporary reviewers compare Rogers' *A Connecticut Yankee* favorably with its silent predecessor, though the two heroes are very different: Harry Myers as Hank Morgan in the silent version is quite the bon-vivant. The film survives in only a few reels.

inventor's doctor (Harris) hovering over him; he leaves the mansion, finds the runaway lovers outside, and helps them to escape in his van.

Rogers' Hank Martin is not only a man of the people, but a man's man. He asserts the prerogatives of the masculine and the homosocial in an aw-shucks kind of way, and avoids the company of women—and their advances—like a pre-pubescent boy who thinks girls are, well, icky. It is Rogers/Martin's problems with the feminine that are my main concern. Martin's emphatic rejection of women opens up an intriguing space: one might well ask, if he is *against* women, what is he *for*? Rogers queers the cowboy—and Rogers is indeed a cowboy in *A Connecticut Yankee*—not necessarily toward homosexuality or even a homoerotic, but away from a consummated heterosexuality. In *A Connecticut Yankee* as well as in many of his other films, Rogers performs a failed heterosexuality; such a failure interrogates male heterosexuality as much as, queerly enough, it reproduces it. Moreover, the crisis of beset manhood as Rogers performs it is played out against—indeed, is dependent upon—a representation of women as dangerous schemers and viragos. Men are men, it seems, because women are trouble.

Rogers' biographers say, often with admiration, that Rogers' screen persona was not much different from his private self; for this reason, a foray into biography may be helpful. Rogers (b. 1879), after a long, equivocal courtship, married Betty Blake in 1908. "When I roped her, that was the star performance of my life," Rogers said. She was an educated, middle-class white woman who made it clear to Rogers that she wanted to live like white folks—that is, not where he was born, in Indian Territory (even though his family were well-off ranchers). After marriage, Rogers was very much the devoted family man. Although he supported women's rights in the abstract, he reportedly said that actress Irene Dunne was the only woman for whom he would vote for congress.[4] Rogers, according to one biographer, was also "prudish and old-fashioned . . . While ahead of his time in most political and social matters, Will was stuck back in the Dark Ages when it came to gender."[5] Myrna Loy describes Rogers as

A rascal . . . who liked to tease me. . . . Perhaps men need that as an excuse for contact, particularly shy men like Will; even little boys do it. . . . This was Will Rogers as far as I was concerned, very much the Connecticut Yankee, very much that character.[6]

---

4 Ray Robinson, *American Original: A Life of Will Rogers* (New York: Oxford UP, 1996), p. 212.

5 Robinson, *American Original*, p. 212.

6 James Korsilibas-Davis and Myrna Loy, *Being and Becoming* (London: Bloomsbury, 1987), pp. 62-63.

Rogers apparently disapproved of Maureen O'Sullivan's wearing trousers to the set of *So This Is London*. She, in turn, judged Rogers to be a "sharp man, with nothing accidental in his behavior." O'Sullivan also said of Rogers: "if he ever said he never met a man he didn't like, he sure didn't care much for women."[7]

Rogers (who was sometimes billed as "The Cherokee Kid") began his career by performing rope tricks in rodeos throughout the United States and elsewhere. He also moved into vaudeville and worked for a time in Zeigfeld's Follies. He sustained his persona from his cowboy and vaudeville routines throughout his silent and talking film career, and even carried it over into his more serious career as a commentator on the world scene in newspapers and radio. As should be clear by now, Rogers participated in, and helped to shape, all of the major venues for popular entertainment in the early twentieth century.

Rogers was never just an actor in the films in which he starred; rather, he intervened in most aspects of production. He routinely wrote his own dialogue, set up his own scenes, and even performed scenes extemporaneously—unheard of in the early days of film. He often infuriated the directors he worked with, including John Ford.[8] His ad-hoc style discomfited fellow actors. Rogers made it clear that he did not enjoy the role of leading man or romantic interest; he much preferred acting as a friend to a clichéd pair of star-crossed lovers. And Rogers consistently kept an emotional distance from other characters in his films, in part through a humorous meta-commentary. Bob Hope, in a hagiographical documentary on Rogers, says that he "was just the same on-screen as off."[9] What we see in *A Connecticut Yankee*, then, as Myrna Loy says, is a palimpsest Rogers.

Rogers' *A Connecticut Yankee* has its roots in vaudeville (at its peak c. 1880-1920); indeed, this is true of the majority of Rogers' films. In fact, *A Connecticut Yankee* tropes misogyny and the limits of gender identification in many of the ways that vaudeville did. Rogers was certainly fond of the sight gag and the witty retort, but he also drew upon another feature of vaudeville: minstrel acts and drag acts, both of which came to influence vaudeville's replacement, silent film. In their heyday in the nineteenth century, minstrel acts did not include women; female parts were played by men. Minstrel sketches invariably included bits lampooning women and women's rights. In vaudeville, sexual orientation

---

7 Robinson, *American Original*, p. 212.

8 John Ford said: "Nobody could write for Will. . . . And what he came up with was so much better than what was written in the script" (qtd. in Bryan and Frances Sterling, eds., *Will Rogers in Hollywood* [New York: Crown, 1984], pp. 151-52). David Butler said of Rogers: "He had quite a time with his lines. You see, he learned them, but they weren't written in his language. He improved his lines" (qtd. in Sterling and Sterling, *Will Rogers*, p. 113).

9 *The Story of Will Rogers*, narrated by Bob Hope (NBC News Presents, 1961).

WILL ROGERS' PINK SPOT: A CONNECTICUT YANKEE (1931)

was fair game. Because explicitly representing homosexuals on stage was illegal, performers developed an elaborate code of mannerisms and dress—such as wearing a red tie—to signal gay characters.[10]

As vaudeville became less popular in the 1920s, there was a renascence of interest in minstrel shows and in "Negro" entertainment in Harlem and then on Broadway. Coincident with Prohibition (which resulted in a network of clandestine clubs), the 1920s also marked what is often called the "pansy craze."[11] Hundreds of New York's social elite attended drag balls in Greenwich Village as spectators, and attended drag and "pansy" revues and burlesques. The popular female impersonator Jean Malin seems to have started a vogue for emcees in drag at fashionable clubs; as one newspaperman described this trend, there were so many that "there was a hand on a hip for every light on Broadway."[12] (I'll be returning to the effeminate, coded body with respect to Rogers' strategies of self-representation later.) The end of the "pansy craze" coincided with the repeal of Prohibition (1933), after which one could get a whisky anywhere, and new, more repressive laws against "pansy" or transvestite entertainment were enacted.

A Connecticut Yankee exploits drag acts in a number of ways. First, male drag is reversed in that we see women dressed as pages at Arthur's court. In one scene, the action stops as a female page enters the court and, elaborately bowing, hands Arthur a message. The scene is framed to foreground the page. Another example: Martin, known as "Sir Boss" after he conjures up the eclipse, employs cross-dressed pages along with decidedly feminine telephone operators and stenographers. In one scene, a coyly named Genevieve (a medieval Mae West) takes dictation from "Sir Boss" while flirting with him. As she eyes him suggestively, the camera slowly pans across his face, registering his look of disgusted suspicion. The film thus represents, and makes fun of, women in their limited roles in the workforce in the 1920s and 1930s—and limited opportunities, if flirting with the boss can be so described. At the Boss's office, perilous female sexuality is held in check by its own hyperbole, and is mitigated by boyish women pages on roller skates.

Cross-dressed pages are also prominent at Morgan le Fay's castle. For example, at Morgan's order, and against Martin's protests, a group of laughing women dressed as pages dress him in silks and finery. I see Zeigfeld's influence on the casting of the pages: women in short tunics and hose serve as a fine

---

10 John Loughery, *The Other Side of Silence: Men's Lives and Gay Identities* (New York: Holt, 1998), p. 39.

11 See George Chauncey, *Gay New York* (New York: HarperCollins, 1994), pp. 301-29.

12 Quoted in Chauncey, *Gay New York*, p. 318. Chauncey also documents the opening of a Pansy Club in 1930 (p. 318).

pretext for showing off good legs. But the presence of cross-dressed pages also reinforces other moments of gender trouble as it is expressed through clothing. For example, in one scene at Arthur's court, just as one has gotten used to women in tights, a row of heralds plays trumpets which obscure their faces and the top part of their bodies. It looks like a row of women wearing gathered skirts. However, as the heralds lower their trumpets, it becomes obvious that they are men. The scene is played for its *frisson* of misrecognition and then adjustment, and is then repeated a few episodes later for emphasis.

The treatment of male drag in *A Connecticut Yankee* is dependent upon a calculated misreading of medieval dress. When Martin boasts that he will blot out the sun, he taps Sir Sagramor, dressed in a long tunic, saying: "Listen Saggy . . . and when I do, you're gonna jump right out of that embroidered nightie you've got on"—an ad-libbed remark by Rogers. The scene is played for a broad laugh, but it also helps Martin establish himself as "properly" dressed in his modern white shirt and overcoat. This scene also captured the interest of the censors; the laws that set limits on live entertainment in the 1920s and 1930s had their parallels in Hollywood. Apparently R. E. Plummer of the Hays Office (soon to become the Production Code Administration) did not hear the above dialogue correctly. The PCA, the censorship board that in effect determined what films were made in Hollywood for almost forty years, was not institutionalized until 1934. However, the conservative activist Will Hays had first formulated the Code as a set of "Do's" and "Don'ts" and "Be Carefuls" in 1927, and the Motion Pictures Producers and Distributors Association began to comply with what was then called the "Hays Code" in 1930. The Code prohibited representations of "sexual perversion or any inference to it," as gay and lesbian acts and identities were branded, but that did not mean that there were no depictions of gays and lesbians. Rather, as in vaudeville, performers depended on speech, mannerisms, costumes, and other props to be decoded by those who chose to.[13] The Hays Office attempted to censor *A Connecticut Yankee*, mainly because of language—Martin, as per the script, says "Where the helleth am I?" and Arthur calls Merlin "spawn of the devil"—and because of several violent scenes. The Hays Office also wanted the allusion to Mussolini (quoted above) deleted, as well as shots of Rogers shooting Morgan's knights. Fox declined to make the cuts. Instead of hearing Morgan's reference to Sagramor as "Saggy," Plummer heard *faggy* and took offense at the word due

13 The Hays Code can be found at www.artsreformation.com, The Motion Picture Production Code of 1930 (Hays Code) <http://www.artsreformation.com/a001/hays-code.html> (last accessed 12 June 2008).

to its "meaning pervert"; Plummer said the word has got to go.[14] However, as I have shown above, the script had simply turned "Sagramor" into a diminutive: "Saggy." Perhaps Rogers' scriptwriter was playing on the possibility of *Saggy* sounding like *faggy*, especially given the "nightie" remark. Or perhaps we might attribute Plummer's mishearing to homosexual panic, a version of Woody Allen's character thinking everyone is saying "Jew" in *Annie Hall* (1977). I would like to think that Plummer recognized that something was decidedly queer about *A Connecticut Yankee*.

In another, more pointed scene, faced with the page Amy (Frank Albertson) in a tunic, Rogers is made uneasy by what he sees as the blurring of gender difference through dress—for indeed, he thinks Amyas le Poulet, who is the only male page in the film—is wearing a dress. (When Rogers first hears Amyas's name, he mangles it as "Amy"; I will refer to him as "Amy" throughout.) We might take Twain's version of the meeting between Hank Morgan and Clarence in *A Connecticut Yankee in King Arthur's Court* as containing the seeds of the corresponding events in *A Connecticut Yankee*. In Twain's novel, Morgan, thinking that he has landed in an asylum, is looking for someone who might help him out. He is directed to

> . . . an airy slim boy in shrimp-colored tights that made him look like a forked carrot, the rest of his gear was blue silk and dainty laces and ruffles; and he had long yellow curls, and wore a plumed pink satin cap tilted complacently over his ear. . . . He . . . said he had come for me, and informed me that he was a page. . . .
>
> "Now, Clarence, my boy—if that might happen to be your name . . ."[15]

This is a deliberately effeminate portrait. In *A Connecticut Yankee*, this encounter is transformed thusly:

Martin: I don't want to be inquisitive . . . ahhh just what is thy sex?

Amy: I understand thee not.

Martin: Say . . . I've seen you somewhere, but I can't place that boyish bob you've got on there. What got you in here for?

---

14 Letter reproduced with permission of the Academy of Motion Picture Arts and Sciences Library, Beverly Hills, CA (Production Code Administration Archive, Special Collections).

15 Mark Twain, *A Connecticut Yankee in King Arthur's Court*, ed. Bernard Stein (Iowa Center for Textural Studies/U of California P, 1979), pp. 61-63.

. . . *[intervening episodes]*

Cut back to dungeon.

Martin: What did you say your name was, sonny?

Amy: Amyas le Poulet, by grace of God, page in the court of his majesty, Arthur, King of Britain.

Martin: Amy! Your name's not Amy! No, there's only one Amy, and you ain't her. From now on your name is Clarence.

Gender is dramatized as unintelligible in this scene. Martin then refers to Amy's "boyish bob," which is the name of a variation on the flapper's short haircut introduced in 1923. A haircut that was considered scandalous and even immoral in the 1920s because of its perceived appropriation of the masculine by the feminine is here a cause for anxiety, in that Martin finds it impossible to read it as either masculine or feminine. Martin, wrongly concluding that *Amy* is a woman's name, tries to restore the order of things by giving Amy what he hopes is a clearly unambiguous masculine name.

However, the notion that women can play pages and men who are pages are unreadable as men may have its origin in Twain's book itself. Daniel Beard, who illustrated Twain's *A Connecticut Yankee*, often used real-life figures as models (Merlin was modeled on Tennyson, for example). His inspiration for Clarence was Sarah Bernhardt (1844-1923), who took on many a cross-dressed role ("trouser parts") during her career. Beard puts Clarence/Bernhardt in a *contrapposto* posture, one hand lingering at his/her hip; this posture, as well as the long curling hair and strangely-suggestive cross-hatched crotch, introduces quite a sexually-ambiguous figure into Twain's book (see Figure 9.1).[16]

---

16 Beverly David and Ray Saperstein, "Reading the Illustrations," Mark Twain, *A Connecticut Yankee in King Arthur's Court* (New York: Oxford UP, 1996), pp. 21-27. Bernhardt played a page in Louis Denayrouse's *La Belle Paule*. By drawing her as Clarence, Beard gives us an intertextual *mis en abîme*.

Figure 9.1 Sarah Bernhardt as Clarence

Later in the film, at Morgan's castle, Martin himself is transformed into an ambiguously gendered figure—and forced to do so at the hands of women, literally. Martin's new costume is over the top, complete with a hat with a feather so large that it curls down to his shoulder. He is the picture of a medieval fop as Hollywood imagines one. The camera tracks quickly to the right, from the women dressed as pages to a group of maidens to a group of knights, and then faster to Morgan, looking ecstatic, and faster still to Martin in his fine clothes. There is nothing subtle about the reversal of gender roles in this scene. In addition, consider how the extravagance of the upwardly-mobile fop or dandy has been consistently coded as effeminate in fiction, on stage and screen, as well as in history.[17] The socially anxious, it seems, invariably overdress, and such sartorial excess can register as drag. And, as Rogers well knew, vaudeville in general loves a gaudy costume, an important semiotic prop in a five-minute sketch. Moreover, the dandy with pretensions to white folks' ways was a recurring character in minstrel shows. Rogers/Martin looks silly; indeed, he counts on the fact that he does. Martin in silks and velvets is a calculated *failed* passing with respect to both class and gender.

It seems to be a rule of genre that, in comedies set in the Middle Ages, costume serves as a way to make jokes about gender difference and sexual identity: period films in general might be said to offer ways to indulge in a Bakhtinian carnivalesque in this respect. And certainly hair in the style of Prince Valiant's—a famous variation on the 1920s bob—has been the focus of cinematic humor. (Perhaps the best-known example of medievalized sartorial anxiety is Mel Brooks's *Robin Hood: Men in Tights* [1993].) The past is indeed another country, and therefore it is much safer to play with the boundaries of gender identity there than here. Bakhtin argues that the inversion of social roles in the pre-modern period, then much more profoundly dangerous compared to today, enabled new forms of discourse that challenge, or offer alternatives to, a dominant discourse.[18] Since Bakhtin, critics have been quick to point out that the upside-down world of carnival time is always emphatically put back to rights: carnival is no more than a state-sanctioned subversion that only reproduces the status quo. As Foucault puts it, the carnivalesque only helps to "*extend* our participation in the present system."[19] We may go to the movies, but we must always come back.

Bakhtin's notion of the carnivalesque and subsequent critiques of it also suggest a way to read Rogers' physicality; namely, the body that he carefully presents in many of his publicity shots and in films. As does Beard's Bernhardt, Rogers often poses in *contrapposto*; that is, he stands in such a way that his shoulders and arms twist off-center from his hips and legs, making his body asymmetrical—a trick accomplished by simply bending one knee. While *contrapposto*, Rogers stands with one or both arms akimbo, or raises his right arm to his head, sometimes to scratch it. What does this pose signify for Rogers

---

17 For an account of the dandy in history, see Ellen Moers, *The Dandy* (1960; Lincoln: University of Nebraska Press, 1978), esp. pp. 36-37.

18 M. M. Bakhtin, *Rabelais and His World*, trans. Helen Iswolsky (Bloomington: Indiana UP, 1985), p. 34.

19 Michel Foucault, "Revolutionary Action: 'Until Now,'" *Language, Counter-Memory, and Practice*, ed. Donald Bouchard (Ithaca: Cornell UP, 1980), pp. 218-34, 230, emphasis mine.

and his immediate audience?[20] Certainly it conveys puzzlement and a shy, self-deprecating modesty. He is the bashful cowboy, a hick who is about to rope in a spectator with a lariat or a joke (see Figure 9.2). But perhaps there is more.

Moe Meyers has explored the connection between Oscar Wilde's development of a "homosexual social identity"[21] and his appropriation of what is known as the Delsartean system, an array of speaking styles, gestures, and poses for actors, singers, and dancers that was quite popular in Europe and the United States at the end of the nineteenth century—and not one to be supplanted until the 1940s when "method" acting became widespread. François Delsarte (1811-71) believed that, as Meyers puts it, "exteriority . . . could create a completely new interiority."[22] As Meyers argues, Wilde came to embody the notion that identity could indeed be performed—which, needless to say, precisely unsettled so many of Wilde's contemporaries. In the Delsartean system, the *contrapposto* stance was the position from which all other positions and gestures followed.

The first and most famous use of *contrapposto* is Polyclitus's Doryphoros (4th c. B.C.E). Helen Gardner describes the *contrapposto* stance as transforming the static figure into "a true acting unit"; the body is able to speak and show emotion in an entirely new way.[23] Perhaps the most famous example of the *contrapposto* stance from the Renaissance revival of the pose is Michelangelo's David, with one languid arm hovering at the hip, the other raised to the shoulder. The Doryphoros has had a long history as a gay icon. Rogers' raised right arm seems to be a kind of follow-through on the Doryphoros's partly-raised left arm, which Michelangelo raises even higher. In fact, early twentieth-century homoerotic photography often represented the male figure in classical costume,

---

20 *Contrapposto* was not unique to Will Rogers. Compare to photographs of Wild Bill Hickok (at Missouri State, http://history.missouristate.edu/FTMiller/LocalHistory/Bios/wildbillshootout.htm, last accessed 10 February 2007) and Buffalo Bill Cody (at the Buffalo Bill Historical Center, http://www.bbhc.org/bbm/biographyBB.cfm, last accessed 10 February 2007). These and other cabinet photographs suggest that the *contrapposto* pose was a deliberate performance, and perhaps one in opposition to the more stiff, hieratic pose that was also popular at the end of the nineteenth century. Corey Creekmur, in his forthcoming *Cattle Queens and Lonesome Cowboys: Gender and Sexuality in the Western* (Durham, NC: Duke UP), compares photographs of Oscar Wilde and Buffalo Bill Cody, arguing that "we have retrospectively isolated them as icons of homosexuality and heterosexuality, despite their shared poses in their own time" (private correspondence). I am grateful for his suggestions, which led me to look at cabinet photographs.

21 Moe Meyer, "Under the Sign of Wilde," *The Politics and Poetics of Camp,* ed. Moe Meyer (London: Routledge, 1994), pp. 75-109, 77.

22 Moe Meyer, "Under the Sign," p. 81. See Joe Williams, "A Brief History of Delsarte," *The Delsarte Project*, <http://www.delsarteproject.com>.

23 Helen Gardner, *Art through the Ages*, 6th edn. (New York: Harcourt, 1975), p. 132.

Figure 9.2 Roger's most famous pose, Ziegfeld's *Midnight Frolic*, 1915

and, when nude, in poses that recalled Greek and Roman sculpture. (I am not claiming that Rogers was an aficionado of classical art and gay iconography; rather, I would argue that he was an acute student of the body and its powers of signification as realized in vaudeville.) *Contrapposto* can be quite swishy, especially when combined with arms akimbo; Thomas King has traced out how bodily affectations such as arms akimbo—what he calls "excessive performances of the self"—came to be coded first as aristocratic and then as effeminate in the seventeenth and eighteenth centuries; his argument is thus grounded in anxieties about both gender and class difference.[24]

However, and to complicate matters, at the turn of the twentieth century, *contrapposto* could also signify the *über*-masculine. Vaudeville usually included novelty acts such as strong men as exemplified by bodybuilder Eugen Sandow, who, like most other bodybuilders of the day, borrowed classical poses for his own.[25] The male body on voyeuristic view is not necessarily gay, but it *is* queer. In vaudeville, it seems, the body was always already a sliding signifier, and it is this aspect of the *contrapposto* pose that Rogers exploits. In Ziegfeld's Follies, for example, Rogers developed a skit in which he cross-dressed as an ingénue trying out for a part; he strikes a feminine pose through *contrapposto*. In the comedic short, *Uncensored Movies* (Roy Clements, 1923), Rogers impersonates a number of stars, and vamps the disturbingly exotic Rudolph Valentino through an extreme *contrapposto* stance while dressed as the Sheik.

In addition, Rogers may have borrowed his arm gesture from minstrelsy.[26] To perfect their routines, the white actors who first put on blackface spent a good deal of time observing African Americans. Minstrelsy holds up a distorted,

---

24 See Thomas King, "Performing 'Akimbo': Queer Pride and Epistemological Prejudice," *Politics and Poetics of Camp*, 23-50, at p. 36. Also see his "The Fop, the Canting Queen, and the Deferral of Gender," *Presenting Gender: Changing Sex in Early-Modern Culture*, ed. Chris Mounsey (Lewisburg, PA: Bucknell UP, 2001), pp. 94-135, especially his discussion of what will become known as "arms akimbo," a gesture built on the *contrapposto* pose: "Enacted on a commercial stage . . . the distance of the elbow from the body was . . . producing effects of gendering *among men*, not male or female but *masculine or effeminate*" (p. 105), and of physiognomer John Bulwer's books on oratorical gestures, which identifies hand-wagging and head-scratching with the middle finger as effeminate and bordering on the sodomitical (pp. 109-12).

25 I am grateful to Corey Creekmur for his suggestions that led me to Eugen Sandow. For photographs, see the Sandow Museum <http://www.sandowmuseum.com> last accessed on 9 February 2007.

26 Eric Lott, in *Love and Theft* (New York: Oxford UP, 1995), argues that minstrelsy offered a safe site for whites to experiment with blackness. His title captures what he calls the "mixed erotic economy of celebration and exploitation" (p. 6). Lott also discusses the "homoerotic charge" (p. 53) of minstrelsy and how minstrelsy mediated homosocial relations, thus reaffirming the status of white masculinity (pp. 53-55, 120-22).

parodic mirror to black folkways. Lincoln Perry, more famously known as Stepin Fetchit, started out in minstrel shows and then vaudeville; he had a way of shuffling and scratching his head while bugging out his eyes to signify a kind of amazed stupidity. On stage and in film, Fetchit played the "coon"—the name given to the stereotyped character of the lazy, inarticulate African-American. We can productively read the coon as subversive, a figure overtly opposed to taking orders from white folks.[27] It may be worth noting that Rogers grew up with ex-slaves and their children in "Indian Territory," and learned roping from an African-American cowboy on his father's ranch.[28] He worked with African Americans throughout his career, and, more to the point, he made four films with Fetchit.[29]

In *A Connecticut Yankee*, Rogers moves into the *contrapposto* posture and raises his arm whenever, I would argue, he must assert himself and his masculinity. We meet Rogers in this pose in the initial "frame" story at the radio station, and see it again when he is first brought before Arthur's court. When he is manipulated into going on the quest to rescue Alisande, he bends his knees and shuffles, saying:

Martin: Wait a minute, king—I, I'm not much on ahh enchantin' women . . . I'm not hardly . . . I'm not the type . . . I'm not I'm not there with the ol' S.A.

Arthur: S.A.?

Martin: No sex appeal.

When forced to joust with Sir Sagramor, Rogers appears in full cowboy regalia, and wins by roping Sagramor. (Bing Crosby, in Tay Garnett's 1949 musical version of Twain's novel, pays homage to Rogers by doing the same.) After Martin wins, he is praised by King Arthur, but responds with an aw-shucks modesty, once again moving into a *contrapposto* pose to emphasize lack in favor of Amy.

Let us revisit a scene I've already discussed, in which Rogers/Martin questions Amy about his gender. In this scene, there is an elaborate visual set-up in which Rogers moves into the *contrapposto* pose right before he asks: "just what is thy sex?" (see Figure 9.3.)

---

27 See Mel Watkins and Donald Bogle, *Toms, Coons, Mulattoes, Mammies, and Bucks: An Interpretive History of Blacks in American Films* (New York: Continuum, 1973/1994), p. 8.

28 The children of Rabb and Houston Rogers, former slaves, were his first playmates. See http://www.willrogers.com/new/articles/book_reviews/stepin_fetchit/perry.html, last accessed on 9 February 2007.

29 *In Old Kentucky* (George Marshall, 1929), *Judge Priest* (John Ford, 1934), *David Harum* (James Cruze, 1939), and *The County Chairman* (John Blystone, 1935).

Figure 9.3 "Just what is thy sex?"

Rogers certainly looks like the shy rube while in this pose, but I also think that he acts the "skippin' twistin' woman actin' man," as Bessie Smith says, to signal his marginality, not in a negative way, but to assert his right to speak from the margins. What looks like a failed, marginal heterosexuality is simply reinscribed as something quite powerful and central, depending as it does upon an emphatic rejection of women in *A Connecticut Yankee* and pushing them to the margins. Bewilderment, I would argue, is not quite white, male, and heterosexual; the dominant discourse has no language for perplexity, so Rogers must go elsewhere to perform it.

We have already looked at the episode in which Martin is dressed as a fop; let us return to its conclusion. As Morgan le Fay caresses him, he pulls away; the more he pulls away, the more she grows ardent and declares her love. Morgan's rush at Martin is punctuated by tortured cries from her dungeon as her henchmen work over various prisoners, including Alisande and Arthur. The juxtaposition of screams with love-talk is very much like aversion therapy: by the end of the episode, the audience feels as jumpy as Martin does. Morgan is evil feminized, a virago who usurps the natural order of things. But Loy's Morgan is comically, hyperbolically alluring, and her dramatic gestures, arch delivery of lines, and lavish costumes highlight the very fact *of* performance.

As Morgan advances upon him, Martin babbles nervously, playing the clichéd beleaguered bachelor. When she kisses Martin full on the mouth, a pink blush blooms on his cheek. This special effect was achieved by laboriously hand-coloring the black-and-white film, frame-by-frame and print-by-print. The idea to tint the screen was director David Butler's. Butler says: "You see, they had no color, and [Myrna Loy/Morgan le Fay] kissed Will, and he had to blush. The only way they could do it was to have a little Japanese girl tint every frame progressively darker pink. This little girl had to do that on every print we sent out."[30] The unusual and labor-intensive use of the blush is both a continuity and a break with the Keystone-Cops Arthurian world created in *Yankee*: the feminine is the abjected motivator for the plot, and must be rejected in the end. It is certainly a good gimmick, but more than that, the pink spot feminizes Martin; the uncontrollable blush brands Martin as a maiden in distress. Morgan is not the only queen in this scene.

Perhaps we can read Morgan's feminizing of Rogers in a larger context. Historian Robert McElvaine argues, "the Depression can be seen as having effected a 'feminization' of American society. The self-centered, aggressive, competitive 'male' ethic of the 1920s was discredited. Men who lost their jobs became dependent in ways that women had been thought to be."[31] Rogers never leaves the problem of the Depression behind in *A Connecticut Yankee*, and makes many visual and verbal allusions to it, as in, for example, the beginning of the film: as Martin lies sleeping, he looks very much like a hobo, one of the many jobless drifters created by the Depression. Also, consider Martin's "spell" at the time of the eclipse: as the sun disappears, he chants: "prosperity, farm relief, freedom for Ireland, and light wines and beer." Martin's pink blush interrupts the film, slows down time so that we can appreciate the technical virtuosity of the effect: a spot of color on a white man's cheek. It is women—Morgan in the film and the "little Japanese girl" outside of it—who are responsible for the innovative effect. One might say that this particular self-centered male is de-centered, aggressed against: it is Morgan who manages the scopic economy. There is a corresponding, slightly earlier moment in which Morgan's gaze on Martin is held for a silent, full thirty-five seconds—a long time in a talking film—before she brings him to sit on the bed and begins her caresses. Morgan controls the gaze, and we look with her at her prey—the length of the shot encourages us to *really* look—at a dependent, helpless male.

Morgan's attempted seduction of Martin parallels her plot to overthrow Arthur. In both instances, unrestrained, undisciplined feminine desire threatens male privilege, a privilege that is made visible precisely because it comes under attack. And this is the paradox in the seduction scene: Martin is able to claim his masculinity through the *loss* of it. It is not Martin's fault that he has a performance problem; it is the voracious Morgan's.

---

30 Sterling and Sterling, *Will Rogers*, p. 113.

31 Robert McElvaine, *The Great Depression*, 2nd edn. (New York: Times Books, 1993), p. 340.

Consider the episode in which Morgan condemns Arthur, Martin, and Alisande to death by hanging, along with a group of other so-called criminals. Morgan raises her arm up in an incantatory gesture, and drops it to signal to the hangman to open the floor of the scaffold. One by one, the criminals die, until only Arthur, Martin, and Alisande are left. The scene is grisly and gratuitous, as gratuitous as the earlier torture scenes in the dungeon to which the film cuts, interrupting that kiss that results in such a dramatic blush. Critics found the hanging scene particularly off-putting, and the censors asked that the torture-chamber scenes and the shots of men being hanged be deleted. Overall, the violence in the film was, and continues to be, unintelligible, although one may resort to allegory easily enough, especially given Twain's end to his *A Connecticut Yankee*.

Surely Rogers was fully aware of the irony of his performance in his adaptation of Twain's *Connecticut Yankee*, a novel in which medievals stand in for Native Americans, no better than "savages," as Twain often characterizes the people his Morgan meets at Arthur's court. Twain's *A Connecticut Yankee in King Arthur's Court* can be read as an allegorized critique of imperialist expansion into the American West: Twain has no sympathy with the aims of government and capitalist commerce. At the same time (and not in opposition to his critique, but folded into it), Twain vilifies Native Americans as no more than animals, not only in his *A Connecticut Yankee*, but in other writings.[32] Consider how the medieval and the Indian come together in the scene in which Twain's Hank Morgan, on observing the abused and neglected prisoners at Arthur's court, reflects:

> The thought was forced upon me: "The rascals—*they* have served other people so in their day; it being their own turn, now, they were not expecting any better treatment than this; so their philosophical bearing is not an outcome of mental training, intellectual fortitude, reasoning; it is mere animal training; they are white Indians." (66)

But David Butler and Will Rogers made a film that suppresses all of Twain's references to Indians and the West. By depicting medievals at war among themselves, Butler and Rogers erase race; instead, hostilities are played out between a king's hollow, effeminate court and a sorceress's violent, brutal court. Moreover, the Amy and Alisande plot suggests that Butler and Rogers' interest lies in critiquing class difference—and in 1931, the lampooning of the

32 See Kerry Driscoll, "'Man Factories' and the 'White Indians' of Camelot: Re-reading the Native Subtext of *A Connecticut Yankee in King Arthur's Court*," *Mark Twain Annual* 2.1 (2004): 7-23.

privileged class would have resonated very well with an audience anxious about the declining economy.

Although always proud to be part Cherokee, Rogers first played the savage Indian in his roping exhibitions on the rodeo circuit, and then switched sides and became the heroic roping white *cowboy*. He then took on a variety of film roles in which he played a white American, often from the East, as he does in *A Connecticut Yankee*. Rogers was not passing; his background was never a secret the more famous he became. Rather, by taking on such "white" roles, Rogers succeeded in making visible the mechanisms of performance in such a way that whiteness, just like any other subject position, including masculinity, is exposed as performance. After all, there was only the shortest of gaps, the simplest pretense of gaps, between Rogers and any cinematic character he played. Rogers' *A Connecticut Yankee* might also lead us to conclude that he was also suggesting that history itself is comprised of a series of performances, and therefore contingent—and if contingent, perhaps able to be seized and shaped. Let us return for a moment to the beginning of *A Connecticut Yankee*, when Rogers/Martin is confronted with the mad inventor's time machine of a radio:

Martin: Nice little set you got here. You—you oughta get China on this.

Inventor: China! That's no distance at all . . . my belief is that every sound that has ever been uttered is still vibrating somewhere in the ether. If I can build a set sensitive enough, I can tune back into the past and hear those sounds. Think! Think of hearing Lincoln's own voice delivering the Gettysburg Address! Of tuning in on Burke's farewell to Parliament!

Martin: You know, what Cleopatra said to Marc Anthony wouldn't make bad listenin' either.

Sound of trumpets.

Inventor: It works! It works! . . . Listen!

Over the radio: Hear ye, hear ye hear ye . . . court of Arthur, King of Britain . . .

Inventor: I've got it! I've got it! I knew I was right! I've tuned back to fourteen hundred years! I've got the court of King Arthur!

Martin: I don't I don't care about listenin' to King Arthur and his court . . . I'm goin' home n' get *Amos n' Andy*.

The mad inventor imagines listening to history at its most stirringly propagandistic, but Rogers/Martin undercuts such desires by his reference to love-talk between Cleopatra and Antony. And note that Martin identifies Cleopatra as doing the talking: as does Morgan le Fay in her encounter with Martin, Cleopatra dominates the realm of erotic discourse. Martin is not interested in a transmittable past. He prefers "real" radio; in this case, the *Amos n' Andy* show (1928-1960), an extremely popular serial comedy with its roots in minstrelsy. Yet this is not "real" at all, for the "African-American" characters Amos Jones and Andy Brown were voiced by white actors (Freeman Gosden and Charles Correll), who, in the initial years of the show, also voiced all of the other male parts. Rogers/Martin (both actor and character are also radio personalities) prefers performance to history, and a performance that suggests that history, while perhaps audible, can never be fully authenticated.

But perhaps history can be *made*, even when one is not at the center of it. Recall that Martin discovers that Amy/Clarence is Martin's distant ancestor at the point that Arthur knights Amy and gives him the title Sir de Claremore—which, as Martin says in an aside, is his own family name. It is at this point that Rogers/Martin becomes anxiously interested in history. He encourages Arthur to take a hand in history that will ensure the survival and success of his own ancestor, Amy/Clarence/Sir Claremore, enabling him to marry Alisande ("Here's a boy right here that loves her and he'd be the very one to rescue her . . . and it would make a great chapter in history, too"). In the end, Alisande, the passive beloved, serves as the exemplary feminine model who replaces the virago Morgan; moreover, in spite of Rogers' doubts, Amy proves man enough to found a dynastic line, and an aristocratic one to boot, for Amy, a common page, is knighted through the intervention of Martin, and is therefore able to marry up. Thus Rogers/Martin facilitates a narrative of normative heterosexuality and reproduction; that is, a proper history—and a white history.

But what about Rogers' Cherokee ancestry? On the diegetic level, Rogers-as-Martin orchestrates a history of his own whiteness, while all the while his audience knows, on the extradiegetic level, as it were—that is, Rogers' own life—about Rogers' Native-American identity. In the film, not only does Arthur bestow a name and title, but he also dispenses land. Rogers, remember, was born on the western edge of the United States, in "Indian Territory" recently absorbed into the United States. When the new state of Oklahoma was established, thousands of Native Americans, including Rogers' own father, lost the majority of their lands, and were given small allotments. the family's 60,000-acre ranch was reduced to a few hundred acres, and his father moved to a nearby town named Claremore, which became Roger's adopted hometown. (When Rogers began to make money, he bought back allotments to increase the family's spread.) Much could be made, following Jane Tompkins, of the problem of "empty" lands that need occupying and governance—lands such as that "Indian Territory" that became Oklahoma.[33] Inserting Claremore into *A Connecticut Yankee* is one of many instances in which Rogers closes the gap between himself and his character, thus allowing us to wonder about Rogers' own identification as a Native American as we watch the film. I do not see Rogers as a Cherokee Uncle Tom; rather, he collapses the diegetic and extradiegetic— extra-cinematic—levels together to insert a minority narrative, another history, into the film. In *A Connecticut Yankee*, through deploying the language of clothes, the semiotics of posture and gesture, and the power of a blush on a white face, Rogers demonstrates that the white masculine body must be read not as natural, but as an epiphenomenon of culture and history. To make this argument, Rogers piggybacks on the dominant signifying practices that set the limits of gender difference. Rogers' body can only signify in this respect, alas, because women serve as his abjected other.

---

33 Jane Tompkins, "'Indians': Textualism, Morality, and the Problem of History," *Critical Inquiry* 13.1 (1986): 101-19.

Chapter 10

Danny Kaye and the "Fairy Tale" of Queerness in *The Court Jester*

Martha Bayless

The Court Jester, a reeling tale of medieval derring-do and the perilous destabilization of identities, was released by Paramount in 1956 and quickly found favor with the public.[1] The film was written and directed by Norman Panama and Melvin Frank, the team responsible for Danny Kaye's previous vehicles *Knock on Wood* and *White Christmas* (both released in 1954). *The Court Jester* remains one of Kaye's most successful films, and an influential source for the longstanding popular assessment of Kaye's sexual identity. The film's central character, played by Kaye, is the jester Hubert Hawkins, a shifting, liminal figure whose ambiguous identity generates considerable narrative anxiety. In both overt and covert ways the jester is challenged to repudiate his unmanly, ambiguous, and ultimately queer ways and prove he is a hero, a role coterminous with masculinity. In this paradigm of normativity it follows the precedent of medieval tales about jesters and entertainers, which depict them as ambivalent, subversive, disguised, and unknowable. The narrative of the film, moreover, intersects with a second historical paradigm, the widespread belief that, like jesters throughout history, Kaye himself was liminal, ambiguous, and ultimately queer. This conclusion was more informed by cultural concepts of masculinity than by his off-screen behavior, but what audiences saw performed on screen reinforced assumptions about the dangerous liminality of comedy, jesters, and entertainers in both the public and the private sphere. Regardless of their private sexuality, such performers were culturally queer, construed through an interpretive paradigm that regards the public construct of sexuality as definitive.

Issues of identity are central to *The Court Jester* as a whole, framing the narrative of the jester's vexed identity. A pretender, King Roderick I, has usurped the throne of England, wiping out the royal family and supplanting its only surviving member, an infant who remains nameless throughout the film. The infant has been whisked away by a band of loyal rebels, led by the

---

1 *The Court Jester*, dir. Norman Panama and Melvin Frank, perf. Danny Kaye and Glynis Johns, DVD (1956; Hollywood, CA: Paramount, 2003).

Black Fox (Edward Ashley), and the care of the infant is delegated to the jester Hawkins. The very identity of the infant would be in question were it not for the royal birthmark, the Purple Pimpernel, on the royal infant's bottom, which the jester Hawkins must display to the infant king's reverent followers. This emblem of royalty apes the Scarlet Pimpernel, that epitome of gallantry in disguise, but its appearance on an infant's bottom symbolizes the upturning of heroic convention that will be the leitmotif of the narrative. Here the hierarchy of rank and estate is overturned, forecasting the inversion of other hierarchies before the tale concludes.

Thus the issue of royal identity and hierarchy serves as a backdrop to the film's more immediate question: the identity of its central character, the jester Hawkins. This issue is embodied in Kaye's first scene, in which he sings the song "You'll Never Outfox the Fox." Clad in a mask, a disguise of forest green, and a swirling cape, he cuts a heroic figure, vaunting the cleverness of his disguise and cunning as well as the changeability of heroic identity. "Any one of us can be at any time the Fox / But I tell you confidentially that I'm the Fox," he sings, while doubles, triples and finally a host of figures appear dressed identically, each chorusing "No, I'm the Fox!" "No, I'm the Fox!" "You'll never outfox the Fox!" reiterates Danny Kaye, and the truth of this claim is proven when the genuine Black Fox returns to the camp and removes his own mask, admonishing the jester: "How many times have I told you to stay out of my clothes?" Hawkins is hence defined by what he is not. He has been cross-dressing as a hero, his theme the claim that anyone can assume the mask of gallantry. But the genuine Fox is not outfoxed by Hawkins' imposture: "Tend to your duty!" he exhorts again. "And get out of my clothes!" Other aspects of the scene reflect the dynamics of his unsuccessful impersonation. In his guise as hero he bounded effortlessly from tree to earth, singing "I'm out on a limb, they think/I'm down on the ground in a wink." But when he is discovered by the real Black Fox, going metaphorically out on a limb to end up at the top of a pyramid of Black Fox lookalikes, he falls from the pyramid, a tumble that represents his fall from the pinnacle of the heroic hierarchy. Now brought low, he is greeted by the concerned questions of his troop of midget companions: "Did you hurt yourself, Hawkins?" "Are you hurt, Hawkins?" Their use of his true name is as revealing as their concern: he is transformed from the Black Fox, valiant hero, to Hubert Hawkins, inept carnival entertainer and companion of midgets.

Like medieval romance, the narrative thus poses the question of the protagonist's true identity: will events prove Hawkins the hero whose guise he longs to assume, or a failed imposter? In particular, *The Court Jester* clothes the issue of identity in gender terms. Is Hawkins at heart a swashbuckling hero or a man-in-tights figure of fun? From the very beginning, when Hawkins capers in the Fox's clothes, his identity as a manly hero is borrowed, and the film must unravel the dilemma of whether he can overcome his fundamental effeminacy, even indeterminacy, to perform the work of masculinity that defines a hero.

Unmasked by the real Black Fox, Hawkins begins the actual narrative figured as feminine, charged with caring for the royal infant. He claims that he would rather be a warrior, but the very timidity of his objections disqualifies him from the manly role. "Don't you think it would look better if a woman . . . ?" he protests meekly when the Black Fox orders him to display the infant's royal bottom to visitors. The display of the naked bottom can be seen as a vicarious action that proclaims Hawkins' own servitude and lowliness; any man whose job consists of displaying a naked bottom, even one not his own, is on the receiving rather than the wielding end of power. The Black Fox admonishes, "Each one serves as best he can," confirming the narrative position that Hawkins' lowly and effeminate role is appropriate to his identity. Hawkins is further unmanned by the arrival of his followers, midgets from the local carnival, as if the only men he can command are miniature, comic, and unthreatening. Hawkins hopes that he can serve the cause with this band of midgets, almost as if he is of a reduced stature himself, but the Black Fox, the embodiment of Hawkins' would-be manliness, deems them inadequate and sends them away.

The narrative is unambiguous in its assertion that masculinity is essential for heroism. This is confirmed in the person of Maid Jean (Glynis Johns), a woman whose participation in outlaw life tranforms her into an honorary man. Like Hawkins, Jean cross-dresses as a hero; indeed, the name *Jean* itself suggests transvestism, recalling the cross-dressing warrior persona of Jeanne d'Arc. Having assumed the clothes and abilities of a man, she becomes superior to Hawkins, who addresses her as "Captain" and "Sir." Before hierarchies and rightful rule can be reestablished the narrative will require the reassertion of gender norms: Jean must relinquish her male identity and Hawkins must overcome his female identity.

The first step toward the reestablishment of traditional gender roles comes when Hawkins and Maid Jean are ordered to take the infant into hiding, a move that separates them from the social group in which their gender status has been constructed. Jean "disguises" herself as a woman, provoking the first stirrings of desire on the part of Hawkins. Although this desire is nominally heterosexual, it retains a queer edge when he continues to address Jean as "sir": "Each time I see you as a woman, sir, I mean with your flowing hair . . ." Jean's disguise as a young woman is accompanied by a false muteness, underscoring the equation of femininity and powerlessness. This is the guise that must be displayed to the world for her to "pass" (and to retain power). Hawkins is disguised as an elderly deaf man, and the two of them, carrying the infant to safety, resemble a carnival version of Joseph and the Virgin Mary. Like Joseph in the medieval mystery plays, Hawkins is relegated to the role of impotent old man.

The shelter in which they take refuge becomes the scene of their first active negotiation of gender identity. At the appearance of Giacomo, the jester heading for the royal court, Hawkins is unable to assume the male role and grapple with the intruder, leaving Jean to enact the warrior's role. Yet Hawkins and Maid Jean, alone with the baby, also begin to explore their possible identities as heterosexual partners. Hawkins voices his fear that his effeminate role rules out any chance of heterosexual romance: "I find it hard to believe that the Captain could ever be fond of a man who isn't a fighter." "Sometimes tenderness and kindness also make a man, a very rare man," the Captain replies encouragingly. In return she confides her own gender indeterminacy: "My father made me everything I am"—teaching her the use of weapons and how to fight—"In fact I really think he wanted me to be a boy," she concludes, confirming that she, rather than Hawkins, is the warrior of the couple. "Too bad, you'd have made a wonderful girl," Hawkins replies, endorsing the beginning of the crossing of their gender identities.

As if the love of a good woman is all that is necessary to unqueer a man, Hawkins is now free to continue his journey toward warrior/hero status. His transformation accelerates when he assumes the identity of the court jester Giacomo, whom Jean has just put out of commission. Giacomo, "king of jesters and jester of kings," is a paragon of mutability, a covert figure of sabotage, secretly hired by court conspirators to assassinate their rivals. Accordingly, in his disguise as Giacomo, Hawkins must adopt the persona of a man whose identity is fluid by nature. Unlike Hawkins' mimicry of the Black Fox, this new identity is within his capacity and serves as a bridge to greater identities. Confronted by questioners, Hawkins mimics Giacomo's fluency in languages, rattling off gibberish and successfully embodying the changeability of the court jester. The jester's powers of transformation prove to be so great, however, that Hawkins loses control of them. Soon after he arrives at court he falls victim to the witch Griselda, who has been charged with the task of finding a manly husband for the Princess Gwendolyn. Seeing a potential candidate in Hawkins, Griselda hypnotizes him to become a dashing swain at the snap of her fingers. Hawkins' new identity as the gallant hero is inconstant, however, as he is vulnerable to the snap of anyone's fingers, so that he spends much of his time toggling helplessly back and forth between identities.

Hawkins's latent quality of submissive effeminacy is underscored by Griselda's instructions: he begins by obeying her command to intone "I am craven and thou art my master." But though this effeminacy remains, it serves as a platform for his transformation, as if it does take a woman to unqueer a man, and a woman's desire—that of Gwendolyn—to enable him to make the leap to manliness. In this instance, the agency of his new maleness is the desire of the princess to marry a paragon of extravagant masculinity: "someone dashing and romantic who will carry me off as a princess should be carried off." Gwendolyn sums up the central issue when she asks him, "What manner of a man are you, Giacomo?" His identity turns on his prowess as a wooer of women and as a warrior. When Griselda implants Hawkins with suggestions, she charges him with this new identity: "Go and make love . . . You are a figure of romance. You are a man of iron!"

In this part of the film, Hawkins' identity is almost literally up for grabs: he is thought to be a celebrated jester by the court, a secret assassin by the court conspirators, an endearing but hapless outlaw by Jean, a dashing suitor by the princess, and a craven subordinate by the witch Griselda. His identity is fluid and protean, determined by his surroundings, against his will and often without his knowledge—the ultimate socially constructed persona. Among these, it is his hypnotized identity as a fearless swain that serves as a stepping-stone to the realization of his newly masculine self. He graduates to a higher grade of identity when he is dubbed a knight by Roderick. The king is anxious for the Princess Gwendolyn to marry Griswold, an unappealing but powerful suitor who would make an advantageous ally for the kingdom. With Gwendolyn's affections focused on Hawkins, disguised as the dashing Giacomo, the king decides to remove the jester from contention by making him fight Griswold in a tournament. Since the kingdom's rules hold that only nobles can challenge men such as Griswold to joust, the king orders Hawkins to be summarily knighted, bringing about an abrupt rise in his status and ostensible qualifications as a warrior. The kingdom's knighting process is supposed to require "tests of manhood, skill, and courage," but these are hurried through—instead of proving that he can climb a wall, Hawkins is simply thrown over it—and the ceremony is literally conducted in double-quick time. Thus ennobled, Hawkins becomes the social equal of Griswold, a fierce and doughty warrior, raising the corresponding question: is he also the manly equivalent of Griswold? When Griselda drops the famous pellet with the poison in the vessel with the pestle, Hawkins' nervous inadequacies indicate that he cannot yet assume the manly role. He repeatedly confuses the instructions about whether the pellet with the poison is in the vessel with the pestle or the chalice from the palace. "It's so easy even I can say it!" says Jean, ever capable of taking on the hero's role. As if acknowledging that Jean is better suited to heroism, Hawkins counters: "Well then, you fight him!"

The final identity assigned to him is that of the Black Fox, bringing his guises full circle. But whereas in the beginning of the film he was unsuccessfully trying to pass as the Black Fox, here his daring and secrecy lead others to "recognize" and identify him as the Black Fox independently. Sir Ravenhurst (Basil Rathbone), the chief of the conspirators, observes Hawkins alternating between clownish and cunning behavior—the result of Griselda's hypnosis, though Ravenhurst is ignorant of this. Thinking this identity-switching is calculated, Ravenhurst exclaims admiringly: "The Black Fox! And still playing the fool!" The irony, of course, is that Hawkins is the fool, still playing the Black Fox.

The pivotal moment comes when Ravenhurst denounces Hawkins to the king as the Black Fox, bringing the question of Hawkins' true identity into the public arena. Has Hawkins played the hero sufficiently to claim it as his enduring status? His answer demonstrates that he has. He proclaims, "For once, Ravenhurst is right—I am! I am the Black Fox!" He is emboldened to declare himself the hero by sighting his troop of carnival midget followers who swarm the castle in the nick of time, proving that it is not size but cleverness and desire that bestow power. Having publicly taken ownership of a heroic identity, he enters fully into the role by commanding the successful take-over of the castle. In the ensuing combat, Hawkins' own swordplay is variable, but here he is aided by the witch Griselda. Griselda's hypnotic spell transforms him into such a dashing hero of legend that he explicitly outdoes even Errol Flynn, whose Robin Hood (1938) set the standard for medieval swashbuckling.[2] Flynn's Robin Hood sliced through a candle with his swordplay; in clear mimicry of Flynn's example, Hawkins as the Black Fox slices through a whole row of candles. The jester inhabits the heroic Robin Hood role even more fully in defeating Basil Rathbone, whose portrayal of Ravenhurst recalls his performance as the malevolent Guy of Gisbourne opposing Flynn's Robin Hood in the 1938 film.

In the end, hierarchy is restored and characters assume their rightful places. The usurper is deposed and submits to the legitimate king. The infant royal is literally restored to the throne, with homage paid to him by the former rebels and the entire court. Maid Jean abandons the warrior status she claimed for the duration of the struggle, and her "disguise" of women's clothes becomes her permanent garb. The jester's masculinity assured, he displays the baby's pimpernel birthmark to those at court without endangering his heroic status. It is now a sign of power, rather than of effeminacy, that he controls the royal bottom.

In the case of the usurper Roderick, the unnamed infant king, and Maid Jean, the end of the narrative brings about the restoration of identities disrupted throughout the story. Roderick resumes his true identity as a subject of the king, the infant his true identity as royal, and Maid Jean her true identity as a woman. It is only the jester who has been transfigured, and who has been exposed as a figure of protean identity. Thus the key question of the narrative is not "Is the jester actually someone else?" but "What precisely is the jester?" Unlike the other characters in the film, the jester's proper function is to play parts, to assume disguises, and to engage in pretense. He is the only figure whose *modus*

---

2 *The Adventures of Robin Hood*, dir. Michael Curtiz and William Keighley, perf. Errol Flynn and Olivia de Havilland, DVD (1938; Burbank, CA: Warner Home Video, 2003).

operandi is play. As a performer and as a would-be hero, he demonstrates the value and even the necessity of play as an agent of transformation, a force that can alter or restore identities and disrupt or affirm hierarchies, as he wills. Thus the jester, possessing the most versatile identity in the realm, actually has the greatest potential for power. The fact that the rightful king is an infant underscores this, in that the infant king may nominally hold the power, but he cannot put himself on the throne even in the most literal sense; he requires the support of the jester. The jester's forces—both his powers of transformation and his midget followers—come straight out of carnival. His jousting victory over Griswold also draws from the world of playacting. Hawkins, standing over the defeated Griswold, refuses to kill him. For this act of mercy he gains Griswold's allegiance when he endeavors to take the castle from the usurping forces, and thus the manner of his triumph over Griswold assures the fate of the kingdom. In enacting his victory in this way, the jester emphasizes the conceptual, playful aspect of the tournament: just as he does not need to be a real knight to triumph, he does not need to kill Griswold to win. The playacting aspect of the tournament will suffice; winning Griswold's verbal acknowledgement of defeat is more powerful than death. Rather than merely vanquishing Griswold, this victory allows him to add Griswold's power to his own, as if playacting allows him to annex Griswold's masculine powers.

The jester's abilities as a shapeshifter hence serve him well; but the fluid, inconstant identity of shapeshifters also makes them enigmatic, unknowable, and suspect. Here *The Court Jester* takes its place in a long history of narratives that highlight the potential guile and shiftiness of jesters and entertainers. As itinerants of unverifiable origin, entertainers stood outside the hierarchy of familiar retainers and the web of kinship; their loyalties were mysterious. Medieval popular narrative provided many examples of the liminality of entertainers. Two such stories are recounted by William of Malmesbury, whose *Gesta Regum Anglorum*, complete by the mid-1130s, used both popular and learned sources. William recounts a version of the motif attached to Alfred, the historical king who ruled from 877 to 899, although this legend is unlikely to have genuine historical value. In the tale Alfred, under threat from the Danes in England, saves the realm by disguising himself as a performer. "Dressed as an entertainer" (*sub spetie mimi*), Alfred infiltrates the camp of the Danish king and spends several days there as a "performer of jests" (*ioculatoriae professor*), gleaning the secrets of the enemy camp.[3]

---

3 William of Malmesbury, *Gesta Regum Anglorum: The History of the English Kings*, ed. and trans. R. Mynors, R. Thomson and M. Winterbottom, 2 vols. (Oxford, 1998), vol. I, pp. 182-84. "Disguise as harper (minstrel)" is K.1817.3 and "Disguise as musician to enter enemy's camp" is K2357.1 in Stith Thompson, *Motif-Index of Folk-Literature* (Bloomington: Indiana UP, 1955), 6 vols.

In the instance of Alfred, the false jester is on the side of good, but in a second example of the legend the jester is an enemy in disguise. This version of the legend is set at the court of Athelstan, grandson of Alfred and king of the English from 924/5 to 939. Athelstan's power threatened the rule of Anlaf, the Viking king of Northumbria, and Anlaf disguised himself as a minstrel to try to gain intelligence about Athelstan's plans:

> Anlaf, perceiving the impending danger, cunningly assumed the office of a spy and, laying aside his royal garments, equipped himself with a harp and made his way to our king's tent. There he stood singing at the door and from time to time "in sweet confusion struck the vocal strings," and easily secured admission, pretending to be an entertainer who won his daily bread by this kind of skill. For some time he entertained the king and his guests with tuneful music, and while playing surveyed the whole scene. When they had eaten their fill, the entertainment was brought to an end, and the serious business of running a war was resumed in discussion between the nobles, at which point Anlaf was told to leave and given what he had earned by his music.[4]

Anlaf's stratagem is discovered and thwarted, but the potential threat posed by entertainers is clear nonetheless.

Geoffrey of Monmouth included an example of this motif in the *Historia Regum Britannie*, complete by 1138. The Saxon leader Colgrin is besieged by Arthur in the city of York, and Colgrin's brother Baldulf resolves to approach the city walls to confer with Colgrin. Geoffrey describes Baldulf's strategy to make his way to his brother:

> ... he cut short his hair and his beard and dressed himself up as a minstrel with a harp. He strode up and down in the camp, pretending to be a harpist by playing melodies on his instrument. No one suspected him and he moved nearer and nearer to the city walls, keeping up the pretense all the time. In the end he was observed by the besieged, dragged up over the top of the walls on ropes and taken to his brother.[5]

Once again the minstrel's disguise hides a threat to the stability of the realm. Yet another version of the motif involves the Anglo-Saxon king Edward the Martyr, who ruled from 975 to 978. Contemporary accounts of Edward's murder make no mention of a jester; the legend does not surface until the 1140s, when it appears in *L'estoire des Engleis*, the verse chronicle composed by

---

4 William of Malmesbury, *Gesta Regum Anglorum*, 1.206-09.

5 Geoffrey of Monmouth, *The History of the Kings of Britain*, trans. Lewis Thorpe (Harmondsworth: Penguin, 1966), 9.1, p. 213.

the Anglo-Norman chronicler Geffrai Gaimar.[6] In this instance the unmanliness of the jester is twofold: he is not only an entertainer but a dwarf. This dwarf jester, Wlstanet [*sic*], refuses to perform his tricks and leaves the castle to repair to the home of Ælfthryth, Edward's stepmother. Edward follows and is murdered outside Ælfthryth's castle; her collusion is implied. (Stepmothers, like entertainers, had dubious loyalties, and thus were a similar source of potential disruption and danger.) Although the dwarf jester is not directly accused of murder, it is clear that he is a turncoat and traitor, a character whose physical existence, like his loyalty, is liminal, uncategorizable, and dangerous. It is as if, in refusing to perform his tricks at court, he refuses to remain subordinate to the throne, and instead performs tricks in the political realm, using guile and mischief to his own nefarious ends.

As anthropologists such as Victor Turner have shown, liminality and inversion are the hallmarks of transitions; and so it is no accident that in each of these narratives the kingship and the stability of the nation undergo transformation.[7] The jester is an agent of this transformation; is, above all, potentially subversive. In the film, the jester is liminal not only in persona, but above all in the realm of sexual identity. This suspicion of liminal sexuality informs the cultural perception of modern entertainers in the real world as much as in fiction. In this Danny Kaye is a prime example: Hawkins' dubious sexuality, his undercurrent of queerness, both drew from and contributed to rumors about Danny Kaye's own sexual identity.

Although Kaye married his songwriter and collaborator Sylvia Fine in 1940, when he was 27, and remained married throughout his life, rumors of homosexuality arose early in his career and followed him for decades. What began as casual show-business gossip assumed a more substantial form in Donald Spoto's 1992 biography of Laurence Olivier, which claimed that Kaye and Olivier carried on a homosexual relationship. Describing the period around 1950, when Olivier was married to Vivien Leigh, Spoto wrote:

> . . . by this time Olivier and Danny Kaye were lovers. At first Vivien [Leigh] had merely thought Kaye rude, since he arrived at their house unannounced at odd hours, without invitation or permission. But Olivier was also spending long, late hours with him, and the affair—at first rampant gossip and then a widespread belief in Hollywood, New York and in the Caribbean (where the relationship continued irregularly for several years)—was no secret to Vivien, nor did Olivier deny it.[8]

---

6 Geffrei Gaimar, *L'Estoire des Engleis*, ed. Alexander Bell (Oxford: Blackwell, 1960), p. 127, lines 3983-96.

7 Victor Turner, *The Ritual Process* (Chicago: Aldine, 1969).

8 Donald Spoto, *Laurence Olivier* (New York: HarperCollins, 1992), p. 228.

Spoto's most specific claim has Kaye allegedly disguising himself as a customs officer at New York's Idlewild airport and giving Olivier a body search when he arrived from overseas, after which Kaye and Olivier supposedly spent the night together at the St. Regis Hotel. This story, along with a number of others allegedly testifying to Olivier's adult sexual escapades, has been examined in detail and dismissed by Olivier's biographer Terry Coleman.[9] Coleman notes that in the supposed Idlewild/St. Regis escapade, records reveal that Olivier was not alone but was accompanied by Cecil Tennant, landed after a trip of thirty-one hours, proceeded to the Sherry Netherland Hotel (not the St. Regis), had a massage and a short nap, and left on a 12:30 a.m. flight for Los Angeles without spending the night at the hotel. Kaye's biographer Martin Gottfried concurs in his skepticism of the story, noting that Kaye cannot have accompanied Olivier to Los Angeles, as Spoto claims, because on the date in question—March 13, 1953—Kaye was in the middle of an engagement at the Palace Theatre in New York, which did not leave him free until early April.[10]

Kaye and his wife did become estranged, though he never formally divorced her, and indeed they continued to share houses at many points. After their relationship weakened, Kaye had a number of well-known affairs with women, including actresses Eve Arden and Gwen Verdon. These are well documented; by contrast, no direct or substantiated testimony of homosexual involvement has come to light from any source. Producer Perry Lafferty reported: "People would ask me, 'Is he gay? Is he gay?' I never saw anything to substantiate that in all the time I was with him." Kaye's final girlfriend, Marlene Sorosky, reported that he told her, "I've never had a homosexual experience in my life. I've never had any kind of gay relationship. I've had opportunities, but I never did anything about them."[11] Yet the idea that Danny Kaye embodied some essential queerness persists. The index of Kaye's latest biography has ten entries under "Kaye, Danny, homosexual rumors about." The book cites the speculations of acquaintances from Farley Granger to Walter Willison, who reported of Kaye, "Gay people were positive he was homosexual."[12]

The growth and persistence of these rumors, in the face of Kaye's open affairs with women, is testimony to the extent to which the performance of liminality becomes tantamount to queerness. Kaye was, in a sense, personally heterosexual, but culturally queer. Although he took a variety of roles throughout his life, his most prominent roles were of a certain type of comic

---

9 Terry Coleman, *Olivier* (New York: Holt, 2005), pp. 478-83. Kaye's biographer Martin Gottfried dismisses the episode as well in *Nobody's Fool: The Lives of Danny Kaye* (New York: Simon & Schuster, 1994), pp. 192-93.

10 Gottfried, *Nobody's Fool*, p. 193.

11 Gottfried, *Nobody's Fool*, pp. 247, 323.

12 Gottfried, *Nobody's Fool*, pp. 178, 299.

character: sheepish, hesitant, hen-pecked, subordinate, changeable, disguised, protean, liminal—suspect. Although the context is very different, the role of the court jester is identical in essentials to Kaye's other famous role, the abject dreamer in *The Secret Life of Walter Mitty*.[13] Like the jester Hawkins, Walter Mitty is outwardly a timid weakling, explicitly subordinate to a woman, in this case his mother, who admonishes him with lines like "Eat your milktoast!" Like Hawkins, Mitty nevertheless yearns to become a more manly hero through a series of transformations. A similar dynamic informs *Knock on Wood*, the 1954 romp by Norman Panama and Melvin Frank, the same team that produced *The Court Jester*.[14] The film is now one of Kaye's lesser known efforts, but was popular at the time and received an Academy Award nomination for best screenplay. In *Knock on Wood* Kaye is once again feminized, playing a ventriloquist, a performer whose livelihood consists of projecting a false identity. Unable to maintain a relationship with a woman, he enters psychoanalysis with a female analyst (Mai Zetterling), with whom he is meek and uncertain. The plot also involves shenanigans with spies and secret identities, and the climax of the picture finds Kaye disguising himself as a dancer in a ballet—definitely the sissy way to evade pursuers. The scene in which Kaye is the least timid and unsure involves a masquerade as a car salesman, where once again he is performing masculinity, as if he only emerges from his timid persona when mimicking gender stereotypes. A similar dynamic operates in Kaye's earlier film *The Inspector General* (1949), in which he plays the hapless underling in a medicine show—itself a paradigm of misrepresentation—who must cope with being mistaken for a more powerful masculine figure, the inspector general, and who becomes powerful as a result of his masquerade.[15]

Even Kaye's role in his "straightest" movie, *White Christmas*, provided grist for doubt about his masculinity.[16] The role had been written for Fred Astaire, and so originally featured none of the comic gender aspects that characterize Kaye's usual roles. Clowning around on the set, however, led to the addition of a scene in which Kaye and Bing Crosby, sporting ostrich-feather fans, parody a performance of Rosemary Clooney and Vera-Ellen singing "Sisters." The lyrics of the song, rendered queer in their new context, are enough to sissify Kaye and Crosby: "Sisters/There were never such devoted sisters . . . Lord help

---

13 *The Secret Life of Walter Mitty*, dir. Norman McLeod, perf. Danny Kaye and Virginia Mayo, DVD (1947; HBO Home Video, 1998).

14 *Knock on Wood*, dir. Norman Panama and Melvin Frank, perf. Danny Kaye and Mai Zetterling (1954). The film is not currently available on video or DVD.

15 *The Inspector General*, dir. Henry Koster, perf. Danny Kaye and Barbara Bates, DVD (1949; Alpha Video, 2004).

16 *White Christmas*, dir. Michael Curtiz, perf. Bing Crosby and Danny Kaye, DVD (1954; Hollywood, CA: Paramount, 2000).

the sister who comes between me and my man!" The scene finds Kaye in his natural element, that of parody, and his imitation of feminine conventions is exaggerated and expert, while Crosby is clearly out of his element. Gottfried, whose biography of Kaye loses no opportunity to emphasize what he regards as the ambiguity of Kaye's sexual identity, suggests that only a man of dubious sexuality would be at ease in such a performance:

> [Kaye and Crosby's] inability to relate as performers is nowhere so evident as when they dress up as females to lip-synch "Sisters," being sung by Vera-Ellen and Rosemary Clooney. Crosby was very uncomfortable with this, and Kaye had to talk him into doing the number. . . . It is the one moment in the movie when the usually cool Crosby looks ill at ease, whereas Kaye is plainly relaxed with the camping.[17]

Gottfried does not reveal the source of his information that Crosby was uncomfortable with the scene. It may be that he assumed that a masculine figure like Crosby would naturally be uneasy with such humor, and that Crosby's awkwardness in the scene is evidence of this. But Rosemary Clooney's own commentary on the DVD soundtrack suggests the opposite. She notes that Crosby was laughing so uncontrollably, unscripted, during the filming of the scene that he thought a different, less riotous, take would be used in the final cut of the film. Viewers preferred the take in which Crosby is broken up by Kaye's mimicry, and so the scene is actually eyewitness testimony to the extent to which Crosby relished the comedy.

Kaye's most prominent film roles, then, were of a type: the timid, subordinate, hapless man who can only make the transition to a more masculine identity by taking on the persona of manliness. In a culture in which men were required to shun any semblance of effeminate behavior, the willingness to portray such a character was almost tantamount to an admission of homosexuality. If this were not enough of an indictment, it was even more suspect for a man to sing, dance, and clown, and modern jesters and comic performers have been regarded with as much suspicion as medieval ones ever were. As Steven Cohan points out, women have traditionally been the subject of the gaze and serve as spectacles—except in the case of these male comics and song-and-dance men, whose role as spectacle essentially feminizes them.[18] Those who wanted to claim heterosexual identities had to employ careful strategies to do so. Fred Astaire required the brazen seductiveness of Ginger Rogers to keep him male in the public opinion. Gene Kelly cultivated a more masculine persona by choosing

---

17 Gottfried, *Nobody's Fool*, p. 213.
18 Steven Cohan, "'Feminizing' the Song-and-Dance Man," *Hollywood Musicals*, ed. Steven Cohan (London: Routledge, 2002), pp. 87-101.

conspicuously athletic dance moves and by such strategies as dancing in sports uniforms.

The equation between comic performers and effeminacy arises from the convention of the performer as the feminized spectacle, as object of the gaze, as well as from stereotypes of masculinity as silent, rough, and serious rather than quick, refined, and comic. But the latent queerness of the comic persona is also the result of a more immediate and pressing requirement, that of humor. One of the chief techniques of humor is to deflate the pomposities of elevated expression or of upper-register stereotypes. Parody in particular operates in this way, mocking the conventions and self-regard of serious genres. Thus male stars singing "Sisters" is a comic travesty of pompous masculinity, as is the behavior of the henpecked Walter Mitty and the hapless ventriloquist. Performers may be identified as queer because they submit themselves to spectacle, but they enter into the queerness because they are comics, and simply because, as comic parody, queerness *works*. In fact comic queerness was one of the few places gayness might register on screen. In one famous instance, Edward Everett Horton's effeminate comic persona was an enduring constant. In *The Gay Divorcee* Horton's character confesses that he was called "Pinkie" as a child, and his nickname is "Auntie" throughout the movie.[19] His effeminate mannerisms offset the fact that Betty Hutton engages him—fruitlessly—in a dance. He ends the movie married, but to a battleaxe, reinforcing his subordinate masculinity. In addition to the comic value of his effeminacy, Horton serves as a queer foil to Astaire, making Astaire's character reassuringly masculine by contrast. The comic Eddie Cantor, though straight and married, capitalized on comic queerness even in such marriage-plot pictures as *Whoopee!*[20] Eddie Cantor's effeminate hypochondriac stole the film, and in fact served as the forerunner of Danny Kaye's hypochondriac character in the film that launched Kaye to stardom, 1944's *Up in Arms*.

Thus Danny Kaye did not adopt the persona of queerness because he could not help himself, because he was too effeminate to project a more masculine image. He projected queerness precisely because he was in control, because he was a consummate performer who knew how to puncture masculinity masterfully. Such expertise could give rise to remarks that were subject to misunderstanding. Gottfried cites an interview in which Kaye showed disdain for the journalist's question. The interviewer began, "Mr. Kaye, you're known for your sophisticated humor . . ." Kaye interrupted: "Yeah, I'm very sophisticated.

---

19 *The Gay Divorcee*, dir. Mark Sandrich, perf. Fred Astaire and Ginger Rogers, DVD (1934; Turner Home Entertainment, 2006).

20 *Whoopee!*, dir. Thornton Freeland, perf. Eddie Cantor and Ethel Shutta, VHS (1930; Samuel Goldwyn Entertainment/HBO Home Video, 1992). Not currently available on DVD.

You know I dress up in ladies' clothes."[21] Gottfried insinuates that this is yet another instance of Kaye's irrepressible effeminacy; but it is far more likely that Kaye was referring to one of the oldest comic tricks in the book, a man dressing in drag.

As a comic performer and song-and-dance man, Kaye was inevitably vulnerable to rumors about his sexuality. Although his biographer acknowledges that "there is no evidence of and there are no witnesses to a Kaye-Olivier sexual relationship,"[22] he describes other aspects of Kaye's life as if they do provide evidence, and as if queerness or effeminacy is simply a deficiency or inadequacy, a matter of lacking enough *nous* to be masculine. He even interprets Kaye's marriage as displaying some of the dynamics shared by Hawkins and Maid Jean, in which the partners have exchanged sexual roles. There is no question that Kaye's wife and sometime collaborator, Sylvia Fine, was assertive in personality. Apprehensive that her own talents and professional identity would be overshadowed by Kaye's career, she refused to take a back seat in Kaye's life, which led many to find her abrasive. Gottfried identifies her as a threat to Kaye' masculinity, going so far as to term Kaye "whipped by obedience" in his marriage. At one point Kaye separated from his wife, and Gottfried speculates: "Perhaps it was to get his manliness in order and finally disobey her." Thus the marriage itself is made to serve as evidence of his heterosexual deficiencies. In such an interpretative context, the innuendo concerning Kaye and Olivier is almost inevitable:

> [Kaye] frequently visited with Olivier in the house next door, and it is hardly surprising that there were whispers about them. Then again, Olivier was also friendly with Spencer Tracy—friendlier than he was with Danny Kaye—and there were no whispers about them. The explanation was simple: Tracy projected an unimpeachably masculine aura, while Kaye, if not effeminate, seemed asexual at least.[23]

This explanation underscores the performative aspects of sexuality in ways that even Gottfried could not have realized. Kaye did not perform masculinity in its narrowest sense, and so he was defined as gay, though every documented piece of evidence shows him to have been exclusively heterosexual. By contrast, Spencer Tracy performed the "unimpeachably masculine" man; yet recent scholarship, including first-hand testimony, reveals that it was Tracy

---

21 Gottfried, *Nobody's Fool*, p. 145
22 Gottfried, *Nobody's Fool*, p. 190.
23 Gottfried, *Nobody's Fool*, pp. 132, 168.

who was bisexual, or even almost exclusively queer.[24] For performers above all, performance determines identity.

Thus the jester's dilemma in *The Court Jester* is the dilemma of male jesters and entertainers everywhere: is it possible to sustain a comic persona of haplessness, subordination, and unmanliness without being pegged as effeminate or queer? Throughout the film, Danny Kaye plays the opposite of a straight man: a comic; but the opposite of a straight man is also a queer man. Can the jester ultimately overcome his own effeminacy? In *The Court Jester*, the answer is yes: in the end he is not effeminate but powerful. He wins the girl and hierarchy is restored—but he is no longer funny.

To continue to be funny, Kaye had to recapitulate the role of the hapless queer man. The transformation of Hawkins at the end of *The Court Jester* was irrelevant to Kaye's own legend, as he himself played the queer role again and again. Thus, as the film's theme song goes, "What starts like a scary tale ends like a fairy tale." The film ends happily, as fairy tales do. But the gender dynamics of the narrative also contributed to the lasting understanding of the film's star as genuinely effeminate, liminal, and queer—a fairy tale just as simplistic as anything in Grimm, yet one that has served to perpetuate yet another legend of the ambiguous, liminal performer.

---

24 Tracy's sexuality is documented with substantial corroborating evidence, including the first-hand testimony from a male sexual partner, in William Mann, *Kate: The Woman Who Was Hepburn* (New York: Holt, 2006), pp. 337-43 and 383-84.

Chapter 11

Mourning and Sexual Difference in Hans-Jürgen Syberberg's *Parsifal*

Michelle Bolduc

The coupling of mourning with sexual difference is an old idea, readily found in both ancient and medieval texts. Perhaps the most well-known is Aristophanes' description of love as a search for healing, predicated on finding one's lost, indeed severed, other half in Plato's *Symposium*. Aristophanes characterizes sexual difference (and desire) as deriving from an original androgynous wholeness: "So you see how ancient is the mutual love implanted in mankind, bringing together the parts of the original body, and trying to make one out of two, and to heal the natural structure of man."[1]

A more complicated and contemporary example of the relationship between memory, mourning, and sexual difference appears in Hans-Jürgen Syberberg's 1982 film *Parsifal*.[2] Made in pre-unification Western Germany, Syberberg's film is a cinematic rendering of Richard Wagner's opera of the same title, which is itself loosely based on Wolfram von Eschenbach's thirteenth-century *Parzival*. Produced during the centennial anniversary of the premier of Wagner's *Parsifal* at Bayreuth (26 July 1882, with Hermann Levi conducting), this film is a visual, theatrical, and musical tour-de-force running over four hours in length.

Looking back to Aristophanes' conception of sexual difference as an altered state of lack is useful for considering Syberberg's *Parsifal*, for this film encapsulates both mourning in sexual difference and the hope of eventual wholeness in a union based on desire. Syberberg's film establishes sexual difference as an emblem of alterity, which is, moreover, thoroughly imbued with a queer mourning of the past. Syberberg not only works with tropes derived

---

1 Plato, *Symposium*, in *Great Dialogues of Plato*, eds. Eric Warmington and Philip Rouse, trans. W. Rouse (New York: Mentor, 1956, 1984), 189D-191E, pp. 85-88.

2 *Parsifal*, dir. Hans-Jürgen Syberberg (W. Long Branch, NJ: Kultur, 1988, 1982); Syberberg, *Parsifal: Notes sur un film*, trans. Claude Porcell (Paris: Gallimard, 1982); in German: *Parsifal. ein Filmessay* (Munich: Wilhelm Heyne Verlag, 1982). See also Solveig Olsen, *Hans Jürgen Syberberg and His Film of Wagner's* Parsifal (Lanham, MD: UP of America, 2006). All translations, unless otherwise noted, are my own. I thank Ruud van Dijk for his assistance with German translations.

from the medieval past, but also works through Germany's recent past under National Socialism. He grapples with Wagner's significance in late twentieth-century Germany, complicating his reception of Wagner (and Wolfram) by reworking Wagner's adaptation of his medieval source.

His *Parsifal* is thus guided by the conception of *Trauerarbeit*, or work of mourning, which not only pervades the specific concept of sexual difference according to Freud, but which also promises the Levinasian idea of an alterity that is fundamentally ethical rather than utopic. By means of sexual difference, Syberberg undermines the anti-feminine and anti-Semitic tropes of Wagner's opera in an attempt to heal the wounds left by Wagner's legacy on 1982 German society. This essay argues, then, that sexual difference in this film symbolizes both an ethical and a historical sense of loss and the (post)utopic search for wholeness.

Exploring the use of sexual difference as mourning in *Parsifal* has here another purpose: it also allows for both a more nuanced assessment of this filmmaker and his vexed reception. Syberberg was, and continues to be, a controversial figure in German art.[3] Leon Wieseltier contends that "Syberberg is determined to show that Parsifal survived Hitler's impersonation,"[4] whereas Mary Campbell argues that Syberberg's *Parsifal* serves as "the state masque of the Nazi cultural revolution."[5] For Thomas Elsaesser, however, Syberberg's cinematic meditations on Wagner's influence on German society offer a "long overdue cultural reparation for Nazism."[6] Further, Michael Gilbert characterizes Syberberg's films, and *Parsifal* in particular, as operating within a redemptive mythology whose underlying gestures of mourning and remembrance extend

---

3 Much of the controversy surrounding Syberberg stems from his 1978 film, *Hitler, ein Film aus Deutschland*. See, for example, Anton Kaes, "Holocaust and the End of History," *Probing the Limits of Representation: Nazism and the Final Solution*, ed. Saul Friedlander (Cambridge, MA: Harvard UP, 1992), pp. 206-22; Hans Vaget, "Syberberg's *Our Hitler*," *Massachusetts Review* 23.4 (1982): 593-612; Fredric Jameson, "'In the Destructive Element Immerse': Syberberg and Cultural Revolution," *Perspectives on German Cinema*, eds. Terri Ginsberg and Kirsten Thompson (New York: Hall, 1996), pp. 508-25; and Susan Sontag, "Eye of the Storm," *New York Review of Books* 27.2 (21 February 1980): 36-43.

4 Leon Wieseltier, "Syberberg's Hitler," *New Republic* 182.10 (8 March 1980): 27-30, p. 29.

5 Mary Campbell, "Finding the Grail: Fascist Aesthetics and Mysterious Objects," *King Arthur's Modern Return*, ed. Debra Mancoff (New York: Garland, 1998), 213-25, at p. 221.

6 Thomas Elsaesser, "Myth as the Phantasmagoria of History: H. J. Syberberg, Cinema, and Representation," *New German Critique* 24-25 (1981-82): 108-54, at p. 108.

beyond Wagner and even German culture to European civilization more generally.[7]

It is clear that Syberberg's *Parsifal* means to engage the viewer in *Trauerarbeit* through his aesthetics of recycling and repetition of past, and emotionally charged, cultural references; indeed, he characterizes his filmmaking in *Parsifal* as nostalgic.[8] As Thomas Elsaesser remarks, "A Syberberg film sets up a network of cultural references, artifacts, and emblems, historical signposts and musical echoes which invite recognition at the level of memory and consciousness, while denying the unconscious identification-projection mechanisms activated by conventional fiction films."[9] And in fact, what also complicates Syberberg's vexed reception is his theatrical film style, often likened to kitsch and surrealism, which makes for a difficult, not to mention lengthy, viewing experience.[10] As Susan Sontag notes, "Syberberg is an artist of excess, making thought into a kind of excess, the surplus production of ruminations, images, associations, emotions,"[11] and Robert Shandley argues that Syberberg's filmmaking techniques respond to Theodor Adorno, who for Syberberg serves as a spectre, the "kill-joy of postwar aesthetics who has stolen Germany's enjoyment of art."[12] Syberberg's use of theatrical pastiche, including photographs, puppetry, sculpture, and paintings within unrealistic and closed sets, challenges Adorno's prohibition against art after the Holocaust.[13] Syberberg's kitsch is, nevertheless, another manifestation of the powerful role of mourning in the film: "Nothing is more saturated with the past than kitsch, whose passing it perpetually regrets and laments. Kitsch cover[s] the gap between past and present."[14]

At first glance, then, it might seem that Syberberg's cinematic art lies behind his jarring insistence upon sexual difference in *Parsifal*. In other words, the reason

---

7 Michael Gilbert, "'Die Wunde ist's, die nie sich schliessen will': Richard Wagner, National Socialism, and the Films of Syberberg," *Yearbook of Interdisciplinary Studies in the Fine Arts* 1 (1989): 355-406.

8 Syberberg, *Parsifal: Notes*, p. 216.

9 Elsaesser, "Myth as the Phantasmagoria of History," p. 145. Similarly, Jameson describes Syberberg's "spiritual method" of filmmaking as a "*dereification*" ("'In the Destructive Element Immerse,'" p. 517).

10 David Schwarz, *Listening Awry: Music and Alterity in German Culture* (Minneapolis: U of Minnesota P, 2006), p. 159.

11 Sontag, "Eye of the Storm," p. 40.

12 Robert Shandley, "Syberberg and the State of the Ghost," *German Studies in the Post-Holocaust Age*, eds. Adrian del Caro and Janet Ward (Boulder: UP of Colorado, 2000), 140-47, at p. 142.

13 Theodor Adorno wrote in 1949 that "To write poetry after Auschwitz is barbaric" ("Cultural Criticism and Society," *Prisms*, trans. Samuel and Shierry Weber [Cambridge, MA: MIT Press, 1981], p. 34).

14 Elsaesser, "Myth as the Phantasmagoria of History," p. 115.

for having two actors play the part of Parsifal, one male, the other female (a third, a young boy, plays the "innocent" Parsifal during the *Vorspiel*) might seem contrived, associated with the puppetry that is a hallmark of Syberberg's films, and especially when the male voice of the singer (Rainer Goldberg) issues forth from the female Parsifal II (Karin Krick). David Schwarz, for one, describes *Parsifal* as "one grand puppet show."[15] However, there are two simultaneous, and mournful, impulses behind the doubled Parsifals, one tied to the film's visual and narrative thematics of the medieval *unio mystica*; the other, representing the way in which the director here grapples with Wagner's legacy.

Admittedly a complicated reading of an already complicated film, this study turns on a single insight: that Syberberg's attempt to come to terms with—to mourn—Wagner and his cultural and historical legacy in a post-Holocaust world hinges on sexual difference. Indeed, Syberberg's mourning is based on an alterity that highlights sexual difference; however, it is also interwoven with questions of racial difference, precisely because Wagner ties the concept of the evil seductress as the origin of sin in this grail story to that of the errant Jew, thereby coupling female sexuality with Judaism in the figure of Kundry. In response, Syberberg presents Parsifal as two separate forms of the same character, one male, the other female; as a result, he navigates the perverse seductive powers of Wagner's Kundry—and by extension, those of Wagner himself—so as to negate and defuse them. In fact, he declares that all the problems of anti-feminism and anti-Semitism inherent in Wagner's Kundry, not to mention Wagner's legacy to German society more broadly, are solved in this idea of the two Parsifals.[16]

My reading is divided into four sections. The first begins with Syberberg's use of the medieval past and explicitly medieval allusions in the film. Because Syberberg's medievalism depends upon—and is mediated by—Wagner's opera, I then explore Wagner's opera, its transformations of its medieval predecessor, and its late nineteenth- and early twentieth-century historical context. Syberberg's mourning of the past, particularly its Wagnerian legacy, is the subject of the third section, as I examine the film as a *Trauerarbeit*. It is within this concept of mourning that I consider the film's presentation of sexual difference, which Syberberg presents as a means of performing the work of mourning necessary to re-envision (but not to rehabilitate) Wagner in a post-Holocaust context. The concluding section treats the film's resolution, which serves as the resolution of both sexual difference and mourning, and this by altering the concept of the medieval *unio mystica* present in Syberberg's reflections on the film.

The reader may wonder why this study enacts a temporal circle of sorts, beginning with the film's medieval allusions to conclude with the medieval

---

15 Schwarz, *Listening Awry*, p. 153.
16 Syberberg, *Parsifal: Notes*, pp. 132-33.

concept of the androgynous union with God, all the while mediated by Syberberg's mournful sense of Wagner and history. This circularity is no accident, as it enacts Syberberg's demands on the viewer in his *Trauerarbeit* (and indeed, those of the theoretical notions of mournful sexual difference): to pay careful attention to a diachronic perspective. Moreover, this diachronic perspective serves to highlight how the film engages the mournful "queer spectrality" of the past.[17] In other words, the film makes use of the past—itself already haunted—not only to disturb the viewer (especially German), but also to disrupt his sense of historical and national identity. Recall too that Judith Butler's neo-Freudian considerations of mourning and melancholy relate the latter specifically to gender identity: "Prohibited by regimes of compulsory heterosexuality, these original homosexual attachments must be lost, yet they are grieved by being secreted inside the subject to constitute the repudiated ground of gendered identity."[18] As a result, it is only through a conception of mourning itself as queer, as shifting and reshaping our sense of identities—here, sexual and historical—that sexual difference may be read as embodying Syberberg's directives of how Germans should mourn Wagner and their recent past.

Indeed, what the film's funereal medieval allusions make clear is that the film's conception of sexual difference is neither ideal nor paradisal, but is rather a (post)utopic means of healing. Sexual difference becomes for Syberberg, as it did for his medieval forebears, not only a concrete sign of the earthly distance from joyous perfection, but also an expression of the hope of eventual reparation (if not the attainment of paradise). In this sense, Syberberg's use of the male/female Parsifal also theoretically and psychologically suggests the queer coupling of the stranger and the neighbor, and in contrast to Wagner, embodies the continued social, historical, and ethical importance of coming to terms with the Other in our midst.

Uses of the past

Syberberg's film is filled with a pastiche of cultural references, many of them medieval; indeed, Syberberg believes that the Grail functions as one of our most sacred nostalgias.[19] While its action is not clearly set in the Middle Ages, the film

---

17 Carla Freccero, *Queer/Early/Modern* (Durham: Duke UP, 2006), p. 101. See also Cary Howie's essay in the present collection.

18 Judith Butler, *The Psychic Life of Power* (Stanford, CA: Stanford UP, 1997), p. 135. See also Michael O'Rourke, "Queer Theory's Loss and the Work of Mourning Jacques Derrida," *Rhizomes(RhizomesC)* 10 (Spring 2005), accessed at http://www.rhizomes.net/issue10/orourke.htm#_edn86.

19 Syberberg, *Parsifal: Notes*, p. 49.

strongly evokes the medieval through its visual symbolism, as Syberberg confirms in his lengthy reflections on the making of *Parsifal.*[20] For example, Parsifal II is meant to recall the medieval image of Christ, made clear by a stained glass image that looms over Parsifal II in Act III, and knights in Templar costume process through labyrinthine paths around and over Wagner's *Totenmaske* (death mask), which serves as the "landscape of the Grail country."[21] Syberberg also engages well-known medieval monuments. The image of the sleeping Herzeleide, who holds the open book of the Grail and the Knights of the Round Table, recalls the stone effigy of Eleanor of Aquitaine at Fontevrault. Amfortas's throne is modeled on Charlemagne's at Aachen, and his wound appears, as Syberberg declares, "bleeding in the manner of relics or medieval allegorical representations or devotional objects used in pilgrimage places."[22] Syberberg also draws the image of Synagogue from the gothic sculpture of Strasbourg cathedral; the Flower Maidens from Bosch's *Garden of Earthly Delights*; the medieval aromatic garden complete with a fountain of life from Jan van Eyck's Ghent altarpiece; and Amfortas and Kundry in death as tomb sculptures of a medieval ruler and consort from the crypt of the Capuchins at Vienna. Further, Syberberg characterizes *Parsifal* as a comedy in the vein of Dante's *Commedia*. Even more striking are Syberberg's references to medieval tropes to describe his filmmaking. He characterizes the production of *Parsifal* in Monte Carlo as following the itinerary of the medieval Parsifal, who looks for the Grail in Rome, Sicily, and Jerusalem. And elsewhere, Syberberg explains that his style of filmmaking is analogous to the "medieval *unio mystica*": "The maker of such documentary films must serve in the archaic, virtually monastic sense . . . One understands here the grand masters of the medieval *unio mystica*."[23]

Parsifal is, then, an instance of "medieval" cinema, for it appropriates the textual topoi and visual iconography of the Middle Ages for its own political and socio-historical reasons. We have only to recall that one of the film's opening images is a photo of Coventry cathedral, which had been destroyed on the night of 14 November 1940, to understand how Syberberg reads the medieval in terms of a recent, and mournful, history. The medieval serves simultaneously as a remembrance of the German nation's cultural history as well as the site of the

---

20 Syberberg, *Parsifal: Notes*, pp. 89-90, 112, 161-62, 185, 203, 221. Syberberg also uses medieval imagery in his *Hitler, Ein Film aus Deutschland*. The two films are interrelated: Syberberg's *Hitler* begins with the prelude from *Parsifal*, and the word "Grail" appears in blocky, but fractured letters; the young girl/grail bearer in *Parsifal* derives from *Hitler*.

21 Donald Hoffman, "Re-framing Perceval," *Arthuriana* 10.4 (2000): 45-56, esp. p. 48.

22 Syberberg, *Parsifal: Notes*, p. 83.

23 Syberberg, *Filmbuch* (Munich: Nymphenburger, 1976), pp. 85-86.

explicitly foreign and strange. For example, when Gurnemanz leads Parsifal to the Grail ceremony in Act I, they walk through a gorge decorated with different flags which, while initially modern, including the swastika flag of the Third Reich, become increasingly heraldic and medieval in nature. The alterity of the medieval thus signifies politically (and, in the case of this film, ethically as well). As John Ganim writes, even "[i]n the nineteenth century, medievalism was constructed as a fierce reproach as well as a utopic escape from the present, and that reproach was framed in explicitly political terms."[24] The visual evocations of the Middle Ages in the film's narrative and cinematography establish the medieval as one of the critical tools of alterity necessary for working through these twentieth-century events of national and historical shame.

However, the significance of this film's medievalism is unquestionably complicated by its relationship to Wagner's dense opera, *Parsifal*. Wagner's *Parsifal* is the *raison d'être* of Syberberg's film. As a result, while *Parsifal* is an adaptation of Wolfram von Eschenbach's medieval *Parzival*, Syberberg's engagement with this medieval narrative is mediated by Wagner and his cultural legacy. Syberberg, in fact, insists that he has made use of Wagner just as Wagner used the texts of the Middle Ages.[25] Syberberg even characterizes his filmmaking—and what we might describe as his Wagnerism—in operatic terms, describing how "At night in bed he is exhausted, often trembling from listening, thinking, conducting. He conducts from the score of another composer with a rhythm of his own."[26] We must therefore look back to Wagner's reshaping and use of his medieval material to better grasp Syberberg's transformations of *Parsifal*.

Wagner: The Story Begins

The medieval Grail story, and in particular Wolfram von Eschenbach's epic poem, is clearly the foundation of Syberberg's story.[27] However, Wagner's transformation of Wolfram's narrative was radical. As Ulrich Müller writes,

---

24 John Ganim, "The Myth of Medieval Romance," *Medievalism and the Modernist Temper*, eds. Howard Bloch and Stephen Nichols (Baltimore: Johns Hopkins UP, 1996), pp. 148-166, at p. 148.

25 Hans-Jürgen Syberberg, "Filmishes bei Richard Wagner," *Richard Wagner: Millter zwischen Welten*, ed. Gerhardt Hekdt (Anit, Austria: Müller-Speiser, 1990), p. 76.

26 Syberberg, *Filmbuch*, p. 86.

27 Syberberg, *Parsifal: Notes*, p. 57. Mircea Eliade considers Wolfram von Eschenbach's *Parzival* "the most complete story and coherent mythology of the Grail" (*A History of Religious Ideas, Volume 3: From Muhammad to the Age of Reforms*, trans. Alf Hiltebeitel and Diane Apostolos-Cappadona [Chicago: U of Chicago P, 1985], p. 105).

Wagner changes Wolfram's global and well-populated epic into a *Weltenschauung-drama*, one that concentrates on only a few characters. His *Bühnenweihfestspiel* advances the notion that sexual asceticism and the renunciation of the world are of the highest merit. . . . Through asceticism, [the opera's hero] gains the power to acquire the Grail and takes on the role of redeemer.[28]

Wagner changed Wolfram's circuitous medieval narrative to focus on what he considered its redemptive elements. His modifications to Wolfram's text accentuate the religious and ascetic nature of the Grail story: he emphasizes the Grail as the chalice used at the Last Supper and by Joseph of Arimathea to catch Christ's blood at the Crucifixion rather than Wolfram's grail stone; he transforms the character of Kundry into a Mary Magdalene/errant Jewess figure rather than Wolfram's learned grail bearer (and bizarrely shaped) Cundrie; and he characterizes the Grail community as entirely masculine, ascetic, and celibate, rather than Wolfram's grail family, which is built around procreation and genealogy, and which includes men, women, and children.[29]

Wagner's own psychology and that of his cultural context also pervade his adaptation of Wolfram's medieval narrative. As Volker Mertens writes, "Wagner believed that he himself was the first person to have extracted the essential mythical meaning of these medieval narratives, and to have portrayed that meaning onstage, whereas what he actually staged . . . were the problems of his own age, even of his own life."[30] It is not the place here to rehearse in detail Wagner's anti-Semitism or the way in which he may have informed the discourses of National Socialism. Suffice it to say, as does Ernst Hanisch, that while there is not a direct, clear path from Wagner to Hitler, "[t]o write about Wagner . . . is to write about a central problem in German and European history."[31] And further, as Sontag notes, "It is true that Hitler has contaminated romanticism and Wagner, that much of nineteenth-century German culture is, retroactively, haunted by Hitler."[32]

28 Müller, "Blank, Syberberg, and the German Arthurian Tradition," *Cinema Arthuriana*, ed. Kevin Harty (New York: Garland, 1991), pp. 157-68, at p. 159.

29 See Volker Mertens for a fuller account of Wolfram's *Parsifal* and Wagner's adaptation, in "Wagner's Middle Ages," *Wagner Handbook*, eds. Ulrich Müller and Peter Wapnewski (Cambridge, MA: Harvard UP, 1992), 236-68, at pp. 262-66.

30 Mertens, "Wagner's Middle Ages," p. 236. Friedrich Nietzsche lamented Wagner's appropriation of old sagas as an escape to the past and indicts *Parsifal* as a "work of rancour" (*Nietzsche contra Wagner, The Complete Works of Friedrich Nietzsche*, trans. Oscar Levy [New York: Russell & Russell, 1964], 8.57-82, esp. pp. 64-65, 73).

31 Ernst Hanisch, "The Political Influence and Appropriation of Wagner," *Wagner Handbook*, 186-201, at p. 186.

32 Sontag, "Eye of the Storm," p. 40.

For our purposes, it is quite clear that Syberberg's use of two Parsifals responds to Wagner's conception of sexual difference as a polyvalent expression of alterity, which is at the forefront of Wagner's conception of the grail narrative. Even Wagner's own romantic notion of the poet at work—the creation of opera as an emotional expression—hinges upon a sense of otherness.[33] More important, Wagner's reworking of Wolfram's narrative inserts racial and sexual alterity into what had been an unusually "multicultural" medieval narrative. The most telling example is that of Kundry, who as we have noted, no longer represents for Wagner a learned Arab woman, but rather a female version of the wandering Jew.[34] This portrayal of Kundry highlights alterity as marked by sexual and racial difference, and it is to this portrayal that the two Parsifals of Syberberg's film respond.

Wagner considered Judaism generally as a manifestation in sociological terms of the foreignness of the stranger within a community. In his essay on Judaism in music, for example, Wagner describes the presence of Jewish composers in pathological terms:

> So long as the separate art of music had a real organic life-need in it, down to the epochs of Mozart and Beethoven, there was nowhere to be found a Jew composer: it was impossible for an element entirely foreign to that living organism to take part in the formative stages of that life. Only when a body's inner death is manifest, do outside elements win the power of lodgment in it—merely to destroy it. Then indeed that body's flesh dissolves into a swarming colony of insect-life.[35]

What is notable here is the way in which Wagner joins such terms of "foreign" and related notions of interiority and exteriority with illness and death, with the last phrase invoking the swarming of maggots over a corpse. As Clifton Spargo explains, "Even when the stranger is another citizen within our society, she occurs to the subject firmly ensconced in culturally determined identity as an exception to ordinary logic and knowledge; she is not yet or perhaps no longer

---

33 Wagner describes the musicality of poetry as created by means of alterity in "Opera and Drama" (*Richard Wagner's Prose Works*, trans. William Ellis [London: Kegan Paul, 1893], 2.375).

34 Richard Wagner, *Sämtliche Schriften und Dichtungen* (Leipzig, n.d. [1871-1883; 1911-1916]), XI, 404; cited in Dieter Borchmeyer, "The Question of Anti-Semitism," *Wagner Handbook*, p. 184.

35 K. Friegedank [Wagner], "Das Judentum in der Musik," *Neue Zeitschrift für Musik*, no. 20 [September 3, 1850]: 107; *Richard Wagner's Prose Works*, trans. William Ellis, vol. 3, p. 99.

the neighbor whom one habitually recognizes."[36] This passage also intimates the way in which alterity in general produces for Wagner, and for such a Wagnerian as Syberberg, disquieted grief.

Consequently, if Syberberg "sets as his goal nothing less than obtaining our undivided attention to, and passionate involvement with, the work of art itself, a quintessentially Wagernian claim," as Johan Deathridge writes, he also insists upon coming to terms with—that is, mourning—Wagner and his legacy on early twentieth-century Germany.[37]

Syberberg's Wagnerian Mourning

Mournful memory is less a part of the content of Syberberg's films than their form: *Trauerarbeit,* the work of mourning, serves as the moral and psychological justification for Syberberg's aesthetics of repetition and recycling.[38] Indeed, Syberberg explicitly links *Trauerarbeit* with his filmmaking. For Freud, whereas the therapeutic and practical work of mourning aims to restore the mourner to the established social narratives that highlight the autonomous self within the culture of the living, the "complex of melancholia behaves like an open wound."[39] The melancholic, trapped in narcissistic regression, can only compulsively desire to "repeat the trauma of loss."[40] For Syberberg, however, *Trauerarbeit* refers specifically to Wagner's legacy, polluted by anti-Semitism and National Socialism. Although Syberberg's notion of *Trauerarbeit* is first emphasized in connection with his film *Winifred Wagner und die Geschichte des Hauses Wahnfried von 1914-1975*, which he calls his "*Trauerarbeit* für Bayreuth,"[41] he is also keenly aware of the profound influence that *Parsifal* had on Hitler. Syberberg explains, "Because it was also of *Parsifal* that Hitler was able to say that he would make of it a religion, and that he had chosen it for the celebration after the happy outcome of the world war."[42] Applying the concept of *Trauerarbeit* to *Parsifal*

---

36 Clifton Spargo, *Vigilant Memory: Emmanuel Levinas, the Holocaust, and the Unjust Death* (Baltimore: Johns Hopkins UP, 2006), p. 182.

37 Johan Deathridge, "A Brief History of Wagner Research," *Wagner Handbook*, 202-23, at p. 218.

38 Sontag, "Eye of the Storm," p. 40.

39 Sigmund Freud, "Mourning and Melancholia," *The Standard Edition of the Complete Psychological Works of Sigmund Freud*, ed. and trans. James Strachey (London: Hogarth Press, 1953-1974), 14.239-58, esp. pp. 244-46, 253.

40 Wendy Wheeler, "After Grief? What Kinds of Inhuman Selves?" *New Formations* 25 (1995): 77-95, at p. 81.

41 Syberberg, *Filmbuch*, pp. 243-96.

42 Syberberg, *Parsifal: Notes*, p. 9.

accentuates its status as a film that is fundamentally marked by mournful, Wagnerian memory. As Michael Gilbert notes,

> the Wagner complex in Syberberg's work is more concretely or precisely a "Parsifal-complex"—a perspective concerned essentially with matters of guilt, knowledge, and redemption in relation to the difficult task of *Trauerarbeit* as it pertains to the legacy and historical consequences of Richard Wagner and Bayreuth . . . and . . . is the logical consequence of Syberberg's attempt to come to terms with Wagner and *by way of Wagner*, with the German past. . . . [T]o Syberberg, the only effective means by which to heal the seemingly unhealable wounds created by Wagner's legacy (i.e., in terms of its overwhelming influence on Hitler) is the critical appropriation and use of that legacy itself.[43]

Further, Syberberg's use of *Trauerarbeit* suggests that he subscribes to the idea (a relatively controversial one) that Germans' inability to mourn means that they are afflicted by mass melancholy. It is to this inability to mourn that his films (and in particular *Hitler, ein Film aus Deutschland*) respond.[44] Elsaesser writes,

> Syberberg's cinema defines both its own historical position and its concrete aesthetic principle. He has clearly recognized that the historical function of the cinema has been to act as a mirror, and to provide self-images for the spectator who engages with the film through projection and identification. . . . Syberberg's cinema . . . hold[s] up to the spectator a mirror in which Germans are reluctant to recognize themselves—the mirror of their own fragmented and disavowed past.[45]

This notion of German society being held captive by its history is strongly felt, and the mourning here has specifically historical, and queer, overtones: "[s]omething of the past always remains," writes Dominick LaCapra, "if only as a haunting presence or revenant."[46] Michael Gilbert characterizes Syberberg's "Parsifal-complex" as both mythical and historical. For Gilbert, the Grail symbolizes "a national-cultural search for deliverance, the tragic consequences of which are themselves a gaping wound, posing the 'grail question' anew for post-war German society."[47] Gilbert's notion of the Grail quest accentuates

---

43 Gilbert, "'Die Wunde ist's, die nie sich schliessen will,'" p. 358.

44 Cited in Sontag, "Eye of the Storm," p. 40.

45 Elsaesser, "Myth as the Phantasmagoria of History," p. 145.

46 Dominick LaCapra, "Trauma, Absence, Loss," *Critical Inquiry* 25 (1999): 696-727, at p. 700.

47 Gilbert, "'Die Wunde ist's, die nie sich schliessen will,'" p. 361.

a queer, and spectral, approach to the past: his use of "gaping wound" has not only Freudian resonances (recall Freud's aforementioned description of melancholia as wound), but also medieval, and even mythological echoes, which are linked to, and surpass, history and identity (national, sexual, and ethical). We also might consider a Levinasian conception of mournful memory as useful in this context: for Levinas, as for Syberberg, both memory and ethics are inherently linked to mourning, which is a disruptive force both for the subject and for history. If Syberberg's conception of history is one of catastrophe,[48] it is, moreover, also not that of Germany alone: Eric Santner argues, for instance, that Syberberg universalizes the wounds of recent history.[49] According to Syberberg, then, *Parsifal* represents "utopia as a society of the dead [*Totengesellschaft*] . . . the liberation, finally, myth as remembrance, myth as memory. Once again the journey into the interior, the world after its decline."[50]

Syberberg's Adaption of Wagner: Sexual Difference and Mourning

Syberberg's cinematic adaptation of Wagner reproduces and yet heightens this sense of death and mourning in connection with Wagner's *Parsifal*; indeed, Wagner's *Totenmaske* [death mask] serves as the set of the film, the "landscape of the Grail country."[51] As Syberberg explains, "In *Parsifal* we already had the idea of everything taking place in the head of a human being, but it was Richard Wagner's death mask. . . . It was the fantasy of projection, it was based on an old idea of utopia, into which the audience had to incorporate its own ideas."[52] Moreover, Syberberg resolutely connects sexual difference to this mourning: for the two Parsifals issue forth from Wagner's death mask. That is, the passage from Parsifal I to Parsifal II takes place by means of the death mask's projection, with Parsifal II appearing like a shadow from the mask, and Parsifal I slowly receding into it.[53] The two Parsifals thus function as an androgynous projection from the mortuary mask of Wagner.[54]

---

48 Sontag, "Eye of the Storm," p. 40.

49 Eric Santner, *Stranded Objects: Mourning, Memory and Film in Postwar Germany* (Ithaca: Cornell UP, 1990), 192n101.

50 Syberberg, *Parsifal: Notes*, p. 11.

51 Hoffman, "Re-framing Perceval," p. 48.

52 Christopher Sharrett, "Sustaining Romanticism in a Postmodernist Cinema: An Interview with Hans-Jürgen Syberberg," *Cineaste* 15.3 (1987): 18-20, at p. 20.

53 Syberberg, *Parsifal: Notes*, p. 132.

54 Marie-Bernadette Fantin-Epstein, "De Wagner à Syberberg: *Parsifal*, ou le masque éclaté," *Mises en cadre dans la littérature et dans les arts*, ed. Andrée Mansau (Toulouse, France: Presse Universitaire du Mirail, 1999), 257-64, esp. p. 260.

The relationship between mourning and sexual difference is critical in psychoanalysis. Indeed, for Freud, mourning and melancholia operate in a fashion similar to the conflict between Thanatos and Eros. In other words, mourning and melancholia replicate the way in which the demands of the death drive (Thanatos) struggle with those of the life instincts (Eros). The intended therapeutic result of *Trauerarbeit* is to allow the ego to become "free and uninhibited again," capable of connecting to new love objects.[55] Healthy mourning restores the bereaved to society as an autonomous being. On the other hand, melancholia is related to the unconscious lost object, and is thus a substitute for the erotic cathexis, characterized by ambivalence toward the lost object and the regression of the libido into the ego.[56] For Freud, mourning is thus intimately connected to Eros and the libido, which are in a healthy fashion withdrawn from the Other *qua* lost love object. Melancholy, on the other hand, functions as a disruption: the melancholic cannot be reintegrated into the society of the living because of his continued and regressive libidinal attachment to the beloved Other. As Santner writes, "What makes the Other *other* is not his or her spatial exteriority with respect to my being but the fact that he or she is *strange*, is a *stranger*, and not only to me but also to him- or herself, is the bearer of an internal alterity, an enigmatic density of desire calling for response beyond any rule-governed reciprocity."[57]

We must emphasize the decidedly Wagnerian hue of this mournful presentation of sexual difference, recalling that for Syberberg, Wagner's *Parsifal*, devoted to the notion of redemption necessitated by the guilty evil Woman as enemy and as wandering Jew, is Wagner's testament.[58] If, as Syberberg notes, the two Parsifals solve the problem of the impossibility of a credible hero, especially one of German origin, they also hinge upon his interpretation of Wagner. We see this particularly in terms of the casting: Syberberg points out, for example, the resemblance of Parsifal I (Michael Kutter) to the original appearance of the character in Kaspar [Clemens] von Zumbusch's sketches. Moreover, Syberberg explains that if Parsifal I follows the traditional iconongraphy of Jean the Baptist, Parsifal II resembles a Flemish Christ, foreshadowed by this John the Baptist. As a result, Syberberg exlains, he has restored Christ to Wagner's opera: Wagner, Syberberg declares, had desired to compose an opera on Christ, but because of fear and phobia, replaced Christ with Parsifal.[59]

The film's cinematography further emphasizes the mournful cast of sexual difference. From its very outset, the film ties sexual difference to mourning. It

---

55 Freud, "Mourning and Melancholia," p. 245.

56 Freud, "Mourning and Melancholia," pp. 239-58.

57 Santner, *Psychotheology of Everyday Life* (Chicago: U of Chicago P, 2001), p. 9.

58 Syberberg, *Parsifal: Notes*, p. 9.

59 Syberberg, *Parsifal: Notes*, pp. 132-33.

opens with a lengthy series of shots of a ruined temple, and then appear yellowed photos and postcards of ruined landscapes (collapsed German highways, St. Peter's in a devastated cityscape) and destroyed monuments (Dresden in 1945, Versailles in ruins, the Statue of Liberty looking over a flooded New York), scattered and floating on water.[60] Even a golden grail chalice appears, seemingly frozen in this river of desolation and memory. Immediately after, an arrow with red feathers enters the ground near the water, and we see the child Parsifal with his mother (Kundry). We follow Parsifal's gaze as he watches the figures of Parsifal I and Parsifal II ride by in a carriage. Clearly, the film's opening sequence links history in the guise of ruined monuments to the sexual differentiation of Parsifal as young child, boy, and girl. If this moment of the three Parsifals represents a triad of "neuter, male, and female components lingering for a moment before splitting off into sexual difference," as David Schwarz argues, what is most striking is the way in which the sexual difference represented by the three characters is resolutely joined to questions of national memory and mourning: sexual difference in the film is seemingly produced out of the apocalyptic ruins of the past.[61] As a result, these opening scenes adumbrate the way in which sexual difference functions symbolically in this film.

The way in which the initial scenes imbue sexual difference with mourning reappears near the end of Act II, when Kundry attempts to seduce Parsifal in a rocky, ascetic setting, itself a conscious departure from the traditional garden scenes of seduction used by Wagner.[62] Kundry convincingly presents herself as a tender mother/lover, and she and Parsifal kiss. However, after the kiss, Parsifal turns away from her. This renunciation of the sexual act is inscribed in sexual difference, as it is this moment when Parsifal II (girl) awakens and appears on the scene. She joins Parsifal I (boy), and the pair stands side-by-side. When Kundry attempts to seduce Parsifal II (girl) she fails outright. For Syberberg, Parsifal I represents "Wound"; however, he notes that Parsifal II's rejection of Kundry transforms what seemed simply a sexual wound into a greater wound, on the level of spiritual, rather than sexual, sublimation, "as if the elements (and not simply masculine and feminine) were reunited to conquer at this moment the original principals of seduction."[63]

John Christopher Kleis calls the transformation of Parsifal into a woman "Syberberg's one big misstep in the film."[64] However, according to David

---

60 Syberberg, *Parsifal: Notes*, p. 56.

61 Schwarz, *Listening Awry*, pp. 151-52.

62 Syberberg, *Parsifal: Notes*, p. 122.

63 Syberberg, *Parsifal: Notes*, p. 132.

64 John Kleis, "The Arthurian Dilemma: Faith and Works in Syberberg's *Parsifal*," *King Arthur on Film*, ed. Kevin Harty (Jefferson, NC: McFarland, 1999), 109-22, at p. 117.

Schwarz, this moment in the film serves a double purpose, both narrational and psychological:

> By having Parsifal II awaken at the moment of Parsifal's recognition of his sexual desire, Syberberg achieves both a diachronic representation of Parsifal's quest, and a regressive fantasy of Parsifal turning back away from his sexual awakening, moving back to a time and place during which / at which the two elements of sexual difference embraced each other in a perfect union. Syberberg achieves a large-scale transformation of time becoming space by combining the forward-moving diachronic trajectory of quest with a backward rewinding of the tape to a moment before sexual difference.[65]

Parsifal II thus defuses and transforms this seduction scene; rather than traumatized by sexual wounding, she offers the possibility of Kundry's conversion from her role as sexual temptress. As a result, Parsifal II allows Syberberg to read *Parsifal* beyond Wagner and his anti-Semitic and misogynist inclinations.

Sexual Difference and the Promise of the *unio mystica*

If Syberberg declares that it is "up to the spectators to see and understand" the gender change, he nonetheless provides many clues as to the multiple meanings behind this sexual difference in his essay on the film.[66] The emphasis here should be on the polyvalence of sexual difference. Syberberg not only appropriates Wagner's legacy in order to heal the wounds caused by that same legacy, but also makes use of sexual difference as a means to address, even heal, those wounds. Recall that Syberberg argues that anti-feminism and anti-Semitism—again, Wagner's conjoining of the idea that the Biblical image of evil Woman with that of the errant Jew in the figure of Kundry—are solved in this idea of mournful sexual difference embodied by the two Parsifals. According to Syberberg, Parsifal has no sex, but is instead an idea.[67] In other words, Syberberg's manipulation of the mournful nature of sexual difference holds the promise of resolution in a (post)utopic union.

---

65 Schwarz, *Listening Awry*, p. 156.

66 Hans-Jürgen Syberberg and Pierre Flinois, "A New Golden Age of Cinema: A Background to Syberberg's *Parsifal*," *Continental Film and Video Review* 29 (11 September 1982): 40-42, at p. 42.

67 Jacques Siclier, "Entretien," *Le Monde* jeudi 20 mai 1982, p. 11, "Propos recueillis par J. Siclier."

The final scenes of the film highlight the notion of reunion: the two Parsifals embrace within Wagner's mortuary mask as it splits open, severed just under the nose. Their embrace appears "like a circle of the utopic redemption of dichotomized life."[68] Marie-Bernadette Fantin-Epstein characterizes this resolution—this idea of rediscovered union—as androgynous.[69] Syberberg, however, explicitly describes the doubling of the two forms of being (male/female) as functioning as an allegory of love as brother/sister,[70] which Syberberg declares as "possible only at this age, situated between the phases of human life, after childhood and before the division into conscious sexual difference."

Suggesting a time before sexual difference, the conclusion of the film has paradisal aspirations: Syberberg notes that the two Parsifals suggest Paradise, realized in the reunion of the two sexes till now separated.[71] It is, then, useful to recall the medieval notion of the *unio mystica*, or the mystical relationship of the soul to Christ, to which Syberberg alludes in his description of his filmmaking. The notion of the *unio mystica* transcends gender to emphasize the promise of complete union with God, a union that is impossible, and thus mourned for, on Earth: recall, for example, Augustine's passionate yearning for God in his *Confessions*.[72]

The *unio mystica* has Biblical foundations in the story of the creation of one flesh in two natures found in Genesis 2.23.[73] In his letter to the Ephesians 5.21-33, Paul invokes this creation story to describe marriage as the joining of the husband to the wife and, moreover, with it creates an equivalent analogy of the intimate relationship of Christ as groom and individuals within the church as the bride. This Pauline conception, which first characterizes the ideal relationship between Christ and the Church, comes to represent in the exegesis of the Song of Songs, and especially in the twelfth century, the relationship of Christ (or Mary) and the individual soul figured as feminine. The two sexual natures of this spiritual relationship have become necessary to "express the metaphysical need for complementarity."[74] It is no surprise, then, that the notion of God and Christ both as animating father and nurturing mother to their "children" gains currency in the High Middle Ages.[75] Most prominent in Cistercian affective

---

68 Syberberg, *Parsifal: Notes*, p. 184.

69 Fantin-Epstein, "De Wagner à Syberberg, " p. 263.

70 Syberberg, *Parsifal: Notes*, p. 133.

71 Syberberg, *Parsifal: Notes*, pp. 200, 132.

72 Augustine, *Confessions,* trans. R. Pine-Coffin (New York: Penguin, 1961), esp. Book 10, pp. 211, 232.

73 See Wayne Meeks, "The Image of the Androgyne: Some Uses of a Symbol in Earliest Christianity," *History of Religions* 13 (1974): 165-208.

74 Ann Astell, *The Song of Songs in the Middle Ages* (Ithaca: Cornell UP, 1990), p. 200.

75 Bynum, *Jesus as Mother* (Berkeley: U of California P, 1982), pp. 112-29.

theology, this conception of the *unio mystica* encourages bridal affection in the soul.[76] In his reading of the Song of Songs 2.2 ("like a lily among thorns"), Bernard of Clairvaux considers the difference between *unum* and *unus*: the first expressing the relationship between Father and Son, the second, between God and man. The latter relationship, declares Bernard, "cannot be said to be a unity, yet they are with complete truth and accuracy, said to be one spirit, if they cohere with the bond of love."[77] However, Bernard then exhorts his fellow monks to join with God in the same terms that Genesis uses to describe the creation of two sexual natures, and that Paul uses to describe the marriage relationship and thus the relationship between Christ and the church:

> There is a saying by one who experienced it, "For me it is good to cleave to God" [Ps. 72.28]. Good indeed, if you cleave wholly to him. Who is there who cleaves perfectly to God, unless he who, dwelling in God, is loved by God and, reciprocating that love, draws God into himself. Therefore, when God and man cleave wholly to each other—it is when they are incorporated into each other by mutual love that they cleave wholly to each other—I would say beyond all doubt that God is in man and man in God.[78]

Bernard here seems to describe the process by which humans, no longer bound by sexual difference, are mystically united with God, recalling Paul's letter to the Galatians 3.28, "There is no longer Jew or Greek, there is no longer slave or free, there is no longer male and female; for all of you are one in Christ Jesus."

Syberberg's two Parsifals, particularly in their concluding androgynous embrace, allude to this mystical, spiritual union with God. As Syberberg declares, "In the film the child is no longer a child but a representation of Faith and of the final unification of ancient opposing worlds—an illuminating and mutually reflecting entity of innocence."[79] However, that the two Parsifals embrace within Wagner's fragmented, ruined death mask is significant: Syberberg invokes and yet alters the medieval *unio mystica* to emphasize that this androgynous embrace is neither paradisal nor transcendent, but rather (post)utopic and diachronic. To stop here, then, is to forget how Syberberg figures sexual difference as a mourning that can come to terms with—that can mourn, ethically—a resolutely historical trauma. We must delve further into the Levinasian conception of

---

76 Astell, *Song of Songs,* p. 112.

77 Bernard of Clairvaux, *On the Song of Songs,* trans. Kilian Walsh and Irene Edmonds (Spencer, MA: Cistercian Publications, 1971-1980), Sermon 71, p. 54. The Latin appears in *Sermones super Cantica Canticorum,* eds. J. Leclercq, C. Talbot, and H. Rochais (Rome: Editiones Cistercienses, 1958), II, 214-24.

78 Bernard of Clairvaux, *On the Song of Songs,* Sermon 71, pp. 56-57.

79 Syberberg, *Parsifal: Notes,* p. 200.

diachronic alterity, which offers an ethics that, unlike the *unio mystica,* is not transcendent.

Turning from pschoanalysis to Levinas is instructive in this context, for Levinas's mournful memory, or what Clifton Spargo has described as "disquieted" and "vigilant" memory, not only hinges upon alterity but even produces the ethical. While in the psychoanalytical terms of Freud and Kristeva, the stranger heralds "an alienation within identity that would unsettle all of our most basic cultural myths, especially our most vehement nationalist commitments," for Levinas, however, alterity is productive, in that it produces Being itself as responsibility for the Other.[80] In other words, in the Other exists a trace of alterity—Otherness—that can never be seized or understood, even in proximity and the face-to-face, which is why the responsibility for the Other always comes before and exceeds subjectivity and ontology.[81] As Wayne Froman argues,

> The restlessness associated with the fission of the Ego . . . which comprises the Self . . . amounts to an other within the Self. . . . It is strange because the very disturbance brought on by the approach of the other, the persecution that precludes recourse to any resources, is what brings on the liberation of my Self and a sense of sameness that would appear not to amount to a sameness with anything that has preceded it.[82]

More important, Levinas describes the alterity of the stranger/neighbor—the spectral stranger within every neighbor—as the operative element of ethics, and thus justice.[83] He writes, "The neighbor that obsesses me is already a face, both comparable and incomparable, a unique face and in relationship with faces, which are visible in the concern for justice."[84]

Indeed, the notion of alterity inherent to sexual difference is essential here, for it allows us to understand more fully both Syberberg's use of the medieval and his insistence upon sexual difference as a way of coming to terms with the past, and in particular with Wagner's cultural legacy. Levinas's suggestion that

---

80 Spargo, *Vigilant Memory,* p. 181.

81 Emmanuel Levinas, *Otherwise than Being, or, Beyond Essence,* trans. Alphonso Lingis (Pittsburgh, PA: Duquesne UP, 1998), p. 92.

82 Wayne Froman, "The Strangeness in the Ethical Discourse of Emmanuel Levinas," *Addressing Levinas,* eds. Eric Nelson, Antje Kapust, and Kent Still (Evanston, IL: Northwestern UP, 2005), 52-60, at p. 55.

83 See Emmanuel Levinas, "Enigma and Phenomenon," in *Emmanuel Levinas: Basic Philosophical Writings,* eds. Adriaan Peperzak, Simon Critchley, and Robert Bernasconi (Bloomington: Indiana UP, 1996), 65-77, esp. p. 74.

84 Levinas, *Otherwise than Being,* p. 158.

"*being's other*, or the *otherwise than being*, here situated in diachrony, here expressed as infinity" is thus useful for thinking through Syberberg's (post)utopic conclusion of *Parsifal*.[85] For when we consider Levinas's notion of alterity as ethical, we understand that, for Syberberg, as for Levinas, responsibility—the mourning for the past—is diachronic, and as such, surpasses temporal boundaries. This differs sharply from the telos of the medieval *unio mystica*, which emphasizes God as Alpha and Omega. As Augustine writes: "I have seen that while each single one of your works is good, collectively they are very good, and that heaven and earth, which represent the Head and body of the Church, were predestined in your Word, that is, in your only-begotten Son, before all time began, when there was no morning and no evening."[86] For Augustine, difference—inscribed and surpassed in the creation of two natures from one flesh—is resolved transcendently, outside of time. However, rather than invoking theological transcendence, Levinas characterizes diachrony as firmly grounded in an ethical relation: "What in fact seems to transpire—after the attempts to think time starting from the face of the Other, in which 'God comes to our minds,' as an authority that there commands indeclinably, but also refuses to compel and commands while renouncing omnipotence—is the necessity to think time in the devotion of a theology without theodicy."[87]

As a result, Syberberg's aesthetics, his film as Wagnerian *Trauerarbeit*, and the way in which he transforms the medieval thematics of the narrative that underlie its cinematography point to its decidedly (post)utopic cast. While it presents sexual difference as the yearning of the medieval *unio mystica* for the mystical union of the soul with God, it negates the possibility of the return to transcendent innocence, precisely because any *unio mystica* must be understood as mediated by Wagner and national ignominy of the Second World War. More important, the mournful nature of Syberberg's sexual difference in *Parsifal* inscribes mystical, even mythical, reunion in the continued ethical position necessary for understanding the place of Wagner in the late twentieth century. Echoing Levinas's conception of alterity, Syberberg thus establishes sexual difference as a means of cathartic mourning. In Levinasian terms, then, we might (queerly) consider the film's final joining of the Parsifals as the stranger/neighbor coupled in this androgynous embrace. As Santner explains, against the background of "my answerability to my neighbor with an unconscious"—this Other who bears an internal alterity—"the very opposition between 'neighbor' and 'stranger' begins to lose its force . . . it is precisely this sort of answerability

---

85 Levinas, *Otherwise than Being,* p. 19.

86 Augustine, *Confessions*, 13.344-45.

87 Emmanuel Levinas, "Diachrony and Representation," *Entre nous: On Thinking-of-the-Other*, trans. Michael Smith and Barbara Harshav (New York: Columbia UP, 1998), 159-77, at p. 177.

that is at the heart of our very aliveness to the world."[88] Syberberg's insistence upon mournful sexual difference thus offers a new way of being alive to both Wagner and history.

88 Santner, *Psychotheology of Everyday Life*, p. 9.

Chapter 12
Superficial Medievalism and the Queer Futures of Film

Cary Howie

It is by now a commonplace of a certain kind of medievalism—the kind of medievalism I tend to like—that the Middle Ages touch us: that medievalism is, in fact, nothing if not a response to being touched by the past, a response that is also reciprocally (and diffusely) tactile. Carolyn Dinshaw gave the first sustained articulation of this tactile medievalism in *Getting Medieval*, where touching consists of "making partial connections between incommensurate entities" and where a specifically queer touch "show[s] something disjunctive within unities that are presumed unproblematic, even natural."[1] The Middle Ages have become, in the wake of Dinshaw's account, particularly well-suited to a queerly tactile historiography because they name and comprise so much "incommensurate" stuff; because so many beginnings and endings get folded into their constitutive "middle." The disjunctions at the heart of that historical juncture we have come, for better or worse, to call medieval provide a number of recent writers—Catherine Brown, Virginia Burrus, Carla Freccero, and Bob Mills, to name a few—with the opportunity to reflect, often eloquently, on the affects that draw some of us toward (and, occasionally, drive us away from) the Middle Ages and the periods they touch upon, "late" antiquity and "early" modernity.[2] Belated, premature, or in-between, the "partial connections" envisioned by Dinshaw are, it turns out, written into the very taxonomies according to which historical and disciplinary "unities" are posited in the first place. There is, in other words, no *impartial* connection to the past, much less within it; no "unity" or "entity" without contingency: without, that is, the bodies and times that rub against them and mark their limits.

---

1 Carolyn Dinshaw, *Getting Medieval* (Durham: Duke UP, 1999), pp. 54, 151.

2 I'm thinking here in particular of Catherine Brown, "In the Middle," *Journal of Medieval and Early Modern Studies* 30.3 (2000): 547-74; Virginia Burrus, *The Sex Lives of Saints* (Philadelphia: U of Pennsylvania P, 2003); Carla Freccero, *Queer/Early/Modern* (Durham: Duke UP, 2006); and Robert Mills, *Suspended Animation* (London: Reaktion, 2006).

In this chapter, I hope to flesh out how such a contingency, how such a touch, might look—and, no less importantly, how it might *feel*. It is my conviction that a queer medievalism, touching across time, does amount to something more—which is to say, something more touching—than mere transgression. It's this latter understanding of what it might mean to have a queer encounter with the past that Karma Lochrie seems to target in her recent book, *Heterosyncrasies*, when she sums up an entire generation of queer medievalism as dependent upon constructions of "medieval sexualities in terms of a normative heterosexuality against which deviant sexualities are posed and configured."[3] Lochrie's answer to this problem is simple: if heteronormativity "slips a modern category into the premodern past in disguise" and "overlooks the historicity of norms as well as sexual categories," then the thing to do is historicize.[4] We need, in other words, to stop slipping. Lochrie's point—that heteronormativity isn't for everyone—is well taken, but it cannot hide the fact that hers remains, to use Eve Sedgwick's terms, a paranoid position.[5] Instead of scouting out the heteronormative, what Lochrie recommends is that we scout out the insufficiently historicist. Lochrie, indeed, declares herself "on a rescue mission," specifically "to rescue the Middle Ages and all of us from the terrible presumption of transhistorical heteronormativity."[6] Vigilance requires a vigilante.

I would argue, instead, that a different kind of response—a more capacious one, less indebted to the rhetoric of heroism and less vigilant about what it is and what it is not—already lies within Dinshaw's "partial connections." The past—inevitably "incommensurate" with us, whoever "we" finally are—speaks to us even as we respond to it, even as our response will only ever be partial, inadequate. We only touch these historical objects because we have already been touched, because our position is inevitably and literally "transhistorical," crossing and crossed by time. Touch names the way in which these crossings of history are always felt, first and foremost, by bodies whose temporal positioning is far from simple. Carla Freccero proposes, in this light, a "queer spectrality" that would give voice to how the past haunts us: "the ghost arrives both from

---

3 Karma Lochrie, *Heterosyncrasies* (Minneapolis: U of Minnesota P, 2005), p. xiv. Lochrie singles out in particular Mark Jordan's *Invention of Sodomy in Christian Theology* for "creating" a normative sexuality where none existed previously. As I will argue implicitly below, there could be no greater temperamental and philosophical difference than that which obtains between Lochrie's historicism and Jordan's more delicate awareness of the ramifications of past desires in our very desires *for* a past. It goes without saying that the theological stakes of Jordan's argument—and their roots in a liturgical present—escape (in every sense possible) Lochrie's critique.

4 Lochrie, *Heterosyncrasies*, p. 2.

5 See Sedgwick's discussion of paranoid and reparative reading practices in *Touching Feeling* (Durham, NC: Duke UP, 2003).

6 Lochrie, *Heterosyncrasies*, p. xxviii.

within and from without as a part of the self that is also—and foremost—a part of the world." If we are haunted, that is to say, then it is no longer possible to say that something is unequivocally in the past. If we are haunted—and we *are* haunted—we are suspended between times, and we are suspended there not over *against*, but *with* our objects. In Freccero's words, a "spectral approach to history" consists of "a suspension, a waiting, an attending to the world's arrivals (through, in part, its returns)."[7] To wait is plainly not the same thing as to rescue. But to be historically and historiographically suspended is, all the same, not exactly to be still. After all, when Renée Fleming sings the old Howard Dietz lyric, "Be still, my haunted heart," she makes it clear that there is a tremulousness to being haunted.[8] The haunted heart wants stillness: it craves stillness and lacks it.

In what follows, I want to linger and wait in the company of several spectral, suspended encounters. These are, yes, encounters with the past, but they are specifically encounters with the surfaces of bodies that are no longer—and perhaps were never—what we thought they were. A spectral encounter with the past may, then, be a specifically *superficial* encounter, inasmuch as it coheres around and within the breaks between bodies, bodies that can only, after all, feel one another at their edges, at the places where they break and, breaking, break out into the world. This is, then, an attempt to theorize an explicitly superficial medievalism: a medievalism whose commitment to the surfaces of things—our bodies and those we find or phantasize in the Middle Ages—would allow new aspects of these things to surface. Such a medievalism would also be an avowedly melancholic one, or at least a medievalism that acknowledges its own constitution through loss and lack, as well as its inability properly to know the full extent of this constitution. But at the same time, through a commitment to the surface, a poetics of the body and its breaks, it may be possible to reach, if not beyond melancholia, then just to one side of it, in our inevitably tactile dealings with the past.

Dante, in this way, thinks he knows what it means to touch a body when, walking on the shore between the ocean and Mount Purgatory, he is approached by his old friend Casella. But he soon learns otherwise: "Io vidi una di lor trarresi avante" (I saw one of them pull himself ahead), Dante writes,

per abbracciarmi, con sì grande affetto,
che mosse me a far lo somigliante.
Ohi ombre vane, fuor che ne l'aspetto!

---

7 Freccero, *Queer/Early/Modern*, pp. 101, 104.

8 Renée Fleming, "Haunted Heart," *Haunted Heart*, produced by Renée Fleming and Elliot Scheiner (Decca 2005).

tre volte dietro a lei le mani avvinsi,

e tante mi tornai con esse al petto (2.76-83)

(in order to embrace me, and with such great affection that he moved me to do the same. Oh empty shadows, except in your appearance! Three times I placed my hands behind him and just as often I pulled them back to my chest).[9]

I want to underscore three characteristics of this strange embrace. First, Dante extends his arms in *response* to his old friend's gesture: Casella literally moves him, "mosse me," to do the same. Second, the character of this embrace is nothing less than an *asymmetrical reciprocity*: asymmetrical, because the bodies in question are not made of the same stuff; reciprocal, because this material asymmetry nonetheless is revealed according to the logic of call and mimetic response, of an "affetto" so great that Dante cannot help doing likewise, "lo somigliante." Third, Casella remains in every way *ungraspable* for the Dante-pilgrim. Their encounter here is an affective, erotically driven negotiation with difference; it is neither a blithe acceptance of an object's inevitable lostness and distance, nor is it an assimilatory annihilation of the possibility that something might separate me from what I hold. Instead, Dante recognizes that Casella is somehow beyond him only by responding to Casella's call; only by reaching out to Casella as a body does Dante literally bump up against the radical difference between them. The erotic response precedes and produces the critical, and here the self-critical, moment.

How do we learn that a body is no longer there, or is not there in the manner we were anticipating? I want to juxtapose this Dantesque fragment with François Ozon's film *Sous le sable* (*Under the Sand*), released in 2000 and starring Charlotte Rampling.[10] In Ozon's film, as in Dante's canticle, it is first and foremost a question of shorelines and appearances, of how what loves us appears to us, and how we in turn respond to it; and how the beach, with its constantly renegotiated, undulant edge, figures the space of our response.

Marie (Charlotte Rampling) and her husband Jean (Bruno Cremer) leave their Parisian home for a vacation in the southwest of France. They spend the morning after their arrival at the beach, where Jean goes for a swim while Marie dozes in the sun. Marie wakes up; Jean never comes back. The rest of the film shows Marie's ongoing refusal to accept what everyone around her acknowledges as Jean's inevitable death. She sleeps with a friend of a friend, but construes their affair as simply adulterous. She continues to buy Jean gifts. In fact, she continues to see Jean, and we are complicit in this too, seeing him

---

9 These are my translations from Dante, *Le Purgatoire* (Paris: Flammarion, 1992).

10 *Under the Sand*, dir. François Ozon. perf. Charlotte Rampling, DVD (2000; Winstar, 2001).

across from her, for example, at the breakfast table. Marie wonders at a certain point if Jean "might be contemplating suicide." When, at the end of the film, she is finally faced with Jean's body, dredged up from the sea several months after their vacation, Marie insists, "Je veux tout voir" (I want to see everything). She is reminiscent, in this way, of the protagonist of Marguerite Duras' screenplay for Alain Resnais' 1959 film *Hiroshima mon amour*, another woman with sharp cheekbones whose first words, forty years before Marie, are: "J'ai *tout* vu. *Tout*" (I've seen *everything. Everything*).[11] And yet, if having seen it all is precisely what *Hiroshima mon amour* demonstrates as impossible, in Ozon's film it is as though exhaustive vision were not impossible so much as insufficient. Despite the horror in Marie's eyes when she does look, despite her commitment to seeing everything, she inspects the articles found on the body—a swimsuit, a watch— and erupts into laughter. The watch, she says, isn't his; it's not Jean: "C'est pas la sienne; c'est pas Jean." Seeing everything is not enough. What is at stake here exceeds the field of vision. The film ends with Marie at the beach again, looking at the waves. A body appears on the horizon. She runs toward it. By the time that long, final shot is over, she still hasn't gotten there. Her encounter with that body remains suspended.

This appears, in one way, to be a relatively straightforward account of melancholia. The principle difference between melancholia and mourning is summed up by Freud as follows: "the obvious thing," he writes, "is for us somehow to relate melancholia to the loss of an object that is withdrawn from consciousness, unlike mourning, in which no aspect of the loss is unconscious."[12] That is to say, when I mourn, I know what I have lost, or at the very least I know *that* I have lost something or someone. In melancholia, on the other hand, I know neither the bare fact of my loss nor its content. This unconscious object-loss, Freud insists, is felt narcissistically by the melancholic as a loss internal to the ego rather than a loss outside it: "In mourning, the world has become poor and empty, in melancholia it is the ego that has become so."[13] If Marie were a classic melancholic, she might shore up this disavowed loss with expressions of self-hatred, finding that it is precisely *she* who is wanting, and not her husband's body. Ozon's film, however, depicts a different but analogous situation: instead of the hollowed-out, inadequate, exposed ego, which Freud likens to an "open wound,"[14] what Marie offers to view, her own view and ours, is a meticulously cared-for bodily surface, as flawless and as empty as a vase. A lost husband manifests himself, in this way, not exactly via the disturbance

11 Marguerite Duras, *Hiroshima mon amour* (Paris: Gallimard, 1960), p. 22.

12 Sigmund Freud, "Mourning and Melancholia," trans. Shaun Whiteside, *The Penguin Freud Reader*, ed. Adam Phillips (London: Penguin, 2006), 310-26, at p. 312.

13 Freud, "Mourning and Melancholia," p. 313.

14 Freud, "Mourning and Melancholia," p. 319.

of self-regard, the ego's sense of its own discontinuity, that Freud notes as the foremost melancholic symptom but, rather, across a series of shots of Marie's hyperbolically *continuous* body, working out, swimming, looking in mirror after mirror, wrapped in red silk. The surface of her body—and, most crucially, the wedding ring that never fails to take its place right at this surface—is what we are given in Jean's place. It is what Marie is working on, instead of working through her loss. It is as if we were to say: Marie hasn't lost a husband; she's just lost weight. What happens to "loss" in that transition?

In one of the film's most stunning sequences, Marie literally comes to grips with what she has and does not have. She has bought a red silk dress and presented her husband (or his shade) with a tie; and she has dined with Vincent, her lover, who has declined the invitation to come up to her apartment. Marie lies down and, as she starts to masturbate (but "masturbate" says this too knowingly), out of the darkness around her, one by one, hands emerge: Jean's, perhaps, and Vincent's, but in any case hands, anyone's hands, joining Marie's own hands in delimiting the edges of her body, in bringing pleasure through this delimitation.

Just as Dante mimetically extends his hands to Casella and repeats this embrace each time it fails, here Marie's hands do not initiate but rather respond to a prior touch or touches. Her hands are, at least at a purely phenomenal level, no more or less present than those that collaborate with her in this meticulous tracing of her body's edges, and it is precisely this collaboration which makes Marie more than melancholic. For here, on the surface of her body, is not just the proof of the loss she's swallowed and stretched herself over like so much taut, fine fabric; here is the proof that her bodily surface is constituted not singularly, not alone, but chorally, in tandem with hands that are not her own. Mark Jordan writes, along these lines, that "all erotic relations, except perhaps the briefest and the dullest, are polyamorous. They bring together multiple erotic roles, sexual identities, and real or fictive persons."[15] Marie shows us not just the extent to which Jordan's observation is particularly applicable to masturbation, but also the extent to which masturbation, historically figured as deeply bound up with both narcissism and melancholia, may actually undo both of these. These *ombre vane*, empty shades, paradoxically give texture and depth to Marie's surface. They do this, as Casella does, by issuing the call to which Marie must respond. If this response—like Dante's—fails, it nonetheless succeeds in constituting her body and its pleasures as given to her, as originating outside her, and belonging (if they belong at all) to an order that cannot be reduced to her own.

What would it mean to suggest, then, that our bodies, summoned by and into love, can only take place in response to what remains beyond their grasp? Jean, in this way, would be less a lost object whose absence Marie melancholically

---

15 Mark Jordan, *Blessing Same-Sex Unions* (Chicago: U of Chicago P, 2005), p. 182.

refuses to own and more, and more fundamentally, the basic proof of the extent to which it is impossible to own what I love; that, on the contrary, what I love owns me, and owns me in a way that preceded my love and is not reducible to it. Jean persists because, like Casella's unembraceable shade, his touch summons Marie's body as such. And it is not only *his* touch that does this. He rarely touches Marie before or after his disappearance. Touch, as this scene makes evident, is fundamentally anonymous; those hands could really be anyone's. Or rather, what those hands show, as they touch Marie, and touch her touching, is the extent to which touch takes place between particularity and generality, between anonymity and the name. There is touch, and there is a body, here, called into being, into consistency by hands that arrive from outside it, by hands that belong to an order that is not its own. These bare facts, beyond mourning and melancholia, beyond that subject/object distinction which alone permits us to speak of loss, inaugurate another kind of embodiment, one that takes place across particular kinds of bodies, takes place as it were transcorporeally, and takes place in the response of one body across and to the other bodies that convoke it erotically, summoning this body to and through the gestures of love.

There is, then, no such thing as a pristine body; no such thing as a body that has not already been crossed, by sight or by touch, that is not somehow at a crossing. (And what can you do at a crossing except wait?) This holds for history too: there is no unadulterated time to be restored or rescued. What does this have to do with film? Only this: the medium is the message here, the flicker of frames strictly analogous to the flicker of hands against Marie's body, producing continuity out of so many sharp cuts. To ask Marie to give up Jean (and, why not, to ask Dante to give up his attempts to get his hands around his old friend) would be akin to asking the picture to stop, to isolate the frame, to validate and quantify and engage in the empirical art of scission and dissection.

There are, of course, precedents for breaking a body—a filmed, lived, or literary *corpus*—in this way. Toward the end of his thirteenth-century life of St. Elizabeth of Hungary, the Parisian poet Rutebeuf shows what a body risks by being touched:

En cele houre qu'ele fina,
Cele qui si douce fin a
Fu tout ausi com endormie,
Qu'au trespasseir n'est point fenie.
Quatre jors fu li cors sor terre
C'om ne le muet ne l'enterre:
Une odour si douce en issoit
Qui de grant dousor ramplissoit
Touz ceulz qui entor li venoient,

Qui envis la biere laissoient.
Au cors covrir n'ot pas riote:
Covers fu d'une grize cote;
Le vis, d'un drap, c'om ne la voie:
N'i ot autre or ne autre soie.
Asseiz i vint grant aleüre
De gent copeir sa vesteüre;
Des cheveux et dou mameron
Li copa hon lou soumeron;
Doiz de piez et ongles de mains
Li copa hon; ce fu dou mainz:
Tout l'eüssent derompue
Qui ne lor eüst deffendue.[16] (1877-98)

(In that hour in which she died, she who had such a sweet end to her life was exactly as if she were asleep, for in crossing over [from this life to the next] she was not at all finished. For four days her body lay above the earth, as no one moved or buried her: such a sweet scent came from it that it filled with great sweetness all those who came and surrounded her, leaving her bier reluctantly. There was no dispute about covering the body: it was covered with a grey dress; and her face with a cloth, so that no man might see her: there was no gold or silk besides these. Quickly plenty of people came to cut her clothing; from her hair and her breasts they clipped the tips; they cut her toes and her fingernails; and that was the least of it: they would have entirely torn her apart if it hadn't been forbidden [or prevented].)

To touch, here, is to cut: that momentary connection with the saint's body is also a severance. Rutebeuf provides in these few lines a stunning summary of the dangers of the appropriative hand: to tear a body to pieces is literally "dou mainz," an idiom I have translated as "the least of it," but that literally reinscribes "two hands" at the site of fragmentation. These devotees seek to shred the surface of the body they surround. This body, touched and retouched, is vulnerable to violence. To be at a crossing, transcorporeally and transhistorically, would risk, in one sense, naming nothing other than these repeated cuts, "copier . . . copa . . . copa," through which Elizabeth is at once severed by and from the community that crowds around her.

This is a scene that resonates with Pier Paolo Pasolini's 1971 film version of Boccaccio's *Decameron*.[17] There, San Ciappelletto (Franco Citti), an unrepentant sinner canonized after an overwrought—and entirely phony—deathbed

---

16 Rutebeuf, *Oeuvres complètes*, ed. Michel Zink (Paris: Poche, 1990), p. 742.
17 *The Decameron*, dir. Pier Paolo Pasolini, DVD (1971; MGM, 2002).

confession, is adored by a horde of people whose outstretched hands at once frame and threaten his newly sanctified corpse. What I want to ask, in the remainder of this chapter, is whether we can have something like an experience of the body's extremities, of the body's surfaces, without making these cuts—without, in other words, this double work of violent appropriation, on the one hand, and distancing, on the other. We may not be able to touch a body, dead or alive, without risking this violence, but there is, I will argue, an account to be given of surfaces that might show how to risk violence and to do violence are not necessarily the same thing, how two hands might touch repeatedly and otherwise than by scission and sundering.

In Judith Butler's *Psychic Life of Power*, psychic interiority—the very sense that we have a kind of inner depth to speak of—is not a precondition for melancholia but, instead, a melancholic effect. "Melancholy," she writes, "is precisely what interiorizes the psyche."[18] In other words, it is what allows me to experience a difference or distance between what I feel and what I feel I *ought* to feel; what allows me, in short, to speak this reflective, reflexive "I" at all. The psychic space inaugurated by melancholy, by what will not be grieved, is paradoxically described by Butler as one of contraction: "In melancholia," she says, "the ego contracts something of the loss or abandonment by which the object is now marked, an abandonment that is refused and, as refused, is incorporated. In this sense, to refuse a loss is to become it." A few lines later, she goes on to say, "In narcissistic love, the other contracts my abundance. In melancholia, I contract the other's absence."[19]

I want to linger with this rhetoric of contraction. To contract, after all, can be to receive, to catch, as when (for example) I contract a disease, but it can also be to shrink; it can be the opposite of expansion. My vulnerability to you and my spatial finitude go hand in hand. When you go away, my world shrinks a little; when I cannot grieve that you have gone—when I do not even really have the coordinates to register that loss—then it's not the world but me that shrinks. I contract your loss, and I contract: melancholia names this spasm, this reflex, which alone enables me to experience something like reflexivity. I can only experience my limits as they diminish; I can only experience this psychic space as it becomes—gradually or in one quick clench—a little smaller.

In a small book entitled *Noli me tangere*, Jean-Luc Nancy also speaks of contraction. Here, though, it is by way of coming to terms with how it might be possible to think the resurrected Christ's refusal to be touched when, confronted by Mary Magdalene in John's Gospel, he insists, "Don't touch me" (*Noli me tangere*). The phrase, Nancy suggests, "résonne moins comme un ordre

---

18 Judith Butler, *The Psychic Life of Power* (Stanford, CA: Stanford UP, 1997), p. 170.

19 Butler, *Psychic Life*, p. 187.

que comme une supplication qui peut être lancée dans l'excès de la douleur ou dans celui de la jouissance. Ne me touche pas car je ne peux pas supporter encore cette souffrance sur ma plaie—ou cette volupté qui s'exaspère jusqu'à l'insoutenable" (resonates less as an order than as a supplication which can be hurled in the excessive moment of pain or enjoyment. Don't touch me because I can't yet endure this suffering at the surface of my wound—or this pleasure exasperated to the point of becoming unbearable).[20] This point is, he will specify, a crossing, a "point de croisement, non pas de contradiction (ni logique, ni dialectique) mais de contraction, de rétraction et d'attraction. La déflagration dans laquelle souffrir peut jouir et jouir souffrir. Ne veuille pas, ne cherche même pas à touche ce point de rupture: car en effet, j'y serais rompu(e)" (point of crossing, not of contradiction—neither logic nor dialectic—but of contraction, retraction, and attraction. The deflagration where suffering can enjoy and enjoyment can suffer. Don't wish it, don't even try to touch this point of rupture: for, effectively, I would be broken).[21]

"J'y serais rompu(e)": just as Elizabeth's body would have been broken, "tout l'eüssent desrompue," if the enamored masses had not been impeded from doing so, here too the untouchable point where suffering and joy cross is also the place where brokenness is risked. This brokenness has something to do with gender: Nancy suggests as much by his parenthetical "(e)"; Rutebeuf, likewise, suspends the body's feminized breaking, "desrompue," in relation to a masculine wholeness, "tout," suggesting that to be *wholly* broken is also to be located at a kind of gender crossing. It's when the stakes are high that gender becomes a problem. If, for Butler, psychic interiority and stabilized gender are the contracted effects of incorporated, unavowed loss, the undoing of this interiority and the suspension of this gender in the barely thwarted moment of total fragmentation would also seem to write melancholic ambivalence at the body's surface. Elizabeth is, after all, at the moment of her death, her "fin," literally "unfinished"—and this is why I think it is possible to make an analogy between psychic surfaces and depths, on the one hand, and those of the body, on the other. Not just because the body is all we've got, all we can get our hands on, but because the crucial thing, the unfinished business of a life (and a death), has not buried or hidden itself away in some place of deep incorporation but has, instead, crossed over, superficially slipped past us. The modern psyche, in other words, may be deep, but what remains of Elizabeth is shallow, and thin as a skin. What remains of Elizabeth is also, paradoxically, what escapes.

I want to ask again: what happens to the surface, the skin of our bodies but also, if I may put it this way, of our psychic life, in accounts of melancholic depth? To what kinds of incorporations and losses do we owe our sense of

---

20 Jean-Luc Nancy, *Noli me tangere* (Paris: Bayard, 2003), p. 88.
21 Nancy, *Noli me tangere*, pp. 88-89.

our surfaces? Might medieval accounts of what it means (and what it looks like) to have a body (or not have one) alter our sense of incorporation? One way, after all, to read this episode of death and adoration would be to say that the crowd's appropriative touch melancholically misses the mark, confuses the surface of the saint's body with that part of her—but again, "part" says this melancholically—which does not die. They touch and retouch this body, make these cuts that only ever bring part of it close, because Elizabeth has already presumably touched them otherwise; because Elizabeth has been cut away from them. But if Elizabeth has already been cut away, this more originary scission is felt neither as deep psychic lack nor as object-loss but, instead, as something between and beyond loss and lack. The crowd, that is to say, feels—in the strongest sense—the frustration of an encounter with something that remains only by crossing over. The paradox is that, for Elizabeth's body as for the cult of saints more generally, what you see is what you get, but (as Elizabeth's covered face attests) what you see is not necessarily what is there to be seen. In this unfinished economy, appearances are everything, but paying attention to them, giving them their due, is harder than it seems.

The surfaces of saints, then, would be these extremities, these summits or "soumeron": toes and tits, fingernails and hair. To touch them is to alter their place in the world; it is also to be altered by them, or at the very least to articulate some of the extent to which that alteration has already taken place. But to speak like this is also to presuppose a closed, immanent economy, an economy in which there's just my hand and this object, in which we can know more or less precisely what these are and what they do. There are differences in such an economy—differences that can be registered as lack or loss, differences that are caused by or cause a cut—but these differences are circumscribed or, at least, theoretically circumscribable. What happens, however, if the economy of sanctity is unfinished, as Rutebeuf suggests, and uncircumscribable? If, in other words, the surfaces we offer to the world—my hand, for example, or your toe—are incomplete not because they lack something, not because they don't measure up, nor because they've lost something (for example, the extra bit of nail that would make them perfect), but because they are inexhaustible? That is to say, are there modes or qualities of touch that might better accommodate the unfinished economy of our transcorporeal, transhistorical lives? Is it possible to speak of a superficial touch that crosses without cutting, that suspends the summit, that holds by putting on hold?

Nancy speaks, in the passage cited above, of "contraction, retraction, and attraction." What kind of touch both pulls and pulls back, recoils as it unfurls? Mary Magdalene is the saint "par excellence," Nancy argues, "parce qu'elle se tient à ce point où la touche du sens est identique à son retrait" (because she holds herself at that point where the touch of sense is identical with its retreat).[22] Touch, sense, and retreat are not innocent words for Nancy: they indicate, elsewhere in his work, various modes and registers of how the world *worlds*—or, we could also say, how shit happens. The fact that there is something rather than nothing, that there are these things and persons around us, and we come to be in irreducible relation to them: this is our extension and retreat, the deferred, diffracted touch that constitutes us, singular and plural. But what does any of this have to do with a superficial medievalism, or a saintly one? How, in other words, do sanctity and its attendant surfaces name—"par excellence" or not—the retreat, the withdrawal, internal to every reaching out toward the world, beyond all distinctions between inside and outside, surface and depth?

Rutebeuf engages with this question again in his version of the life of Mary the Egyptian, a repentant prostitute whose legend comes down to us from late antiquity in a variety of twelfth- and thirteenth-century Old French versions. Mary wanders the deserts of Palestine in atonement for years of whoring around. In Rutebeuf's version of the story—the only other saint's life attributed to him—Mary appears to a monk named Zosimas, whom she repeatedly enjoins to keep her secret to himself:

> "Peire Zozimas," dit Marie,
> "Juqu'a tant que soie fenie
> A nelui ne me descouvrir
> N'a ton abein pas ne l'ouvrir.
> Par toi vodrai estre celee
> Ce Diex ma a toi demontree." (933-38).[23]

> ("Father Zosimas," Mary says, "Until my life is finished, don't disclose me to anyone, not even your abbot. I wish to be hidden by you, even if God has shown me to you.")

The saint, that is to say, is ambivalent about the disclosure of her body—this body that, now burnt and covered only by her increasingly long hair, is the strongest visible testament to her penance—even as she recognizes that this disclosure is not strictly under her control. Moreover, her body, and her life, remain—like Elizabeth's—unfinished business; she's not yet "fenie," and it is unclear, at any rate, what it would mean for her to be done, and therefore when her unequivocal disclosure would be authorized.

When Mary dies, it's with an analogous gesture of bodily extension and withdrawal:

---

22 Nancy, *Noli me tangere*, p. 72.
23 Rutebeuf, *Oeuvres complètes*, p. 508.

Lors c'est a la terre estendue
Si com ele estoit, presque nue.
Ces mains croisa seur sa poitrine,
Si s'envelope de sa crine. (1133-36)

(Then she stretched herself out on the ground, just as she was, nearly naked. She
crossed her hands over her breast and thus wrapped herself in her hair.)

Mary literally "extends" and "envelops" her body: hands and hair collaboratively
make her perceptible to the world and gather her into herself, away from the
world. This equivocal manifestation—together with the embodied response it
might be said to solicit—speaks itself most lyrically in the description of Mary
"just as she was, nearly naked." To be almost naked, "presque nue," is to be
literally close to nakedness; it is to inscribe a kind of proximity ("pres") and
contingency into the body's self-disclosure. One can be naked alone, but in
order to be nearly naked, naked with a difference, there needs to be someone
or something else, real or phantasized, visible or invisible, somehow nearby.
Furthermore, for Rutebeuf, this near nakedness, the imminence of the body's
self-presentation, is essential: it is how Mary is; it is, in fact, her being-thus, her
estre-si. In this gesture of extension and envelopment, Mary displays precisely
that process which Maurice Merleau-Ponty describes in the *Phenomenology of
Perception* as transcendent: she takes in hand the radical contingency of her
body—the world it touches—and makes it necessary, makes it thus.

If Rutebeuf's version of Mary's life leaves the erotics of this transcendence
largely implicit, an earlier French version is more candid.[24] Crucially, in this
earlier version (T) of her life, Mary's body is not nearly but, instead, *entirely*
naked when she dies:

Dont s'est a le tere estendue
Si conme ele estoit tote nue,
Ses mains croisa seur se poitrine
Et s'envolepa en se crine. (1295-98)[25]

---

24 In *Retelling the Tale* (London: Duckworth, 2001), especially pp. 111-118, Simon
Gaunt gives beautifully clear parallel readings from Rutebeuf and version T. He notes:
"Rutebeuf seems to have hesitated, in a text designed to express his devotion to a saint,
to dwell on her [Mary's] physical beauty and erotic charms" (116). What I am suggesting
here is not in opposition to this claim; it merely requires a different understanding of
the erotic.

25 Peter Dembowski, ed., *La vie de Sainte Marie l'Egyptienne* (Geneva: Droz, 1977).

(Thus she stretched herself out on the ground, since she was [just as she was,] entirely naked, she crossed her hands over her breast, and wrapped herself up in her hair.)

It is worth noting, first of all, that the differences between Rutebeuf and the anonymous writer of the earlier version are, here, extremely slight: one conjunction ("lors") is substituted for another ("dont"); and "presque" takes the place of "tote" in the description of Mary's nakedness. This serves, on the one hand, to make the totality of this nakedness in the earlier version all the more striking. It shows, moreover, what a difference editorial punctuation can make. Whereas Michel Zink's edition of Rutebeuf isolates and ontologizes Mary's near nakedness with a comma—"Si com ele estoit, presque nue"— Peter Dembowski enfolds her total nakedness into the narrative dynamic of the passage, so that there appears to be a causal relation between her body's exposure and her final enveloping gesture. The overall effect—admittedly, the effect of a comma—is that *near* nakedness gets weighted toward contingent disclosure to the world, whereas *total* nakedness gets weighted toward the body's retreat from and resistance to that world. There is, as a result, a greater phenomenological skepticism in the putatively more erotic of the two accounts; less faith, in version 'I', that the body's appearing will refuse to be reduced to an objectifiable appearance.[26]

Of course, Mary does enclose herself in her "crine" in Rutebeuf's account as well. There's no getting away from that retreat. Still, there is a sense in which Mary's body, gathered up into itself, nonetheless continues to extend, to link itself blindly to the earth—and, perhaps, to this earth's contingent bodies, human and inhuman. This extension occurs not in spite of her hair's envelope but, instead, precisely *as* this envelope: Mary's enclosure is also her means of extension and disclosure toward the world. She takes her body in hand, conforms her grasp to it, and releases it—out toward other bodies, including those of subsequent writers (like Rutebeuf) and editors (like Dembowski and Zink) who will touch it up and touch it again. Mary's grasp, in other words, restores the hand to the process of scribal and editorial revision: she puts the *main*, the hand, back into the Old French word for revision, *remaniement*.

In Mary's and Elizabeth's lives, bodily surfaces mark and produce the sense that someone or something is nearby, close, offered to my body and yet, even so, withdrawn into his or her own: offered precisely in this withdrawal. Not lost but *retracted*, which is also to say *retraced*. In Eve Sedgwick's words, "to touch is

---

26 This may be another way of accounting for the restlessness of Mary's body in the earlier version, where she is constantly turning away from the monk Zosimas's gaze. I've engaged with this at some length in "As the Saint Turns," *Exemplaria* 17.2 (2005): 317-46, especially pp. 321-31.

always already to reach out, to fondle, to heft, to tap, or to enfold, and always also to understand other people or natural forces as having effectually done so before oneself, if only in the making of the textured object."[27] All touching is, in this account, a retouching. Every object I hold—and every body—bears the deposits and effacements, the gentle and less gentle traces, of other hands. What Martin Seel has called the here and now of aesthetic perception, this lingering in the object's presence,[28] does not, then, exclude the fact that this object may very well have been present to others in the past, however differently, and that my outstretched hand may very well depend upon other hands, perhaps those represented in the picture or on the screen, or those of editors, scribes, and even friends who have literally handed these texts and images down to me. These "other people" and "natural forces" may, in addition, become erotically present to me in the presence of any beloved *corpus*. The pages that stick together in some well-worn magazine (or the frayed images of a secondhand video) might summon me to a new kind of erotic imagining, just as those whorls of hair (on a spine or a clavicle) might appear across a set of remembered images and textures—my lips on that skin, in that place—whose force startles my body into reflexivity.

This reflexivity is, of course, quintessentially melancholic. Yet if we take seriously the challenge of a superficial medievalism—the wager that to be embodied is to be crossed and crossing, subjects and objects of histories of handling that contract us and expand us, too—then it becomes possible to suggest that there is also another account to be given of incorporation, one that would begin with the riddle that remains at the heart of the word. To incorporate is literally to take, to bring, to fold, to subsume, to sublate, to invite, but most crucially to *become* into, inside a body. What does that mean? Can we know what it is to *be* inside a body before this becoming? Above all, can we know this in a sense that would be distinct from being at the body's surface— our own body's or someone else's?

In her *Queer Phenomenology*, Sara Ahmed observes, "The 'here' of bodily dwelling is thus what takes the body outside of itself, as it is affected and shaped by its surroundings: the skin that seems to contain the body is also where the atmosphere creates an impression."[29] Our interiors, in other words, are ecstasies of the skin, superficial ecstasies. But if "here" also inevitably means "more than here," if I am inevitably "affected and shaped" by spaces and surfaces that touch upon mine, then so too is "now" also more than just this moment; so too does my time, our time, respond to and bear the traces of other times. These other

---

27 Sedgwick, *Touching Feeling*, p. 14.

28 Martin Seel, *Aesthetics of Appearing*, trans. John Farrell (Stanford, CA: Stanford UP, 2005).

29 Sara Ahmed, *Queer Phenomenology* (Durham, NC: Duke UP, 2006), p. 9.

times are not lost. They are within reach. We may just need to develop new ways of reaching toward them: what Ahmed might call new orientations. These orientations cannot help being shaped by, even as they shape, their objects. Ahmed writes elsewhere that bodies are "shaped by contact with objects and with others, with 'what' is near enough to be reached," even as "what gets near is . . . shaped by what bodies do."[30] What would happen if, in the spirit of this collection of essays, we allowed the past to "get near," or acknowledged the ways in which it is already close, without worrying about whether this is the correct past, the right one? What if, in other words, we exchanged the juridical sense of right—the opposite of wrong—for the directional sense of right, of right-handedness, which would also be the sense of orientation, the surface, and that which comes literally out of left field?

A superficial medievalism—a queer medievalism attuned to these ecstasies of the skin—is one that takes seriously "the intimate and materially consequential bonds we have (whether we deny or embrace them) with all others and all things."[31] Our finitude is such that we cannot touch everyone or everything. Nonetheless, it may be the case that we frequently underestimate our reach. In the breaks between bodies and times, in these variously spectral, anachronistic, and erotic encounters, we discover what binds us; we discover just how easy it is to be bound, just how extensive our embraces, like our denials, may be. If we have, in Adam Phillips' words, become "obsessed by, indeed obsessional about, loss,"[32] if we have become more comfortable with denial than with embrace, then perhaps a sense of the surface, of all that it might accommodate, might be exactly the untimely thing we need: a reminder and a promise of our connectedness. A superficial medievalism, then, might help us bear witness to the haunted hearts within our skins, past and present, and how those hearts will not be still. It is—like film, like time, like love—unfinished business.[33]

30 Ahmed, *Queer Phenomenology*, p. 54.

31 Vivian Sobchack, *Carnal Thoughts* (Berkeley: U of California P, 2004), p. 3.

32 Adam Phillips, *The Beast in the Nursery* (New York: Pantheon, 1998), p. 15.

33 This chapter would not have happened without Bettina Bildhauer and Carla Freccero. My thanks to both of them, and to the audiences at the medieval film conference at the University of St. Andrews in July 2005, as well as to the faculty and students associated with the Pre- and Early Modern Studies Program at the University of California, Santa Cruz, who showed me exceptional hospitality in January 2007.

Afterword

Glenn Burger and Steven F. Kruger

Queer Movie Medievalisms opens an extremely various and thought-provoking set of discussions regarding how twentieth-century film negotiates a specifically medieval past in ways that entail an examination, questioning, and (sometimes) queering of gender and sexuality. The volume emphasizes especially how the temporal disjunction of modern or post-modern movies meeting the premodern enables a variety of queer effects, effects that might lead us to rethink not only dominant histories of sexuality but also the certainties of period division and of progressive historical narratives. Each chapter has its own, individual way into this broad field of inquiry, but we will here focus largely on some general conclusions that the chapters, in the aggregate, suggest.

Perhaps unsurprisingly, the "art films" and film "auteurs" represented here are European—Bertrand Tavernier, Luc Besson, Hans-Jürgen Syberberg, and François Ozon. English film makers—Anthony Harvey and the Monty Python troupe—occupy a space between the "artistic" and the popular. U.S. film—along with the New Zealand director Peter Jackson's version of Tolkien's *Lord of the Rings*—is represented consistently by "Hollywood" movies, directed largely toward mass audiences. *Queer Movie Medievalisms* in fact focuses most of its energy on popular entertainment, and, fittingly, the medieval material these movies engage with tends to be not the "great" authors of literary tradition— Dante, Chaucer, Boccaccio, Chrétien de Troyes. (The single exception is Wolfram von Eschenbach, though, even here, it is not primarily Wolfram's *Parzival* that is at issue, but rather Richard Wagner's operatic restaging of Wolfram.) Instead, it is largely anonymous romance, popular culture (the Robin Hood stories), and historiographical traditions that provide the material for the filmmakers taken up here. One could, of course, construct a different canon of medievalist movies that would emphasize authors like Chaucer and Boccaccio: Pasolini's *Canterbury Tales* and *Decameron* would stand at the center of that canon, but this could also include such popular entertainments as *A Knight's Tale*. The current volume's focus, however, points up the ways in which a certain Middle Ages— what we might call a "Hollywood Middle Ages"—is identified not with high, poetic or narrative art but rather with myth and popular legend, romance, grand historical conflict, and courtly intrigue.

At the same time, the films considered focus their attention largely on public, "historical" material. Even when they are quite clearly fictions, and based on fictional material—*A Connecticut Yankee in King Arthur's Court*, or the Robin Hood legend—they tend to take on questions about nation, kingship, international conflict, and courtliness. The medievalist films considered here thus largely construct history as a history of public, masculine action, even when—as, for instance, in *The Court Jester*, *The Conqueror*, or certain of Sean Connery's performances—a heroic, chivalric masculinity is lampooned, undermined, or taken apart. To what extent might such an emphasis reflect the structures of gender within the modern regimes of heterosexuality organizing the films, occluded within high culture but less controlled within the popular culture of Hollywood? That is, does the popular address of the Hollywood film allow particularly bald and boldly drawn constructions of "normal" gender and sexuality to dominate the screen, without the qualifications and complexities of more nuanced and introspective genres? And do the bold strokes of such movies allow, paradoxically, for undercutting moves—the camp effects that circulate around John Wayne as Genghis Khan, for instance—that allow us to see "normal" gender and sexuality quite clearly as fictional constructs? Furthermore, do the othering effects of the medieval within these films—the potential for imagining men and women, masculinity and femininity, as transformed by historical difference, or the strange relations that might be produced when modern gender and sexual stereotypes are simply transported as with the Connecticut Yankee to a radically different historical/cultural moment—do these othering effects provide new points of access and angles of vision for understanding the interimplication of sexuality and gender within modernity? The chapters' attention to public, masculine action is also interestingly different from the preoccupations of much recent medievalist gender and queer studies, which tends to focus on the domestic and the feminine or deviant. And while there has been innovative, challenging work recently on medieval historiography and romance, this has often remained separate from gender and sexuality studies. Might attending to movie medievalism in this way help us take another, queer look at medieval public masculinity and historiography in less monolithic and predictable ways?

Two exceptions to the focus on history as the history of public, masculine action—Bernard Tavernier's *La Passion Béatrice* and Luc Besson's *Jeanne d'Arc*, each of which has a woman at its center—point us in other useful directions. Besson's *Jeanne d'Arc*, while centered on a woman's story, demonstrates a notable form of "female masculinity" (to use Judith Halberstam's formulation) at work at a crucial moment in the formation of French nationhood (and nationalism altogether). And Tavernier's *La Passion Béatrice*, by "medievalizing" an Early Modern "true crime story" of the Cenci family, later famously taken up by nineteenth- and twentieth-century authors such as Shelley, Stendhal, and Artaud, crosses and re-crosses the lines between the historical and domestic, real-life and fictional, high art and popular culture, patriarchal hegemony and queer revisionism. As Lisa Manter presents the film, the "popular" here, to the extent that it is not bound by "the same historical or academic constraints as scholarly analysis of medieval texts," both tellingly resembles the methods of medieval historiography at a time before historicism had been invented and produces its own complex analysis of the medieval, one queerly stepping outside of prevalent unconscious assumptions about the medieval world and its regimes of gender and sexuality.

The movies focused on in this volume are also largely concerned with secular, rather than religious, matters. The Middle Ages associated with the Gothic cathedrals, monastic life, and a trans-European Catholicism is largely absent. That queer analysis of movie medievalism points in this direction, rather than toward a consideration, for instance, of celibacy as a sexuality (as gender and queer medievalist analysis has begun to do), suggests a concern for thinking about how queerness might intervene in the larger histories of (mostly European) politics and secular cultures. It would be interesting, for example, to bring queer movie medievalism up against such queer and postcolonial medievalism as Kathleen Biddick's or Jeffrey Cohen's. At the same time, it would be interesting to bring this medievalist movie canon concerned largely with the political and secular up against alternative cinematic medievalisms: *The Name of the Rose*, for example, which would engage with another—clerical and celibate—masculine public world; or *Anchoress*, which would take up the queer dynamics of another domestic, feminine, and celibate medieval form of religious life.

These chapters also engage broadly and variously with issues of periodization, temporality, and with how past and present meet, touch, engage with each other. Several of the chapters explore how movies, as a genre developing out of modern popular culture, bring together medieval and modern in a hybridity that interimplicates the medieval and modern in boundary-blurring ways. Thus, Jane Chance argues for a directorial citation of a present-day film and its masculinity as queering Tolkien's presentation of Hobbit feudalism. Or Anna Kłosowska investigates the temporal and spatial displacements that occur when medieval Mongol East meets Hollywood Western. Or Barton Palmer explores how the otherness of the medieval Richard I to 1960s America allowed James Goldman and Richard Harvey to articulate a proto-gay subject position as something other than automatically abjected. And the earlier Richard I of Cecil B. DeMille's 1935 *The Crusades*, as analyzed by Lorraine Stock, allows us to recognize, with a certain surprise, the ways in which American film, in an era before the clamping down on gay and lesbian sexualities that followed World War II, might engage quite directly with the possibilities of "ambiguous sexualities" and dissonant, butch and femme, genders. All of this suggests, as we have discussed above with Tavernier's *La Passion Béatrice*, that movie medievalism, encountering the Middle Ages, as it does, by way of distinctly modern genres and concerns, can provide alternative modes of analysis for the Middle Ages themselves. Equally, however, analyzing the medieval in such movies produces another engagement with their present (both the historical moment from which they arise and the performative present created by medievalists viewing these films in the current moment).

As these chapters consistently recognize, movies that take up medieval material tell us as much or more about their own moments as about the medieval past they reinterpret. Susan Aronstein shows in exemplary fashion how *Monty Python and the Holy Grail* engages with the British politics of its moment in ways that enable its thoroughgoing social and political satire to reverberate queerly in relation to gender and sexuality, even against what may be the explicit intentions of its creators. Kathleen Coyne Kelly shows how Will Rogers's public persona, shaped by his well-known involvement in political causes and his Native-American ancestry, colors his performance in *A Connecticut Yankee*. Other, surprising, historical conjunctions emerge in a more aleatory fashion from the variety of chapters brought together here. Thus, for instance, the coincidence, in the chapters by Palmer, Stock, and Tison Pugh, of several Robin Hood/ Richard the Lionhearted films from very different twentieth-century moments might provide the opportunity for a writing of the comparative history of normative and dissident genders and sexualities from the 1930s to the 1990s. Or we might note with some surprise that both John Wayne's *The Conqueror* and Danny Kaye's *The Court Jester* are dated 1956. Simply the reminder that the extremely different styles of masculinity of a John Wayne and a Danny Kaye are contemporaneous has the potential to raise questions. But more specifically, how might the moment of 1956 be reflected in, elucidate, and be elucidated by, these two very different films? That year (like most years) is characterized both by big political movements—the Cold War, the threat of nuclear destruction, the Korean War remembered intensely and the Vietnam War on the horizon— and by significant domestic developments—deeply enmeshed in the social conservatism we identify with "the Fifties," we should remember, too, that 1956 saw the publication of Allen Ginsberg's *Howl and Other Poems* (Jack Kerouac's *On the Road* would appear in 1957), and that, by 1957, Betty Friedan was beginning the research for *The Feminine Mystique* (Simone de Beauvoir's *Second Sex* had been published in French in 1949, and in English in 1953). Some of the intensities of this moment are seen more explicitly in one movie or the other, with *The Conqueror* resonating more strongly with the North American/ Eurasian politics of the moment and *The Court Jester* more strongly with the challenges to traditional men's and women's roles and sexualities that we might see developing, at least subculturally, by the mid-1950s. But further, what would it do also to read across the two movies—to take the "domestic" questions of *The Court Jester* more explicitly into *The Conqueror* and the international questions of *The Conqueror* more intimately into *The Court Jester*?

The double, even triple, move *Queer Movie Medievalisms* enables—simultaneously toward the medieval and the modern, and toward the hybrid "now" being created by this simultaneous viewing—suggests that queer movie medievalism is, and should be thought of as, profoundly historicist and archival, but in quite different terms from "straight" history. We might think of movies as an archive of both popular and "high" cultural material that is not removed from public circulation in the way that manuscript collections or documentary archives are, and thus as an archive that records particular moments in ways that relate quite intimately (if often not at all straightforwardly) to their own moments and to those moments' fantasies and understandings of more and less distant past moments, including the medieval. Such fantasies and understandings are themselves more or less closely linked to other archives, including the traditional ones that shape medieval studies and enable, for instance, the production of "authoritative," critical editions of medieval texts and scholarly histories, but also less traditional, more popular archives, like the more or less continuous, largely oral traditions that have been handed down about a figure like Robin Hood. One of the challenges of *Queer Movie Medievalisms*, specifically addressed to scholars of the Middle Ages, is to think about how movies as an archive shape our work. In part, this might be by disavowal—a scholarly insistence that the movies, like other popular forms of "medievalism" (the Society for Creative Anachronism, for instance), have it "wrong." But the movies are with us, and with our students, nonetheless, and their medievalism necessarily colors our thinking about the past in ways of which we might not be fully conscious.

Queer Movie Medievalisms might also lead us to think about movies as a technology of seeing that incorporates a hybridity that traditional high art, as well as "serious" scholarship, seeks to avoid or occlude, but which might correspond more to the hybrid genres, mixed medias, and performative reading practices of the Middle Ages. Might we take our readings of the movies and their medievalism as challenging us to rethink some of the ways in which we understand medieval reading and writing, which, after all, intimately touch oral composition and oral performance and often blur any clear line between private and public, "sentence" and "solace?" And might we recognize that one productive way of encountering the medieval past is, like these movies, to do further creative, cultural work with them, to fantasize new presents and futures through the taking up of the past? Rather than gaining agency via a research figured as mastery of a discipline or via a passive acceptance of the alterity of the past and the right of others to interpret it to us, movie medievalism reorients us in a more phenomenologically figured way. Both Michelle Bolduc's and Cary Howie's articles are suggestive attempts to theorize what such a practice might look like.

Howie's formulation of medievalism as "superficial," and as involving a certain touch that suggests conjunction but not necessarily similarity, raises the possibility of interaction across alterity without moving into a violent interrogation of the past like that entailed in some kinds of critical, historicist practice (as well as in the metaphors we use to describe them). Howie's formulation resonates strongly not only with Carolyn Dinshaw's queer touch and the Derridean spectrality that has reshaped recent thinking about historicism like Carla Freccero's but also with the work of film theorists like Steven Shaviro, who, in response to the dominance of theories of spectatorship and the gaze in film studies, emphasize instead the visceral, embodied, and not merely visual effects of movies. We wonder, however, whether a return to the gaze, with an awareness of recent critiques of the too simple ways in which spectatorial relationships have been understood within much film theory, might now also be productive. The gaze is, interestingly and strikingly, absent from most of the chapters in this volume, even those like Kłosowska's that take up questions of audience response and participation. Would it be useful to think about the ways in which movies—in presenting a long-past world to us *visually*, as well as aurally and viscerally—allow us to "touch" the past specifically by negotiating visual similarities and differences, cultures made exotic by the filmmakers' medievalist costume and scene design, cultures brought close to us by giving us places (and faces?) that further spectatorial identification and disidentification? What might a more formalist and technical film studies approach to movie medievalisms give us that the largely thematic and "literary" readings of the bulk of these chapters have not yet provided?

Focusing on the formal and the technological might also remind us that, at the present moment, film is, perhaps, an obsolescent form, or at least a form that is rapidly changing in ways that are difficult to predict. *Queer Movie Medievalisms* is a volume about twentieth-century film; what will the twenty-first century bring in terms of cinematic encounters with the medieval past? As the relationship of "the movie" to popular culture changes in the face of new market practices (the demise of the Hollywood studio, rise of independent cinema, globalization of cinema and proliferation of non-European, non-Hollywood models, new technologies such as digital film and computer/Internet, and so on), would it be right to see the movie, even in its more popular incarnations, as now itself somehow a "high art" form in relation to newer technologies? Must we recognize movie medievalism as largely a past chapter in the history of popular cultural "takes" on the Middle Ages, and if so, can we think about what the future might hold? *Digital* movie medievalism is already here with Robert Zemeckis's *Beowulf* (2007). Internet medievalism is here as well. On July 31, 2008, searching "YouTube" for "medieval" turns up 322,000 results, many no doubt not "medievalist," but all telling us something about the meaning of the medieval in the current moment. *Queer Movie Medievalisms*, in taking seriously the popular movies of the twentieth century calls us, too, to be alert to the development of new, related forms of visual medievalism.

We will end with a brief cautionary note. The chapters in *Queer Movie Medievalisms* energetically and persuasively show the rich queer potential that emerges when a modern form like the movie encounters the medieval past. Even the most mainstream and politically conservative of movies here yields itself to queer effects—whether these emerge from commercial calculations (as when the studios, and the star himself, invent new masculinities for Sean Connery that will maintain him as a box-office draw) or from the resistant readings of audiences (and of some of those involved in making a film), as in *The Conqueror*. But film, and medievalist film, even some of the films queered here, might nonetheless participate strongly in maintaining dominant ideologies of gender and sexuality. Understandably, the chapters here are more interested in uncovering "fairy tales" and "pink spots" than they are in analyzing the ways in which popular, filmic engagements with the past might bolster, rather than destabilize and undermine, constrictive constructions of gender and sexuality. And yet might not part of the work of queer analysis be to recognize and describe the armor of those constrictive constructions, even as we move to recognize, and revel in, the ways in which, queerly, there are always chinks in that armor?

Index